FOOD
COMMODITIES

FOOD COMMODITIES

Second Edition

Bernard Davis
B.A., M.H.C.I.M.A.

HEINEMANN PROFESSIONAL PUBLISHING

Heinemann Professional Publishing Ltd
Halley Court, Jordan Hill, Oxford OX2 8EJ

OXFORD LONDON MELBOURNE AUCKLAND SINGAPORE
IBADAN NAIROBI GABORONE KINGSTON

First published 1978
Reprinted 1981, 1982, 1984, 1986
Second edition 1987
Reprinted 1988
© Bernard Davis 1978, 1987
ISBN 0 434 90306 X

Printed in Great Britain by
Redwood Burn Ltd, Trowbridge, Wiltshire

This book is dedicated to

DOROTHY, NIGEL, CHRISTINE and NEIL

Foreword

Most students and practitioners learn about commodities and their uses in catering, whether in the classroom or on the job, in one of two ways: either by viewing them as a subject on their own, or as an element in the learning of food preparation and cookery. Whichever of the two approaches they have adopted, so far they have lacked a sound textbook on the subject. This gap has now been filled by Bernard Davis, whose book is both authoritative and comprehensive.

Bernard Davis spent ten years of his early working life in the kitchen, rising to a senior position in a leading London hotel. In the twenty years that followed, he formulated and developed as a teacher the study of commodities in catering, and lectured widely on the subject, not only to those new to catering, but also to the many experienced men and women who attended his short courses, and to other audiences. What is contained in this book is, therefore, based on a first-hand knowledge of the best practice, and on a thorough understanding of student needs.

It is no easy task to write for students of different backgrounds on different levels of courses, and for students and practitioners, at the same time. The author has succeeded in embracing these varying needs by adopting a structure and approach, which makes the same volume relevant to all of them. Apprentices, City and Guilds students, and others who need the main basic facts can concentrate on those parts of each chapter which provide them, and stop short, for example, of the scientific aspects, which are intended for the more advanced student. Classification and grading of commodities are of particular value to those responsible for purchasing and receiving deliveries; sections dealing with catering uses to those concerned with food production; and storage requirements of various foods to those responsible for storing them.

For a number of years Bernard Davis was a valued colleague of mine who contributed much to the pioneering work of the Department, of which I was Head for ten years. I am, therefore, very glad to have the opportunity to introduce and commend this book to students, teachers, and to those working in the industry; it is a competent and reliable guide both for systematic study and for frequent reference, which they will find an indispensable tool in their catering careers.

Professor S. Medlik
formerly Head of Department of
Hotel, Catering and Tourism Management
University of Surrey

Preface

This book has been written for all who are interested in food, but it is primarily intended for students and teachers of courses in hotel, catering and institutional subjects, and has been planned to cover the examination requirements of the following courses:

City and Guilds of London Institute Certificates in catering and cookery;
Ordinary and Higher National Diplomas in hotel, catering and institutional studies;
Membership of the Hotel, Catering and Institutional Management Association;
University and C.N.A.A. degrees in hotel and catering studies;
BTEC/SCOTBEC Diplomas and Certificates.

In addition, it is hoped that the book will also serve as a basic text on food commodities for students of home economics, nutrition and dietetics.

Last but not least, it will be of value to practising chefs, food and beverage managers, those responsible for purchasing, and other catering managers and supervisors who may wish to formalize their knowledge and bring it up-to-date, in order to improve the profitability of their operations and to enhance their customers' satisfaction.

While writing this book I have been conscious of the fact that whilst there are hundreds of books on cookery there are very few books available that examine in detail the subject of 'Food Commodities'. My goal has been to introduce the subject to the reader in a structured way so that from this book he or she may be encouraged to go forward to research further in areas of interest. Each chapter, in the main, contains a brief introduction, various classifications, methods of production, grading, catering uses, storage requirements and scientific and nutritional aspects. The appendixes contain details of legislation relating to specific foods, further reading and a glossary of scientific terms.

No one author can produce a text-book of this type without the help of many others. My grateful thanks are given to the following:

Professor S. Medlik, previously of the University of Surrey, who gave me valuable help and encouragement to start writing this book. To the many organizations and firms who so willingly provided help and information: the Ministry of Agriculture and Fisheries/The British Bacon Curers Federation/

ix

Henry Telfer Limited/Associated Health Foods Limited/The Milk Marketing Board/The Dairy Produce Advisory Service/The Meat and Livestock Commission/The Tea Council/Lyons Tetley Ltd/Twining and Co. Ltd/The Flour Advisory Board Ltd/The Rice Council/MenuMaster Ltd/The White Fish Authority and Unilever Ltd. Also to my many colleagues in teaching and in industry who have helped and influenced me over the years, my indebtedness is nonetheless gratefully acknowledged.

Bernard Davis
Guildford, Surrey

Preface to the Second Edition

Since the first publication of *Food Commodities* in 1978 and its subsequent reprinting, changes of public interest and fact have occurred necessitating the preparation of this second edition.

The basic structure and approach of the book has been retained. The choice of material selected for this edition was influenced by two main considerations. First, it was essential for the book to still remain as a basic text on food commodities for students, practitioners and others with a specific interest in foods, and to present the information in a structured way. Second, there was a need to completely update the information in the first edition and add relevant new material.

Two particular changes have taken place in recent years which have affected the content of this edition. As members of the European Community more of the food legislation of the UK has now been brought into line with that of the other member countries. This has resulted in changes being made in the main text and legislation section of most chapters. Also, there has emerged an international concensus, particularly within the developed countries, of linking certain aspects of diet with that of general health. In the UK concern with diet and health resulted in the publication in 1983 of the James Report (or NACNE report) and in 1984 the publication of a report by the DHSS Committee on Medical Aspects of Food Policy (COMA) *Diet and Cardio-vascular Disease*. It is with some reflection on diet and health that this book should be studied.

Bernard Davis
Guildford, Surrey

Author's Special Acknowledgements

I would like to place on record my deep appreciation of the assistance that I have received from two colleagues in the preparation of this second edition of the book:

To Michael Kipps, B.Sc. (London); M.Sc. (Surrey), Senior Lecturer in Food Science, University of Surrey, for assistance with the updating of the sections on Scientific and Nutritional matters in each chapter; and

To Terry Kirby, M.Inst.M; M.Nat.Fed; Trade Development Officer, Meat and Livestock Commission for assistance with the updating of the chapters on Meat and Poultry.

Bernard Davis
Guildford, Surrey

Contents

List of Figures

List of Tables

1

Cereal Products

Cereals or grains are the seeds of grasses and include the many species of wheat, rye, maize, oats, barley, and rice. They are without doubt the most important group of the vegetable kingdom and in some countries are the staple food diet, providing at least two-thirds of a person's energy and protein intake.

The structure of cereal grains is similar, with each cereal differing in detail only. Grains of wheat, rye, and maize consist of a fruit coat (pericarp) and the seed consisting of the seed coat, endosperm, and the germ, whilst grains of oats, barley, and rice have in addition, a husk outside the fruit coat. Each of the main parts of a grain, the fruit coat, seed coat, germ, and endosperm can be further divided into various layers and tissues. Thus the skill of the processor, usually the miller, lies in being able to separate out the parts of the grain from each other and at times to make further separations from within each individual part. With today's technology it is now possible to process cereals so that the finished product (e.g. a special type of wheat flour) can be standardized in its nutritional content and for a particular purpose (e.g. for the making of a particular type of bread or cake).

The various parts of grain in general are perhaps easiest to understand by examining the structure of a wheat grain. This will vary slightly depending on the species of wheat grown and to a lesser extent where it was grown. The wheat grain is a seed used by nature for the continuity of its species and it contains all of the food necessary for the early stages of growth.

The structure of the grain can be divided into three main parts: bran coatings; the germ (or embryo); and the endosperm. The bran itself consisting of six layers of cells, the outer three forming the pericarp and the inner three the seed coat. The endosperm which is the major part of the grain consists of tightly packed cells amongst which are found soluble and insoluble proteins, oil, sugar, mineral matter, and some moisture. The inner starch cells are small and fine whilst the outer cells are large and coarse. The germ, from which a new plant would grow, under ideal conditions is a very small part of the total

1

grain. It is itself divided into three main parts, the radicle which could develop into a rootlet, the plumule which could develop into a green shoot and the scutellum which contains most of the vitamin content of the grain. Figure 1.1. shows a longitudinal and cross-section of the wheat grain.

A wheat grain consists of approximately:

			% by weight	
		Epidermis	0·5	
	Pericarp	Epicarp	1·0	
		Endocarp	1·5	3%
(1) Bran				
		Testa	2·0	
	Seed Coat	Nucellar layer	1·0	
		Aleurone layer	7·0	10%
(2)		Germ		2%
(3)		Endosperm		85%

Because there are differences between the various grains, mainly in their products and catering uses, each will be discussed separately in order of general importance to the catering industry.

Wheat

Wheat is the most valuable grain for the British: some 62% of which we are able to grow, the remainder is imported. The consumption of flour has increased slightly, although the consumption of bread shows a small decrease:

	All flour *kg per capita p.a.*	*Bread* *kg per capita p.a.*
1982	59.4	45.8
1983	60.5	45.3
1984	62.4	45.1

(Data from *Annual Abstract of Statistics* and National Food Survey.)

Wheat may be classified under some seven headings.

(i) BY SPECIES. There are three main commercial species of wheat. *Triticum vulgare, Triticum durum* and *Triticum compactum.* Triticum being the botanical name given to all grasses. *Triticum vulgare* is the name given to varieties within the species that on milling produce a flour particularly suitable for bread and general cake production. *Triticum durum,* a species not grown in the U.K., produces a flour very suitable for the production of spaghetti, macaroni, and other pastas. *Triticum compactum* or club wheat produces a flour that is unsuitable for breadmaking but ideal for the production of cakes.
(ii) AS A WINTER OR A SPRING WHEAT. Winter wheats are planted in the autumn and harvested in the early summer in countries such as Canada,

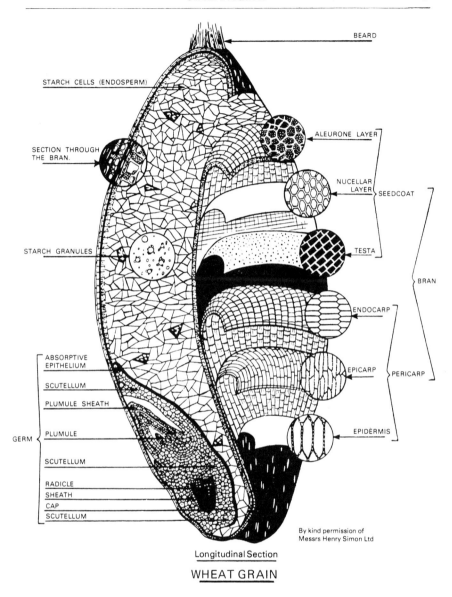

BEARD

STARCH CELLS (ENDOSPERM)

ALEURONE LAYER

SECTION THROUGH
THE BRAN.

NUCELLAR
LAYER } SEEDCOAT

STARCH GRANULES

TESTA

BRAN

ENDOCARP

ABSORPTIVE
EPITHELIUM

SCUTELLUM

EPICARP } PERICARP

PLUMULE SHEATH

GERM { PLUMULE

SCUTELLUM

EPIDERMIS

RADICLE
SHEATH
CAP
SCUTELLUM

By kind permission of
Messrs Henry Simon Ltd

Longitudinal Section

WHEAT GRAIN

Figure 1.1 A longitudinal section of a wheat grain

U.S.A., and Russia, where they have severe cold winters and hot, dry summers. Winter wheats give a strong flour with a high percentage of quality protein.

Spring wheats are planted in the spring and harvested in the late summer in countries such as the U.K. and southern parts of the U.S.A., where there are mild winters, a fairly high rainfall and rather damp harvesting periods. Spring wheats give a soft flour with a lower percentage of quality protein than that of winter wheats.

(iii) BY THE COLOUR OF THE GRAIN, white, red or yellow.

N.B. The colour being referred to is the colour of the testa, the fourth skin or layer of bran, not the colour of the flour.

White grain is associated with flours of excellent colour. Red grain is associated with the strength of flour and a good bloom. Yellow grain is associated with flours that are somewhat harsh and have a particular dryness. It should be noted that the colour of the flour purchased by the caterer or householder is dependent on the grist, (or mixture of grains used) the grade and granularity of the flour, whether the flour has been chemically treated and also the particular purpose for which the flour has been milled.

(iv) BY ITS STRENGTH, which is determined by the quality and quantity of the gluten forming proteins present.

Strong flours come from winter wheats mainly and are capable of producing good bulky bread type products after a long fermentation period. Strength refers to a strong gluten that will give a very good support to the cooked product.

Medium flours which are imported from sources such as the South American 'Plate' region but are often mixtures of strong and weak flours are used to produce goods such as aerated buns and scones which could not be produced satisfactorily using strong or weak flours on their own.

Soft flours come from spring wheats and are used to produce short paste and sponge type goods. Quality in soft flour refers to a flour that has the ability to contain a high ratio of fats and sugar.

N.B. See pp. 4–5 for an explanation of gluten.

(v) BY ITS CATERING USE. This in particular is an extension of Section (iv) above combined with Sections (i) and (vi). A summary in table form of the types of flour used for particular catering uses is given on pp. 14–15.

(vi) BY THE PART OR PARTS OF THE GRAIN USED. The grain consists of three main parts: the bran; the germ; and the endosperm; each of which can be separated from each other. Thus a flour could contain the whole grain, the whole grain minus the bran or part of it, the whole grain minus the bran and germ, etc. The types of flour available are listed on pp. 8–10 and they make this clearer.

(vii) BY THE COUNTRY WHERE IT WAS GROWN, e.g. England, Canada, U.S.A., Australia, etc.

Gluten Content of Flour

When selecting a flour, the colour and fineness of the flour are easy to see. However, the most important characteristic is invisible, it is called gluten.

Gluten consists of two insoluble proteins glutenin and gliadin, and is formed when the flour is mixed with water. Glutenin has the characteristic of giving strength and stability to the structure of a loaf, cake or other bakery product, whilst gliadin has the properties of elasticity and is a softer, stickier substance to which the other materials adhere.

Without gluten in wheat flour there would be no bakery products as we know them today, for it is the gluten in a dough which expands when gas is generated by baking powder or yeast and coagulates at about 60° C (140° F) and thereby forms the structure of the cooked product.

Gluten from a good type of breadmaking flour will rise on cooking to form a bold spherical shape, whilst gluten from a cake flour will produce on cooking a rather flat and spread-out product. Gluten has another important property and that is its ability to absorb water, therefore the more gluten in a flour, the more water that can be added and the greater the volume and yield of cooked products.

Fortunately, gluten can be conditioned by the caterer to his advantage to get the best results from flours. It can be toughened by salt, by long contact with water, by handling, e.g. by kneading, rolling, mixing etc., and by the slight acidity of an ingredient such as sour milk. It can be softened by fat, sugar, and by the enzymes from yeast, malt, bran, and wheat germ. Gluten quality can be improved by the miller by the addition of small quantities of oxidizing substances, known as 'improvers'. The most important point is that both the *quantity* and *quality* of gluten are significant.

Flour Milling

Milling is the controlled conversion of the grain into a variety of flours for particular purposes and by-products.

There are some three distinct methods of milling wheat, stone-milling, roller-milling, and fragmentation-milling. Although all three methods are still in use today, they will be explained in order of historic use and of least importance (i.e. fragmentation milling is a relatively new process and is widely used today for the bulk of flour produced whereas stone milling is the oldest of commercial methods known to be used but is not so common today).

Irrespective of the method of milling all wheat grain whether home produced or imported will go through two main stages before being milled.

Cleaning
The grain on arrival at the flour mill will be dirty containing usually some if not all of the following: grains of other cereals; seeds from a variety of field weeds; straw; dust and mud from the fields; stones; live and dead insects, small rodents and their excreta; string and small pieces of metal. All of these must be removed before the grain is milled.

The processing stage of cleaning is usually broken down into four separate operations.

(*a*) SCREENING. The grain is passed through several sieving operations to remove items both larger and smaller than itself. It is then passed along a conveyor belt where any pieces of metal are removed magnetically and dust, rodent hairs etc., are removed by the use of currents of air.
(*b*) SORTING. At this stage all non-wheat grains such as barley and oats are removed by passing through a range of separators which remove all foreign grains by virtue of their size.
(*c*) SCRUBBING. The grain is processed through scourers which remove any

mud or dirt and the beard and beeswing from each grain (the beeswing is the epidermis or outer layer of the bran coatings).

(*d*) WASHING. This operation cleans the grains by removing any fine dust and hairs, and also any stones which have not been removed previously. After washing the grain is centrifuged to remove excess surface water.

Conditioning

The purpose of conditioning is to ensure that the grain is in such a physical condition that the milling stage can be easily and efficiently performed. As the grains to be milled are often mixed (a grist) by country of origin and species, it is necessary for them all to be of the same moisture content and for there to be the correct distribution of their moisture in the grain because of quality requirements of the end product. This may be done by moistening the grain and allowing it to lie in a bin for some 24–72 hours depending on the air temperature, or by heating the wheat to a temperature of up to 49°C for approximately $1\frac{1}{2}$ hours in a special type of machine. Conditioning will assist in toughening the bran so that it can be easily separated from the endosperm and germ; it will also facilitate the further processing of the endosperm.

The cleaned and conditioned wheat is then ready to be milled in one of three ways.

(i) Stone-milling

This was the first commercially known method of milling in the U.K., using geared water mills or wind mills. The method is still used today to produce wholemeal, wheatmeal and many speciality flours, but the power to operate the mills is usually electric.

In the stone mill two circular stones are used, each with its surface corrugated radially, with the distance between the stones being smaller towards the outer edge of the stones. In operation, the cleaned, conditioned grain enters from above into an aperture in the centre of the top stone. The bottom stone is stationary at all times whilst the top one revolves grinding the grain more finely as it is pushed to the outside of the stones. The resulting flour is then sieved before being bagged.

The flour produced by this method (often termed 'wholemeal) contains all of the constituents of the grain (the bran, endosperm and grain) mixed together, and has five characteristics:

- (*a*) All the parts of the grain are contained in the flour.
- (*b*) The flour will have a dark colour.
- (*c*) The gluten-forming proteins (contained in the endosperm) are mixed with proteins from the germ and the bran during milling, and the resultant gluten formed on dough making is of a lower quality.
- (*d*) The flour will have a characteristic flavour as a result of the mixing of all the constituents of the grain and of the heat generated during milling.
- (*e*) Because of the ground (and raw) germ, it will have a storage life of only 6–8 weeks.

(ii) Roller-milling

This method has been used in this country for almost 100 years and is different from stone-milling in some three main ways:

(a) It is particularly concerned with the milling of white flour.
(b) It aims to make as efficiently as possible the separation of the bran, the endosperm, and the germ.
(c) Flour of any extraction rate can be produced.

Roller-milling is a much more complicated method than stone-milling and involves a large amount of specialized equipment. For economic reasons therefore there are fewer but much larger flour roller-mills operating today, than those operating in the past.

The process can be broken down into two clear stages:

Breaking

The cleaned and conditioned grain is passed through a series of break rolls. These are grooved rollers which operate in pairs, rotating in the opposite direction to each other, the top one rotating two and a half times faster than the lower roller. It is usual for the mill to have five sets of break rolls with each set being more finely set than the previous set of break rolls.

At the first break roll the grain is sheared open and all the product is sieved in a process known as 'Scalping'. The large particles, split open grains from which a very small part of the endosperm has been extracted, then go into the second break rolls. At this and the subsequent stages more of the endosperm will be extracted each time – the product of each of the following breaks being sieved with the coarser particles going into the next break. The final product after the fifth break is just the outer skin of the grain with a small percentage of endosperm attached.

'Scalping' is the technical term given to the special sieving operation that takes place after each stage through a break roll. It separates the main product into three specific products:

(i)   the coarse particles which would go into the next break rolls for more endosperm to be extracted;
(ii) some flour which could be bagged;
(iii) coarse flour (or semolina) which is divided by particle size into (a) dunst – a fine grade of endosperm particle but larger than flour; (b) break middlings of intermediate particle size to semolina and dunst; (c) semolina which is endosperm of a coarse particle size.

Each of the above are passed through purifiers where by means of air currents any minute particles of bran are removed to ensure purity of the white flour end-product.

Reduction

The purpose of this stage is to reduce the endosperm to a fine flour and to extract the germ. The reduction stage is less complicated than the breaking stage (one of the three main parts of the grain having been removed). It consists of a series of reduction rollers, which are smooth and each pair is set more finely than the previous set. After passing through each set of reduction rollers the product is sieved, the coarse particles going to the next set of rollers for finer reduction. This process is repeated until all the semolina which was fed into the reduction rollers is reduced to fine white flour, germ and a small amount of branny by-product. The germ is extracted early in the reduction stage where it is easily sifted off because, being of a tough and oily nature, it is flattened on the rolls with little fragmentation taking place.

The flour is ready for sale after it has been treated with improvers and the statutory addition of specific minerals (*see* p. 19) and has been suitably packaged.

(iii) Air Classification, or Fragmentation-milling

This is a relatively new method of milling by which it is possible to control the protein quality and quantity in the production of a particular flour.

In the standard roller-milling method, the protein quality of the end-product depends very much on the skill of the miller in blending the grist (mixture of grain), remembering that the protein quantity and quality will differ according to the country of origin and the species of the wheat.

In milling, the break rollers splinter the endosperm into particles that can be separated by size. Air classification or fragmentation-milling is a refinement of roller-milling in that after producing the white flour it is then processed a further stage, and is separated by means of air classification into particles of three broad size ranges. The measurement of the particle size is in microns (1 micron = one millionth of a metre). Fortunately the particles divide themselves into three bands of sizes, those that are larger than 40 microns and are similar in composition to the endosperm from which they have splintered, those that are between 15–40 microns and are almost completely starch and therefore low in protein, and those that are smaller than 15 microns and are both starch and protein. The protein content of the smaller particles is higher than the average for the endosperm and makes up for the medium-sized particles which are low in protein. Thus it is possible to increase the protein content of a particular flour by either adding to a flour a higher percentage of the smaller particles or by removing from a flour a percentage of the medium particles. Further, it means that the miller is now able to produce a flour to a particular specification for processing into a specific cooked item by the caterer. To the caterer it means that by being able to buy flour to a specification he will be able to perfect his method of processing very efficiently and obtain a standard yield and volume of product consistently, and hence give satisfaction to his customers.

Types of Flours Available

Brown Flours or Meals

(i) WHOLEMEAL. This is flour which by law must contain 100% of the whole wheat grain; it is light brown in colour, and has become much more popular again in recent years with the increasing interest in nutrition and with the growth of health food shops in the U.K. Stone-ground wholemeal flour is usually regarded as the quality wholemeal because of the developed flavour caused by the generation of heat during milling.

(ii) WHEATMEAL. Similar in appearance to wholemeal, it must contain in excess of 85% of the grain, the very coarse bran particles being removed during milling. Like wholemeal the granularity of the bran affects the general colour and appearance of the flour. Most of the brown flours available are wheatmeal. The use of the term 'wheatmeal' should not be applied to brown bread (C.O.M.A. Report 1978).

(iii) GERM MEAL. There are several germ meals available on the market and are sold under brand names such as Hovis, Daren and Vitbe meals. They all contain a higher percentage of germ than is usually found in flour, which will have been cooked with salt (to reduce the development of rancidity) and then mixed with the flour. The addition of a higher percentage of germ (cooked) makes the meal more nutritious and fuller flavoured.

(iv) MALTED MEAL. There are a few malted meals available being sold under brand names such as Bermaline. They are usually made from wholemeal and white flours plus soya and malt flour. Often sugar and salt are added to the meal before it is sold.

White Flours

(i) WEAK FLOUR. Milled mainly from English and Australian wheats, this grade is low in protein content, about 8%.

(ii) MEDIUM FLOUR. Milled from a mixture of wheats which will produce a flour with an average protein content of about 10%.

(iii) STRONG FLOUR. Milled from Canadian and American wheats, this grade is high in protein content, up to 17%.

It should be noted that in white flours although there are three main types there are grades of quality within each. These grades are based on the proportion of flour extracted from the wheat and the amount of bran and germ in the flour. The two main grades are:

(*a*) *Patents Grade.* This refers to the finest grade and is the flour which comes from the first, second and third break rollers, i.e. early in the milling process. A typical patent would be a 25–40% extraction, i.e. from a 100 lb of wheat only 25–40 lb of quality flour would be extracted. The remaining 60–75 lb of by-product being processed to make a lower grade of flour. Patents grade is available for both bread and cake manufacturing.

(*b*) *Bakers Grade.* This is the main grade of white flour produced being of a 70–72% extraction, i.e. nearly all the endosperm has been removed from the grain. It is not so highly refined as patents grade and is therefore cheaper.

(iv) STRAIGHT-RUN FLOUR. This is a general purpose flour and as its name implies it has not had any of the patents grade removed from it. It contains all of the white flour extracted from a particular grist.

(v) SELF-RAISING FLOUR. This is a medium strength flour which has had carefully blended with it chemical agents (usually slow action baking powders). The purpose being that on being made into a dough, the chemical agents will react producing carbon dioxide and make the dough expand and become porous.

(vi) HIGH RATIO FLOUR, or special cake flour. This is milled from high grade wheats having an extraction rate of less than 50%. It has a low gluten content, but is of high quality. The flour is milled more finely than usual and then heavily chlorinated. The fine milling increases the granule number to a given weight and so increases the absorption properties of the flour, whilst the chlorination increases the acidity and renders the starch more soluble and so increases its absorption properties. As the name implies, it is a flour which will take a high ratio of liquid, fats and sugar to itself.

As well as increasing the absorption properties, chlorination brings about oxidation, improving the gluten quality, and also bleaches the flour, thus increasing its whiteness.

(vii) HIGH PROTEIN FLOUR. This flour has been available only since fragmentation or air separation milling has been known. The small particles of the endosperm, being less than 15 microns in size contain a much higher percentage of protein and it is this that is used. It should be noted that because of its small particle size it is not satisfactory on its own for breadmaking in spite of its high protein content.

Other Cereals

Rice

The growing of rice is different from other cereals in that it is capable of being grown in standing water or on dry land like other cereals. Rice grown on dry land is known as 'upland' rice and accounts for only some 10% of the total rice acreage. Rice is imported into the U.K. mainly from the U.S.A., Italy, South America and Far Eastern countries, with the majority today being from the U.S.A. It is imported either as a raw product requiring milling or in varying forms as a finished product.

The milling process is similar to that of other cereals. After cleaning and conditioning the outer husk is first removed exposing the grain covered by a brown bran layer. It is sold in this condition as Brown rice. It can then be milled further in a stage known as 'pearling' to remove the bran, leaving a white grain which is sometimes milled further when it is polished with mineral substances such as talc to give the grain a bright shining surface. The protein content is similar to that of weak, low protein wheat and it is unsuitable for breadmaking.

Two factors determine the types of rice available to the caterer.

(i) THE SIZE AND SHAPE OF THE GRAIN i.e. long, medium or short grain.

(a) *Short Grain Rice* (originally known under the name of Carolina Rice, but today referred to in the U.K. as round grain rice). This variety is a short, plump grain which when cooked is tender and moist with the particles of grain clinging together. It is the variety that is used to make rice puddings, rice croquettes and many other rice based sweet dishes.

(b) *Medium Grain Rice.* This variety is slightly narrower and longer than the short grain and is often mistaken for long grain. It is imported from Italy and South America and may be used for the same purposes as short grain and for some savoury rice dishes such as a risotto.

(*c*) *Long Grain Rice.* This variety is four to five times as long as the grain is wide. On being cooked the grains tend to remain separate and are light and fluffy. It is the main rice used in savoury rice dishes.

N.B. All of the above three sizes and shapes are available as whole or broken grain.

(ii) THE TYPE OF PROCESS THAT THE GRAIN HAS UNDERGONE i.e. to what extent it has been milled and whether it has been subjected to a cooking process before being packaged.

(*a*) *Regular Milled Rice.* This would be rice that has been cleaned and graded during the milling process but has not been subjected to any form of cooking process.

(*b*) *Parboiled (usually long grain) Rice.* In this process the rice has been subjected to a combination of steam and pressure, and drying before it is milled in the usual way. The process gelatinizes the starch in the grain aiding the retention of much of the natural vitamin and mineral content. Surprisingly parboiled rice takes longer to cook, but has the advantage of taking up more liquid during cooking and therefore increasing the yield. On being cooked the grains tend to be fluffy, plump in appearance and separate. It can be used for the same purpose as long grain rice.

(*c*) *Precooked or Instant Rice (usually long grain).* After being milled the grain is completely cooked and then the moisture is removed. It is reconstituted by adding water or stock and allowing the rice to absorb it. The reconstitution time usually being less than ten minutes. It can be used for the same purposes as long grain rice although the usual recipe would have to be modified.

By-products of Rice

RICE FLOUR. This is clean milled rice, usually broken grain, that has been ground and sifted into flour. It is used as a thickening ingredient for soups and the making of special cakes and macaroon goods.

RICE CONES. This is a coarse rice flour and is used in the bakery trade for dusting yeast goods, preventing them from sticking together.

RICE PAPER. An edible paperlike base for macaroons and sweets.

Rye

This is a prominent cereal in parts of Europe and Russia, mainly because it will grow better than wheat in poor soil and harsh weather conditions. The grains are longer and thinner than wheat grains and yield a flour that is darker than wheat flour, having a low protein content.

Its main use is for the manufacture of rye bread.

Barley

This is a hardy cereal, but not processed commonly into a flour because it has little protein content. Its particular products are:

(*a*) Malt products, made by allowing the barley grain to sprout changing much of the starch to a sugar (maltose). The germinated grains can then be dried and milled to make a malt flour, or soaked in water and concentrated to make a malt extract.

(*b*) Pearl barley which is the polished endosperm, after the bran and germ has been removed. It is used in soups and stews.

(*c*) Scotch or pot barley which is the cleaned whole grain with only the outer husk removed. It is used in stews requiring a long, slow cooking time.

Maize

Not a prominent cereal in Europe but is extensively cultivated in the U.S.A., Argentina, Egypt, and India. It is the tallest of the six cereal plants discussed in this chapter, growing usually to a height of some 6 ft and bearing some four to six large cobs within which are contained the hard yellow grain. The starch of maize is similar in properties to that of oats. The flour produced is the source of cornflour and is usually the main ingredients of custard and blanc-mange powders.

Oats

This is not a very important crop for man, having more use in animal feeding nowadays. However it is used to some extent for food in the U.K. Although containing about 12–13% protein it is non-gluten forming and is therefore unsuitable for breadmaking. The main products of oats are:

(*a*) Rolled oats. The dehulled grain is steam-treated prior to rolling into flakes and is principally used for the making of porridge.

(*b*) Ground oatmeal has the husk removed and is available in three grades, coarse, pinhead and fine.

(*c*) Oatflour has the husk and most of the bran removed.

Processed Cereals

Pasta Products

There is a great variety of pasta products available to the caterer, of which varieties such as spaghetti, macaroni, noodles, and lasagne are among the most well known.

Pasta products are normally made from amber durum wheat (high gluten quality and content) which is milled into semolina and mixed with water, salt, eggs, vegetable oil, and at times vegetable colouring. Semolina is preferred to flour because less water is required to make the pasta dough, which greatly helps in the drying stage. The process of manufacture is in four stages:

(i) The initial mixing of the ingredients into a dough with a final temperature of about 38°C (100°F).

(ii) The kneading of the dough for 10–20 minutes to bring it to the correct consistency and homogeneity (similar to that of putty).

(iii) The pressing of the dough into the required type of pasta. This is done by placing the dough into a waterlined press at a temperature high enough to keep the dough in a plastic form, and extruding the dough under pressure into the required shape.

(iv) The drying or curing of the extruded dough. This is done in two parts. Firstly there is a preliminary drying which helps to prevent sourness and the development of any mould growth. Secondly there is the major drying stage which may take up to 90 hours, depending on the type of product. Dried macaroni for example will have a moisture content of about 10 per cent.

A quality pasta, e.g. macaroni or spaghetti, will be translucent, a rich yellow colour, be hard and brittle and break with a clean glassy fracture. Long pasta should be quite pliable. Pastas such as ravioli which are often made by the caterer will not be hard and brittle but have a texture similar to that of short paste. One of the main criteria for the quality of a pasta is its behaviour on being cooked. In general, it should swell to almost twice its size, retain its particular shape and remain firm without breaking up.

Pasta products may be classified according to their size and shape.
(i) LONG PASTA. This group includes smooth, solid rod forms, e.g. spaghetti, vermicelli; tubular forms of which the outer surface may be smooth or corrugated, e.g. macaroni, mezzoni, zitori rigati; and flat forms, e.g. noodles.

N.B. It is possible to purchase most of this group in varying thicknesses and sizes.
(ii) SHORT PASTA. This group contains large cut macaroni which may be straight or slant cut and a large variety of fancy shaped pieces of pasta, e.g. farfallette — which is in the shape of a butterfly.
(iii) PASTAS SUITABLE FOR STUFFING WITH A FORCEMEAT. These are of two types:

> (*a*) Those that are stuffed while the pasta is in the raw state and then cooked, e.g. ravioli, tortellini.
> (*b*) Those that are partly cooked before being stuffed and then the cooking completed, e.g. canneloni, marricotti.

N.B. This group is often made by the caterer on his own premises.
(iv) SMALL FANCY PASTAS. This group consists of a large variety of small pastas which are used almost exclusively for garnishing soups, e.g.

> Capellini — fine hairlike vermicelli
> Alfabeto — letters and numbers
> Stellette — small stars

Breakfast Cereals

There is a wide variety of cereal breakfast foods available to the caterer, the various types being known under brand names. They are made from grain, maize, wheat, rice, oats, barley, and rye in the whole grain form, milled or from a cereal premix. The grains can be puffed, flaked, shredded or produced in a granular form and have sugar, honey, and vitamins added.

Breakfast cereals may be firstly classified according to whether they are in the ready-to-serve form (e.g. Cornflakes) or whether they require some cooking before being served (e.g. Porridge). The ready-to-serve breakfast cereals may be classified according to their method of manufacture.
(i) PUFFED PRODUCTS These are made from either the whole grain (e.g. wheat, rice) or from a stiff dough from ground cereals (e.g. wheat, rice, etc.) which has been extruded like pasta products into different shapes. The product is placed in a 'puffing gun' chamber, sealed, and the vapour pressure increased.

The pressure is then suddenly released and the products swell to many times their original size. The product is then toasted and may be further treated by coating with sugar in some form.

(ii) FLAKED PRODUCTS. These are made from the whole grain (e.g. wheat rice) or from pieces of the maize endosperm (also known as hominy or as grits). The cereal (cleaned and cracked in the case of whole grain) is cooked under pressure together with salt, sugar in some form, etc., and then cooled before being flaked between heavy rollers. The product is then toasted and cooled.

(iii) SHREDDED PRODUCTS. Shredded products are mainly made from the wheat grain. The clean grain is pressure cooked until the starch has completely gelatinized and then cooled. It is then passed through special rollers and emerges as long strands which are collected to form a mat of the desired thickness. The mat is then cut into 'biscuits' of the required size and these are then baked and cooled.

(iv) GRANULAR PRODUCTS. These are made by making a special type of malt loaf which on being cooked and cooled is broken up into small pieces and further dried and then ground and sieved.

All of the above types of breakfast cereals are ready-to-eat simply by adding hot or cold milk or single cream to the cereal. One breakfast cereal however requires cooking before it can be eaten and that is porridge.

Porridge

This is prepared from coarse-milled oats. The de-hulled oat grain is steam-treated prior to rolling into flakes and drying. In this form it would require quite a long cooking time to gelatinize the starch and make it readily digestible. To reduce the cooking time manufacturers gelatinize the starch to varying degrees from those that require some cooking, to the 'instant' type of porridge.

Catering Uses of Cereal Products

Table 1.1. The main cereals, their products and catering uses

Cereal	Product	Main Catering Uses
WHEAT	Weak flour	Short paste goods, sponge goods
	Medium flour	Slab cakes, scones, aerated buns, queen, and Madeira cakes
		N.B. A mixture of weak and medium flours is often used for wedding, birthday, and simnel cakes.
	Strong flour	Bread, rolls, puff pastry, thickening soups, and sauces, batters, etc.
	Brown flour	Brown bread, rolls, scones, special germ breads
	White flour	'Patents grade' — may be used on its own or mixed with other flours for bread and cake making.
		'Bakers grade' — the main grade for bread making
		'Straight run' — a general purpose flour

Table 1.1 cont.

Cereal	Product	Main Catering Uses
		'Self-raising' — a general purpose flour used mainly by the domestic market 'High ratio' — a special cake flour for making very light cakes, e.g. angel and golden cakes 'High protein' — for the production of high ratio fruit cakes, e.g. cherry, wedding, Christmas cakes
	Semolina	All varieties of pasta, semolina puddings
	Processed grain	Breakfast cereals, e.g. 'Puffed Wheat', 'Sugar Smacks', 'All-Bran'
BARLEY	Malt product	Malt flour for bread making, malt extract for the brewing industry
	Pearl barley	Soups and stews
	Scotch barley (or pot barley)	Stews
MAIZE	Corn flour	For thickening of sauces, soups and the main ingredient in custard powder, blancmange
	Maize endosperm	Also known as 'hominy' and 'grits' Used to produce breakfast cereals, e.g. 'Cornflakes', 'Frosties'
OATS	Rolled oats	Porridge
	Ground oatmeal	Oatcakes, gingercake, parkins
	Oat flour	Not commonly used but an alternative to wheat flour
RICE	Grain	Short grain — mainly for rice based sweet dishes Medium grain — rice based sweet and some savoury dishes Long grain — savoury rice dishes
	Flour	Thickening of soups and sauces. Special cakes and macaroon goods
	Cones	Mainly for dusting bakery items during production
	Paper	Base for macaroons and sweets
RYE	Flour	Rye bread

Storage of Cereals

All cereals should be stored in a cool dry storeroom that is kept scrupulously clean.

If purchased in large quantities they should be stored in mobile steel bins with straight sides and with a close over-fitting lid. This is because cereals, and flours in particular, soon become the home of pests and rodents if care is not taken. When purchased in small quantities the same applies as above, with strict control over stock rotation being necessary.

Wheatmeal and wholemeal flours should be purchased in small quantities as the shelf life is limited to two months owing to the germ being present in the flour.

Scientific and Nutritional Aspects

Wheat Grain

The principal component of the wheat grain is carbohydrate in the form of starch; it is this component which provides man with energy when wheat is his staple food.

The next component present in order of quantity is protein (Table 1.2 shows the composition of wheat flours for various extractions. The values for 100% extraction can be taken as also representing the proportion of nutrients in the whole grain). Protein is the constituent that is necessary for repair of the body, and is also needed for growth in children. The protein in wheat is reckoned to be of adequate Biological Value, having a value of approximately 50 (compared with whole egg of 100 — the highest value, and millet of 40).

Table 1.2. Nutrients (g per 100 g) in various flours
(Data from McCance and Widdowson, 1978)

Flour	Extraction Rate (%)	Protein (g)	Carbohydrate (as starch) (g)	Fat (g)	Moisture (g)	Fibre (g)	Energy (Kcal)
Wholemeal	100	13.2	63.5	2.0	14	9.6	318
Brown	85	12.8	66.9	2.0	14	7.5	327
White, breadmaking	72	11.3	73.3	1.2	14.5	3.0	337
White, household plain	72	9.8	78.4	1.2	13.0	3.4	350
White, household, self-raising	72	9.3	76.1	1.2	13.0	3.7	339
Patent (mixed sample)	40	10.8	76.6	1.3	14.1	*	347
Cornflour	n/a	0.6	92.0	0.7	12.5	0	354
Oatmeal	100	12.4	72.8	8.7	8.9	7.0	401
Rye flour	100	8.2	75.9	2.0	15.0	*	335
Soya flour, full fat	n/a	36.8	12.3	23.5	7.0	11.9	447
Soya flour, low fat	n/a	45.3	14.5	7.2	7.0	14.3	352

* = not available
n/a = not applicable

Other nutrients present in the wheat grain are fat (wheat germ oil), minerals and vitamins (mainly of the B group).

Table 1.3 attempts to indicate the range of percentage composition of wheat grains used as human food.

Table 1.3. Range of percentage composition of wheat grain

	%
Carbohydrate	65–78
Protein	8–17
Fat	1–2·5
Minerals and vitamins	1–2
Moisture	8–15

The distribution of the nutrients in the wheat grain is by no means uniform – this is clearly indicated by a consideration of Table 1.2. The endosperm contains mainly carbohydrate and most of the protein of the grain, although the protein is not so concentrated in the endosperm as in the germ and the outer layers of the grain. The germ contains the fat along with traces of fat soluble vitamins. It is this fat (or oil) which can cause flours of high extraction to go rancid on prolonged storage. The germ is also rich in B group vitamins and protein.

The scutellum, the tissue separating the germ from the endosperm contains more than half of the total quantity of vitamin B_1 (thiamine) contained in the grain. The outer layers of the grain contain a higher concentration of protein, vitamins, and phytic acid than the endosperm.

Wheat Flours

Clearly the distribution of nutrients in the flour from the wheat grain will not necessarily be the same as that in the grain, since the composition of the flour will depend entirely on the extraction rate. As can be seen from Table 1.2, the extraction rate of 100% will give a flour containing all the nutrients and bran contained in the original grain; whereas lower extraction rates, although giving a more refined flour, with a more suitable combination of proteins for gluten formation, will necessarily be low in bran and those nutrients contained in the outer layers and in the germ.

White Bread versus Brown Bread

Much has been said and written on this topic, and what follows is merely a brief summary of the facts of the case, and by no means an exhaustive analysis.

It may be asked, 'Why white bread at all, when brown – or wholemeal and other high extractions – are perfectly good for food? Why bother to refine when the basic raw material is just as acceptable?'.

First consider the historical development of white flour (*see* McCance and Widdowson's interesting monograph on the history of milling (1956) for further details). As far back as Greek and Roman times white flour has been used to produce bread — it was produced by painstaking and time-consuming sieving of stone milled flour. Obviously white flour was more expensive to produce than wholemeal, hence it was only used by the rich. A similar pattern developed in Britain and Western Europe during the Middle Ages. In all societies the less privileged try to emulate the more privileged when they can afford it and so it was that the poor aspired to eat white bread.

During the Industrial Revolution it became easier to produce white flour and soon white bread became the staple of the poor, besides being part of the diet of the rich. Moreover white flour was seen by the millers to have some advantages over wholemeal as discussed below, added to which they could sell the by-product of the low extraction processes to farmers for cattle fodder. However, throughout history it is evident from literature that some people have always regarded wholemeal bread as being part of the good wholesome simple country life.

Advantages and Disadvantages of White and Wholemeal Flours

Compared to high extraction flour (brown), low extraction flour (white) may be said to have the following advantages:

(a) Obviously they are whiter. Products from them are said to be more attractive.

(b) The gluten developed in them during processing allows products to have a better cellular structure and texture.

(c) They contain less fat, and are therefore not so prone to rancidity during storage.

The disadvantages of white flours against those of higher extraction rates may be listed as follows:

(a) They contain less bran or cereal fibre. This at one time was certainly not considered to be a disadvantage, but recently attention has been focussed on diseases of the digestive tract which are associated with Western man's refined diet. Since the fibre is indigestible it adds bulk to the faeces and so exerts a mild laxative effect. It is thought by some authorities that this effect helps to prevent the onset of certain diseases such as diverticular disease, which, although common in developed countries where a refined diet is prevalent, is rare in developing countries, where a much less refined diet is the norm.

(b) They contain less vitamins.

(c) They contain less minerals.

(d) They contain less protein.

Examine Table 1.2 to see example variations in values of nutrient composition for various extraction rates.

Nutrient Supplementation

In order to minimize the loss of nutrients in flour of low extraction rate, the lost nutrients can be added back as pure chemicals.

The flour from which a standard white loaf of bread is made in the United Kingdom is normally of 70% extraction to which the following nutrients are added according to the Bread and Flour Regulations, 1984.

Table 1.4. Essential ingredients of flour according to the Bread and Flour Regulations, 1984

Substance	mg per 100 g flour
Calcium carbonate	between 235–390
Iron	not less than 1.65
Thiamin (Vitamin B_1)	not less than 0.24
Nicotinic acid or Nicotinamide	not less than 1.60

N.B. These nutrients must be present naturally in wholemeal, and must be added as necessary to other types of flour.

The controversy over the relative merits of white and brown bread will no doubt go on for a long time. Certainly it must be admitted that in the prevalent use of low extraction flours for white bread, even though they are fortified with some nutrients, some trace nutrients and some nutrients in larger quantities are missing from our diet. This may constitute an avoidable risk which we ought not to take. On the other hand it also must be admitted that there is no evidence, apart from that already mentioned in connection with cereal fibre and diverticular disease, to suggest that there has been an increase in illness due to a loss of nutrients from low extraction flour, since most people enjoy a mixed diet which will provide those nutrients removed during the milling process.

Changes Occurring in Flour During Bread Making

The two principal proteins which control the quality of the final product are gliadin and glutenin. When the flour is mixed with water and kneaded these two proteins become hydrated and form an elastic complex. This complex compound substance, consisting of about 60% gliadin and 40% glutenin, is called gluten.

The quantity and quality of the gluten formed controls the quality of the finished loaf. The elastic gluten is distributed uniformly throughout the dough as a three-dimensional network, therefore when the dough begins to leaven because of yeast action (fermentation), carbon dioxide is trapped by the framework of gluten. The elastic dough begins to rise as the trapped gas pockets begin to expand.

When the dough is baked, initially the yeast activity increases giving off more carbon dioxide, as the temperature rises to about $55°C$ ($130°F$) the yeast is killed, but the gas obviously continues to increase in volume. Vaporization of alcohol and water also aid the further expansion of the loaf, until at a temperature of about $75°C$ ($170°F$) the gluten coagulates, losing its elasticity.

Other components are changed by the baking process. Starch is gelatinized. Dextrinization and caramelization occur at the surface of the loaf, imparting to it the characteristic brown colour together with certain flavour compounds.

The Chorley Wood Breadmaking Process

In 1961 the British Baking Industries Research Association, which is centred at Chorley Wood, published details of the above process. Traditionally after the dough has been mixed initially, it is left for some time to allow yeast fermentation to occur. The yeast fermentation produces the volatile products, carbon dioxide and ethyl alcohol (thousands of gallons of these products escape daily into the atmosphere from bakeries!) which contribute to the risen structure of the final product.

Essentially the Chorley Wood process dispenses with the standing period. The same effect is obtained by very intense mechanical mixing of the dough. The amount of mechanical energy put into the mixing process is critical and therefore calculated carefully for given dough weight (5 watt hours per lb). The process requires extra yeast (total of 5lb per 280lb sack of flour) to be added initially to make up for that not grown during the fermentation period. More water is used than in the traditional process (1 gallon extra to 280lb of flour sack). Other differences include the addition of fat (2lb to 280lb sack of flour) and vitamin C [ascorbic acid at the rate of 75 parts per million (p.p.m.)].

Advantages of this process are as follows:

(*a*) an increase in yield of about 5%;
(*b*) more soft English flour can be used;
(*c*) a time saving of about 60%;
(*d*) space saving;
(*e*) products have very good consumer acceptance.

Flour Improvers

It has already been stressed that the quality of finished products depends largely on the quality of the gluten formed. The quality of gluten formed can be improved by the addition of 'improvers', basically these are oxidizing agents. Although the nature of the chemical reactions that bring about an improvement in gluten quality are complex and not fully understood, it is true to say that they bring about a greater degree of cross-linking between the protein molecules. The increased cross-linking clearly increases the stability of the gluten framework of the product made from the flour to which 'improvers' have been added, thus producing a better product.

Improvers besides increasing the stability of the gluten framework, generally have a bleaching effect on the flour. White flour produced by the milling process contains small quantities of pigmental materials which can be bleached by oxidizing agents, thus increasing the whiteness of the flour.

It should be noted that legislation controls the nature and quantity of improvers permitted in flour (Bread and Flour Regulations, 1984). They are presented in very small amounts, i.e. between 10–500 p.p.m.

In the past, improvement in the gluten quality was achieved to some extent by storing the milled flour for some weeks to permit natural oxidation of the air to improve the gluten quality. This process was known as 'ageing' the flour. A number of other permitted additives may be present in a flour in small quantities, to improve its storage properties and enhance its characteristics for a particular use.

Other Cereals

It is clear that wheat is the most important grain in the U.K. and therefore its scientific and nutritional aspects have been discussed to some extent. It is worth noting that the nutritional losses mentioned as being associated with the milling and refining processes of wheat flour, are closely paralleled with other cereal commodities, e.g. polished (white) rice is very much more deficient in minerals, vitamins, and protein, when compared with brown rice (rice with its husk intact). These aspects are important when a society is dependent upon such a cereal for its staple diet.

Dietary Fibre

An increasing emphasis on the role of flour and bread in a healthy diet has been placed by doctors and nutritionists following the recommendations of the C.O.M.A. Reports of 1981 and 1984. Table 1.5 illustrates the amounts of dietary fibre, fat, carbohydrate and protein found in the three main types of bread.

Table 1.5. Composition per 100 g grammes of bread

	White	Brown	Wholemeal
Carbohydrate	49.7	44.7	41.8
Protein	7.8	8.9	8.8
Dietary fibre	2.7	5.1	8.5
Fat	1.7	2.2	2.7

Table 1.6. Flour production by type
(data from M.A.F.F.)

| Type of flour | % volume | | | |
	1982/83	1983/84	1984/85	1985/86e
Breadmaking				
White	59.7	60.0	56.3	55.0
Brown	3.5	3.1	2.5	2.9
Wholemeal	4.9	6.2	7.3	7.3
Biscuit	13.1	12.9	13.7	12.9
Cake	2.0	1.7	1.8	2.2
Pre-packed household	2.3	2.1	1.5	2.8
Self-raising	2.9	3.1	3.3	3.1
Others	11.7	10.9	13.6	*13.8

*Includes flour for starch manufacture
e all 1985/86 figures estimated

2

Sugars, Preserves, and Confectionary Gums

Sugar

Sugar occurs naturally in nearly all plant structures, in the fruit, leaves and stems, however sugar for general commercial use is obtained from two major sources, the sugar cane and the sugar beet. After extraction and refining the two sugars are alike in every way and only rarely when impurities are found in a sugar can its source be determined and even then only after detailed analysis. Some 60% of the world's supply of sugar is obtained from sugar cane and 40% from sugar beet. Sugar cane itself contains approximately 18% sugar whilst sugar beet contains approximately 15% sugar.

Sugars may be classified under one or a combination of the following:

- (*a*) The source – beet or cane sugar.
- (*b*) The country of origin – West Indies and Guyana, England, etc.
- (*c*) The method of processing, which in turn determines the type of sugar produced, e.g. cube sugar, icing sugar, etc.
- (*d*) The catering uses. Specific types of sugar should be purchased for particular purposes. For example, cube sugar would usually be purchased for table use to serve with tea and coffee, and icing sugar would usually be purchased to be used as a decorative dusting for cakes or to be made into an icing such as royal icing to decorate birthday and wedding cakes.
- (*e*) The chemical group. Sugars may be classified chemically into two groups (i) monosaccharides, and (ii) disaccharides. (*See* pp. 32–3 for further information.)

The Functions of Sugar

Sugar is one of the most versatile ingredients used in food preparation. The reasons for its popularity are its constant and acceptable level of sweetness without any other taste or unpleasant flavour traces plus the fact that it has a very high level of purity.

Its main functions are:

(a) To sweeten beverages, cakes, pastries, sweet drinks, etc.

(b) To soften the gluten in flour and to make the baked product more tender to eat and lighter in texture.

(c) To colour the cooked product. For example, the addition of sugar will assist bread and cakes having a good colour (the addition of a brown type of sugar will assist in making rich fruit cakes dark in colour).

(d) To retain moisture and prevent in particular baked goods such as cakes from drying out.

(e) To act as a preservative, e.g. in jams, marmalades, canned fruit, etc.

(f) To act as an activator. Sugar helps yeast to grow faster by providing it with a readily available source of nourishment.

(g) As an anti-coagulant. Sugar helps to delay the coagulation of the proteins in eggs, e.g. in making an egg custard the sugar helps to prevent the custard from breaking down during cooking to form a firm coagulum, thereby providing a smooth texture.

(h) As the main ingredient for cake decorating, e.g. water icing, royal icing, fondant icing, etc.

The Extraction and Refining of Sugar

The extraction from the two main plant sources differs although the method of refining is the same.

Extraction

EXTRACTION FROM SUGAR CANE. The sugar cane is a tall (12–15 ft) grass-like plant which is grown extensively in a number of tropical and sub-tropical countries such as Fiji, Mauritius, West Indies, and Guyana. When the cane is fully grown and the sugar content analysed as being high, it is cut, trimmed and crushed by passing it through rollers to extract all of the juices. Some further juice is extracted by soaking the residual canes in hot water. The liquid is filtered and then treated with lime to remove organic acids and then heated to coagulate any unwanted protein matter.

The clear liquid is then further heated to reduce the moisture content before transfering it into vacuum pans where it is further reduced and then allowed to crystallize. The resulting mixture of crystals and dark coloured syrup, known as 'massecuite' is then transferred to centrifugal machines where the syrup is spun off leaving the crystals covered with just a surface film of syrup. At this stage it is known as raw brown or 'muscovado' sugar. The syrup that has been spun off is known as mollasses and is used for processing into rum, yeast, etc. The raw brown sugar is then sent to refineries. EXTRACTION FROM SUGAR BEET. The sugar beet is a root crop similar in external appearance to a large swede. It grows in the more temperate parts of the world such as England and Europe. The sugar beet is harvested and partially cleaned before being sent to the factory where it is further cleaned and then sliced. The slices are then placed in warm water in diffusion tanks and the sugar slowly diffuses out into the water.

The liquid from one tank is then run into a second tank containing fresh slices of sugar beet and the operation repeated many times until the sugar concentration is about 18%. The liquid is then treated in a similar way as that obtained from the sugar cane, that is, it is filtered, treated with lime, heated and the raw sugar then crystallized out from the molasses. The raw sugar is then refined.

Refining

The refining process is illustrated in Figure 2.1. It can be shown in four major stages.

(i) The raw sugar is mixed with a raw syrup to soften the adhering molasses and the molasses spun off in centrifugal machines.

(ii) The sugar crystals, plus any recovered sugar is dissolved in water and then treated to produce a colourless liquid.

(iii) The syrup is then concentrated and crystallized. The crystallization being in the charge of a skilled pansman who judges the correct degree of concentration of the syrup and at the correct moment induces the growth of crystals by letting into the pan a small quantity of sugar crystals called the 'seed'. The crystals are boiled and grown to the required size and then separated from any remaining liquor in a centrifugal machine and then dried in hot air driers.

It should be noted that the various kinds of sugar as well as the crystal size depend largely upon the quality of the concentrated sugar liquor, the time and temperature attained during the process.

(iv) The last stage is often one of milling during which the sugar is milled and sieved to grade the sugar into various known types, e.g. granulated, fine castor, icing sugar etc. An exception to this is the many types of cube sugar which are usually made by compressing the moist sugar crystals into moulds and then drying them.

The types of sugar commonly available with their catering uses are shown in Table 2.1.

The Cooking of Sugar

Sugar is boiled to various degrees by pastry chefs and bakers for the making of various sugar syrups, marzipan, fondant, petit fours, modelling pastes, etc. The density of a syrup may be tested by a saccharometer (a hydrometer) or for measuring high temperatures by a sugar thermometer. The type of sugar usually used is lump sugar and the cooking takes place in a special sugar boiler, with special care being taken to prevent any sugar crystallizing out.

Table 2.2 sets out the degrees baumé for specific syrups and the temperatures for cooking of sugar.

Preserves

The term 'preserves' in this book has been chosen to include all types of jams, marmalades, fruit curds, table jellies, mincemeat, and fruit pie fillings.

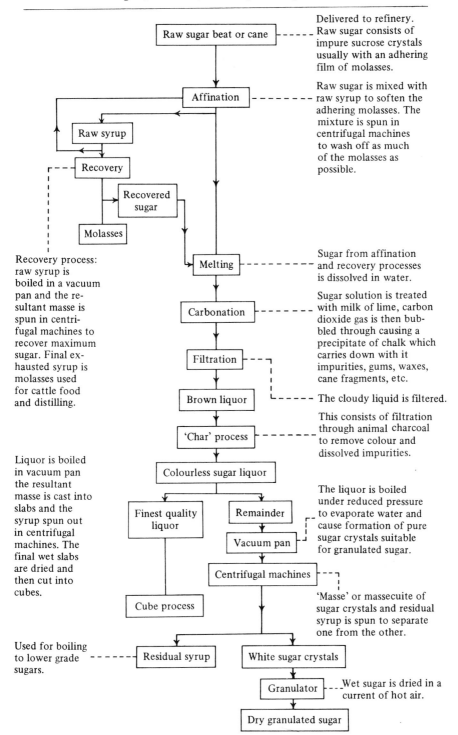

Delivered to refinery. Raw sugar consists of impure sucrose crystals usually with an adhering film of molasses.

Raw sugar is mixed with raw syrup to soften the adhering molasses. The mixture is spun in centrifugal machines to wash off as much of the molasses as possible.

Recovery process: raw syrup is boiled in a vacuum pan and the resultant masse is spun in centrifugal machines to recover maximum sugar. Final exhausted syrup is molasses used for cattle food and distilling.

Sugar from affination and recovery processes is dissolved in water.

Sugar solution is treated with milk of lime, carbon dioxide gas is then bubbled through causing a precipitate of chalk which carries down with it impurities, gums, waxes, cane fragments, etc.

The cloudy liquid is filtered.

This consists of filtration through animal charcoal to remove colour and dissolved impurities.

Liquor is boiled in vacuum pan the resultant masse is cast into slabs and the syrup spun out in centrifugal machines. The final wet slabs are dried and then cut into cubes.

The liquor is boiled under reduced pressure to evaporate water and cause formation of pure sugar crystals suitable for granulated sugar.

'Masse' or massecuite of sugar crystals and residual syrup is spun to separate one from the other.

Used for boiling to lower grade sugars.

Wet sugar is dried in a current of hot air.

Figure 2.1 A flow chart for the refining of sugar

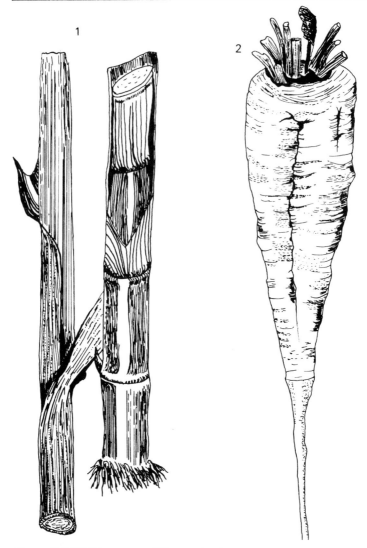

Figure 2.2 (1) Sugar cane; (2) sugar beet

The manufacture of preserves is controlled by 'The Jam and Similar Products Regulations, 1981' which prescribes the minimum permitted standards.

The Manufacture of Jam and Marmalade

The type and quality of a jam or marmalade depends on the careful selection of a suitable variety of the fruit, its degree of maturity and the amount of treatment required before being manufactured. Ideally, sound, medium ripe fruit should be used as this will be easier to handle, have a good flavour and colour, and any gel-forming pectin content would be high.

Table 2.1. The types of sugars commonly available with general notes and their catering uses

Product	General Notes	Catering Uses
Granulated	Produced by the standard refining process	General table use. Slab cakes, macaroon goods, sauces, etc.
Fine Granulated	As above but smaller crystals	Sponge and cake batters
Castor	Produced by boiling a very fine crystal or milling granulated crystals and sieving	Table sugar for fruits, cereals. Ideal for sponges, cake batters, short pastry, shortbreads, and biscuits
Fine	Crystal size between granulated and castor	Table sugar, sponge and cake batters. Vending machines
Extra Fine (in sachets)	Screened from granulated. Readily dissolvable and packed in paper sachets containing about $\frac{1}{4}$ oz	Table use
Icing	Produced by milling	Mainly cake decoration
CP Icing	With the addition of a small proportion of calcium phosphate to prevent hard lumps forming during storage	Mainly cake decoration
Pulverized	Produced by milling. Coarser than icing sugar	Cake decoration, short pastry, and biscuits
Coffee Crystals	Produced as granulated in several successive boilings. A large true crystal ten times the size of granulated. Amber brown in colour	Coffee drinks
Preserving	Produced as granulated in several successive boilings. Dissolves slowly to allow correct boiling of fruit	Domestic jam making and bottling
Cube	Moist granulated moulded into the required cube shape and dried. Available in different sizes and individually wrapped	Table use for drinks
Nibs	By-product of cube sugar	Cake decoration, e.g. Bath buns
Soft Brown	Made from sugar syrup after white sugars have been extracted. Fully refined. Light brown in colour and moist	Coffee drinks. Birthday and wedding cakes
Demerara	Produced similarly to soft brown sugars. The colour is a pale amber and the crystal	Coffee drinks. Rich fruit cakes

Table 2.1. cont.

Product	General Notes	Catering Uses
	size is coarse. May be pur-chased unrefined	
Fondant	Fine crystals held in a glucose syrup and or an invert sugar syrup. A white plastic mass	Coating of tea cakes, gateaux, petit fours, etc., giving a high gloss finish
Drifon	A special dry fondant made by Tate and Lyle Refineries Ltd	As fondant, but a high gloss finish can be retained more easily and easier to use than fondant
Golden Syrup	Processed from selected refinery syrups, partially inverted	Table syrup, puddings, and sponges
Black Treacle	Partially inverted filtered molasses	Ginger cakes and to darken rich fruit cakes
Glucose	Confectioners' glucose is a thick viscous, clear, trans-parent syrup. A complicated mixture of simple sugars and dextrin	Used in some cake making to keep cakes moist. Used also in sugar boiling
Honey	Obtainable as a clear, golden-coloured syrup, or as a thick opaque crystalline mass	Honey cakes, nougats etc. Table syrup

Table 2.2 The temperatures and catering uses for cooked sugar

Sugar Syrup	Catering Uses
Density by Degrees Baumé	
17°	Water ices
20°	Syrup for compôtes of fruit
22°	Syrup for soaking of babas and savarins
28°	Stock syrup for making the basic pâte à bombe mix for ice creams
Temperature °C (°F)	
115 (240)	Soft ball. Making of marzipan and fondant
121 (250)	Hard ball. Making of nougat, petit fours, etc.
138 (280)	Soft crack. Making of Italienne meringue
143 (290)	Pulled sugar for making baskets, roses, ribbons, bows, etc.
154 (310)	Hard crack. Dipping of fruit and marzipan for petit fours. To make spun sugar for decoration of gateaux St. Honore, etc.
177 (350)	Caramel. Used for crème caramel, etc.

The manufacture may be broken down into eight stages:

Sorting
The removal of leaves, stems, foreign matter, and defective fruit.

Washing
The initial cleansing of the fruit.

Preparation
This will differ, depending on the fruit and type of jam being made which may involve cutting, destoning, etc.

Pre-cooking
This is often done for several reasons such as:

    (*a*) to soften the fruit tissues to make any subsequent sieving easier;
    (*b*) to kill off by heat any micro-organisms;
    (*c*) to inactivate any enzymes which would affect the stability of the pectin during the storage of the jam;
    (*d*) as a measure to prolong the storage life of the fruit during the busy fruit season, prior to making it into jam at a later date.

Boiling
This is done today in vacuum pans as a lower boiling temperature can be used. Since it is a closed process the flavour may be more controlled. The fruit or fruit pulp is weighed out, the required quantity of water added and the fruit boiled for a few minutes before adding the required amount of sugar. Some five minutes before the end of the boiling period a measured quantity of liquid pectin is added (if required). The completion of the boiling is regulated by the boiling temperature reached by the jam — the higher the sugar content, i.e. of fruit and added sugar, the higher the final boiling temperature necessary, e.g. strawberry jam should have a final boiling temperature of 105–108°C (220–225°F). A further check is the finished weight of the jam after boiling.

Cooling and Filling
The jam is allowed to cool partially and is then transferred into sterilized containers, and then further cooled quickly.

Capping
When sealing jams a super heated steam injection is used to sterilize the head-space between the top of the jam and the inside of the metal cap, and on cooling to form a partial vacuum.

Labelling and Packing
This is the final stage.

    N.B. The texture of jam depends on a good gel formation which is dependent on the correct proportions of pectin, acid, and sugar in the final produce.

The Manufacture of Fruit Curds
Fruit curds are gels of an easily spreading consistency which are used for the
same purpose as jam for a filling in tarts, afternoon pastries, sponges, etc. The
most commonly made curds are lemon and orange. The composition of fruit
curds is controlled by 'The Jam and Similar Products Regulations, 1981'.

They can be made by mixing sugar, glucose, and margarine together, and
adding a solution of flour and water, and a solution of dried egg yolk powder
and water. The total mix is then gently heated and stirred continuously to
about 88°C (190°F) then passed through a fine sieve into a cooling vessel
where it is cooled and blended with any necessary colouring and flavouring
such as orange or lemon oil. The finished curd is then filled into sterilized
containers and sealed.

The Manufacture of Table Jellies
A table jelly is a stiff jelly made with a fruit juice or flavour, acid, sugar,
colouring, water, and gelatine.

It is made by soaking the gelatine in cold water so that it swells, maintains
its strength and will readily dissolve in a hot sugar solution. To this is added
an acid, usually citric or tartaric, some colouring, some clarified fruit juice and
flavouring if necessary. All of this is thoroughly mixed, passed through a series
of fine sieves, and then poured into shallow tray moulds to set. It is then cut
into tablets and packaged.

It is also possible to buy table jellies in a powder or crystal form, requiring
only the addition of boiling water to make it into a jelly.

The Manufacture of Mincemeat
Mincemeat is a traditional English preserve made with currants, sultanas,
candied peel, apples, sugar, spices, and suet. Its composition is governed by
the same food order as that for jams.

It is made by mixing together all of the ingredients after they have been
cleaned, dried and diced, or coarsely chopped. The apples require the most
preparation, i.e. washing, de-coring, peeling and dicing. Mincemeat is not heat-
treated at all, nor is it permitted to contain preservatives, and relies completely
on its own compositional factors to safeguard itself against microbiological
spoilage. After mixing of all the ingredients it is placed into sterilized cans or
glass jars and sealed.

The Manufacture of Fruit Pie Fillings
Fruit pie fillings are made from fruit (fresh, frozen, canned, and dehydrated)
sugars, stabilizers (modified starches, gum mixtures, etc.), colourings and
flavouring. Their special characteristic are their consistency at a wide range of
temperatures, they should not set when cold like a jam, nor be too runny
when hot. They can be made from a very wide range of fruits.

They are manufactured by first boiling the sugar and water together, adding
the pectin (if required) and colouring, then adding the clean, prepared fruit
and re-boiling. The suspension of starches, gums, etc., with water is prepared
and strained, and then added to the boiling fruit and stirred in. The fruit filling
is then partially cooled before being canned.

Confectionary Gums

'Confectionary gums' are a generic name given to a group of foodstuffs which have particularly useful gelling properties. Some gums are further useful in that they are used also as stabilizers and thickeners.

Confectionary gums can be classified by their:

- (*a*) catering uses, e.g. gelatine can be used in making table jellies, bavarois, aspic, etc.
- (*b*) source of origin
    - (i) animal, e.g. gelatine
    - (ii) marine, e.g. agar-agar, alginates
    - (iii) vegetable, e.g. arabic, tragacanth, pectin
    - (iv) synthetic, e.g. sold under 'trade' names.

The gums most frequently used are the following.

Gelatine
This is produced as a by-product from slaughter houses and is made by soaking hide trimmings and bones in a series of solutions of lime water to remove all undesirable matter and then soaking in hot water before filtering. It is available in sheet, flake and powdered forms.

Agar-agar
This is produced from a particular seaweed found along the coasts of Japan, U.S.A. and New Zealand. The seaweed is very well washed to remove any traces of salt, then pounded and boiled in water for 24–36 hours. It is then filtered and purified before being set in trays.

Alginates
This is also produced from a seaweed found off the coast of the U.S.A. The seaweed is washed, treated with chemicals until the salts of the alginic acids are fully extracted.

Gum Arabic
This is a substance which exudes from the stem of the acacia tree which grows in the Sudan and Australia.

Grum Tragacanth
This is also an exudate coming from the astragalus shrub which grows in Iran and Turkey.

Pectin
Pectin is a by-product of the cider and orange juice industries being found in the pips of apples and in the pips and pith of oranges (most citrus fruits are useful sources of pectin).

Synthetic Gums
These are produced to have specific standards of purity and gelling properties as well as being almost non-putrefactive.

Catering Uses of Preserves and Confectionary Gums

The catering uses of preserves and confectionary gums are shown in Table 2.3.

Table 2.3. Catering uses for preserves and confectionary gums

Product	Catering Uses
Preserves	
Jams	Table preserves. As a filling for tarts, sponges, etc. Jam sauces and glazes
Fruit curds	Table preserves. As a filling for tarts, sponges, etc.
Table jellies	Table jellies, glazing of prepared cold fruit
Mincemeat	Mince pies, mincemeat tarts, eccles cakes, etc.
Fruit-pie fillings	Filling for fruit pies and tarts
Confectionary gums	
Gelatine	Fresh fruit jellies, bavarois, aspic jelly, etc.
Agar-agar	Marshmallows. Mainly used as a stabilizer and thickener by food manufacturing industry
Alginates	Confectionary jellies. Thickener, by the food manufacturing industry
Gum arabic	Glazing macaroon goods
Gum tragacanth	Pastillage. Thickener, by the food manufacturing industry
Pectin	Jams. Proprietary brand sauces, etc.
Synthetic gums	Almost exclusively used by the food manufacturing industry

Storage of Sugars, Preserves, and Confectionary Gums

The storage of sugars, preserves and confectionary gums are shown in tabular form (*see* Table 2.4).

Scientific and Nutritional Aspects

The sugars which commonly occur in food products belong to chemical groups known as monosaccharides and disaccharides, which are members of the larger chemical group called carbohydrates. Examples of these common sugars are as follows.

Monosaccharides
(i) Glucose (dextrose) — occurs in grapes, onions, honey.
(ii) Fructose (laevulose) — found in most fruits and honey.

Both the above sugars have the same basic molecular formula $C_6H_{12}O_6$ but their molecular structures differ (i.e. the way the atoms are arranged in the molecule), giving rise to different properties.

Table 2.4. Approximate storage times for sugars, preserves and confectionary gums

Product	Satisfactory Storage Time
Sugars	
All varieties of sugar	2–3 months if kept in their original packaging unopened
Fondant	3 months if unopened
Drifon	1 year if unopened
Golden syrup/black treacle	1 year if unopened
Glucose	1 year if unopened
Honey	1 year if unopened
Preserves	
Jam	8–12 months if unopened
Fruit curds	6 months if unopened
Table jellies	6 months if unopened
Mincemeat	6 months if unopened
Fruit-pie fillings	6 months if unopened
Confectionary gums	
Gelatine and all confectionary gums	6 months if unopened

N.B. As sugars are hygroscopic (that is they absorb moisture from the air), and are packed usually only in paper or cardboard, they should always be stored in a cool and very dry storeroom.

Disaccharides

    (i) Sucrose (cane or beet sugar – the fundamental substance of granulated, castor, and icing sugars) found in fruits, sugar cane, sugar beet, maple.

    (ii) Maltose (malt sugar) – found mainly in malt.

    (iii) Lactose (milk sugar) – found mainly in milk.

The above disaccharides all have a common basic formula of $C_{12}H_{22}O_{11}$, and it is their different molecular structures which accounts for their differing properties.

Invert Sugar

This is a mixture of glucose and fructose which can be made by heating sucrose solution with acid (this occurs in jam making for example, with fruit acids). It may also be formed when sucrose solution is acted upon by the enzyme 'invertase' or 'sucrase' – an action which also occurs in the small intestine during digestion. Honey consists mainly of invert sugar which has been produced by the enzyme secreted by the bee.

Invert sugar is essential for satisfactory jam production — about 20% being
necessary to prevent crystallization of the sucrose when the jam has set.

The formation of invert sugar may be summarized by the reaction:

'hydrolysis'

enzyme or heat

sucrose + water with acid ⟶ glucose + fructose

invert sugar

$$(C_{12}H_{22}O_{11}) + (H_2O) \longrightarrow (C_6H_{12}O_6) + (C_6H_{12}O_6)$$

Similarly, the other disaccharide sugars may be hydrolysed to monosaccharides
by heating with acid, or by enzyme action.

maltose + water ⟶ glucose + glucose
(2 molecules of glucose)

$$(C_{12}H_{22}O_{11}) + (H_2O) \longrightarrow (C_6H_{12}O_6) + (C_6H_{12}O_6)$$

lactose + water ⟶ glucose + galactose

$$(C_{12}H_{22}O_{11}) + (H_2O) \longrightarrow (C_6H_{12}O_6) + (C_6H_{12}O_6)$$

Both the above reactions also occur normally in the small intestine during
digestion.

Commercial Glucose or Glucose Syrup

This is made on a large-scale basis by the hydrolysis of starch using enzymes
or acids. The acid is neutralized and the resulting solution concentrated by
evaporation, leaving a viscous liquid, containing the following substances:

glucose/maltose   — 35%
water   — 17%
other carbohydrates
  of varying types — 47%

This syrup is used extensively in the manufacture of confectionery, jam,
ice-creams, cakes, and other foods.

Properties and Characteristics of Sugars

Relative Sweetness

The characteristic property associated with the term 'sugar' is that of sweetness
— however, all sugars do not have the same degree of sweetness. The relative
sweetness of sugars may vary apparently from one individual to another, and
details quoted by authorities often differ. The figures given below will, however, give an idea of how the sweetness of sugars relate to each other
approximately.

If one gives sucrose — the most widely used sugar — a sweetness score of 100, the following may give a reasonable approximation of relative sweetness:

fructose	170
invert sugar	130
sucrose	100
glucose	70
maltose	30
galactose	30
lactose	15
saccharin	30,000
cyclamate	3,000
sorbitol	60

ARTIFICIAL SWEETNERS. These materials often replace sugars in manufactured foods, sometimes because of the high cost of sugar, but often because they can be easily tolerated by diabetics. For the most part they also have the distinct advantage for 'weight-watchers' that they have little or no calorific value to impart to the diet. This is either because they are not metabolized by the body, or because they are used in very small quantities as a consequence of their great relative sweetness, *see* above.

Saccharin is the most widely used material since it is synthetically produced and has a sweetness variously quoted as 300 times or 500 times greater than sucrose. It is not metabolized by the body and consequently has no food value, and is very suitable for diabetic and slimming-aid foods.

Sorbitol is a natural product occurring in some fruits, for example in plums and apricots. It is, however, metabolized in much the same way as sugars and therefore has a similar calorific value, but it is apparently tolerated by most diabetics, and consequently used widely in jams and preserves for such people.

Cyclamate, another synthetic product, was for some time preferred to saccharine until animal experiments in America suggested it had carcinogenic properties. It was preferred principally because it had little or no after taste as have some forms of saccharine and because it was heat stable in processing unlike saccharine.

The regulations in the U.K. on sweetners were revised in 1983, when four more new products were added to the permitted list; aspartame, thaumatin, xylitol and acesulfame potassium. These all have relative sweetnesses many times that of sucrose.

Action on Wheat Gluten in Doughs

By competing with the proteins for the water present in the dough, sugar affects the rate at which gluten forms. It is found in such doughs that since the gluten structure is somewhat limited in its development, the resultant product has a less elastic quality. It is sometimes stated that the gluten has been tenderized. This is only of significance in high sugar doughs.

Preserving Action

This phenomenon relies on the fact that sugar (normally sucrose) used in high concentrations exerts a dehydrating effect upon both food and micro-organisms. This osmotic effect dehydrates the cells of micro-organisms, certainly preventing them from multiplying, and often destroying them, and consequently preserving the treated food from spoilage. The common uses of sugars as preserving agents consist of the making of fruit preserves, jams, candies, condensed milk, etc. The storage life of certain other products, such as pies and cakes, owes something to the preserving effect of high concentrations of sugar, which like salt, make water unavailable to micro-organisms.

However, some yeasts and moulds can grow in the presence of as much as 60% sucrose, while most bacteria are inhibited at much lower levels. Yeasts (particularly *Saccharomyces cerevisiae*) involved in fermentation processes, e.g. in converting sugar to alcohol as in wine and beer manufacture, can be inhibited by the presence of high sugar concentrations.

Roles in Jams and Preserves

Beside their preserving action, sugars play another important role in successful jam manufacture. The texture of jam depends upon how satisfactory the gel formation has been, and this in turn relies upon the correct proportions of three principal components:

(*a*) pectin
(*b*) acid
(*c*) sugar

Pectin is a long-chain carbohydrate with a structure similar to that of starch and cellulose (*see* chapters on cereals and fruit and vegetables), and the gel is formed when sufficient pectin molecules are present (usually 1 or 2% of the total weight of the jam) and loosely form a stable three-dimensional framework which traps water containing the soluble solids of the jam, most of which are sugars (usually about 70% of the weight of jam is sugar).

It must be stressed that the amount of pectins and acids in fruit which will be made into jam is of crucial importance, as is the amount of sugar to be added, because gel formation only occurs when concentrations of pectin, acid, and sugar in mixture are within certain limits. Fruits high and low in pectin are listed in Table 2.5, those rich in pectin and acid are more easily made into a stable jam, than those poor in pectin content.

Table 2.5. Examples of fruit high and low in pectin content

High	Low
Lemons	Strawberries
Seville oranges	Cherries
Apples	Raspberries
Gooseberries	
Damsons	
Plums	
Currants	

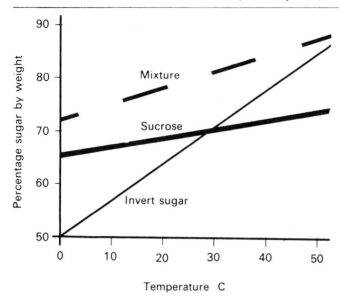

Figure 2.3 Solubility of sucrose, invert sugar, and mixture of sucrose and invert sugar

N.B. The solubility graphs clearly show that the mixture is much more soluble than either sucrose or invert sugar alone. Therefore the mixture that is caused to occur in jam manufacture stabilizes the sugars in solution, and prevents crystallization.

The nature of the sugar content is also important. Jam is usually made with the addition of sucrose, and the boiling stage in the process, in the presence of fruit acids brings about inversion to fructose and glucose — usually to the extent of 25–40%. (If significantly more than this, the invert sugar would precipitate out on cooling — rather like crystallized honey in texture.) This mixture of sucrose, fructose, and glucose (sucrose between 60–75% and invert sugar between 25–40%) is very stable and remains dissolved in the water of the gel, and does not crystallize out on storage of the jam — this is very important for a satisfactory jam (*see* Figure 2.3 on sugar solubilities).

Thus with the correct balance of components a jam can be made which is neither tough in texture, nor runny; which neither weeps on cutting (syneresis), nor crystallizes on storage.

Some Nutritional Aspects
Sugar provides energy in the human diet, but granulated sugar (and brown sugar for that matter) contains little else but sugar; similarly confectionary products provide few, if any, nutrients besides carbohydrate — the energy such foods provide is therefore often called 'empty calories'. Sugar consumption has fallen in recent years to an annual consumption per head of approximately

35 lbs or (16 kg). The consumption of preserves also continues to fall slightly. Tables 2.6 and 2.7 indicate the amount of sugar in the average diet and in selected foods.

Table 2.6. Approximate proportions of digestible carbohydrate in the average U.K. diet

	Per cent
Sugars and preserves	18
Vegetables including potatoes	15
Cereals	49
Fruit	5

Table 2.7. A sample of sugar contents for various foods (clearly actual values will depend on many factors, e.g. variety, ripeness, etc.)

	Per cent		Per cent
*Granulated sugar	99·9	Ice cream	19·8
Demerara sugar	99·3	English eating apples	11·4
Golden syrup	79·0	Onions	10·1
Honey	76·4	White grapes	16·1
Jam	69·0	Black grapes	15·5
Boiled sweets	86·9	Oranges	8·5
Milk chocolate	53·8	Green gooseberries	3·4
Plain chocolate	49·8		

*Castor and icing sugar will have very similar values, since the main difference between these and granulated sugar is crystal size

Since, in the U.K., we obtain just over half our energy from food in the form of carbohydrates, and of this, about 40% is from sugar, it can be seen that sugar plays a major role in providing energy in the average diet. However, this has not always been the case, over the past hundred years while the consumption of cereals in the U.K. has fallen, the consumption of sugar has doubled! It has been suggested by some that this great increase in sugar consumption has led to a greater incidence in our society of atherosclerosis, diabetes, obesity and dental caries.

Confectionary Gums

As their name suggests these materials have 'gummy' characteristics. They rely mainly for their properties on their hydrophilic capability, that is the ability with which their molecules, usually polysaccharides or their derivatives, attract water.

They are widely used in the food industry in general, and valued for their ability to swell and form gels or viscous solutions or dispersions when mixed with water.

Examples are listed below.

GUM ARABIC. An exudate as previously explained, has the ability to form solutions of high viscosity and to recrystallize, and this together with the fact that it is non-toxic, odourless, tasteless and colourless make it very suitable for a variety of uses from 'gum drops' to preventing the recrystallization of sugar in many food products. It is also able to act as an emulsifier in certain applications.

GUM TRAGACANTH. Again a complex polysaccharide exudate. This substance too, has the ability to absorb water to form gels, and it is used in foods because of its thickening power and ability to hold suspended particles in suspension over a wide range of pH and temperature.

AGAR-AGAR. Perhaps best known to many college students as the base gel material used in microbiological cultures. Agar is also a complex polysaccharide, and although almost insoluble in cold water, it dissolves in boiling water. The resulting gel it forms on cooling, and its uses in foods are related to its emulsifying and gelling properties, and also to the thermal stability of its gels.

Another gelling agent which has a long history of usage in foods, is gelatine, a protein formed by hydrolysis from collagen, the connective material protein of animals. In food preparation dry gelatine is usually allowed to swell in a small amount of cold water. When hot water is later added the gelatine disperses and upon cooling a gel forms. Gelatin is used extensively in food preparation as a gelling agent; as a stabilizer in whipped foams, to increase viscosity of sauces, in aspic jelly, as added jelly in meat pies and to prevent large ice crystal formation in frozen desserts.

Since these materials are often mixed with other food constituents, the resulting gels are very good growth media for bacteria, as one would expect since they resemble the nutrient agar media used in microbiological cultures. Therefore extreme care must be taken to keep them at temperatures below $10°C$ and free from bacterial contamination, to prevent them from becoming possible causes of food poisoning.

3

Fats and Oils

Types and Sources of Fats and Oils

Edible fats and oils are obtained from three main sources: vegetable; animal; and fish.

Vegetable Oils

These are derived from the seeds of plants which grow in many parts of the world but mainly in tropical and sub-tropical regions. The main vegetable oils are obtained from the following.

Coconut Palm

The coconut is harvested when ripe, the outer fibrous husk is removed and the nut exposed. This is then cut in half, exposing the thin white fleshy layer, known as the 'meat'. This is the endosperm of the nut. This may be eaten raw, or processed into products such as desiccated coconut, or dried in the sun or in kilns. When dried it is known as copra in which state it is exported to countries who extract and refine the oil. The main sources of supply are the Philippines, Oceania, Malaysia, and Sri Lanka.

Oil Palm

The fruit grows in large bunches of some 150–200 fruits weighing in total up to 40lb. The structure of the oil palm fruit consists of an outer skin, an inner layer of fibrous pulp (pericarp) which is rich in oil, and a nut of which the inner kernel is also rich in oil – the more valuable 'palm kernel oil'. The main sources of supply are Nigeria, the Congo, Malaysia and Indonesia.

Olive Tree

The ripened fruit of the olive tree produces one of the finest of all vegetable oils. The first crushing of the fruit gives the highest grade oil which needs no refining. It is exported mainly by Italy, Spain, and Greece.

40

Groundnut or Peanut Plant
The plant produces pods containing the nuts a few inches below the surface of the soil, which makes harvesting more complicated than for those sources previously mentioned. It is exported as nuts, and as oil, by such countries as Nigeria, West Africa, and China.

Soya Bean
The soya plant, a member of the pea family, produces many pods which each contain three to four beans on each plant. Although relatively low in oil content (between 13–20 per cent) the soya bean has recently become the leading source of vegetable oil in the world. It is mainly exported by the U.S.A., China, and Brazil.

Animal Fats
Animal fats are one of the many by-products from the slaughtering of animals for human consumption. Fat in animals occurs naturally and is found mainly as a layer under the skin and also surrounds and protects vital organs of the body such as the kidney and the intestines. The three main sources are from the following.

Beef Animals
These are the largest of animals commonly killed for human consumption and a high quality fat is obtained as a by-product. Suet is obtained from around the kidneys and shredded. The intestinal fat is processed at low temperatures to produce two products, oleostearin and also oil, both of which can be used in the manufacture of margarine.

Pigs
This species of animal tends to have a higher fat to meat ratio than other animals and therefore large quantities are available.

Sheep
Very small quantities of sheep's fat are used. This is mainly because the fat tends to be harder than beef or pork fat and has a stronger flavour and odour.

Fish Oils
These are obtained by the extraction of oil from the whole fish. The fish most suitable are those with a high fat content and these are mainly pelagic type fish such as the herring, pilchard, sardines, and anchovies. Unfortunately these are unsaturated oils and are susceptible to oxidative attack and must therefore be carefully refined and hydrogenated before being used in margarine and cooking fats. Fish oils are imported from Peru, Norway, and Iceland.

Classification

Fats and oils may be classified under the following headings:

    (i) by their original natural source when possible, e.g. animal fats, vegetable oils or marine oils;

(ii) by their physical state at room temperature and by their chemical nature, i.e. whether they are fats or oils;

(iii) by their catering uses.

In order to obtain satisfaction about the quality of the end-product, the correct fats and oils should always be used.

The Functions and Uses of Fats and Oils

There are two main functions for fats and oils as follows.

An Ingredient

Fats and oils are used as an ingredient in bread, cakes, pastry type goods, etc., for many reasons, in particular the following.

Flavour

If the fat contains flavour as does margarine, it will impart that flavour to the goods of which it is an ingredient. Any off-flavour such as that from fats that are mildly rancid will also be imparted.

A Good Appearance

The correct quantity of a quality fat will assist in giving a cooked product an even texture, a better bloom, and a good saleable appearance. Some research has indicated that the presence of fat will raise the temperature at which the product sets in its final shape.

Keeping Qualities of the Product

Fat by its emulsifying action, holds the moisture content of a bread dough and cake batter and assists in preventing the bread, cake, etc., from drying out too quickly.

Shortening Property of the Product

All fats are shortening agents, that is they reduce the extensibility of the gluten in the flour. The gluten is split up by films of fat which weakens the structure sufficiently to make it tender, giving a product which when cooked is friable and easily broken, e.g. shortbread, short pastry, etc.

To Obtain a Good Volume

When products are made by the creaming process it is the fat which holds the air. Therefore the creaming properties of a fat, or its ability to entrap air, will result in rising taking place uniformly and sufficiently throughout a mixture giving a cooked product of good volume and of uniform grain and texture.

To Add Nutritional Value to a Product

Fats are important in the diet, being a concentrated source of energy and a carrier for some important fat soluble vitamins.

A Cooking Medium/Ingredient

Shallow Frying
The oil or fat acts as the medium for the transfer of heat to the food, although the item being processed is only partially immersed in the oil or fat.

Deep Frying
In this method of cooking the oil acts as the medium for the transfer of the heat from the fryer to the food (the food being fully immersed in the hot oil). Oils used for deep frying should have a high smoke point (*see* pp. 51–2), be stable oils and be mainly bland in taste so that there is no evident transfer of flavour from the oil to the food product.

Basting or Roast Meats etc.
Basting serves the function of preventing the meat drying out, giving colour to the cooked meat, and adding flavour.

The Manufacturing Processes for Fats, Oils, and Margarine

The fats and oils that are used in the catering trade come from a variety of sources, from vegetables, animals, and fish. It is rarely that the raw, unprocessed fat or oil is in a form that can be used straight away without being treated in some way.

The Refining Process
The objective of this process is to produce oils and fats which are pure and completely free of taste, smell, and colour.
   The process is in five main stages.

Degumming
This is the removal of impurities from the crude oil or fat and of substances which will cause the end product to develop 'off' flavours and odours. The crude oil is mixed with a weak salt solution and the impurities are precipitated off into the salt solution which is then strained off.

Neutralization
This stage does two important things. It removes the free fatty acids from the oil which would cause rancidity (*see* p. 52) and it partly bleaches it.

Bleaching
The oil is bleached in a process using Fuller's earth. This is added to the crude oil while it is under vacuum and the earth absorbs the colour pigments.

Filtration
The oil is passed through a series of filter presses to remove the Fuller's earth.

Deodorizing
This is the final stage in refining in which the volatile impurities are removed by a steam distillation process. The deodorized oil is then filtered again. On

completion of this stage the oil, e.g. a salad or cooking oil is completely ready for any suitable edible purposes.

The Manufacture of Margarine

Margarine is a fat bearing a close resemblance to butter. The fat content of margarine is not dairy fat although a small proportion of it is permissible. Margarine was invented in the nineteenth century by Mege-Mouries, a Frenchman, who was competing in a competition organized by the French government for a substitute for butter. As margarine is a substitute for butter its contents and labelling are strictly controlled by legislation.

The manufacture of margarine is in six main stages.

Hydrogenation

This is the process by which oils can be hardened by the addition of hydrogen to give them a higher melting point and to make them more stable (*see* pp. 48–9).

Final Refining

After hydrogenation it is usual to process the oil again through the stages of neutralization, bleaching, and filtering to remove the breakdown substances from hydrogenization.

The Blending of Oil and Fats

The manufacturer makes his selection of which oils and fats to use on two main criteria, the cost of the raw ingredients and the particular required properties of the margarine to be produced. The wide selection of oils and fats available to the manufacturer enables him to control his raw material costs. The type of margarine to be produced determines the blend of different fats and oils that may be used to give a particular melting point, acceptable spreading ease, and plasticity.

Aqueous Phase

This can be just water when the margarine is produced for religious or dietary reasons. Usually, however, it consists of cultured, sweet skimmed milk or reconstituted milk powder. In addition, salt as a brine can be added if required to give a salt content in the margarine of up to 2%. The percentage of salt depends on the type of margarine being produced and which part of the country it is to be sold in.

Addition of Special Ingredients

Four special ingredients may be added to the fat after the hydrogenization. They are:

- (a) Vitamins A and D. The quantities of Vitamin A and D are laid down by the Margarine Regulations.
- (b) Colouring matter. A colouring ingredient may be added to give an overall satisfactory colour to the finished product.
- (c) Flavouring agents. These are usually some of the constituents found in butter such as butyric acid.
- (d) Emulsifiers. These are to ensure that the fat and liquid parts of the margarine do not separate out at a later stage.

Emulsification

The fat blend and the aqueous phase are next mixed and solidified in special apparatus known as a Votator. The mass of fat is then mixed further to become homogeneous. The margarine is then packaged.

Figure 3.1 shows the manufacture of fats and margarine in diagrammatic form.

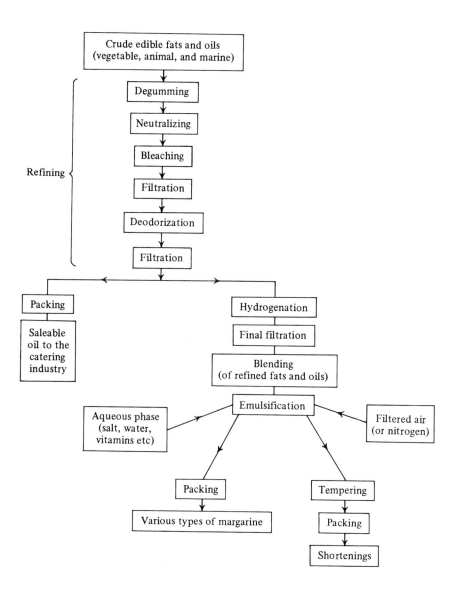

Figure 3.1 The manufacture of oils, fats, and margarine

Types of Margarine
The manufacturing process of margarine allows many types of margarine to be made by:

(*a*) varying the refined and hydrogenated fats and oils to be used so as to obtain margarines of different plasticity and melting points;
(*b*) adding if required the permitted 10% milk fat (by weight);
(*c*) adding salt if required;
(*d*) varying the quantity of water (maximum of 16%).

The common types in use are listed under the section on Catering Uses for Fats and Oils.

Shortenings
These are also known as 'fat compounds' or 'bakery utility fats' having originated in the U.S.A., as a lard substitute. Shortenings are usually made from vegetable oils with at times the addition of lard. The manufacture is very similar to that for margarine, except that shortenings contain no water (*see* Figure 3.1).

The manufacture of shortenings provides the basic method of classification. The improvement on ordinary lard being by the aeration of shortenings. Moulded shortenings containing up to 10% trapped air, and liquid filled shortenings from 10–30% trapped air.

A special shortening known as high ratio shortening allows a much higher ratio of sugar to flour to be used in the manufacture of cakes than is usual. This is possible by the addition of certain emulsifiers to the shortening which gives the cake dough a higher strength.

Lard
This is the original shortening which lost favour mainly because of the advancement of food technology making the hydrogenization of oils possible. Lard is the processed fat of pigs, the fat mainly coming from the loin and kidney regions. It is processed mainly by the wet method of processing in which the fat is rendered in large vats by live steam at a high pressure. Lard in recent years has been partially hydrogenated to improve its plasticity and also to make it more resistant to rancidity. The creaming properties of lard are usually not as good as many of the special shortenings.

The catering uses of fats and oils are shown in Table 3.1.

Scientific and Nutritional Aspects

Fats and oils are chemically very similar, the difference between them being that fats are normally solids or plastic semi-solids, at normal temperatures [i.e. around 20°C (or 70°F)], whereas oils are liquids at similar temperatures. These edible oils are distinct from mineral oils (which are hydrocarbons containing only the elements carbon and hydrogen) and cannot be used by the body, and are a health hazard. Mineral oils are therefore specifically prohibited in foods under the 'Mineral Hydrocarbons in Foods Order'.

Table 3.1. Catering uses of fats and oils

Product	Main Catering Uses
Vegetable oils	
coconut oil	Margarine
palm oil	Margarine
palm kernel oil	Margarine
olive oil	Salad and cooking oil
groundnut oil	Cooking fats and oils. Margarine.
soya bean oil	Salad and cooking oils. Margarine.
Animal fats	
beef suet	Suet for confectionary mincemeat, suet pastry, and ingredient in stuffings
beef oleostearin } oleo oil }	Margarine
beef dripping	Shallow frying, basting of roast meats, etc.
pig – lard	Cooking fat, savoury pastry
Fish oils	Margarine and cooking fats
Margarines	
soft margarine	Domestic table use – as a butter substitute
general purpose	Substitute for butter – general purpose fat
pastry	Particularly for puff pastry products – a higher melting point and capable of standing heavy mechanical working
cake	As a cake fat requiring high creaming properties
saltless	Ideal for use in pastry creams for gateaux etc.
Kosher	For members of the Jewish faith
Low calorie spreads	Not a 'true' margarine. Containing less than statutory amount of fat.
Shortenings	
moulded shortenings	General cake and pastry making
liquid filled shortenings	Special cake making
high ratio shortenings	Special 'light' cakes

Edible fats and oils are known chemically as 'glycerides', and occur widely in most animal and plant foods – some of the sources are given in Table 3.1. In animals, fat is often found as a protective layer around vital organs, e.g. suet around the kidneys, as well as being dispersed between layers of muscle (meat) and occurring beneath the skin as adipose tissue. Fish oil is often associated with the liver, e.g. cod liver oil, and while the flesh of white fish has very little associated with it, *see* Table 3.2, some fish such as herring and mackerel have quite oily flesh.

Chemically fats and oils (or glycerides) are composed of the elements carbon, hydrogen and oxygen (not in the same proportions as carbohydrates, *see*

Chapter 2). All molecules of glycerides consist of what might be termed a glycerol 'back-bone' to which three fatty acid molecules have been attached, Figures 3.2 and 3.3 illustrate this.

Table 3.2. Approximate percentages of fats and oils in some common foods in the U.K. diet

Cooking oils	100	Cod	1
Margarine	92	Herring	12
Lard, etc	99	Sardine	24
Butter	82	Cream	42
Bacon	45	Eggs	12
Lamb	30	Milk	4
Beef	28	Cheese	34
Veal	4	White bread	1
Pork	40	Wholemeal bread	2
Liver	6	Rice	1

The characteristics of the fat or oil depend upon the nature of the acid molecules attached to the glycerol. It should be noted, that when a fat or oil is discussed in terms of its fatty acid content, the acids are chemically attached to the glycerol and are not free, unless otherwise stated.

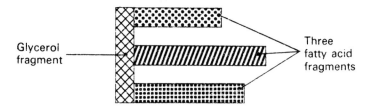

Glycerol fragment — Three fatty acid fragments

Figure 3.2 A crude diagrammatic representation of a glyceride molecule, showing glycerol 'backbone' to which three dissimilar fatty acid molecules have been attached

There are two principal factors concerned with the fatty acids which govern a fat or oil's properties.

The Molecular Weight of the Fatty Acid
The longer the carbon chains are, that are attached to the glycerol, clearly the heavier will be the resulting fat molecule. The heavier the fat molecule, the more likely it is to be a solid at normal temperatures of say 20°C (approximately 70°F); conversely, the lighter it is, the more likely it is to be liquid at normal temperatures. To summarize fats containing long carbon chain fatty acids will tend to be solids, while those with short carbon chains will tend to be liquids at room temperatures.

The 'Degree of Saturation' of the Carbon Chain of the Fatty Acids
Briefly 'degree of saturation' is a term which describes whether or not all the

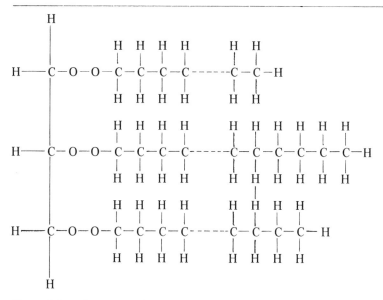

Figure 3.3 A diagrammatic representation showing possible arrangements of atoms in a typical glyceride molecule

carbon atoms in the carbon chains of the acids have the maximum number of hydrogen atoms associated with them. If the maximum number of hydrogen atoms is present in the carbon chains of the acids, then the fat or oil is said to be 'saturated'. However, if there are less than the maximum number of hydrogen atoms that can be accommodated present in the carbon chains, the fat or oil is said to be 'unsaturated'. Therefore 'the degree of saturation' or 'the degree of unsaturation' of a particular fat or oil, will depend upon how far short of the maximum number is the number of hydrogen atoms in the carbon chains of the constituent fatty acids.

The more unsaturated a fat or oil, the more likely it is to be a liquid at normal temperatures, e.g. mutton fat has a high degree of saturation (or a low degree of unsaturation) and is a brittle solid fat at $20°C$ ($70°F$), whereas corn oil has a high degree of unsaturation and is liquid at $20°C$.

Of the two factors discussed above, molecular weight and 'degree of unsaturation', it is the latter which has the greater effect. This can be clearly illustrated by considering two fatty acids which commonly occur in natural fats and oils — both of animal and plant origins. Consider the following data:

Acid	Formula	Molecular Weight	Melting Point ($°C$)
Stearic Acid	$C_{17}H_{35}COOH$	284	69
Oleic Acid	$C_{17}H_{33}COOH$	282	15

The fact that oleic acid, the major fatty acid in olive oil, contains only *two* less hydrogen atoms than stearic acid, a constituent of beef tallow, accounts for the great disparity in melting point — i.e. oleic acid is a liquid at $20°C$

whereas stearic acid is a brittle solid. Such characteristics as these similarly govern the physical properties of the fats, of which the acids form a part.

Hardening Oils

Until fairly recently vegetable oils were reasonably cheaply and readily available. Largely, they were imported from developing countries at prices which were well below those charged for animal fats in most western countries. It was therefore an attractive proposition to try to incorporate them in such products as margarine and manufactured shortening products. However, some naturally occurring vegetable oils were unsuitable because of their low melting points caused by their degree of unsaturation. To overcome this difficulty, so that the oils will have a more solid consistency at normal temperatures, hydrogen has to be introduced into the unsaturated molecules. This can be done by bubbling a stream of hydrogen gas through the heated oil, to which has been added finely divided metallic nickel to catalyse the reaction. In this way liquid oils with a high degree of unsaturation can be converted by this process of 'hydrogenation' into fats of a more solid consistency, with a lower degree of unsaturation.

Emulsifying Agents

As has been previously discussed margarine is a mixture of processed vegetable oils or animal fats or both, cultured milk, salt, colouring and vitamins (in regulated amounts). In order for these ingredients, especially the oil/fat and water phases to remain stably mixed, another type of substance must be added – this class of compounds is known as 'emulsifying agents' or 'emulsifiers'. Margarine is a water in oil emulsion, i.e. water droplets dispersed in oil. For this situation to be stable, another substance which has an affinity for both water and oil must be interposed between the water and the oil (Figure 3.4 shows this very simply). Such substances are lecithin (a substance which occurs naturally in egg yolk) and mono- or diglycerids; any one or all of them might be used in margarine.

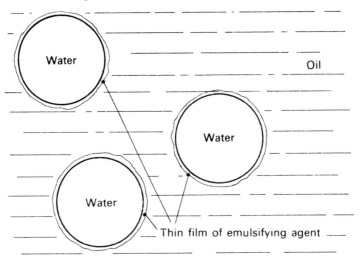

Figure 3.4 A simple diagram showing relationships between oil/emulsifying
agent/water in a stable water/oil emulsion, such as margarine

Plastic Properties

Many different oils and fats may be used in the manufacture of margarine and other shortening agents, such as animal fats, peanut, sunflower, coconut, palm kernel, palm and rape seed oils. Partially hydrogenated soya bean, cotton seed, or maize (corn) oils are generally used. These may be balanced with soft oils, such as sunflower or maize, to control plastic properties and increase the content of unsaturated oils.

The trend today is towards the production of softer margarines which spread easily, and shortenings which 'rub-in' easily, over a wide temperature range and release flavour rapidly. For diet-conscious consumers a margarine can be produced which contains about half as much fat as normal margarines, and consequently much more water.

Shortening Properties

One of the major factors which accounts for the difference in texture between a shortbread biscuit and a bread roll is the fat content; it is much higher in the former than the latter. The properties and nature of gluten has been described earlier (*see* Chapter 1), and it was seen that it was the long strands of gluten which gave bread its characteristic elastic open texture.

In bread, the gluten molecules were able to soak up water during the mixing of the dough to form the characteristic elastic mass. If, however, a larger proportion of fat is added, which will coat the gluten, water penetration is prevented and long elastic strands of gluten are not formed. The gluten remains in short lengths, and the elastic complex is not formed. Hence the texture of a baked product containing a higher amount of fat will be more crumbly or 'short' — the texture of shortbread is a good example.

Creaming Properties

When beaten vigorously fats have the ability to form quite stable foams with air. The incorporation of air may be initially helped by the presence of sugar granules in the beaten mixture, but the stability of the foam will be greatly increased for example by the presence of the emulsifying agents present in margarine, if margarine is the fat being used. The plasticity of the fat also helps in the formation of foam, and as previously mentioned, this in turn is dependent on the nature of the fatty acids in the constituent fat molecules, which governs their range of melting points.

While a low melting point range might be preferred for the preparation of products where creaming is an essential step, high melting point fats have been manufactured with a low degree of unsaturation (hard fats) for particular purposes, e.g. in the production of 'flaky pastry', where the fat is required not to melt or flow and soak into the dough, but simply to separate layers of pastry, to give the required flaky texture.

Heating Characteristics

When fats and oils are heated they melt at first (if they were solid at room temperature), then if heating is continued, their surface begins to 'shimmer' and a faint blue haze may be seen above the surface — the 'haze' point temperature has been reached. It is at this sort of temperature that deep frying should be carried out. If heating is continued above the haze point, smoke will begin to rise from the surface of the heated fat — the 'smoke' point temperature has been reached, and the fat or oil has begun to decompose. The decomposition takes place in *two* stages:

(i) the fat splits into glycerol and fatty acids; and
(ii) the glycerol further decomposes to form a toxic substance, acrolein, which has a nauseating smell.

If this decomposition has been allowed to occur, the fat or oil should no longer be used, but discarded. It is worth noting that food debris in the oil or fat will lower the smoke point, and similarly prolonged use will cause breakdown of the oil or fat, with obvious effects on products cooked in it. (In fact, current research suggests that this may well constitute a real health hazard.)

The example data given below may illustrate the deep-frying principles described above:

Oil	Smoke Point °C (°F)	Approximate Recommended Frying Temperature °C (°F)
Groundnut	199 (390)	182 (360)
Cottonseed	182 (360)	160 (320)
Pure edible dripping	177 (350)	170 (340)

Storage Properties
Fats and foods containing fats are subject to spoilage in various ways. Among them is the property that fats have of picking up strong odours and flavours from other goods stored nearby.

Fats are also subject to rancidity — the result of which gives rise to very unpleasant flavours and odours. There are two types of rancidity.

Hydrolytic Rancidity
This is due to the fat or oil splitting up into glycerol and free fatty acids. Such reactions are often brought about by moulds or bacteria. This is best prevented by keeping oils and fats, and products containing them, cool and dry, and by practising good hygiene.

Oxidative Rancidity
This is caused by oxidation and is much more common. It occurs in unsaturated fats and oils (and their products), where oxygen from the air joins on to the carbon chains of the fatty acids which are short of hydrogen atoms. The oxygen absorbed by the fat in this way forms 'peroxides' which give rise to the rancidity. Fats therefore which contain a high proportion of unsaturated acids, such as maize, soya, and sunflower seed oils are especially prone to this type of rancidity, as are products containing them.

It has been discovered that nature has a way of preventing such rancidity — naturally occurring highly unsaturated vegetable oils contain natural antioxidants. One of these is Vitamin E. Often processing removes the natural anti-oxidants, and manufacturers now add these or, more often, cheaper synthetic anti-oxidants to processed fats and oils to prolong their shelf-life.

Storage of Fats and Oils

Table 3.3. The approximate storage times for fats and oils

	Cool, dry store 12°C (55°F)	Refrigerator 4–7°C (40–45°F)
Oils	2–3 months	not applicable
Lard	7 days	1 month
Suet – shredded	1 month	not applicable
– fresh	not applicable	2 weeks
Margarine	7 days	1 month
Shortenings	7 days	1 month

N.B. Fats and oils should be kept in sealed containers to reduce exposure to light and air which would cause rancidity, and also to prevent picking up undesirable odours and flavours from other foods, etc.

Nutritional Aspects

Fat is important in the human diet, and performs a variety of functions. It is a concentrated source of energy, providing over twice as much as the same weight of carbohydrate. Fats and oils are carriers of the fat soluble vitamins, A, D, E and K. The function of the most important fat soluble vitamins are often given as:

(i) Vitamin A being concerned with building of body cells, particularly in the skin, and also associated with good vision.
(ii) Vitamin D helping to maintain bones and teeth in a healthy condition.

Vitamins E and K are widely distributed in the average diet, but most of A and D come into the diet via butter, cheese, meat, eggs and fish, and now, since the 1920s, also in margarine. Manufacturers in the U.K. add vitamins A and D to margarine – the law demanding a minimum rate of:

(i) Vitamin A – 27–33 International Units per gram of margarine.
(ii) Vitamin D – 2·8–3·5 International Units per gram of margarine.

Fat also helps to make food palatable and at the same time, satisfying, producing a feeling of 'fullness' after eating.

Today, much research on the possible connections between the nature of a fat and heart disease is being carried out. Studies so far appear to show that people with a high cholesterol level in their blood, run a high risk of heart disease. It has been found that oils with a high proportion of unsaturated fatty acids tend to reduce the cholesterol level in the blood, when taken in the diet. These oils are of vegetable origin, e.g. soya bean, sunflower, and cottonseed and are now used widely in specially prepared soft margarines.

Table 3.4. Approximate percentage distribution of fats and oils in the U.K. diet

	Per cent
Fats and oils	36
Milk, cream, cheese	20
Meat (all types)	25
Fish (all types)	1.3
Eggs	3
Cereals	11
Fruit	1
Vegetables	2

Table 3.5. Summary of N.A.C.N.E. guidelines

Food component	Short-term advice	Long-term advice
Fat Currently providing nearly 40% total energy	34% of energy intake	30% of energy intake
Saturated fat	15% of energy intake	10% of energy intake
Sucrose Currently nearly 40 kg per head per year	34 kg per head per year	20 kg per head per year
Salt Estimated at a total of 12 g per day per head	Decrease by 1 g per day per head	Decrease by 3 g per day per head
Alcohol It should provide no more than:	5% of energy intake	4% of energy intake
Fibre Currently about 20 g per head per day	25 g per head per day	30 g per head per day

Table 3.6. Summary of C.O.M.A. guidelines

Food component	Advice
Fat	35% of energy intake
Saturated Fat	15% of energy intake
(Polyunsaturated fats should be increased as a proportion of total fat intake)	
Sucrose	Should not be increased
Salt	Ways should be found to decrease amounts consumed
Alcohol	Excessive intake to be avoided on general health grounds
Fibre	It is advantageous to increase fibre-rich foods such as bread, fruit, cereals, fruit and vegetables

4

Dairy Type Foods (Milk, Cream, and Ice-cream)

Milk

Milk is the natural food for young mammals during the first stages of life when they are unable to obtain food for themselves. It is a near perfect single food containing proteins, carbohydrates, fats, mineral elements, etc., but is lacking in iron and vitamins C and D. It is an emulsion, a suspension of minute droplets of fat in a watery solution. Milk from several species of animals is used for human consumption in different parts of the world (e.g. goats, sheep, mares, water buffalo, etc.), but in the U.K. it is obtained from dairy cows with a very small amount of goats' milk available in some parts of the country.

Cows' milk purchased in the U.K. is a 'safe' food in that all milk sold comes from attested herds. A farmer is unable to obtain a licence to sell milk until all his herd have been officially tested individually and certified as being free from tuberculosis infection.

The Milk Marketing Board (M.M.B.)
The board was formed in 1933 with the main objective of guaranteeing a market at a fair price for every dairy farmer's milk. This still remains the board's primary function today despite its extensive activities into other milk products, butter and cheese production.

Every farmer who produces milk for sale must by law sell it through the M.M.B. A farmer who wishes to sell milk by retail direct to the consumer must first be licensed by the board to do so. The vast majority of the dairy farmers, some 37,000 have a yearly contract with the board which is responsible to find a market for all the milk offered by the milk producer, whether it is to a retail milk distributor or to a manufacturer. Sales to a manufacturer are only permitted when all liquid milk and cream demands are satisfied, with markets bringing in the highest price taking preference, e.g. the demand by a cheese producer being met before that of a butter producer. Approximately two-thirds of the milk from farmers is used for liquid milk and cream. The remainder is made into milk products with some two-thirds of it being processed into cheese and butter and the rest into condensed milk, dried milk, and cultured milk products, e.g. yoghurt.

The M.M.B. has increased its functions beyond that of buying milk produced on farms and selling it to distributors and manufacturers. It also provides assistance to farmers with breeding and herd management schemes by providing an artificial insemination and a milk recording service; it operates a milk quality control scheme and operates a collection and distribution service for the milk.

Milk Pricing in England and Wales

Milk is the only food that is subject to Government price control at the various stages of its journey from the producer to the consumer. The price that the M.M.B. pays for milk brought from the dairy farmers is largely determined by government guarantees which are fixed annually; the price at which the board sells milk to distributors is fixed by the Minister of Agriculture Fisheries and Food (N.B. milk to be used for manufacture into dairy products is not subject to these controls) and the maximum sale prices of liquid milk at various stages of the distribution process, including the retail stage are also fixed by the Minister.

The Composition of Milk

The composition of milk obtained from a cow is not the near standard product which is purchased by the caterer or member of the public from his dairy supplier. Milk is required to contain some 8·5% (minimum) solids not fat and 3% (minimum) fat under the Drinking Milk Regulations, 1976, otherwise it is presumed to have been adulterated. The largest percentage constituent is water, 80—85%, containing the proteins, carbohydrates, fats, mineral elements, etc. Should milk be sold specifically under the names of Channel Islands or South Devon milks it must legally contain 4% fat.

The variations in the composition of the milk are caused mainly by the following.

The Breed of Cow

Jersey, Guernsey, and Ayrshire cows are noted for producing milk that is high in butter fat content and solids not fat, but low in milk yield, whilst cows such as Freisians produce milk that is low in butter fat content and non-fatty solids but high in milk yield. The typical yield from a cow is about 850 gallons during the period of lactation. The price paid to a farmer for his milk is based on the percentage of non-fatty solids and the total solids present in the milk.

The Phase in the Lactation Period

The period lasts for approximately 40 weeks during which the maximum yield is obtainable around the third to fourth week followed by a gradual decline in yield. Therefore to produce a reasonably standard daily/weekly yield of milk the dairy farmer needs to stagger calving by the cows so that the lactation periods of a dairy herd is balanced.

The Type of Feed

To obtain milk containing at least the minimum statutory amounts of fat and non-fatty solids with as high a yield as possible, it is necessary for the diet of the cow to be controlled. In the winter cows tend to live indoors and to be fed on hay, silage, oilcake, and some root vegetables, all of which are expensive but result in milk rich in fat content. In the spring and summer the cows live outdoors and feed mainly on grass (of differing quality depending mainly on the weather) and produce a high yield of milk richer in vitamin A than in the winter, but frequently low in fat content as a result of a lower roughage content in the diet.

The composition of milk, although almost a complete food for man, makes it an ideal medium for the growth of bacteria and other micro-organisms. In order to ensure that liquid milk sold for human consumption is a safe product it is necessary to have a system that reduces the number of harmful bacteria and micro-organisms often found in milk and then to process it in such a way that all the harmful bacteria and micro-organisms are destroyed. This is done by taking the milk from fit, clean animals under hygienic conditions, collecting the milk in sterilized containers and then cooling and keeping the milk at a temperature of less than 4·5°C (40°F). On receipt of the milk at a dairy or creamery it is always checked for appearance and smell and undergoes a chemical test for freshness if there is any doubt.

Grades of Liquid Milk

Milk is graded according to the heat treatment that is applied to it prior to being sold. The various grades are defined by 'The Drinking Milk Regulations, 1976' and are identifiable in bottles by the different coloured metal foil caps.

There are four main grades of fresh liquid milk that are heat treated and one that is not.

Pasteurized

This is milk that has been subjected to the pasteurization method of heat treatment. The process heats the milk to a temperature high enough to kill any pathogenic organisms and reduces the number of any others present so as to make the milk safe for human consumption without spoiling its accepted flavour and appearance. It is done in one of two methods, either heating the milk to 63–65°C (145–150°F) for 30 minutes (the Holder method) or more usually by heating it to not less than 72°C (161°F) for 15 seconds (the High Temperature Short Time – HTST). As soon as the heating time ends the milk is rapidly cooled to below 10°C. The rapid cooling is to restrict the growth of heat-resistant organisms and to ensure that the cream line will be distinct in bottled milk.

These two groups of milk are sold as pasteurized milk.

ORDINARY MILK. This is milk of no special description but fully complying with the minimum standards of butter fat (3% minimum).
CHANNEL ISLANDS AND SOUTH DEVON. This is milk from Jersey, Guernsey or South Devon breeds of cow which is being sold under this description and therefore is required by law to have a 4% minimum butter fat content.

Homogenized

This is milk which has been treated to make it of uniform composition, i.e. the cream is distributed evenly throughout the milk. The process consists of heating the milk to about 60°C (139°F) and then forcing it through a very small tube at a high pressure breaking up the fat globules into very small droplets. The droplets remain suspended in the milk and do not float to the top forming a cream layer as in ordinary pasteurized milk. The treatment produces a milk which has a smoother creamier taste. The milk is then subjected to heat treatment being either pasteurized or sterilized.

Sterilized

This is milk that has been heated to a temperature higher than boiling temperature to ensure the destruction of all micro-organisms (i.e. more completely than pasteurization). The milk is first pre-heated, homogenized and then filled into bottles which are closed with a hermetic seal. The 'sterilization' is then done in two main ways.

(*a*) In-bottle sterilization in which the milk is filled into bottles and then heated for 30–40 minutes at a temperature of 104–110°C (220–230°F) in large autoclaves or pressure steam chamber and then allowed to cool.

(*b*) Continuous flow sterilization by an ultra-high-temperature method (*see* UHT below).

Because of the high temperature to which the milk has been subjected it will have a 'cooked' flavour due to the slight caramelization of the sugar (lactose) and a creamy appearance.

Ultra-heat-treatment (UHT)

This is milk that is first homogenized and then subjected to a high temperature of between 135–150°C (276–304°F) for at least 1 second. The UHT process kills off all micro-organisms and the very short holding temperature reduces the changes in colour and flavour that occur with the in-bottle sterilization process.

The shelf life of UHT milk can be extended to several months by filling the milk into specially designed Tetra-pak cartons which are plastic coated and lined with an aluminium foil. The packs are usually date stamped. This reduces the need for daily deliveries of milk and for refrigeration.

Untreated Milk or Farm-bottled Milk

This is raw milk which has not been subjected to any form of heat treatment at all before being offered for sale. A special licence is required by the farmer or supplier to produce and sell this milk and it is therefore unlikely to be readily available in all parts of the country.

Legislation

The composition of milk depends on the provision of E.E.C. Regulation No. 1411/7, as amended by E.E.C. Regulation No. 566/76, and the Drinking Milk Regulation, 1976.

It should be noted that the Food Labelling Regulations, 1984 do not apply specifically to milk itself. There are, however, special designations for milk (e.g. 'pasteurized', 'sterilized', etc.) prescribed in the Milk Regulations, 1977 and the Milk and Dairies Regulations, 1982.

Semi-skimmed Milk

This is milk which has had some of the cream content removed reducing its calorie content per pint from 380 to between 263–280. The Regulations require that its milk fat content be a minimum of 1.5% and a maximum of 1.8%.

Skimmed Milk

This is milk that has had virtually all of the cream removed and with it the vitamins A and D. It has a calorie content per pint of 195 and a maximum fat content of 0.3%.

Concentrated Milks

The concentration of milk serves four main purposes:

(a) it reduces bulk by the reduction of the water content;
(b) the heat treatment (and high sugar content in condensed milk) gives the product a very good shelf life;
(c) it is a convenient outlet for skimmed milk from the production of butter and cream;
(d) it requires no special form of storage.

There are two main types of concentrated milks (evaporated and condensed) both being produced from whole milk (full cream) or skimmed milk.

Evaporated Milk

This is an unsweetened concentrated milk. It is produced by first pasteurizing the milk, evaporating it under reduced pressure in steam-heated vacuum pans until the volume has been reduced to 60% when it is then homogenized, cooled, and canned.

Condensed Milk

This is a sweetened concentrated milk. It is produced by a similar process to that of evaporated milk except that prior to the evaporating stage sugar is added. The sugar content in condensed milk is about a 62% concentration in the water of the condense'd milk. The milk is then cooled very carefully so that the crystallization of the lactose is in very fine crystals before being canned.

Dried Milk

The drying of milk serves similar purposes to that of the liquid concentrated milk. In this case the water content is removed entirely and thereby the bulk is reduced. It requires no special storage facilities and is an outlet for the skimmed milk from butter and cream production. It includes any milks which have been sweetened, modified, or compounded (Dried Milk Regulations, 1977).

Table 4.1. A summary of the varieties of fresh liquid and concentrated milks available, their butter fat content and processing method

Grade or Type of Milk	Legal Minimum Fat %	Heat Treatment	Processing
Fresh Liquid Milk			
Pasteurized Ordinary	3	Pasteurized	Mild heat treatment 72°C (161°F) for 15 seconds and rapid cooling
Pasteurized Channel Islands and South Devon	4	Pasteurized	As above
Homogenized	3	Pasteurized	Milk heated to about 60°C (139°F) then forced through fine tubes under pressure to break down fat globules. Then treated as above.
Sterilized	3	Sterilized	Homogenized then sterilized in bottle at 104–110°C (220–230°F) for 30–40 minutes or by UHT at 135–150°C (276–304°F) for 1 second, then cooled.
Ultra-heat-treatment	3	Ultra-heat-treatment	Homogenized then heated to 135–150°C (276–304°F) for 1 second, then cooled
Untreated ordinary or Channel Island and South Devon	3 or 4	No heat treatment	Cooled to below 10°C (50°F)
Semi-skimmed	1.5	Pasteurized or sterlized	As above
Skimmed	0.3 (max.)		Homogenized
Concentrated Milk			
Evaporated Full cream	9	Pasteurized	Pasteurized, then evaporated to reduce volume to 60%, homogenized and cooled.
Evaporated Skim milk	—	Pasteurized	As above
Condensed Full cream	9	Pasteurized	As above, except that sugar is added before the evaporating stage. Very careful cooling after homogenizing.
Condensed skim milk	—	Pasteurized	As above

There are two main processes for drying milk.

ROLLER DRYING. The milk is usually concentrated in an evaporator until it has about 17% total solids (as against 11·5% minimum in fresh liquid milk) before it is then homogenized. The milk is then fed on to the very smooth surface of single or twin heated drums operating at a temperature of about 150°C (303°F). The water content in the milk evaporates very quickly leaving a very thin film of dried milk which is scrapped off by a blade fixed to the roller. The thin film is then quickly cooled before being ground into a powder and sieved before being packed in air-tight containers. (Milk powders are hygroscopic, i.e. they will quickly absorb moisture from the atmosphere and the powder will deteriorate becoming stale in flavour and less soluble on reconstitution.)

Roller drying is the cheaper process of the two and produces a product that is practically free from bacteria owing to the severe heat treatment it receives. However it has the disadvantages of having a slight 'cooked' flavour, it does not reconstitute easily having a solubility of about 85%, and the structure of the fat globules in the milk is destroyed causing an oily layer to form on the surface when reconstituted in warm water.

SPRAY DRYING. The milk is pre-heated to a temperature of 80–90°C (175–196°F) for some 10 seconds, homogenized and then concentrated at about 43°C (110°F) to about 40 per cent total solids. The milk is then atomized to a fine mist in a drying chamber containing hot air at 165°C (330°F). The very minute particles of milk give off their moisture almost instantaneously and drop to the bottom of the drying chamber as tiny grains of dried milk. The powder is removed to cool as quickly as possible before being packed into air-tight containers.

Spray drying is the more expensive process but it has a very good solubility of over 98% with less pronounced flavour changes than roller dried milk.

Description and composition of dried milk

Dried high fat milk	– Dried milk:
High fat milk powder	min. 42%, max. 65% milk fat max. 5% water
Dried whole milk	– Dried milk:
Whole milk powder	min. 26%, max. 42% milk fat max. 5% water
Dried partly skimmed milk	– Dried milk:
Partly skimmed milk powder	min. 1.5%, max. 26% milk fat max. 5% water

'INSTANT' MILK POWDER. A more recent development has been the production and marketing of instant non-fat (skimmed) milk powders which dissolve easily and completely when added to water, tea, coffee, etc. The process used is based on a modification of the spray-drying method in which the dried milk powder is moistened with steam to give a lumpy porous structure, the lumps of powder then being dried, cooled, and then reduced to a more standard size. When added to a liquid they quickly absorb it and dissolve completely. The cost of this type of milk powder is higher than that of the conventional milk powders and its main use appears to be in hot beverages.

SUBSTITUTE MILK POWDER. This is also a relatively recent development being aimed specifically at the hot beverage market. The products do not contain any milk constituent at all but are specially processed from products such as dried glucose, syrup, and vegetable fat. A particular claim for this type of product is that it is low in calories (11 calories per teaspoonful) as against other forms of milk.

Cultured Milk

The commercial production of some of these milks in the U.K. has mainly been since the early 1950s, but it has been common in European countries for centuries. Cultured milk is produced from the milk of cows, goats, ewes, and mares. The process consists in general terms of deliberately souring milk by adding specific harmless bacteria which will then produce an acid and so control the growth of possible harmful bacteria. The process originated by man's attempts to prevent milk from being totally unusable and developed into a variety of products in different countries which were not only palatable but nutritious and easily digestible. Many of the products although not well known are available in some continental delicatessen shops.

Cultured milks can be classified into three groups based on:

(*a*) butter cultures;
(*b*) yogurt cultures and related strains (N.B. yogurt is also spelt as yoghurt and yoghourt).
(*c*) weak alcoholic sour beverages.

Butter Cultures

These include buttermilk, cultured cream, and European cultured milks such as lacteral (Poland), ymer (Denmark), and nordische sauermilch (Switzerland)

(*a*) Buttermilk is a by-product from the manufacture of butter. It is made from pasteurized skimmed milk which is incubated with an acid producing butter culture. It can be obtained either as sweet or sour buttermilk depending on whether fresh or ripened cream was being used to manufacture the butter (*see* p. 76).
(*b*) Cultured cream is prepared by a similar process to that of yogurt (*see* below). It is made from pasteurized single cream which is incubated with an acid producing butter culture. It is often marketed as 'fresh' soured cream to distinguish it clearly for the purchaser from cream which has soured by accident or carelessness. It may be used in recipes in place of soured cream.

Yogurt Cultures and Related Strains

These include yogurt (in many forms and flavours), curdled milks (Germany and Russia), and soured milk drinks (Germany).

(*a*) Yogurt can be made from whole, partially skimmed milk, skimmed milk, evaporated milk, dried milk, or a mixture of these. It is common, however, for it to be made of skimmed milk to which solids are added to give it a total solids content of between 12–16%.

The milk is homogenized, then heated to 88–105°C (190–200°F) for about 30 minutes, cooled to 41–45·5°C (106–114°F) then innoculated with two special laboratory cultures and held at this temperature for about $1\frac{1}{2}$ hours. It is then poured into cartons and left in a warm atmosphere until the milk has fully clotted. The cartons are then cooled in stages and held in cold store at 5–8°C (40–46°F) during which the yogurt sets firmly.

Various types of yogurt are available, natural yogurt made only of milk products, natural yogurt sweetened with sugar, fruit yogurt which may be flavoured with pieces of fruit or just fruit juice or a flavouring essence.

Weak Alcoholic Sour Beverages

The manufacture of this group of cultured milk products differs from the previous two groups in that,

(a) yeast cultures which produce alcohol are introduced in addition to bacterial cultures;

(b) the conditions of manufacture are often not so strictly controlled, as many are still made in local areas on a small scale.

This group includes Kefir (Poland), Koumiss – also spelt as Kumys and Kumiss (Russia), whey champagne (Poland), and Felisowka (Poland).

KEFIR. Kefir is made from whole or skimmed cow's milk to which the Kefir grain is added. The milk is incubated with the grain for about 20 hours at 16–20°C (61–68°F) until a clot is formed. It is then left for 1–3 days to mature during which time the alcohol and acid content percentage increases. The finished product resembles single cream in appearance, is slightly gassy and has a lactic acid (sour) flavour.

KOUMISS. This was originally made from mare's milk but is now produced also from skimmed cow's milk. To the milk is added two cultures and it is then incubated at 37°C (99°F) for about 4–6 hours. It is then cooled to 30°C (86°F) and yeast is added and it is incubated for a further 4–6 hours at 25°C (77°F). Like Kefir it is left for one to three days to mature during which time the alcoholic and acid percentage increases. The product resembles single cream in appearance, but is slightly grey in colour and has small gas bubbles throughout. It is sour to taste and has a faint alcoholic smell.

WHEY CHAMPAGNE. This is made from clarified whey – a by-product of cheese-making. It has yeast and caramel added in its preparation. The product is of a clear light amber colour with a 'slight sparkle' to it and a faint caramel flavour.

FELISOWKA. Felisowka is made from buttermilk – a by-product of butter manufacture. The milk is fermented at 15–18°C (59–64°F) for 8–10 hours until the required acidity is reached. The liquid that has separated to the top is siphoned off and sugar and yeast added. The buttermilk is then bottled, sealed, and kept at 18–20°C (64–68°F) for some 4 hours. The product is then cooled to below 8°C (46°F) and stored. The final product should foam strongly due to CO_2 production and have a sweet, yeasty, and refreshing taste.

Cream

Cream is the lighter portion of milk containing all the main constituents of milk but in which the butter fat content is high and the solids (not-fat) content low.

Cream is commercially separated from the milk at a creamery by means of a mechanical separator. The milk is first heated to between 32–49°C (90–120°F) before being run into the separator which operates like a centrifugal machine rotating at a high speed and forcing the milk (heavier) to the outside whilst the cream (lighter) remains in the centre. The cream and skimmed milk are drained off by separate outlet pipes, and by means of a control valve the fat content of the cream is adjusted. The skimmed milk is then heated to about 79·5°C (175°F) to kill off any harmful bacteria and then cooled to 4·5°C (40°F) before being processed into dried milk, etc.

There are a variety of fresh creams available to caterers and the retail trade each having a particular legal minimum butter fat content as required by the Cream Regulations, 1970. Each cream will also have been further processed in a particular way, such as being homogenized, to thicken the cream and to ensure that the cream is evenly distributed.

Table 4.2 summarizes the varieties of cream and their legal minimum butter fat content.

Whipping Cream
Although whipping cream and whipped cream are available for purchase, ready for use, many caterers attempt to whip other types of cream without success. In order to whip cream efficiently the following points should be observed.

(*a*) Cream containing a total average butter fat content of 38%–42% is required.

(*b*) Homogenized cream will not whip at all satisfactorily. This is because when whipping cream tiny bubbles of air are trapped and surrounded by the fat globules in the cream. Homogenized cream will have had the majority of the fat globules broken in the homogenizing process and therefore there are not sufficient available to surround and trap the air.

(*c*) The cream and the utensils to be used for whipping should be cooled to below 8°C (46°F).

(*d*) The utensils used should first be sterilized.

Manufactured Creams

Reconstituted Cream
This is specifically mentioned in Section 47 of the Food and Drugs Act, 1955 as being a substance that is not true cream as the general public would understand, but a substance that resembles it in appearance. It must contain no ingredient that is not derived from milk other than water and other ingredients which have not been added to increase bulk or to conceal inferior quality.

Table 4.2. A summary of the varieties of fresh cream available, their legal butter fat content and processing method

Type	Legal Minimum Fat % (by weight)	Heat Treatment	Processing
Cream or single cream	18	Pasteurized	Homogenized and pasteurized by heating to $79.5°C$ ($175°F$) for 15 seconds and rapidly cooling to $4.5°C$ ($40°F$). Filled into bottles or cartons and sealed
Whipping cream	35	Pasteurized	Pasteurized only
Double cream	48	Pasteurized	Slightly homogenized before being pasteurized
Double cream 'thick'	48	Pasteurized	Heavily homogenized before being pasteurized
Sterilized half cream	12	Sterilized	Homogenized, filled into cans and sealed, heated to $115°C$ ($240°F$) for some 20 minutes and then cooled rapidly
Sterilized cream	23	Sterilized	As for sterilized half cream.
Cream or single cream	18	Ultra-heat-treated	Homogenized and then heated to $132°C$ ($270°F$) for 1 second and cooled rapidly. Aseptically packed in foil lined containers
Clotted cream	55	Special	Heated to $82°C$ ($180°F$) and then cooled slowly for 5 hours when the cream is skimmed off. Alternatively the milk is allowed to stand for 12–24 hours for the cream to rise and it is then scalded (heated to $77–88°C$ ($170–190°F$) for 30–40 minutes). After slow cooling the cream is skimmed off
Aerosol-cream	35	Ultra-heat treated	May contain 13% sugar plus permitted additives. Capable of 400% volume increase

It is made by emulsifying butter or butter fat with skim milk or skimmed milk powder.

Imitation or Synthetic Cream

This is also specifically mentioned in Section 47 of the Food and Drugs Act, 1955. It is a substance that is not cream nor reconstituted cream, but resembles it in appearance and is usually made by emulsifying vegetable fats with dried egg, gelatine, etc. and adding to sugar and flavourings.

It is a product which is frequently used in the catering and baking trade but which is very easily contaminated and liable to cause food poisoning.

Ice-Cream

The term 'ice-cream' is unfortunately used loosely to cover a very wide range of products which are available as confections or frozen desserts. The range extends from ice-lollies to the true ice-creams and to special ice mixtures usually of a particular shape such as bombes.

The composition of ice-cream is controlled by 'The Ice-Cream Regulations, 1967' that states what the permitted minimum contents are to be for particular described types. Table 4.3 sets out the requirements. It will be noticed by the reader that the regulations do not include items such as ice lollies, sorbets or water ices.

Table 4.3. A summary of the compositional requirements from 'The Ice-Cream Regulations, 1967'

Type	Minimum Fat Content (%)	Minimum Milk Solids (other than fat) Content (%)
Ice-cream	5	$7\frac{1}{2}$
Fruit ice-cream	5 or $7\frac{1}{2}$	$7\frac{1}{2}$ 2
Dairy ice-cream/Dairy cream ice/Cream ice	5 milk fat	$7\frac{1}{2}$
Milk ice-cream	$2\frac{1}{2}$ milk fat	7
Parev ice (or Kosher ice)	10	None (N.B. No milk or milk derivatives permitted.)

N.B. The regulations also state that 'No ice-cream of any kind nor any Parev ice shall contain any artificial sweetener'.

Ice-creams can be classified under the following five headings:

    (i) Those containing milk solids, e.g. dairy ice-cream, fruit ice-cream, etc;

    (ii) Parev ice, e.g. Kosher ice;

(iii) Those containing no milk solids and not covered by 'The Ice-Cream Regulations, 1967', e.g. water ices, sorbets, punches, granit;
(iv) Speciality ice-cream mixture, e.g. bombes, etc;
(v) 'House-made' ice-cream sweets, e.g. coupes and sundaes, etc.

The manufacture of ice-cream is controlled by 'The Ice-Cream (Heat Treatment etc.) Regulations, 1959 and 1963' which in particular is concerned with the ingredients being either pasteurized or sterilized early in the process, then cooled to below $7 \cdot 1°C$ ($45°F$) within $1 \cdot 5$ hours and kept at that temperature until frozen when it must be held at less than $-2 \cdot 2°C$ ($28°F$). If at any time in the manufacture the temperatures should be exceeded the total ingredients must be pasteurized or sterilized again.

Commercially made ice-creams are of two main categories, hard ice-cream and soft ice-cream of which hard ice-cream is the most commonly used by caterers. The typical composition for a hard ice-cream is shown in Table 4.3. The main difference in composition of the two categories is that the soft ice-cream usually contains less fat, more milk solids, and more water.

The manufacture of ice-cream by a caterer is also controlled by the same regulations as regards composition and heat-treatment. The differences are that the equipment used is of a much smaller size and is less sophisticated, that the ice-cream produced will usually be made for consumption either the same day or within a few days and that the ingredients used will most likely be 'fresh' and of a high quality. There are three basic types of ice-cream made by caterers; cream ices; water ices; and bombe type ices.

Dairy Ice-Cream, Fruit Ice-Cream, etc.
There are many types of dairy ice-cream made by manufacturers and based on the recipe for a vanilla ice-cream substituting the vanilla flavour by chocolate and coffee extracts, etc., or by adding fruit juice and pulp such as from strawberries, raspberries, blackcurrants, etc.

The manufacture of a commercial hard ice-cream is in five stages.

(a) The ingredients are mixed together and the solid ingredients dissolved or dispersed in warm water. The purpose of adding a stabilizer to the mix such as gelatin is to obtain a smooth texture and improve the body of the ice-cream.
(b) The mixture is then either pasteurized or sterilized.
(c) The mixture is then homogenized to reduce the size of the fat particles present and to disperse the ingredients evenly.
(d) The mixture is then frozen at about $-5°C$ ($22°F$) in either a batch or continuous freezer process. During the freezing of the mixture air is bubbled in to lighten the texture. This increases the volume of the mixture by as much as 90–100% and is known as the 'overrun'. The 'overrun' in soft ice-cream is only about 50%. The mixture at the end of this stage becomes a stiff, plastic, semi-frozen product and in this state is packaged into cartons, etc.
(e) The packaged 'ice-cream' is then 'hardened and conditioned'. This is done by submitting it to a temperature of $-46°C$ ($-50°F$) for one

hour and then storing it at −29°C (−20°F) for some two to three days after which it is ready for sale.

Parev Ice

Parev or Kosher ice is a type of ice-cream that is made specifically for customers who are members of the Jewish faith. The Ice-Cream Regulations, 1967 specifically state that Parev ice shall contain not less than 10% fat and contain no milk fat nor other derivative of milk. It may be served on its own, or as the ice-cream content in coupes and sundaes.

Water Ices, Sorbets, Punches, Granit

This group of ices is not specifically covered by the 1967 Regulations. They are available from ice-cream manufacturers and are also commonly made by caterers on their own premises. They are manufactured in a similar way to ice-cream but from a mixture consisting largely of water to which is added sugar, fruit pulp, a stabilizer (often sodium alginate), synthetic flavourings, and colourings. When made by a caterer they would be made from a stock syrup with fresh fruit and egg whites only. The success of this group depends on the density of the stock (sugar) syrup, in that it should not measure more than 18° Baumé or else it will be difficult to freeze. The lower the degree Baumé the firmer and more solid the texture will be.

The composition of the four types in this group is usually accepted as being the following:

Water Ices

These are made from a stock syrup with fresh fruit juice, fruit pulp, and egg whites. Examples include lemon, orange, raspberry, etc.

Sorbets and Punches

These are very similar to water ices. They are made with a stock syrup, with fresh fruit juice or a wine, and after being frozen a small quantity of Italian meringue is added to the mixture to make it light and fluffy. The completed mixture is piped into chilled sorbet glasses or coupes to be served. E.g. lemon sorbet − the addition of lemon juice and zest to the stock syrup and punch romaine − the addition of rum prior to freezing the liquid.

Granit

This is simply a water ice with a lower percentage of sugar in the mixture. Before freezing the liquid should register 14° Baumé. Examples include lemon, pineapple, and strawberry granit.

Speciality 'Ice-Creams'

This group includes bombes, biscuits, parfaits and cassatas. They are the richest of all ices, as they are made from stock syrup and egg yolks (the two forming the basic pâte à bombe mix) plus cream and fresh fruit juice or pulp.

The composition of the types within this group include these.

Bombes

These are composed mostly of two different ices. One of the ices is used to line the bombe mould and the second to fill the centre of the mould. The two ices chosen have a complementary but contrasting flavour and colour. For example, bombe leopold – a coating of pistachio cream ice with a filling of orange biscuit ice, and bombe jamaique – a coating of pineapple cream ice with a filling of rum flavoured coffee biscuit ice.

Biscuits and Parfaits

These are made from the basic pâte à bombe mix to which is added cream and beaten egg whites plus fruit juice or pulp and liquors. The mixture when completed is placed into special biscuit or parfait moulds and then frozen. Biscuit ices are either single or multi-flavoured whereas parfaits are usually of one flavour only. For example, biscuit glace tortoni – vanilla and raspberry biscuit ices in layers and parfait princesse – a praline biscuit ice.

Cassata

These are usually made in bombe moulds, lined with two or three different types of ice-cream, with the final filling being of a meringue and cream mixture containing diced glacé fruits and nuts. E.g. Cassata Tosca – a bombe mould lined in layers with pineapple, apricot and praline ice-cream with the centre filling of glacé cherries and diced pineapple.

'House-made' Ice-Creams

This group include coupes and sundaes. They are 'made-up' ice-cream sweets consisting of ice-cream, fruit and a sauce, and are decorated with fresh whipped cream, nuts, crystallized fruits, etc.

The difference between these types is just the serving dish in which they are offered to the customer. Coupes are usually served in silver coupe cups or tall glasses, whereas sundaes are served on shallow dishes, for example, coupe andalouse – orange segments soaked in maraschino covered with lemon ice-cream; coupe royale – macedoine of fresh fruits soaked in kirsch covered with a vanilla ice-cream.

Catering Uses of Milk, Cream, and Ice-Cream

As explained in this chapter there are a great variety of different types of milk, cream and ice-cream available to the caterer to meet his many requirements. The caterer can save money for his organization by specifying the type or grade of ingredient to be used in the preparation of every dish produced and not allowing his staff to use a more expensive type or grade when a lower (and cheaper) grade would serve the same purpose.

Milk

The main uses for milk are:

To serve as a refreshing drink either chilled or hot;
To serve with non-alocholic beverages, e.g. tea, coffee, cocoa, etc;

The main ingredient for some basic sauces, e.g. bechamel sauce, cheese
sauce, etc;
For adding to soups to enrich and give a smooth texture;
The main ingredient for milk based sweets, e.g. rice pudding, junket, ice-
cream, etc.

Dried milk may be used as an alternative (and cost saver) for fresh milk in
most cases as long as care is used in reconstituting it properly.

Cream
The main catering uses for cream are:

To serve with hot or iced coffee or chocolate;
To serve as an accompaniment to sweets, e.g. fruit salad;
To use for decorative purposes on cakes, gateaux, etc;
To add to soups and sauces to enrich them and to give a smooth creamy
texture;
As a main ingredient of dairy ice-cream, cream ice, etc.

Ice-Cream
The main uses are:

To serve by itself as a sweet on lunch, afternoon tea, or dinner menus;
Served by itself or with other ices or fruits to make up coupes, sundaes, etc.
for example, coupe bebe — half raspberry, half pineapple ice-cream
garnished with fresh strawberries and decorated with whipped cream
and crystallized violets;
Served as an accompaniment to hot and cold sweets, e.g. Apple pie, fruit
salad, etc;
As the main ingredient in hot/cold speciality sweets, e.g. Baked Alaska, etc.

The Storage of Milk, Cream, and Ice-Cream

Milk
Fresh milk should be purchased daily, used strictly in rotation and ideally new
and old milk should not be mixed. It should be kept in the container it is
delivered in and in a refrigerator or cold room at a temperature of about 2°C
(35°F). When the container is opened, the milk should be kept away from
strong smelling foods and covered to protect it from dust and flies.

UHT milk and condensed milks should be kept in a cool, dry storeroom
until opened, and then kept in a refrigerator and used within two days.

Dried milk should be kept in a sealed, air-tight container in a cool, dry
storeroom.

Cream
Fresh cream should be treated in the same way as fresh milk.

Whipped cream should be kept in a sterilized container, covered against
dust and flies, and used the same day.

Synthetic and imitation cream should be kept in a refrigerator and only
small quantities whipped when required for immediate use.

Ice-Cream

Ice-cream should be stored in a deep freeze or an ice-cream conservator at a temperature of −12 to −6°C (10–20°F).

N.B. Never attempt to refreeze ice-cream if it has melted, as not only will the texture and volume be different it could contain harmful bacteria.

Scientific and Nutritional Aspects

Cow's milk as has already been stated contains a number of the nutrients essential for human health, and Table 4.4 below shows the sort of ranges of composition of cow's milk that can be expected.

Table 4.4. Possible ranges and averages of percentage composition of cow's milk

	% Range	% Average
Protein	2·5—4·5	3·3
Carbohydrate	4·2—6·8	4·7
Fat	3·5—6·0	3·6
Minerals and vitamins	0·6—0·8	0·7
Water	85—88	87

Proteins

The protein present in cow's milk is of very high Biological Value, and is given a value of 80. A number of different proteins have been identified in this fraction.

CASEIN. This is a conjugated protein, that is to say that it has other chemical groups attached to the molecule, notably phosphate (providing the mineral element phosphorus) and calcium. This protein is only just soluble in water, and is therefore very easily precipitated, for example with acid. This is amply illustrated when fruit acid is added to milk, or when the milk sours, producing lactic acid which causes the familiar curdled appearance. However, this protein is not so easily affected by heat as those below. The enzyme rennin, however, causes the rapid coagulation of casein — this can be the basis of cheese making. When casein coagulates the milk it sets to form a junket-like semi-solid, which separates into a curd and whey, the latter containing lactoproteins, lactose and fat.

LACTALBUMIN AND LACTOGLOBULIN. These are simple proteins and are easily heat coagulable — these form the skin on milk when it is boiled.

Carbohydrates

Lactose, milk sugar, is the only carbohydrate present in milk. It is significant that this is the least sweet of all the common sugars, for this reason it would be better to add lactose to cow's milk for baby feeds, rather than the much sweeter sucrose. This might go some way to prevent the desire for sweet things developing in the young.

Lactose is not very water soluble, hence in condensed milk products it is liable to crystallize out and produce a 'gritty' texture; this can also happen in ice-cream, because of the low temperature. In the latter case it is possible that this enhances the texture.

Fats

The fat constituent of milk forms the cream. It is dispersed as fine globules forming fat or oil emulsion in water. When this emulsion is unstable, as in normal milk, the fat droplets coalesce and rise to the top as the familiar layer of cream. The fat globules are stabilized to some extent by a monomolecular layer of protein — but in normal milk this is not sufficient to prevent separation of the fat from the water in milk. However, in homogenized milk, where the fat particles are very much smaller, they are completely stabilized by this layer of protein, and remain uniformly dispersed throughout the milk, i.e. the fat/water emulsion is homogeneous.

The fat contains the fat-soluble vitamins (vitamins A and D), of which it is a useful source, and together with lactose, the fat provides energy in the diet. It has the added advantage of being easily digestible, because of its fine dispersion in globular form.

When the cream of milk is churned as in butter making, the fat lumps together because of the mechanical action, and the emulsion of the milk changes from a fat/oil in water emulsion to that of water in fat/oil (which is the butter). Excess water runs away as butter-milk.

Minerals and Vitamins

Milk is very rich in calcium, which is very important for the growth and repair of teeth and bones. One pint of milk provides all the daily requirement for most people, *see* Table 4.5.

Table 4.5. The average composition of a pint of pasteurized milk

Protein	19g
Fat	22g
Carbohydrate	28g
Calcium	700mg
Phosphorus	540mg
Iron	0·60mg
Vitamin A	260μg*
	220μg[†]
Vitamin D	0·29μg*
	0·06μg[†]
Thiamine (vitamin B_1)	0·23mg
Riboflavine (vitamin B_2)	0·88mg
Nicotinic Acid	5·30mg
Ascorbic Acid (vitamin C)	5·90mg[‡]
Kilocalories of energy	380

(Figures based the Manual of Nutrition, 1970)

Key: g = grams

mg = milligrams = $\frac{1}{1000}$ or 10^{-3} grams

μg = micrograms = $\frac{1}{1,000,000}$ or 10^{-6} grams

* = summer value; † = winter value;

‡ = value based on pasteurized milk stored for 12 hours.

Milk is also rich in phosphorus, and contains traces of iron, sodium, and potassium. Table 4.5 also shows that milk is a good source of vitamins, most significantly, the fat soluble one, vitamin A. Vitamin C, although present in fresh milk, is probably only present in trace amounts in milk consumed by most of the population, since it is destroyed by oxygen in the presence of light and heat. (Riboflavine too is destroyed by light.)

Since milk contains a great deal of water it is a very dilute food, because of this it is very easy to consume and then digest. As a good source of the principal nutrients, which can be easily given, digested and absorbed by the body, milk is an ideal food for all, especially invalids and young children. There is, however, no evidence that it is an indispensable constituent of the adult diet.

Changes Taking Place when Milk is Cooked

Although casein is not very heat coagulable, the other proteins are. As the milk is warmed a skin begins to form consisting of partially coagulated lactalbumin, with some casein and fat globules which have become entrapped in the forming skin. The skin surface dries out during continuing heating because of evaporation from the surface, and forms a barrier, preventing vapours from escaping from the bulk of the milk. As the milk continues to heat up and eventually boils, expanding steam is trapped beneath the skin, causing the skin to bubble up and 'boil over'.

Changes in colour and flavours also occur during cooking, because of:

(i) slight caramelization of lactose; and
(ii) the so-called Maillard–Browning reaction which occurs between protein and certain sugars when heat is applied.

These changes are particularly noticeable in milk products that are heated at high temperatures for lengthy periods, e.g. some sterilized milk, baked milk puddings. These changes also occur in homogenized milk, but often the effects are enhanced compared with normal milk because of the fat particles being broken down into a very small size, and being dispersed uniformly throughout the milk, e.g. custards are thicker, similarly a more stable gel is formed in egg-custard, skin on milk puddings is a little tougher and not so brown.

Yogurt

This is milk to which a culture of bacteria has been added. Normally heat treated milk is used so that unwanted micro-organisms are killed prior to the yogurt process. To this heat treated milk is added a specially prepared culture of *Lactobacillus bulgaricus* and *Streptococcus thermophilus*. In order to ensure a product of acceptable consistency additional milk solids are added, usually about 12% of dried milk powder. The mixture is incubated for a set time in carefully controlled conditions. During incubation acids are produced, bringing about some denaturation of the proteins causing a thickening in consistency, as well as imparting the characteristic flavour to the product.

As yogurt contains the same nutrients as milk it has a very good food value and has become a popular product in the U.K. in recent times, but some of the claims of certain sectors of the health food industry for the health-giving qualities of yogurt are unfounded.

Ice-Cream

Fundamentally this product is a mixture of milk, fat, sugar, stabilizer and emulsifier, flavouring, and colouring agents. The milk part usually comes from liquid or powdered skimmed milk. The fat comes from a vegetable source in the case of the standard product, but from butter in 'dairy ice-cream'. Stabilizers are usually cellulose derivatives. Egg, lecithin and glyceryl mono-stearate (G.M.S.) can be used as emulsifiers.

As one writer put it 'Present day ice-cream is one of the triumphs of food technology, and it is noteworthy as the only major food product in which air is the principal ingredient'. Table 4.6 shows the approximate composition by weight of a typical ice-cream. It should be noted that after processing approximately half the volume of the product is air, but since ice-cream is sold by units of volume this is not disadvantagous to the manufacturer!

Table 4.6. Percentage composition by weight of a typical ice-cream

	per cent
Fat	12
Non-fat milk solids	11
Sugar	15
Flavour Colour Emulsifier Stabilizer	1
Water	61

The Ice-cream Regulations, 1967 govern the composition of the product in the U.K. They state:

    (i) Standard ice-cream must contain at least: (*a*) 5% fat; (*b*) 7·5% milk solids not fat (MSNF).

    (ii) In dairy ice-cream all fat must derive from milk.

When ice-cream is made the ingredients are initially mixed together to form an oil in water emulsion, which is pasteurized to prevent microbiological hazard. This emulsion is then frozen while air is whipped into it. The resultant foam is frozen further and the product hardens and ice crystals form. The stabilizers cause the water in the emulsion to remain homogeneously dispersed in the mixture in very fine droplet form, hence the ice crystals formed are very small, ensuring a smooth textured product.

Because of the high proportion of sugar present, ice-cream provides 56 kilo-calories of energy per ounce, compared with milk's 19, and low fat yoghurt's 15. However, dairy ice-cream will contain many of the nutrients present in milk and butter and must therefore be nutritionally acceptable in these terms.

5

Dairy Type Foods (Butter and Cheese)

Butter

Butter is the product made from churning fresh cream. It consists of more than 80% butterfat and contains vitamins A and D and small amounts of protein, minerals and milk sugar (lactose).

The composition of butter produced in the U.K. is controlled by 'The Butter Regulations, 1966' which states that butter must have a minimum milk fat content of 80%, a maximum of milk solids other than fat of 2% and a maximum water content of 16%.

The flavour and colour of the butter produced will vary depending on:

(a) the breed of cow from which the milk was obtained;
(b) the type of feed that was available for the cow;
(c) the method of manufacture of the butter, i.e. whether it was made from fresh or ripened cream (*see* p. 76);
(d) the efficiency of manufacture, e.g. overworking or wrong manufacturing temperatures can affect the colour and texture of the butter;
(e) whether the butter is blended or not;
(f) whether salt or colouring matter has been added;
(g) the grade of the butter;
(h) the method of packaging and storing.

Butters can be classified under the following four headings:

(a) Fresh or sweet cream butter ⎫ creamery butters
(b) Ripened cream or lactic butter ⎬
(c) Blended or milled butter
(d) 'Special' butters

although the first two are the main types.

Fresh and Ripened Cream Butter
The manufacture of creamery butters is in four main stages.

'Holding'
Cream used for buttermaking will contain 35% butterfat content. It is pasteurized at 95°C (203°F) for 2–4 seconds and then cooled to a temperature of about 4·5°C (40°F) and held there for several hours to ensure a uniform hardening of the fat globules and to prevent any fat losses in the buttermilk.

'Ripening'
When the end-product is going to be a ripened cream butter, a 'starter' will be added during the holding stage, in which case the holding temperature will be 15·5–18·5°C (60–65°F) for 3–4 hours before being cooled to 4·5°C (40°F). A 'starter' is a laboratory prepared culture of an acid-producing bacteria which will give the butter produced by this method a much fuller flavour. Unfortunately the flavour 'fades' and the butter has therefore a shorter keeping quality compared with sweet cream butter.
        N.B. This stage is omitted in the manufacture of sweet cream butter.

'Churning'
The churning of the cream is done in large stainless steel churns containing at least 1,000 gallons of cream at a temperature of about 4°C. The churns are rotated whilst internal rollers pass through the cream. The effect of this is to break the envelope of solids-not-fat around each of the very small fat globules in the cream so that they coalesce and form larger groups of butterfat. The envelope is then dispersed in the thin liquid part of the cream and becomes the buttermilk. After about 30 minutes the butter separates out in the form of grains and floats in the buttermilk. The buttermilk is then carefully drained off and is a useful by-product.

'Washing and Salting'
The butter grains are then washed with iced water to remove any buttermilk left on the surface of each grain in order to maximize the keeping quality of the butter produced. The washing with iced water also assists in the hardening of the butter grains. If the butter is to be salted it is done at this stage in one of two ways, either by adding fine dairy salt, or by adding a brine water for some 10–15 minutes and allowing the butter grains to absorb it. The quantity of salt added will depend on the particular part of the country for which the butter is being manufactured, but will usually average 1% for ripened cream butter and 1·5% for fresh (sweet) cream butter. The buttergrains are then worked into a smooth solid mass by rotating the churns slowly for some 10–15 minutes before being packaged for sale.
        Sweet cream butter is produced in the U.K. and imported from New Zealand and Ireland. Ripened cream butter is imported from Denmark and other European countries.

Blended or Milled Butters
This is a blend of butters from different countries and of varying quality

grades which are mixed together to produce a product which is of a fairly standard quality for the consumer at a competitive price. Blended butters are frequently sold under a brand name label, usually as a salted butter.

'Special' Butters
This group includes the butters that are not so commonly available and those which are not true butters.

Whey Butter
Whey is the watery liquid which separates from the curd in cheesemaking (*see* p. 85). The butterfat recovered from the whey may be made into butter, or it can be added to cream or fresh milk prior to it being processed into butter. Due to its origin, whey butter will have a slight cheesy aroma.

Milk Blended Butter
This is imported butter to which a quantity of milk has been added in this country, increasing its moisture content up to a maximum of 24%.

Butter/Vegetable Fat Spreads
A butter product, which will spread at normal refrigerator temperature, developed using cream and lower melting point vegetable oils such as soya. The manufacture is similar to that for butter with the vegetable oil comprising 15% of the final fat content of approximately 38%.

Compound Butters
These are made by adding a particular natural flavour and colouring to butter which is to be served as an accompaniment usually to a savoury type dish, e.g. with grilled meat and fish. It is made, for example, by passing blanched fresh herbs through a fine sieve, adding a small quantity of lemon juice, mixing with softened creamery butter and correcting the seasoning. It is then shaped into a roll of about 1 in. diameter, wrapped in greaseproof paper and placed in a refrigerator to harden. It may also be made using raw lobster coral, tinned anchovy fillets, fresh horseradish, fresh garlic, etc.

Cocoa Butter
This is not a true butter. It is a pale coloured solid brittle fat obtained by pressing the ground cocoa nib during the manufacture of cocoa powder. It is used almost exclusively for the manufacture of chocolate and is the most expensive ingredient. It is a hard and brittle substance at ordinary room temperature but has the particular property of melting sharply at a few degrees below that of the human body temperature. Because of its high cost cocoa butter substitutes are now man-made using palm oil.

Peanut Butter
This is not a true butter. It is a straw coloured paste-like substance obtained from grinding roasted peanut kernels that may be further emulsified and flavoured. It may be used in place of preserves on bread or scones.

Grading of Butter Produced in the U.K.
The National Association of Creamery Proprietors operates a grading service
for butter produced in the U.K. The creamery manufacturers are required to
submit their entire output for grading if they are members of the association.
The butter that is graded is of three types only, sweet cream butter (salted and
unsalted), ripened cream butter (salted and unsalted), and whey butter.

The grading is done on a points system, with the 'grader' awarding points
as follows:

	Maximum points
Flavour and aroma	50
Body and texture	20
Colour, appearance, finish, and salt	20
Absence of free moisture	10
	100

Depending on the type of butter and the points awarded by the 'grader' the
butter will then be graded by complying with one of the following standards.

Creamery Butters
There are four grades.
EXTRA SELECTED. A total score of not less than 93 points, including not less
than 47 points for flavour and aroma.
SELECTED. A total score of not less than 85 points or more than 92 points of
which not less than 44 points for flavour and aroma.
GRADED. A total score of not less than 75 points or more than 84 points
including not less than 40 points for flavour.
NO GRADE. A total score of less than 75 points and less than 40 points
awarded for flavour.

Whey Butters
There are two grades only.
GRADED. A total score of not less than 75 points with not less than 40 points
for flavour.
NO GRADE. A total score of less than 75 points or when less than 40 points
have been awarded for flavour.

Imported Butter
Any imported butter sold in the U.K. has to comply with the British legal
requirements in regards to composition and labelling. Depending on the exporting country it will frequently have its own grading system which although
helpful can be misleading to the caterer if he is not careful, e.g. the grade
'selected' for creamery butters in the U.K. is the second (high) quality butter
available, an exporting country however may grade its butter in which the
grade 'Selected' is of a third (poor) quality.

In general terms a good quality butter should have a clean flavour and aroma characteristic of the type of butter, have a close body, a waxy texture, be of a uniform colour, have a uniform distribution of salt (if any), be clean and bright in appearance and have an absence of any free moisture.

Cheese

Cheese may be defined as the fresh or matured product made by coagulating any or a combination of any of the following substances, namely milk, cream, skimmed milk, partly skimmed milk, concentrated milk, reconstituted dried milk and buttermilk, and then partially draining the whey resulting from any such coagulation.

This definition would not be suitable for whey cheese.

Cheese was probably made accidentally in the first instance by the carrying of milk in the stomach of a previously slaughtered animal, when the milk-clotting enzymes of the stomach would have converted the liquid milk into a soft mass or junket. This soft mass containing protein and fat was then drained to remove the excess liquid (whey) and it was then dried in the sun to form a harder mass which could be eaten fresh or salted and stored for later use when the food supplies were less plentiful.

Cheesemaking is a very convenient method for converting a considerable part of the milk nutrients into a product that is less bulky, will keep well, is of a high nutritive value and is palatable and easily digestible.

There are over 400 varieties of cheeses listed as being made in different parts of the world. They are made from a variety of different milks, cows, sheeps, goats, buffalo, etc., by different methods of manufacture, are ripened for different periods of time in different conditions and are made in different sizes from a few ounces to the very large size of 70lb or more. They will also differ by colour, texture, hardness, odour, and taste.

The Names Given to Cheeses

Before attempting to classify cheeses it is of value and interest to study briefly and be aware of the origin of cheese names. Names have been given by one of the following:

The Region

Most of the famous varieties have been taken from the region or county where the production of a particular type of cheese established a name for itself, for example, England: Leicester, Wensleydale, and Dorset Blue; Switzerland: Emmental, etc.

N.B. Although the name and the variety may still exist, the cheese may well be produced in a different region now.

Towns Within a Cheesemaking Region

Towns sometimes have given their names because they were the market towns for the region, for example, England: the best example is Cheddar; France: Camembert, Coulommiens, Roquefort, etc.

The Type of Milk

When varieties of cheese are made from whey, the word 'whey' will be used on the labelling and description of the cheese so as to make it distinctive to the customer.

Also when using the milk of goats or sheep for cheesemaking the name will often include wording to identify the cheese as containing a particular milk. E.g., 'Zieger' in Germany indicates that the cheese is made of goat's milk; 'Quark' in Germany indicates that the cheese is made from skimmed cow's milk; 'Pecorino' in Italy indicates that the cheese is made of sheep's milk.

Type of Cheese

There are many varieties of cheese which are internally blue-moulded and are similar in many ways. The word blue being included in the name for the cheese, e.g. England: Blue Stilton, Dorset Blue; France: Bleu de Bresse, Bleu d'Auvergne.

Similarly there are cheeses which have a permitted colouring added to the cheese to make it distinctive from its competitors, e.g. England: Red Leicester, Red Cheshire and Red Windsor.

Appearance

A few varieties have a characteristic external appearance which is incorporated in its name, e.g. France: Tome au Raisin, Tome de Savoie are both semi-hard cheese covered with dried grape skins and pips.

Originally these small cheese were placed in the debris (marc) from the making of wine where they were left to develop the flavour of the grapes at little cost to the producer.

Addition of Flavourings

Herbs, vegetables and spices are added to cheese in some countries and then incorporated in the name of the cheese, e.g. England: Derby Sage, Sage Lancashire.

Additives in continental cheeses include, herbs, carraway seeds, fennel, etc.

For example, France: Poivre d'ane — a goat's milk cheese flavoured with savoury and rosemary
Tomme au fenouil — flavoured with fennel
Germany: Tilsit — flavoured with carraway seeds
Hopfen — flavoured with carraway seeds
Italy: Pepato — flavoured with peppers.

Trade Names

Some well-known cheeses have been named by the firm's trade name, e.g. England: 'St. Ivel'; Italy: 'Bel Paese'.

These firms produce a variety of cheeses under their trade names.

The Classification of Cheeses

Cheeses may be classified under one or a combination of the following.

The Country of Origin

It is helpful to be able to classify cheeses in this way so that cheeses from different countries may be featured on the menu or cheeseboard of a restaurant. Confusion does arise, however, when a traditional cheese of a country is made and exported by another country. Blatant examples of this is the English Cheddar which is now made and exported by New Zealand and Canada; the French Roquefort which is made and exported by Denmark as 'Danish Roquefort'; and the Swiss Emmanthaler which is made and exported by France and New Zealand.

The Method of Manufacture

This system of classification is based on how the cheese has been manufactured, which in turn determines the type of cheese produced. This classification identifies six main groups of cheeses, hard, semi-hard, soft, surface mould, surface slime, and blue-veined (i.e. internal mould and includes acid coagulated cheeses).

The important features in the manufacture of cheeses are:

- (*a*) the type of milk being processed (*see* definition of cheese on p. 79);
- (*b*) whether the milk is ripened or not;
- (*c*) whether rennet is added or not;
- (*d*) whether the curd is scalded or not;
- (*e*) whether the cheese is pressed or not.

The main features in the manufacture of some traditional cheeses are shown in Figure 5.1.

General Aspects

The general appearance of a traditionally made cheese is important for the recognition of it by the consumer and the selling of it by the caterer. To this end the cheese manufacturers aim at a high standard of consistency for their products. Cheeses may be recognized by:

SIZE. Fortunately the traditional cheeses have nearly always been made of the same size and shape and so are easily recognizable. For example, the English Cheddar is usually made in the shape of a small drum, being 13 in. high and 11 in. in diameter. The English Leicester is usually made in the shape of a wheel, being 4 in. high and 18 in. in diameter.

COLOUR. The colour of the cheese internally and externally is another point of recognition. E.g. the English Stilton has a wrinkled brown coat and a blue-veined creamy—white body. The Dutch Edam has a red wax coat and a rich straw coloured body.

FLAVOUR. The flavour of cheeses when fully mature is quite standardized, although only minor changes in the manufacture can affect the flavour considerably. However, considerable experience is needed to appreciate fully the description given to cheeses by the cheesemakers (e.g. 'slightly nutty', 'mildly fruity'), although the basic aspects of flavour such as a cheese being mild, very rich, salty and tangy are usually quite evident to most consumers.

For example, the English Stilton is described as having a flavour which is rich, mellow, and creamy. The French Camembert is described as having a full flavour which is often ammoniacal.

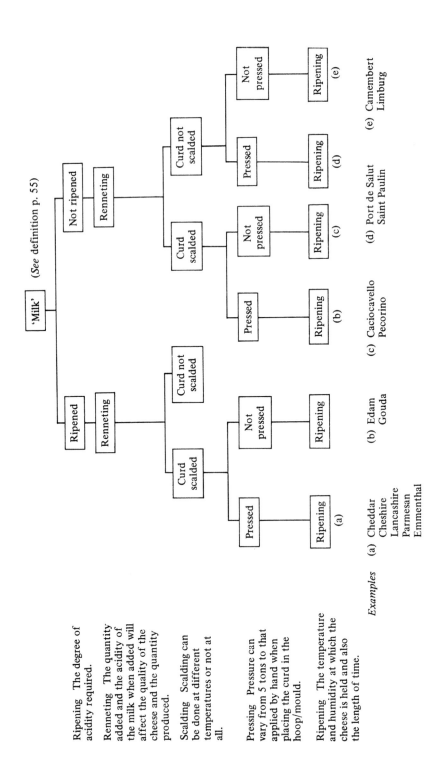

Ripening The degree of acidity required.

Renneting The quantity added and the acidity of the milk when added will affect the quality of the cheese and the quantity produced.

Scalding Scalding can be done at different temperatures or not at all.

Pressing Pressure can vary from 5 tons to that applied by hand when placing the curd in the hoop/mould.

Ripening The temperature and humidity at which the cheese is held and also the length of time.

Examples (a) Cheddar (b) Edam (c) Caciocavello (d) Port de Salut (e) Camembert
  Cheshire Gouda Pecorino Saint Paulin Limburg
  Lancashire
  Parmesan
  Emmenthal

Figure 5.1 The major stages affecting the type of cheese produced

TEXTURE. This is seen when examining the cut surface of a cheese and in greater detail when cutting a portion of the cheese. Typical textures are hard, semi-hard, semi-hard with gas holes, rubbery, close, loose and crumbly, buttery, and open.

For example, the English Lancashire has a soft and crumbly texture; the Dutch Edam has a semi-hard and rubbery texture.

THE CATERING USES. Specific types should be purchased for particular uses.

For example, the Italian Parmesan should be purchased as a cooking cheese, i.e. it is the ideal cheese for cheese sauces, for adding to farinaceous dishes, etc. The English Stilton is the ideal cheese for serving at the completion of a lunch or dinner and to accompany port. The English Derby Sage is ideal for serving with fresh fruit and for featuring on the cold buffet table at Christmas time.

See Table 5.1 for a classification of the main varieties of cheeses by the country of origin and method of manufacture.

The Manufacture of Cheddar Cheese
The reasons why the manufacture of Cheddar cheese has been chosen are:

(*a*) It is probably the most well-known of English cheeses.
(*b*) Its method of manufacture is the most documented and so further details of the manufacturing process are readily available.
(*c*) It is a cheese that is produced after going through all of the major stages of cheesemaking (*see* Table 5.2).

The manufacture of Cheddar cheese is in ten stages.

The Treatment of the Milk
Cheesemaking begins when the fresh cow's milk arrives at a creamery from many different farms. It is tested on arrival and if found satisfactory will be pasteurized and cooled to 21°C (70°F) before being pumped into large stainless steel cheese vats, which are jacketed for either cooling or heating purposes, and which hold up to 2,000 gallons of milk.

The Ripening (souring) of the Milk
Originally milk for cheesemaking was allowed to ripen (to go sour – to develop acidity) naturally, as milk is always contaminated by acid-producing bacteria. The speed at which this would happen, however, would depend on the number of bacteria present, the temperature in the creamery, the quality of the milk, etc., and would not be at a standard rate. This is far from desirable today in large modern creameries where the quantity of output is important as well as the quality of output.

In order to overcome this a laboratory prepared culture (starter) is added to develop the acidity in the milk to the right amount. When the acidity is correct the temperature of the milk is raised to about 29°C (85°F).

Renneting
Rennet is then added to the milk and stirred in. Rennet is a natural extract

Table 5.1. A classification of the main varieties of cheese by country of origin and by type

Country of Origin	Soft	Semi-hard	Hard	Internal Mould	External Mould
U.K.	Cream York Cambridge Colwick	Caerphilly Lancashire White Wensleydale White Stilton	Cheddar Cheshire Derby Sage Double Gloucester Leicester	Blue Stilton Blue Wensleydale Dorset Blue (or Blue Vinny)	Lymeswold Somerset Brie
Belgium		Limburg			
France	Bondon Coulommiers Géromé Gervais Neufchâtel	Saint Paulin	Cantal Gruyère	Roquefort	Brie Camembert
Germany	Quarg	Münster	Sapsago		
Holland		Edam Gouda			
Italy			Parmesan Provolone	Gorgonzola	
Switzerland			Emmenthal Schabzeiger		
U.S.A.		Brick Jack			

containing rennin which has the property of clotting milk. Natural rennet is obtained from the stomach of calves, sheep, and goats.

Cutting the Curd

After about 45 minutes the curd is set like a solid junket and when firm enough it is cut using two mechanical cheese knives. These are sets of parallel blades, which are arranged vertically and horizontally. The curd is cut into ½ inch cubes which frees the whey held in the curd.

Scalding

The curd is then stirred continuously whilst the temperature is raised slowly to about 43°C (110°F) and held there for about 1 hour. The scalding helps to expel the whey from the curd and to obtain the desired texture. Stirring of the curd is continued for 20 minutes after the heat is turned off to prevent the curd on the outside of the vats becoming 'cooked'.

N.B. A lower scalding temperature would leave more moisture in the curd (e.g. English Cheshire is scalded at 32–35°C (90–95°F) and so gives a softer cheese; a higher temperature as for Cheddar cheese gives a drier, harder curd resulting in a longer-keeping cheese).

Settling

The whey is then run off and the curd particles are allowed to settle (or pitch) on the bottom of the vat where they begin to matt together.

Cheddaring

The settled curd is cut into 8 in sq. blocks and then piled on top of each other on each side of the vat and re-piled at 10 minute intervals to ensure a complete draining of the whey. During the piling process, the curd shrinks a little and takes on a rubbery texture which later disappears and the curd acquires a silky texture.

Milling and Salting

The drained, silky textured curd is then milled into small pieces and fine dairy salt is added and well mixed in to enhance the flavour, improve the keeping qualities and to check further acidity.

Moulding

A fixed weight of curd is then filled into hoops which are lined with a cloth and then pressed to drive out the remaining whey. More whey is released from the curd as a result of the addition of salt. The hoops are then placed in powerful horizontal presses, sprayed with steam and left for 24–36 hours under a pressure of 2–5 tons. The spraying of steam on the moulds produces a thin hard rind on the cheese which helps its keeping properties.

Ripening

The immature cheese is then removed from its hoop, date stamped and placed in a ripening room at a temperature of about 10°C (50°F) and with a humidity of 80–90%. The cheeses are turned frequently to ensure a uniform ripening of the cheese and left to mature for about three months. A comparison of the main characteristics of English cheeses is shown on pp. 86–7.

Table 5.2.

Cheese	Notes on Manufacture	Ripening times
Cheddar	Hard pressed. High scalding temperature of $43°C$ ($110°F$) Special 'Cheddaring' process.	3–12 months
Cheshire	Hard pressed. Low scalding temperature of $32-35°C$ ($90-95°F$). Annatto, a red colour, is often added.	6 weeks
Derby	Hard pressed and scalded. The green extract pressed from sage leaves is added giving a green layered appearance for traditional 'Derby Sage' cheese.	4–6 weeks or more
Double Gloucester	Hard pressed and high temperature scalded. Manufacture is very close to Cheddar.	3–4 months
Leicester	Hard pressed and scalded. Curd in vat is drained under pressure from weighted wooden racks. Very finely milled.	10–12 weeks
Caerphilly	Lightly pressed and scalded. Soaked in brine for 24 hours after one day's pressing (packed whilst still warm into hoops).	2 weeks
Lancashire	Lightly pressed and scalded. After cutting curd particles simply fall to the bottom and are collected together twice. Double and single curd types commonly available.	4–8 weeks
White Wensleydale	Lightly pressed and scalded. Less starter is used than in most English cheeses. Milled curd is packed into hoops and left to drain for 2 hours before being lightly pressed.	2–3 weeks
Blue Stilton	Drained curd left overnight. Broken by hand into small pieces, salted and packed gently into hoops. Hoops drained on calico squares placed on boards, being changed daily for 10 days. The hoop is then removed, sides of cheese scraped, the scrapings being used to fill any crevices. Cheese is then bandaged and replaced in hoops. Cheese is rebandaged and turned each day until a white mould starts to grow on the surface. Cheese allowed to ripen slowly.	3–6 months
White Stilton	Similar to above but not fully matured.	3 weeks
Blue Wensleydale	Similar to Stilton. Light pressure applied to the curds in the hoops.	6 months
Dorset Blue (Blue Vinny)	Similar to Stilton, but made from skimmed milk.	4–6 months

U.K. cheeses

Minimum percentage of milk fat in the dry matter	Maximum percentage of water calculated on the total weight	Traditional shape and size (in.)	Appearance		
			Colour	Texture	Flavour
48	39	12 high 15 diameter	Cream to deep yellow	Close, firm and smooth	Clean, mellow, and nutty
48	44	13 high 11 diameter	Orange–red or white	Loose and crumbly	Mild, mellow, and slightly salty
48	42	5 high 14 diameter	Cream or green	Firm and close	Clean and tangy
48	44	4 high 15 diameter	Orange–red	Buttery and open	Very delicate and creamy
48	42	4 high 18 diameter	Rich red	Buttery and open	Mild and mellow
48	46	3 high 9 diameter	White	Close	Clean, mild, and slightly salty
48	48	8 high 13 diameter	White	Soft, crumbly	Clean and mild
48	46	6 high 8 diameter	White	Moderately close	and slightly salty
48	42	9 high 8 diameter	Blue veined	Soft and close	Rich, mellow, and creamy
48	46	9 high 8 diameter	White	Soft and close	Clean and mild
Not spec. in schedule	Not spec. in schedule	6 high 8 diameter	Blue veined	Soft and close	Rich, sweet, and creamy
Not spec. in schedule	Not spec. in schedule	6 high 8 across	Blue veined	Crumbly	Strong and rich

Stages Involved in General Cheese-making

Basically as has been previously discussed, cheese is made by forming a curd by the action of the enzyme rennin, or acid, upon pasteurized milk. This curd is then ripened by the enzymes produced by the addition of a culture of micro-organisms. During ripening, the constituents of the curd are modified to produce characteristic flavours and textures.

In more detail, the steps in the process may be explained as follows.

Curd Formation

This is brought about by the addition of rennin which catalyses changes in the protein content of the milk, causing coagulation of the curd. Suitable cultures of micro-organisms may also be added at this stage, these bring about ripening or souring of the milk.

This mixture may be held at varying temperatures; during what is called the 'setting' period.

    (i) 20–26°C (70–80°F) for soft cheeses
    (ii) 30–32°C (86–90°F) for hard cheeses

The setting temperature, the quantity of rennin added, and the amount of acid produced by the micro-organisms largely govern the rate at which the curd and whey separate, and also affect the texture of the curd.

Cutting the Curd

This process allows further separation from the whey – the finer the curd is cut, the greater is the whey separation. Retention of excess whey can permit excess acidity to form in the curd resulting in defective flavours in the ripened cheese.

Cooking the Curd

This again aids the removal of whey. The curd begins to compact and become elastic rather than crumbly. During the heating, the lactic acid-producing bacteria increase. The higher the temperature the more firm the cheese becomes, e.g. Cheddar at a temperature of 38°C (100°F) becomes firm.

Separating the Curd

All excess whey is removed finally from the curd.

Curd Piling

The curd is cut into blocks and piled up; this allows the curd to form a solid mass and further development of the starter culture. The curd begins to develop characteristic properties of texture and flavour.

Milling and Salting
The now dry curd is milled into small fragments and salt is added (sometimes in *aqueous solution* which permits homogeneous absorption). Salting influences many factors: flavour, moisture content, texture; it checks lactic acid formation by inhibiting acid-producing organisms (also reducing risk of spoilage), and at the same time permits the development of specific ripening micro-organisms.

Pressing the Curd
This gives the cheese its characteristic shape and texture.

Special Characteristic Parts of a Process
A particular treatment may be necessary to produce a particular variety of cheese. For example, the addition of bacterial or mould cultures to certain cheeses (Swiss cheeses are often characterized by bacterial cultures, whereas Camembert and Roquefort are good examples of mould-ripened cheeses). Some cheeses have mould cultures smeared over their surfaces, e.g. surfaced-ripened types like Limburger.

Maturing
(Some texts call this stage 'ripening'.) During this stage the immature or 'green' cheese develops the characteristic texture and flavour of its variety. As has been previously discussed the main constituents of cheese are proteins, fats, and lactose, and these are converted into simpler products by the action of the enzymes of the cheese's characteristic micro-organisms.

$$\text{e.g. proteins} \longrightarrow \text{amino-acids}$$
$$\text{fats} \longrightarrow \text{fatty acids}$$
$$\text{lactose} \longrightarrow \text{lactic acid}$$

Many other by-products such as alcohols, aldehydes, ammonia, and sulphur compounds are also formed during the maturing stage. Although these products are formed in relatively small quantities, they are sufficient to impart characteristic flavours and texture to the cheese.

General Notes on the Manufacture of Cheeses
Further scientific information is given on this subject on pp. 96—7.
Some general points affecting the type of cheese produced may be helpful and are summarized below.

(i) The percentage of fat in the milk has an effect on the quality of the cheese produced. A low percentage of fat will produce a hard leathery type of cheese, whereas a high percentage of fat will produce a soft smoother type of cheese.

(ii) The moisture content is also a major factor affecting the quality of the cheese produced. The lower the moisture content left in the curd the firmer the cheese, the milder the flavour, and the longer its keeping properties. The more moisture left in the curd the more active will be the bacteriological and enzyme action, and the faster the ripening period resulting in a short storage life.

(iii) The more open the texture of the cheese the greater will be the chance for internal moulds to develop. This can be helped further by little or no pressure being applied to the curds when moulding the cheese.

(iv) The percentage of salt present will also affect the end product. Salt, when added, will help to bring out the flavour of a cheese and help to preserve it. Cheeses made without salt tend to have a short shelf-life, to ripen quickly and to develop strong odours.

(v) The method of salting is particular to the type of cheese being made. It is added in one of three ways, by adding to the milled cheese, e.g. English Cheddar; by dry salting of the moulded cheese, e.g. Roquefort; or by placing the moulded cheese in a brine solution, e.g. Edam, Gouda.

A Brief Description of Well-known Cheeses

U.K.

See in particular Table 5.2 (pp. 86–7).

York	A soft cheese with a mellow, slightly acid flavour, and, a soft spreadable texture. Made of full cream cow's milk.
Lymeswold	The first really new natural English cheese, available as a white or blue cheese. It is a soft, mould ripened cheese with a creamy texture. Made from milk and fresh dairy cream.

Belgium

Limburg	A semi-hard cheese made of a mixture of whole and skimmed milk, ripened by a surface slime which forms as a result of dry salting the moulded cheese frequently whilst keeping it in a damp ripening room. The ripening is carried out over some six weeks until the cheese is a reddish-yellow colour and has a very strong and characteristic odour.

France

Bondon	A popular soft cheese made from whole or partly skimmed cow's milk. Often dry salted and ripened on straw.
Coulommiers	A soft cheese made from whole cow's milk. Often made by ripening the curd before moulding, or ripening by an external mould.

Géromé	A soft cheese made from cow's milk, although some goat's milk may be added. During ripening it is washed with salt water to prevent growth of moulds. Takes up to 16 weeks to ripen and is usually greenish when fully ripe. Cloves or aniseed are added to give a characteristic flavour.
Gervais (or demi-Suisse)	A soft cheese made from two-thirds cow's milk and one-third cream. Ripens within three days and because of the soft creamy texture and mild flavour, is frequently eaten with sugar as a spread on biscuits.
Neufchâtel	A soft cheese made from whole cow's milk often enriched with some cream. Dry salted after moulding and ripened on straw. Will take up to six weeks to ripen.
Saint Paulin (or Port du Salut)	A semi-hard, lightly pressed cheese, made from whole cow's milk. It has a strong rind but a soft rubbery like texture and a mild flavour.
Cantal	A hard pressed cheese made from whole or partly skimmed cow's milk. Cylindrical in shape and often weighing up to 100lb. It is of a whitish colour and has many small crevices in the body of the cheese. It has a rich flavour which is particular to itself.
Gruyère	A hard pressed cheese made from whole or partly skimmed cow's milk. Made into huge grindstone shaped blocks often 3ft in diameter. It is of a pale yellow colour with a mild but sweet flavour. Recognized by its large 'eyes' or cavities which are due to proprionic bacteria with which the milk is innoculated. Similar to Emmenthal. Also produced in Switzerland.
Brie	A soft cheese ripened by an external mould. Made from whole or partly skimmed cow's milk. Similar in many ways to Camembert cheese. A large flat whitish cheese often served on a straw mat, having a characteristic sharp taste and a powerful ammoniacal aroma.
Camembert	A soft cheese ripened by an external mould. Made from whole cow's milk plus usually some skimmed milk. Similar to the Brie cheese but smaller in size. Made of curd from two separate days. Whitish in appearance, often semi-liquid when fully ripe, possessing a full flavour and an ammoniacal aroma.
Roquefort	A semi-hard pressed cheese ripened by an internal mould. It is one of the classical blue-veined cheeses. It is made from ewe's milk with two layers of

'mouldy' breadcrumbs being added to the curd
when placing into the hoops. The cheese is dry
salted after being moulded. The cheese is often
pierced with long needles to accelerate the growth
of the mould. The ripening of the cheese in a cool,
damp room takes up to six months.

Germany

Münster

A semi-hard cheese usually made from whole cow's
milk but sometimes with a mixture of goat and
cow's milk. It has a strong flavour which is often
the result of adding carraway seeds to the curds.

Sapsago

A hard-pressed cheese made from skimmed and
sour cow's milk, buttermilk, and whey. It is usually
of a small cone shape. It is a green cheese, as a result
of powdered dried leaves of an aromatic clover
being added to the curd, which also gives the cheese
a characteristic flavour. It is also produced in
Switzerland.

Holland

Edam

A semi-hard cheese made of partly skimmed cow's
milk. Salted by immersion in brine for three days.
Globe-shaped, red or yellow skinned as a result of
being plastic coated or being dipped in paraffin
wax. The cheese itself is usually orange in colour,
firm, leathery and dry in texture and mild in
flavour.

Gouda

A semi-hard cheese made of whole cow's milk.
Salted by immersion in brine for up to six days. It
is made in a disc shape with rounded edges and may
also have a red or yellow skin. It has a paler
interior colour to Edam, a softer texture and a mild
flavour. The ripening takes up to six weeks.

Italy

Gorgonzola

A semi-hard cheese available as a blue veined or
white cheese when ripened or unripened. It is made
from full cow's milk using two different curds. It
has a characteristic sharp flavour and a softish texture. Although a quality cheese it is usually rated
lower than Stilton and Roquefort.

Parmesan

A very hard-pressed cheese made from skimmed
cow's milk. It is a large cylindrical shaped cheese,
weighing as much as 120lb and often has a hard
black oiled surface. It has a granular texture and a
sharp flavour. The ripening period is usually in

	excess of one year. It is usually so hard that it is extremely difficult to cut. Its major use is, when grated, for cooking.
Provolone	A hard pressed cheese made from full cow's milk. It is usually made using rennet obtained from goats. The cheese is usually moulded into a pear shape and is smoked.

Switzerland

Emmenthal (or Emmental)	A hard pressed cheese made from whole and partly skimmed cow's milk. Similar to Gruyère cheese in many ways. Made into huge grind-stone shaped blocks. It has a mild but sweet flavour. Easily recognized by the 'eyes' or cavities in the body of the cheese which are usually smaller than in the Gruyère. Also produced in New Zealand and the U.S.A.
Schabzieger	A hard pressed cheese made of full cow's milk. It is greenish in colour and has a very strong smell and taste. The flavour and colour are due to Coumarin which is cut up and added to the curd.

U.S.A.

Brick	This is a semi-hard cheese made from whole cow's milk. It has a smooth texture and a flavour similar to Cheddar. Its name is derived from its brick shape.
Jack	A semi-hard cheese made of whole cow's milk. It has a smooth texture and is very mild in flavour.

Processed Cheese

This is a manufactured product and not a true variety of cheese. It is made from ripened hard or semi-hard cheeses which, for a variety of reasons, are not saleable. Processed cheese is, therefore, a manufactured cheese made from cheeses of an inferior quality.

It is made by grinding down the natural cheese and emulsifying it with salts, water, whey powder and dried milk. It is then heated to $85°C$ ($185°F$) and mixed into a pliable mass. The mixture may then be coloured and flavoured with spices, chopped meat etc., before being packed into blocks or individual portion sizes.

Grading of Cheese Produced in the U.K.

The grading of cheese produced in the U.K. is carried out under two voluntary schemes.

Creamery produced cheese made from full cream is graded by The National Association of Creamery Proprietors and Dairymen. The cheeses graded are Caerphilly, Cheddar, Cheshire, Derby, Double Gloucester, Lancashire, New

Lancashire, Leicester, and White Wensleydale. Apart from Caerphilly, the cheeses must be of 7 lb minimum weight.

The grading is based on a points allocation system as follows:

Flavour and aroma	45 points
Body and texture	40 points
Colour	10 points
Finish	5 points
	100 points

There are four main grades.

'Extra Selected' for a cheese of superlative quality for which a minimum of 91 points must be awarded, including 41 points for flavour and aroma.

'Selected' for a cheese of good quality for which a minimum of 85 points and a maximum of 90 points must be awarded including not less than 38 points for flavour and aroma.

'Second grade' for a cheese not of such high quality, for which not less than 70 points or not more than 84 points have been awarded.

'No Grade' for a cheese that has been awarded less than 70 points or which fails to attain the standard of cheese prescribed.

Farmhouse produced cheeses are graded by the Milk Marketing Boards for English and Scottish Cheddar, English Cheshire, and Lancashire cheeses that are made on farms under contract. There are three mains grades, 'Superfine', 'Fine', and 'Second Grade'.

Catering Uses of Butter and Cheese

Butter

The catering uses for butter are endless and, without doubt, it enhances the product of which it is a part. It is available to the caterer in a variety of package sizes, from individual portion packs to $\frac{1}{2}$ lb packets, to 28 lb blocks of butter.

Its main catering uses may be summarized as follows:

(i) As a spread, e.g. on slices of bread, rolls, toast, scones, etc.

(ii) As a basic ingredient in all types of pastry pastes, e.g. puff paste, etc.

(iii) As a basic ingredient in all types of cakes, e.g. from wedding cakes, birthday cakes, etc. to rock cakes.

(iv) As an ingredient for making basic sauces and cream soups, e.g. bechamel sauce, vegetable soups, etc.

(v) As the main ingredient for making buttercream, brandy butter, etc., and special rich sauces such as sauce Hollandaise, sauce Bearnaise, etc.

Cheese

The catering uses for cheese are threefold:

(i) As a cheese course for lunch or dinner. The cheeses would be served to a customer on a cheese board containing U.K. cheeses only, continental cheeses only or a variety of U.K. and continental cheeses.

For example, U.K. cheeseboard: cream cheese, Caerphilly, Leicester, Cheddar, Double Gloucester, and Blue Stilton. Continental cheeseboard: Brie, Camembert, Edam, Saint Paulin, Roquefort, and Gorgonzola. A 'mixed' cheeseboard: Cheddar, Blue Stilton, Double Gloucester, Brie, Camembert, Roquefort, and Edam.

(ii) As a feature item on a cold buffet. E.g. Blue Stilton, Sage Derby, Dorset Blue.
(iii) As a 'cooking' cheese.

(*a*) To add to a basic cream sauce to make a cheese sauce.
(*b*) To serve as an accompaniment to soups and farinaceous dishes, e.g. minestrone soup, spaghetti bolognaise, etc.
(*c*) To serve sprinkled on dishes to be gratinated, e.g. French onion soup, ravioli au gratin, sole cubat, etc.
(*d*) To serve on toast, e.g. grilled, Welsh rarebit, etc.

The Storage of Butter and Cheese

Butter

As butter is a perishable food the following points should be noted:

(i) It should be stored in a cold store room away from any strong smelling foods at a temperature of about 2°C (35°F).
(ii) If purchased in bulk it will keep for several months if stored at −25 to −30°C (−10 to −20°F).
(iii) It should be kept in the container in which it was sold as exposure to light will cause the butter to go rancid and destroy the vitamin A content.
(iv) Ripened cream butter has a shorter keeping quality.
(v) Salted butters keep better than non-salted butter.

Cheese

All cheeses should be eaten fresh and in their prime condition. This means that they must be stored correctly so that they will reach the customer in a good condition with a full flavour. Cheeses should be wrapped in separate clean polythene bags to prevent their drying out and then stored at a temperature of 5−10°C (40−50°F). Before being served to a customer the cheeses should be removed from the bags and placed in a room at normal temperature in order for the full flavour to be maximized. Particular care must be taken with soft cheeses, e.g. Brie, Camembert, etc., as they can soon become over-ripe and unacceptable to customers. The very hard cheeses, e.g. Parmesan, and unopened processed cheeses, do not need to be refrigerated and may be kept in a clean, cool, dry storeroom. Blue cheeses require a lower temperature of around 4°C (38°F) and a higher relative humidity of 80%.

Scientific and Nutritional Aspects

Butter

As previously mentioned whereas milk is an oil in water emulsion, butter is a water in oil emulsion; the 'inversion' of the emulsions resulting from the mechanical churning process, the mechanism of which is still not fully understood.

The average percentage composition for a typical butter is given below.

Fat	82·5
Protein (casein)	1·5
Lactose .	2
Salt (added)	2
Water	12

Butter, like milk and cheese, is useful source of the fat soluble vitamins A and D, especially the former.

The Butter Regulations 1966 govern the composition of butters sold in the U.K., and they state that:

'butter shall contain:
(a) not less than 80% milk fat
(b) not more than 2% milk solids other than fat
(c) not more than 16% water.'

For low salt butters (unsalted) the milk fat percentage can be as low as 78.

Cheese

Cheese can be regarded as concentrated milk and because of this it has an excellent nutritional value (about 1 pint of milk converts to 2 oz of cheese). The composition of English Cheddar cheese is given in Table 5.3.

Table 5.3. Composition of 100 g of English Cheddar cheese
(McCance and Widdowson 1978)

Protein	26 g
Fat	33.5 g
Carbohydrate − lost in the whey	
Calcium	800 mg
Phosphorus	520 mg
Iron	0.4 mg
Retinol	342 μg
Carotene	126 μg
Vitamin D	0.261 mg
Thiamine	0.04 mg
Riboflavine	0.5 mg
Nicotinic Acid	6.2 mg
Vitamin C	0
Kilocalories of energy	406

Coagulation of the protein lies at the heart of the cheese-making process. Initially the milk has to be soured or ripened, this is usually done by the addition of a particular bacterial culture. The milk proteins are then coagulated or clotted by the addition of the enzyme rennin. The clotted curds are separated from the whey and compressed into a solid mass, and matured by storing for a set period of time. During this process the water content may be reduced to about 40%, compared with that in the original milk of 80+%.

In summary there are over 400 different named cheeses and the basic process of manufacture is similar in most cases. The flavours of the cheeses are governed mostly by the type of micro-organism used and the nature of the maturing process, while the texture is often governed by the amount of pressure placed on the curds during the process. The flavours themselves consist of many substances which are formed by the action of enzymes, secreted by the cheese's characteristic micro-organism, upon the chemical constituents of the cheese. Some of the proteins are broken down to amino acids, and fats to volatile fatty acids; it is these which contribute to the characteristic flavour and aroma of a cheese.

Table 5.4. Composition of various cheeses

Cheese	Grams per 100 g		
	Fat	Protein	Water
Camembert	23.2	22.8	47.5
Cheddar	33.5	26	37
Danish Blue	29.2	23	40.5
Edam	22.9	24.4	43.7
Stilton	40.0	25.6	28.2
Cottage	4	13.6	78.8
Cream	47.4	3.1	45.5

6

Fresh Fruit and Vegetables

The fresh fruit and vegetable markets are perhaps the most difficult markets in which the food buyer has to operate. This is because:

(a) The produce is very perishable, which if not handled quickly and properly will deteriorate in quality.

(b) The markets react very quickly to outside influences:

  (i) The weather can and does affect the crops being produced; in particular the quality and quantity available in the market. Any scarcity or glut affects the price that the produce will fetch.

  (ii) The quality and volume of imported produce will vary according to the state of the exporting country's own market and the price the produce could fetch in the U.K.

  (iii) The supply of one type of produce to the U.K. market will frequently change from one country to another during the year so that a continual supply is available. The failure of an exporting country to meet the U.K. demands creates a scarcity, and a price rise on the little supply that is available.

(c) There is a great range of produce available of which not all is graded. Where there is no grade the buyers experience becomes very important as he will have to assess the quality of the produce himself.

(d) The grading standards are rather broad. Because of this the purchaser needs to know the classes within a grade very well and in particular the permitted tolerances for each class.

(e) There is a great range of varieties of produce even within a type of fruit and vegetable – each which may well have special uses to the caterer, e.g. melons – the common melons are Honeydew, Cantaloup, Ogen, Charentais and Watermelons. All these differ in size, appearance, flavour, etc., and have a different appeal to different sectors of the catering market.

(*f*) The purchasing units for fruits and vegetables are numerous and confusing. Many of the sizes and weights of produce evolved by the tradition of various sectors of the horticulture industry and not as a result of planned marketing by the industry as a whole.

Fresh Fruits

Fruits develop from the flowers of plants and consist of the ripened seed or seeds contained within a large amount of edible tissue. Like vegetables the term 'fruit' has, through common usage, come to apply to some fruits which are not truly botanically fruit, e.g. a pumpkin which is a member of the vegetable marrow family is frequently used as a fruit and served in a sweet dish 'pumpkin pie'.

The common classification (non-botanical) of fruits is as follows:

Citrus Fruits
This group includes lemons, limes, citrons, oranges, grapefruit, ortaniques, ugli-fruit, kum-quats, mandarines, satsumas, clementines, tangerines, wilkins, etc.

Stone Fruits
Apricots, peaches, nectarines, plums, damsons, greengages, persimmons, mangoes, cherries, etc.

Berry Fruits
Black, red and white currants, cranberries, bilberries, strawberries, raspberries, blackberries, loganberries, gooseberries, grapes, etc.

Fleshy Fruits
Apples, pears, bananas, figs, granadillas, medlars, paw paws, melons, pineapple, etc.

Nuts
Coconuts, hazelnuts, filbert nuts, sweet chestnuts, almond nuts, walnuts, pistachio nuts, pecan nuts, brazil nuts, cashew nuts, pine kernels, etc.

Fresh Vegetables

Vegetables are plants or parts of a plant used for food. The term 'vegetable' has, through common usage, come to apply to plants or parts of a plant which are served to customers either cooked or raw as part of a meal. This means that this generalization allows foods which are not strictly vegetables to be included, e.g. tomatoes which are botanically fruits, rice and sweetcorn which are botanically cereals, etc.

Various parts of the plants are used as vegetables and the simple classification by such parts has the value that it provides some guide to the structure and composition which may influence the use of the vegetable.

The classification (non-botanical) of vegetables by the part of the plant commonly used as a vegetable is as follows:

Roots
This group includes beetroot, celeriac, carrot, parsnip, radishes, scorzonera, salsify, swede, kholrabi (not a true root, swollen base of the stem), etc.

Tubers
Potatoes, sweet potatoes, Jerusalem artichokes, etc.

Bulbs
Garlic, leeks, onions, shallots, etc.

Leaves
Brussel sprouts, cabbage, corn salad, chinese cabbage (Pak-Choi), endives, kale, lettuce, spinach, watercress, etc.

Flowers
Broccoli, calabrese, cauliflower, globe artichoke, etc.

Fruits
Cucumber, avocado pear, gherkins, courgette, pumpkin, marrow, aubergine, peppers, tomato, etc.

Seeds (legumes)
Beans, asparagus peas, peas, etc.

Blanched Stems
Asparagus, celery, sea-kale, chicory, etc.

In addition to the above there is also the following.

Fungi
Truffles, ceps, chanterelles, morels, mushrooms, etc.

The Grading of Fresh Fruits and Vegetables within the E.C.

Since February 1973 there has been a gradual introduction of the E.C. quality grading for fresh fruit and vegetables on the British market. To date these include:

Vegetables
Artichokes
Asparagus
Aubergines
Beans (other than shelling beans)
Brussel sprouts
Cabbage
Carrots
Cauliflowers
Celery
Courgettes
Chicory
Cucumbers
Garlic
Lettuce, endives, and batavia
Onions
Peas
Spinach
Sweet peppers
Tomatoes

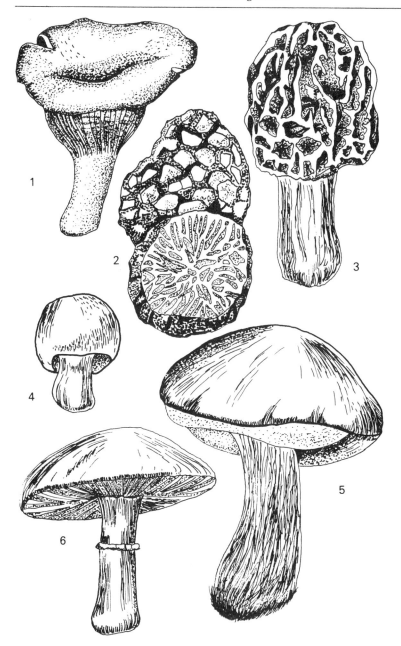

Figure 6.1 (1) Chantrelle; (2) truffle; (3) morel; (4) button mushroom; (5) cep; (6) field mushroom

Fruit   Mandarins
Apples   Pears
Apricots   Peaches
Cherries   Plums
Grapes   Strawberries
Lemons   Satsumas, clementines and
Oranges   similar citrus hybrids

The advantages of providing standards for horticultural products are two-fold.

(*a*) It protects the buyer by providing an item of uniform and legally defined grade so that the buyer is aware of what he is buying and he may limit his inspection of the grades to spot checking.

(*b*) The second advantage is that it brings about a general improvement in quality by the rejection by the producer or packer of all that is below the minimum standard.

There are four main quality classes for produce:

Extra Class for produce of excellent quality.
Class I for produce of good quality with no important defects.
Class II for produce of reasonably good quality.
Class III for produce of a lower marketable quality.

Not all of the classes are always in operation for each type of produce. For example, at the time of writing, for peas and spinach there are only two quality classes, Class I and Class II. Also the Class III for any produce may be suspended if it is decided on a Community basis that the supplies of produce in the higher classes are adequate to meet the consumer requirements for the community as a whole. Class III is also used at times when supplies of the higher classes are not sufficient to meet consumers quality requirements.

There are exemptions from the grading and labelling requirements, in particular for:

(*a*) sales to manufacturers for processing;
(*b*) sales on growers' holdings to consumers for their personal use.

The published standards for the produce is in nine sections.

   (i) States the varieties from which the produce may be grown and the classes for the produce, e.g. celery. The standards apply to fresh celery being varieties of *Apium graveolens L.* var. *dulce Mill* of which two classes are marketed, Class I and Class II.
  (ii) The quality requirements for each class (*see* pp. 103–5 for an example).
 (iii) The size requirements for each class.
 (iv) The tolerances permitted for each class.
  (v) The packing and presentation for each class.
 (vi) The labelling – to give details of the packer/dispatcher, the nature of the produce, e.g. 'French Beans', the origins of the produce, e.g. Vales of Evesham, and the class (and minimum and maximum sizes if applicable).

(vii) Exemptions from the grading and labelling requirements.
(viii) Conditions for exporting the goods.
(ix) References to E.C. regulations.

Table 6.1. E.C. standards for fresh cherries

Extra	Classes I	III (when applicable)

Quality Requirements

MINIMUM REQUIREMENTS
(i) The fruit must be:

whole
of fresh appearance
firm (according to the variety)
clean (in particular, free from traces of pesticides and fungicides)
free from excess external moisture
free from foreign smell or taste
free from pests or disease
with stalk attached (except sour varieties in Class III)

(ii) The fruit must be sufficiently mature. It must be capable of being handled and of travelling without damage.

ADDITIONAL REQUIREMENTS

The fruit must be:	The fruit must be:	The fruit must be:
of superior quality	of good quality	of marketable quality
free from any defects	typical of the variety	meet the requirements
characteristic of the	free from cracking,	of Class I except that the
variety in	bruising and hail	following defects are
shape	damage or sun scorch	permissible so long as
size		the fruit retains the
colour	The following are	characteristics of the
	permissible:	variety:
	slight malformation	slight surface
	slight defects in	blemishes
	colouring	defects in shape
		defects in develop-
		ment and colouring.

Fruit of the sour
varieties without stalks
may be included in this
class, provided that the
fruit is undamaged. Such
fruit should be packed
separately.

Table 6.1. cont.

Classes		
Extra	I	III (when applicable)

Size Requirements

MINIMUM PERMITTED SIZES. Size is measured by the diameter at the widest part of the fruit. The following are the minimum permitted sizes:

20 mm   17 mm except for early   15 mm
                         varieties
                         15 mm for early varieties

SIZE UNIFORMITY. Fruit in any one package must be reasonably uniform in size.

In any one package, quality and size tolerances are allowed as follows:
QUALITY

5% by weight of fruit not meeting the requirements of the class but meeting the requirements of Class I. Of this 5% not more than 2% may be split or pest damaged and none may be over-ripe or unfit for consumption.	10% by weight of fruit not meeting the minimum requirements. Of this 10% not more than 4% may be split or pest damaged and none may be over-ripe or unfit for consumption.	15% by number of weight of fruit not meeting the minimum requirements of the class. Of this 15% not more than 4% may be over-ripe or pest damaged and not more than 10% split fruit. All must be of marketable quality and fit for consumption. Sour varieties packed separately without their stalks may contain 10% by number or weight of fruit with stalk attached.

SIZE. In any one package 10% by weignt of fruit not satisfying the requirements for the class but having a diameter of not less than:

17 mm	15 mm fcr other than early varieties 13 mm for early varieties	In any one package 15% by number or weight of fruit having a diameter of less than 15 mm

Table 6.1. cont.

Classes		
Extra	I	III (when applicable)

COMBINED TOLERANCES. In no circumstances may quality and size tolerances together exceed

10%	15%	

Packaging and Presentation
UNIFORMITY. The contents of each package must include only fruit uniform in

variety	variety	variety
size	size	The visible content of
ripeness		a container must how-
colouring		ever be representative
		of the whole

PACKAGING. Packaging must be such as to give the produce suitable protection. Any paper or other material used inside the package must be new and harmless to human food.

No printing must come into contact with the fruit.

Packed containers must be free from leaves, twigs or other extraneous matter.

Labelling
Each package must bear the following particulars, legibly and indelibly marked on the outside of the container on one side or end

A.   Identification
      Packer
      Dispatcher   Name and address or identifying mark

B.   Nature of produce
      'Cherries' — where the contents are not clearly visible
      Name of variety (optional) but where sour varieties in Class III are
      packed without stalks 'sour variety' or the name of the variety must be
      shown.

C.   Origin of produce
      District of origin or national, regional or local trade name
      (e.g., British, English, Kent, Vale of Evesham)

D.   Commercial specifications
      Quality class

The information required as to marking may be given by means of:
      (i) a label firmly fixed to the container
      (ii) an ink stamp or printing on to the container or
      (iii) a combination of the above methods.

Table 6.2. A summary of the E.C. common quality standards for fresh fruit and vegetables showing the foods which are graded with the specific classes and the general requirements for the grading of each item

Fruit	Extra Class	Class I	Class II	Class III	General Requirements
Apples	✓	✓	✓	X	Grading for size is by the diameter at the widest part of the fruit with minimum sizes for each class. There are two minimum sizes stated for each fruit depending on whether the apple is a large fruited variety or not.
Apricots	✓	✓	✓	O	Grading for size is by the maximum diameter or the circumference. The minimum size for Classes I and II is 30 mm diameter (10 cm circumference). The minimum size for Extra Class is determined by each country according to the variety, but it must not be smaller than that of the other classes.
Cherries	✓	✓	O	✓	Grading for size is measured by the diameter at the widest part of the fruit. *See* pp. 103–5 for details of the common standard of quality for cherries.
Grapes	✓	✓	O	✓	Grading is for table grapes only. Sizing is by minimum weight per bunch depending on whether the grape is hot-house or open ground grown.
Lemons	✓	✓	✓	✓	There is a minimum juice content of 20% by weight required. Grading for size is by the maximum diameter of the lemon. Class III must have a minimum of 42 mm and all others 45 mm. The fruit is also required to be graded by a scale from 0 to 8 for which fruit of a minimum and maximum size are required. (e.g. Size 0 a diameter range of 83–86 mm and size 7 a diameter range of 45–52 mm.)

Mandarins	√	√	√	√	X	There is a minimum juice content for each variety of this type of citrus fruit. Grading for size is by the maximum diameter of the fruit. The fruit is also graded on a size scale from 1 to 10 similar to that for lemons.
Oranges	√	√	√	√	√	A minimum juice content is required for each variety. Grading for size is by the maximum diameter of the fruit. The fruit is also graded on a size scale from 0 to 13 similar to that for other citrus fruits with the smallest range being size 13 with a diameter range of 53–60 mm.
Peaches	√	√	√	√	X	Sizing is determined by circumference or maximum diameter. Peaches are also graded according to a size scale, like citrus fruits but with a letter coding for each size range.
Pears	√	√	√	√	X	The grading is exactly as that required for apples, except that the minimum permitted sizes are different.
Plums	√	√	√	√	O	Size is measured by the maximum transverse diameter of the fruit. There are minimum permitted sizes depending on the variety of plum.
Satsumas, clementines, tangerines and similar citrus hybrids	√	√	√	√	√	
Strawberries	√	√	√	O	√	Size is measured by the maximum diameter or the equatorial section. The minimum permitted sizes within a class depend on whether the fruit is from a large fruiting or small fruiting variety. There are no size requirements for wild strawberries.

N.B. X = A Class III has been defined but does not operate at present.

Table 6.2. cont.

Vegetables	Extra Class	Class I	Class II	Class III	General Requirements
Artichokes	✓	✓	✓	○	This grading is for globe artichokes only. Sizing is by the diameter of the head.
Asparagus	✓	✓	✓	✓	Asparagus shoots are divided into three colour groups: (i) green asparagus; (ii) white asparagus; (iii) violet asparagus, having tips of a colour between pink and violet or purple but otherwise white Quality requirements stress the degree of straightness of the shoots and the compactness of the tips. The grading is also by size of the length and diameter of the shoot. Packaging can be in either bundles, or loose within a package. When in bundles they must be firmly bound in weights of 500g, 1 or 2 kg.
Aubergines	○	✓	✓	✓	Sizing is by diameter or weight.
Beans (other than shelling beans)	✓	✓	✓	○	The standard does not include broad beans. Grading is in two groups: (i) fine or 'needle' beans; (ii) other beans including runner beans, french beans, snap beans and kidney beans. All of which are graded into Classes I and II only. 'Needle' beans are graded by size 'very fine' for beans of less than 6 mm width (into Extra Class, Class I and Class II), 'fine' for beans of 9 mm and less in width (into Classes I and II only) 'average' for beans exceeding 9 mm in width (into Class II only).
Brussels Sprouts	○	✓	✓	✓	Sizing is determined by the maximum transverse diameter with minimum permitted sizes of (*a*) trimmed 10 mm (*b*) untrimmed 20 mm for Classes I and II only. The difference in diameter for produce in a package not to exceed 20 mm. The labelling must specify whether the contents are 'trimmed' or 'untrimmed' unless the contents are visible.
Cabbage (round-headed)	○	✓	✓	○	Sizing is by weight 'summer type' cabbages — not less than 350g. 'Other cabbages' — not less than 500g.

Carrots	○	✓	✓	✓	Carrots are graded for size by the diameter at the widest section or by the net weight per root, without foilage. The standards specify the minimum and maximum diameters and weights (e.g. minimum 10mm/8g, maximum 40mm/150g) for (i) small root varieties and early pullings (ii) maincrop and large root varieties. Packaging may be by (i) bunches, for small root varieties, or (ii) topped.
Cauliflowers	✓	✓	✓	✓	Quality requirements stress the shape, colour and size of the curd. The size requirements state the minimum diameter of the curd, 11 cm for Extra Class and Classes I and II, 9 cm for Class III; and further states the variation in sizes which are permitted within any one package. The presentation of the cauliflowers in a package is in one of the following (i) with leaves; (ii) without leaves; (iii) trimmed.
Celery	○	✓	✓	○	Size requirements: No celery head to be less than 150g. Class I celery is graded into three size groups, large: over 800g; medium: 500–800g; small 150–500g. Packaging may be by boxes, containers, or in bundles.
Chicory (witloof)	✓	✓	✓	✓	There are specific size requirements (length and maximum diameter) for the produce to be placed in a particular class.
Courgettes	✓	✓	✓	○	Sizing is by length or weight.
Cucumbers	✓	✓	✓	✓	Grading for size is obligatory for Extra Class and Class I, with minimum weights of outdoor cucumbers 180g and greenhouse/frame cucumbers 250g; with the difference in weight between the largest and smallest in a package not exceeding 150g. Grading for size is optional for Classes II and III but the minimum weights and sizes must be met. There is an additional requirement for greenhouse/frame cucumbers marketed between 1 June–30 September of minimum length of 30 cm and a diameter of 4 to 7 cm (measured midway along the length). Extra Class and Class I cucumbers must be packaged.
Garlic	○	✓		✓	Minimum diameter of 45 mm for Extra Class and 30 mm for Classes I and II. May be sold loose, in bunches of 6 bulbs for fresh or semi-dry or 12 bulbs for dry garlic, or in strings of not less than 24 bulbs for dry or semi-dry garlic.

Table 6.2. cont.

Vegetables	Extra Class	Class I	Class II	Class III	General Requirements
Lettuce, endives and batavia	O	✓	✓	✓	The standards do not apply to lettuce harvested by the leaf, e.g. Lamb's lettuce. Sizing is determined by the net weights of 100 units or a single unit, e.g. Classes I and II minimum weights Lettuce: open ground 15 kg per 100 or 150 g each glasshouse 8 kg per 100 or 80 g each Curl leaved and broad-leaved (Batavian) endives: open ground 20 kg per 100 or 200 g each glasshouse 15 kg per 100 or 150 g each Details of the minimum weight per 100 units or single units or alternatively the number of units must be displayed on the labelling.
Onions	O	✓	✓	✓	The standards do not apply to green onions with leaves (salad onions). Onions are graded for size which is determined by the maximum diameter at the equatorial section. The minimum permitted size for all classes is 10mm. There is also a maximum permitted variation in size with each package in any of the three classes.

Peas	○	✓	✓	○	The standards apply to fresh peas in the pod to be supplied to the consumer, but excludes the mangetout types. The quality requirements are quite general apart from stating that a minimum of five seeds per pod are required for Class I and three seeds per pod for Class II produce.
Spinach	○	✓	✓	○	The standards do not apply to spinach beet. There is a maximum length of stack of 10cm for Class I produce. The contents of a package to be free from detached stems, yellow leaves seeds. There are no size requirements for spinach.
Sweet peppers	○	✓	✓	○	Sizing is by diameter or width across the shoulder.
Tomatoes	✓	✓	✓	✓	There are very detailed standards for the size requirements for tomatoes based on the tomato being either of a round or ribbed variety or an elongated variety. There are also exceptions with Classes II and III not necessarily being required to be sold by size. Extra Class and Class I are required to have additional protection in packaging.

Table 6.3. Fruit and vegetable supply calendar (N.B. **X** = significant supplies; O = small supplies). This shows the major supplying countries for fresh fruit. Supplies may also be available from other countries but not for longer periods than those of the countries listed.

Produce	Country of Origin	Jan.	Feb.	Mar.	Apr.	May	June	July	Aug.	Sept.	Oct.	Nov.	Dec.
Apples	Home grown	X	X	X	X	X	X	O	X	X	X	X	X
	Australia				X	X	X	X	O	X	X	X	X
	France	X	X	X	X	X	X	X	O	X	X	X	X
	Italy	X	X	X	X	X	X	X		X	X	X	X
Apricots	South Africa	X	X										X
	Spain						X	X					
	Hungary							X	X				
Avocado	Israel	X	X	X	X	X	X	X		X	X	X	X
	South Africa				X	X	X	X	X	X	X	O	O
	Kenya						O	O	O	O	O		
Bananas	Columbia	X	X	X	X	X	X	X	X	X	X	X	X
	Ecuador	X	X	X	X	X	X	X	X	X	X	X	X
	Jamaica	X	X	X	X	X	X	X	X	X	X	X	X
	Windward Islands	X	X	X	X	X	X	X	X	X	X	X	X
Blackberries	Home grown							O	X	X	O		
Cherries	Home grown						X	X	X				
	France					X	X	X					
	Lebanon					X	X	X					
	Italy					X	X						
Currants: Red, Black, White	Home grown							X	X				
Gooseberries	Home grown					X	X	X	X				
Grapes	Spain	X	X	X	X	X	X	X	X	X	X	X	X
	South Africa	X	X									X	X
	Italy								O	O	O		
	Belgium	O	O	O	O	O	O	O	O	O	O	O	O

Fruit	Source	Jan	Feb	Mar	Apr	May	Jun	Jul	Aug	Sep	Oct	Nov	Dec
Grapefruit	Cyprus	X	X	X			X	X	X	X	X	X	X
	Israel	X	X	X	X	X	X	X	X	X	X	X	X
	South Africa						X	X	X		X		
	U.S.A.	O	O	O	O	O	O	O	O	O	O	O	O
Lemons	Italy	X	X	X	X	X	X	X	X	X	X	X	X
	South Africa	O	O	O	O	O	X	X	X	X	X	X	X
	Spain	O	O	O	O	O	X	X	X	X	X	X	X
	U.S.A.	O	O	O	O	O	X	X	X	X	O	O	O
Limes	Kenya	O	O	O	O	O	O	O	O	O	O	O	O
	Dominica	O	O	O	O	O	O	O	O	O	O	O	O
	Seychelles	O	O	O	O						O	O	O
	South Africa	O	O										
Mandarins	Australia					X	X	X			X		
Mangoes	Kenya	O	O	O	O	O	O	O	O	O	O	O	O
	South Africa	O	O	O	O	O	O	O	O				
Melons	Canteloupe (Netherlands)					O	O	O	O	O			
	Charentais (France)	X				X	X	X	X	X	X		
	Honeydew (Spain)	X	X	O	X	X	X	X	X	X	X	X	X
	Ogen (Israel)	O	O	O				X	X	X	X		
	Water (Italy)					X	X	X	X	X			
Nectarines	France						X	X	X	X	X		
	Italy	X	X	X		X	X	X	X	X	X		
	South Africa	X	X	X	X								
	Spain					X	X	X	X	X			
Oranges	Cyprus	X	X	X	X	X	X	X	X	X	X	X	X
	Israel	X	X	X	X	X	X	X	X	X	X	X	X
	South Africa						X	X	X	X	X	X	X
	Spain	X	X	X	X	X	X	X	X	X	X	X	X

Table 6.3. cont.

Produce	Country of Origin	Jan.	Feb.	Mar.	Apr.	May	June	July	Aug.	Sept.	Oct.	Nov.	Dec.
Ortaniques	Jamaica	O	X	X	X	O							
Passion Fruit	Kenya	O	O	O	O	O	O	O	O	O	O	O	O
Peaches	France						X	X	X	X			
	Italy						X	X	X	X			
	South Africa	X	X	X									X
	Spain					X	X	X					
Pears	Home grown	X	X	X	X					X	X	X	X
	Australia			X	X	X	X	X	X				
	Italy	X	X	X	X	X	X	X	X	X	X	X	X
	South Africa	X	X	X	X	X	X						
Pineapples	Azores	O	O	O	O	O	O	O			O	O	O
	Ivory Coast	O	O	O	O					O	O	O	O
	Kenya	X	X	X	X	X	X	X	X	X	X	X	X
	South Africa	X	X	X	X	X	X	X	X	X	X	X	X
Plums	Home grown								X	X	X		
	Italy							X	X	X	X		
	South Africa	X	X	X									
	Spain					X	X						
Raspberries	Home grown						X	O	O	O	O		
Rhubarb	Home grown	X	X	X	X	X	X	X				O	X

		1	2	3	4	5	6	7	8	9	10	11	12
Strawberries	Home grown					O	O	O	O	O			
	Israel	O	X	X	O		O	X	X	X	X	O	O
	Kenya	O	O	O	O	O	O	O	O	O	O	O	O
	U.S.A.	O	O	O	O					O	O	O	O
Artichokes (Globe)	Home grown	O	O	O	O				O	O	O	O	O
	Cyprus	O	O										
	France	O	O	O	O		X	X	X	O	O	O	O
	Spain	O	O	O	O					X	X	O	O
Asparagus	Home grown		X	O	O	X	X	X	X	O	O		O
	France	X	X	X	X	X	X	X	X	X			
	Mexico	O		O	O	O			O	O			
	U.S.A.		X	X	X								
Aubergines	Canary Islands	O	O	O	O	O	O	O	O	O	O	O	O
	France	O	O					O	O	O	O	O	O
	Kenya					O	O	O	O	O	O	O	O
Beans Broad	Home grown			X	X	X	X	X	X	X			
	France			X	X	X	X	X					
Beans French	Home grown	O	O	O	O	O	O	O	O	O	O	O	O
	Kenya	O	O	O	O	O	O	X	X	X	O	O	O
	Morocco				O	O	O		O	O			
	Spain	O	O	O	O	O	O						
Beans Runner	Home grown				X	X	X	X	X	X			
Beetroot	Home grown	X	X	X	X	O	O	O	X	X	X	X	X
	Cyprus					X	X	X	X				
Broccoli Sprouting	Home grown	X		X	X	X							
Brussel Sprouts	Home grown	X	X	X	O	X	X	X	X	X	X	X	X

Table 6.3. cont.

Produce	Country of Origin	Jan.	Feb.	Mar.	Apr.	May	June	July	Aug.	Sept.	Oct.	Nov.	Dec.
Cabbage													
Savoy	Home grown	X	X	X	X	X	X	X			X	X	X
Spring		O	O	X	X						O	O	O
Summer/ Autumn		X	X	X	X			X	X	X	X	X	X
Winter		X	X	X	X						X	X	X
Winter White		X	X	X	X	X					X	X	X
Winter White	Netherlands					X	O		X	X			X
Capsicums	Home grown					O	O	O	O	O			
	Bulgaria				O	O	O	O					
	Kenya	O	O	O	O	O	O	O					
	Netherlands	O	O	O	O	O	O	O	O	O	O	O	O
Carrots	Home grown	X	X	X	X	X	X	X	X	X	X	X	X
	France			X	X	O	X	X					
	Italy	O	O	O	O	O	X	X					
	Netherlands	X	X	X	X	X	X				X	X	
Cauliflower	Home grown	X	X	X	X	X	X	X	X	X	X	X	X
	Channel Islands	X	X	X	X	O					O	O	X
	France	X	X	X	X							O	X
	Italy	O	O	O								O	O
Celery	Home grown	X	X	X	X	O	X	X	X	X	X	O	O
	Israel	X	X	X	X	X	X						
	Spain	X	X	X		O	O						
	U.S.A.	O	O	O	O								
Chicory	Belgium	X	X	X	X	X	O			X	X	X	X
Courgette	Home grown						X	X	X	X	X		
	Channel Islands						X	X	X	X	X		
	France	X	X	X	X	O	X	X	X	X	O	O	O
	Kenya					X						X	X

Cucumbers	Home grown	×	×	×	×	×	×	×	×	×	×	×
	Canary Islands	○	×	×	×	×	×	×	×	×	×	○	○
	Netherlands	○	×	×	×	×	×	×	×	×	×	×	○
	Rumania	○	×	×	×	×							
Endives													
Curly	France	○											○
	Italy	○											○
	Spain	○	○										
Garlic	Egypt	×	×	×	○	×	×	×	×	○	×	×	×
	France	○	×	×	×	×	×	×	×	×	×	×	×
	Italy	×	×	×	×	○	○	×	×	○	×	×	○
	Poland	○	○	○	○								
Leeks	Home grown	×	×	×	×	×	×	×	×	×	×	×	×
	Belgium	○	×	×	○	×	○	×	×	×	×	×	×
	Netherlands	×	×	×	×	×	×	×	×	×	×	×	
Marrows	Home grown						×	×	×	×	×	×	
Mushrooms	Home grown	×	×	×	×	○	×	×	×	×	×	×	×
	Eire			○	○	×	○	×	○	×	○	×	×
	N. Ireland	×	×	×	×	×	×	×	×	×	×	×	×
Onions	Home grown	×	×	×	○		○	○	×	×	×	×	×
	Netherlands	×	×	×	×	×	×	×	×	×	×	×	×
	Poland	×	×	×	○	×	×	×	×	×	×	×	×
	Spain	×	×	○	○	×	×	×	×	×	×	×	×
Parsnips	Home grown	×	×	×	×	○	○	×	×	×	×	×	×
Peas	Home grown								×	×	×		
Radishes	Home grown	○	○	○	×	×	×	×	×	×	×	×	×
	U.S.A.	○	○	○	○					○	○	○	○
Salsify	Belgium	○	○	○	○	○			○		○	○	○
Spinach	Home grown	○	○	○	×	×	○	○	○	×	×	○	○
Sweet Corn	Home grown								×	×	×		
	Spain				×	○	○						

Table 6.3 cont.

Produce	Country of Origin	Jan.	Feb.	Mar.	Apr.	May	June	July	Aug.	Sept.	Oct.	Nov.	Dec.
Sweet Potatoes	Canary Islands	O	O	O	O	O	O	O	O	O	O	O	O
Swedes	Home grown	X	X	X	X	X	O	O	X	X	X	X	X
Tomatoes	Home grown			O	O	X	X	X	X	X	X	O	O
	Channel Islands		O	O	O	X	X	X	X	X	X	O	
	Canary Islands	X	X	X	X	X	X	X	X	X	X	X	X
	Netherlands				O	X						O	
Turnips	Home grown	O	O	O	O	O	O	O	O	O	O	O	O
Water Cress	Home grown	O	O	O	O	O	O	O	O	O	O	O	O

Some Less Common Fruits

Bilberry
Also known as blueberry and whortleberry. A small dark blue berry with a single seed in the centre having similar uses as cranberries and black currants. It grows wild in the U.K., Europe, and U.S.A.

Cape Gooseberry
Grown in South Africa and New Zealand. The fruit is round, yellow, the size of a cherry, but contained within an inflated calyx, making it look a little like a miniature Chinese lantern. Used for jam, as a dessert fruit and for petit fours.

Custard Apple
A tropical fruit from India, Malaya, Australia, Africa, and the U.S.A. It is about the size of an apple, heart-shaped, light green in colour and has a scaly surface. The flesh is white and juicy with a pineapple flavour. Ideal as an unusual dessert fruit.

Granadillas or Passion Fruit
Grown in Australia, Brazil, U.S.A., and the Mediterranean region. It is dark purple in colour, of a similar size to a plum, but with a leathery wrinkled outer skin. The inside is a mass of small seeds surrounded by a yellow/green aromatic juicy pulp. Used as a dessert fruit, for water ices, and made into a beverage.

Kumquats
A member of the citrus family, grown in Japan, U.S.A., South Africa, and Australia. The size of a large gooseberry with the skin and flesh orange in colour with a sharp taste. Used as a dessert, for decorating meat dishes and as a preserve.

Lychee or Litchee or Litchi
Grown in India, China, South Africa, and U.S.A. A small oval/round fruit $1\frac{1}{2}-2$ in. in diameter, with a brown outer shell containing a white juicy flesh and a single seed. Mainly eaten as a dessert but also canned and dried.

Mangoes
Grown in India, South Africa, Israel, and the U.S.A. The fruit is quite large often 1 lb in weight and is oval or kidney shaped. The outer skin is tough, smooth, and a green or red colour. The flesh is yellow/orange, juicy, fibrous and has a spicy aroma and a taste between apricot and pineapple.

Nectarines
Grown in South Africa, Cyprus, Israel, and Spain. Originated as a mutation of the peach, but differs by having a tight, smooth skin, a firmer and brighter coloured flesh. Eaten as a dessert.

Ortaniques
Grown mainly in Jamaica. It is a citrus fruit being a hybrid between an orange and a tangarine. It has the same uses in catering as oranges.

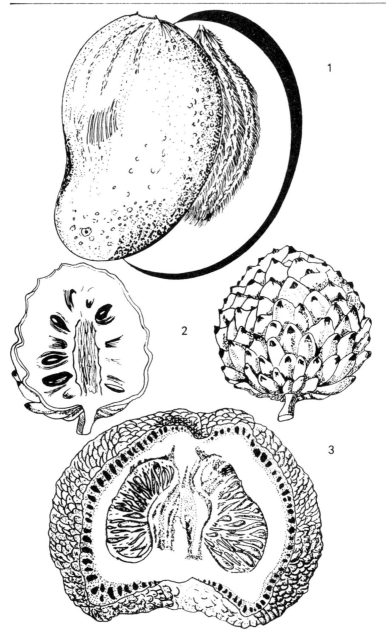

Figure 6.2 (1) Mango; (2) custard apple; (3) ugli fruit

Pawpaw or Papaya

Grown in most tropical countries. A large fleshy fruit often the size and shape of a large rugby ball, it has a green/yellow skin and a flesh similar to a melon yet often only 1 in. thick. Used as an alternative to melon, is canned with other fruits, and also crystallized.

Pecan
Grown in the U.S.A. It is a large nut used for cakes, ice-cream, sweets, etc.

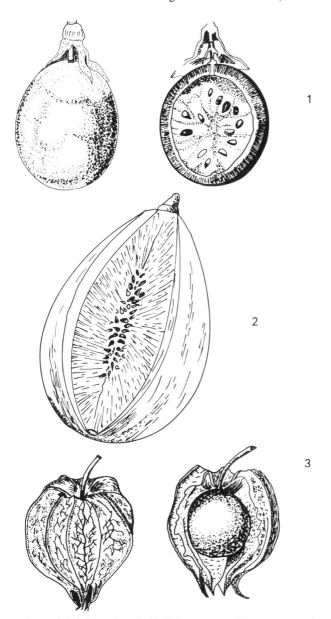

Figure 6.3 (1) Passion fruit; (2) paw-paw; (3) cape gooseberry

Persimmons or Date Plum
Grown in the Mediterranean region and the U.S.A. The size of a large plum, it is usually orange in colour, but should only be eaten when fully ripe and a dull brown colour. The flesh being juicy and a dull orange colour.

Pistachio
Grown in the U.S.A., and the Mediterranean regions. It is a small green nut contained within a dark purple skin. It is widely used in ice-cream, nougats, cakes, and in galantines.

Ugli
A large citrus fruit grown in the U.S.A. It is a hybrid between the grapefruit and the tangarine. It is of a similar size and shape to a grapefruit, but has a loose, corky skin. The flesh is orange coloured. It is used as an alternative to a grapefruit.

Some Less Common Vegetables

Asparagus Pea
A small twin podded member of the pea family grown in the U.K., and in southern Europe. The pods are 1–2 in. in length, have four longitudinal ribs and contain very small peas. Like 'mangetout' the pods are eaten whole.

Aubergines
A distant member of the potato family with edible fruits. It is grown in the U.K., under glass but mainly imported from France, Canary Islands, and Kenya. Usually a dark purple colour, up to 9 in. in length and either egg or sausage shaped.

Artichokes – Globe
A thistle-like plant grown in the U.K., and Europe, the flower heads (or chokes) which are 3–5 in. in diameter having numerous large green bracts. It is the fleshy bases of each bract which are eaten.

Artichokes – Jerusalem
A sweet-fleshed member of the tuber family mainly imported into the U.K. It is whitish in colour, knobbly in appearance like several small new potatoes joined together.

Calabrese or Green Sprouting Broccoli
This is grown specifically for quick freezing.

Celeriac
A root-like crop grown in the U.K., which is closely related to celery except that it is the swollen base of the stem which is eaten. It is similar in size to a large turnip but it has an irregular and roughened surface and a strong celery and nutty flavour.

Chicory

(*a*) A large elongated root which is washed, peeled, chopped, roasted, and ground and blended with some coffees.

(*b*) A salad vegetable which is blanched and has the appearance of a small compact white cos lettuce. Some confusion arises in that in the catering trade it is often referred to as endive.

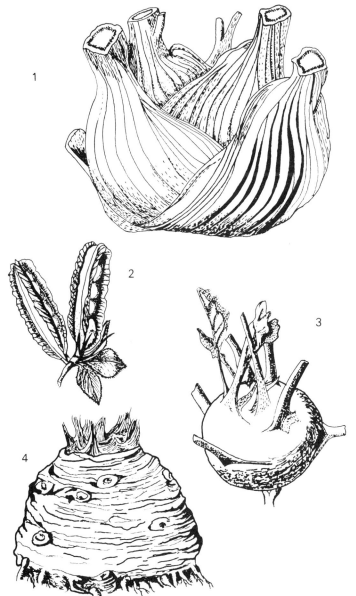

Figure 6.4 (1) Fennel; (2) asparagus pea; (3) kholrabi; (4) celeriac

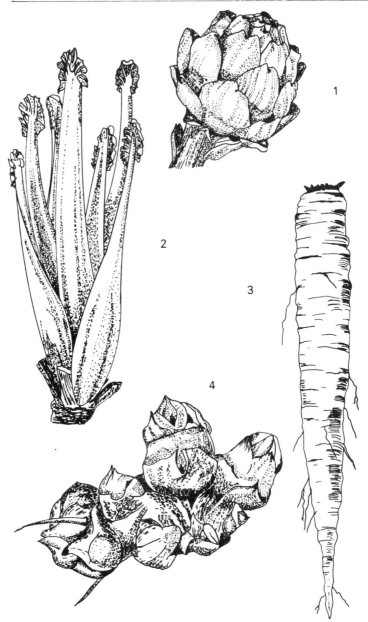

Figure 6.5 (1) Globe artichoke; (2) sea kale; (3) salsify; (4) Jerusalem artichoke

Endives
A salad plant having the appearance of a well developed round lettuce of which all the leaves are divided many times and curled. Confusion also arises here in that in the catering trade it is often referred to as chicory.

Fennel
A short stocky plant with a swollen leaf-base. It resembles the base of a stick of celery, is white/green in colour and smells and tastes slightly of aniseed.

Kholrabi
Often referred to as 'turnip-rooted cabbage'. It is similar in size to a turnip and has small cabbage-like leaves growing from it. The edible part which is really the swollen base of the stem is used as an alternative to turnips. There are two kinds, green and purple.

Pumpkin
A member of the cucumber and melon family, being the largest in size. It is a large round and yellow/orange vegetable with the flesh like that of a melon, which is frequently used as an ingredient in sweet dishes such as pumpkin and apple pie.

Salsify
Also known as 'oyster plant' because its root is supposed to have the same taste as oysters. The root is whitish in colour, about 12 in. in length and at the thickest end is no greater than 1 in. in diameter.

Scorzonera
Also known as 'black salsify'. Similar in appearance and use to salsify except that it is black skinned.

Seakale
It has some slight resemblance to a young immature stick of celery. It has broad, white/green blanched leaf stalks about 10 in. in length and when cooked has a nutty yet slightly bitter flavour.

Truffles
This exotic, expensive, edible fungi is imported from France. It is about the size of a plum, dark brown/black in colour, a shrivelled warty appearance with a solid flesh throughout containing a network of pale veins. Available fresh, frozen, and canned.

Catering Uses

The catering uses of fruits and vegetables are shown in tabular form (*see* Table 6.4).

Table 6.4. Catering uses of fruits and vegetables

Produce	Main Catering Uses
FRUITS	
Citrus Fruits	
citrons	Candied peel
clementines	Fresh fruit
grapefruit	Fresh fruit, fruit cocktail, served hot grilled
kumquats	As a preserve, fresh fruit, garnish for cold meats
lemons	As a garnish for fish and meat dishes, water ice, soufflés
limes	As a garnish for fish and meat dishes, water ices
mandarines	Fresh fruit, soufflés, water ice
oranges	Marmalade, fresh fruit, fruit cocktail, water ice, bavarois
ortaniques	Fresh fruit, fruit cocktail
satsumas	Fresh fruit
tangarines	Fresh fruit, petit fours
ugli	As an alternative to grapefruit
wilkins	Fresh fruit
Stone Fruits	
apricots	Fresh fruit, jam, pies, flans, compôte
cherries	Fresh fruit, jam, pies, flans, garnish for meat dishes
damsons	Jam, pies, flans
greengage	Fresh fruit, pies, flans
mangoes	Fresh fruit
nectarines	Fresh fruit, ice cream
peaches	Fresh fruit, pies, flans, ice cream, garnish for meat dishes
plums	Fresh fruit, jam, pies, flans
persimmons	Fresh fruit
Berry Fruits	
bilberries	Pies, flans, tarts
blackberries	Fresh fruit, pies, flans, tarts
currants — black, red	Jam, flans, tarts, compôte, ice cream
cranberries	Sauce for turkey dishes
gooseberries	Jam, flans, tarts, compôte
grapes	Fresh fruit, fruit salad, garnish for cold poultry, petit fours
loganberries	Fresh fruit, flans
raspberries	Fresh fruit, flans, ice cream, bavarois, soufflés
strawberries	Fresh fruit, flans, ice cream, bavarois, soufflés
Fleshy Fruits	
apples	Dessert varieties eaten as fresh fruit. Cooking varieties for pies, flans, etc.
bananas	Fresh fruit, flans, garnish for chicken and fish courses
figs	Fresh fruit, compôte
granadillas	Fresh fruit, water ice

Table 6.4. cont.

Produce	Main Catering Uses
melons	Fresh fruit, fruit salad
paw paws	Fresh fruit, fruit salad
pineapple	Fresh fruit, fried as a fritter, garnish for ham, etc.
Nuts	
almonds	Salted for use at receptions, decoration for cakes and petit fours, ground for marzipan, frazipan, etc.
brazil	Dessert
cashew	Salted
chestnut	As a garnish for turkey dishes and ice cream, petit fours, etc.
coconuts	Meat dishes, petit fours, cakes
filbert	Dessert, praline
hazel	Dessert, praline
pecan	Dessert, cakes, ice-cream
pine-kernels	Salted, chocolates, meat dishes
pistachio	Decorating galantines, petit fours, ice-cream, nougat
VEGETABLES	
Roots	
beetroot	Soup, hors d'oeuvre, salads
carrot	Soup, hors d'oeuvre, hot vegetable
celeriac	Soup, hors d'oeuvre, salads
kholrabi	Hors d'oeuvre, hot vegetable
parsnip	Hot vegetable
radishes	Hors d'oeuvre, salads, for decoration of cold fish and meat
salsify	Hot vegetable
scorzonera	Hot vegetable
swede	Hot vegetable
Tubers	
artichokes (Jerusalem)	Soup, hot vegetable
potatoes	Soup, hors d'oeuvre, hot vegetable, salads
sweet potatoes	Hot vegetable
Bulbs	
garlic	Used as a flavouring agent rather than as a vegetable
leeks	Soups, hors d'oeuvre, hot vegetable
onions	Soups, sauces, hors d'oeuvre, salads, hot vegetable
shallots	Hors d'oeuvre, sauces
Leaves	
brussels sprouts	Hot vegetable
cabbage	Hors d'oeuvre, hot vegetable
corn salad	Salad
chinese cabbage	Hot vegetable
endives	Salad, hot vegetable

Table 6.4. cont.

Produce	Main Catering Uses
kale	Hot vegetable
lettuce	Salad, hot vegetable, garnish to meat dishes
spinach	Soup, hot vegetable, garnish to meat, fish, egg dishes
watercress	Soup, garnish to meat dishes
Flowers	
broccoli	Hot vegetable
calabrese	Hot vegetable
cauliflower	Soup, hors d'oeuvre, hot vegetable
globe artichoke	Hors d'oeuvre, garnish for meat dishes, hot and cold vegetable
Fruits	
aubergines	Hors d'oeuvre, hot vegetable, garnish for fish and meat dishes
avocado pear	Hors d'oeuvre, soup
courgette	Hors d'oeuvre, hot vegetable
cucumbers	Hors d'oeuvre, soup, salad, garnish for hot and cold fish dishes
gherkins	Hors d'oeuvre
marrow	Hot vegetable
peppers	Hors d'oeuvre, hot vegetable, salads
pumpkin	Savoury or sweet pie
tomato	Soups, hors d'oeuvre, salads, hot vegetable, sauces, garnish for fish and meat dishes
Seeds (legumes)	
asparagus peas	Hot vegetable
beans, broad	Hot vegetable
beans, French	Hot vegetable, salad
beans, runner	Hot vegetable
peas	Hors d'oeuvre, soup, salad, hot vegetable
sweet corn	Hors d'oeuvre, hot vegetable, garnish for egg and meat dishes
Blanched stems	
asparagus	Hors d'oeuvre, soup, hot and cold vegetable, garnish for fish and meat dishes
celery	Hors d'oeuvre, soup, salad, hot vegetable
chicory	Salad, hot vegetable
sea-kale	Hot and cold vegetable
Fungi	
ceps	Soups, hot vegetable
chanterelles	Hot vegetable
morels	Hot vegetable
mushrooms	Hors d'oeuvre, soups, sauces, hot vegetable, garnish for meat dishes
truffles	Sauces, hot vegetable, decoration of hot and cold fish and meat dishes

The Storage of Fresh Fruits and Vegetables

The storage of fruits and vegetables is shown in Table 6.5.

Table 6.5. The short-term storage of fresh fruits and vegetables

Produce	Number of Storage Days 0–1°C (32–34°F)	Notes
FRUIT		
Apples	10	Imported varieties
Figs (fresh)	10	
Gooseberries	10	
Grapes	10	
Pears	10	
Soft fruits:		
including blackberries, loganberries, currants	4	Condensation on removal from store encourages mould growth. This does not include raspberries and strawberries
Stone fruits:		
including apricots, cherries, peaches, plums	10	
VEGETABLES		
Artichokes (Globe)	10	
Asparagus	4	
Beans, broad	10	
Beans, French	4	
Cauliflower	10	
Celery	10	
Green vegetables:		
including cabbage, brussels sprouts, etc.	10	
Leeks	10	
Mushrooms	4	Condensation can cause damage
Onions	10	Ideally stored in low humidity
Peas (in pod)	4	
Rhubarb	4	
Root vegetables:		
including carrots, parsnips, turnips, swedes, etc.	10	
Salad types:		
including chicory, endives, lettuce, watercress	4	Require a high humidity to prevent wilting – sprinkle with crushed ice twice a day

Table 6.5. cont.

Produce	Number of Storage Days 4–7°C (40–45°F)	Notes
Apples (English)	10–30	
Citrus fruits:		
including grapefuit, mandarin oranges, etc.	10	Not including lemons
Pineapple (ripe only)	10	Unripe grapefuit should not be stored below 10°C (50°F)

Produce	Number of Storage Days at above 10°C (50°F)	Notes (effects if placed in cold storage)
FRUIT		
Tropical fruits:		
including avocado pears, paw-paws, mangoes	7	Deteriorate if stored below 10°C (50°F)
Bananas	10	Lack true flesh colour. Ideally stored above 12°C (54°F)
Lemons	10	Develop brown flecks between sections of the fruit
Green pineapple	10–14	Flesh colour remains grey and dull on ripening
Raspberries, strawberries	2	Deteriorate rapidly if cold stored
VEGETABLES		
Aubergine	4–7	Sunken depression in the skin
Peppers	4–7	
Cucumbers	4–7	
Tomatoes	4–7	Unripe tomatoes will not ripen to a good quality if stored below 10°C (50°F)

N.B. The above recommended storage times and temperatures, although important, assume that the storage room is kept clean, that produce is stacked so that circulating cooled air can flow around all produce and that only sound produce is stored.

Scientific and Nutritional Aspects

The skeletal structure of fruit and vegetables is provided by cellulose. The molecules of cellulose are made up from thousands of glucose units joined together, but joined together differently from those making up the starch molecule. The difference in structure renders cellulose indigestible to humans, whereas starch is easily digested to simple sugars which are readily absorbed in the human stomach and small intestine. Associated with cellulose in the cell walls of the plant, especially in fruits, are pectic substances. These are large molecules made up from many molecules of a derivative of an acid with a structure similar to that of a monosaccharide sugar (galacturonic acid).

Texture

The above substances together with moisture content of the plant tissue contribute to the complex system of properties of fruit and vegetables, which the eater describes as the 'texture'. When the living tissue contains all the water it requires, the cells exert a force on each other, which gives erectness to healthy growing plants and 'crispness' of texture to harvested fruit and vegetables. The relative importance of the water content effect just described, and that of skeletal materials, varies from type to type, e.g. the crispness of lettuce depends largely upon water content effects, while the texture of carrots depends more upon the nature of the skeletal materials of the plant.

Vitamins and Minerals

Fruits and vegetables in the main do not provide us with much protein or fat, but their carbohydrate content is often significant as Tables 6.6 and 6.7 show. However, their major importance in our diets must be thought of in terms of vitamins and minerals, as Table 6.7 clearly indicates.

Table 6.7 shows the quantitative importance of fruit and vegetables in the diet in Britain, in the provision of vitamins, especially vitamin C. This table also highlights the role of potatoes in supplying the diet with adequate quantities of this essential vitamin.

The storage of these commodities will be discussed briefly in the next section; however, it is relevant to point out here that the nutrient content alters with the length of storage time. The way in which this does change varies from nutrient to nutrient, but Figure 6.6 shows the change in vitamin C content of potatoes over a period of time.

Flavour

The development of flavours in fruit and vegetables usually involves a decrease in acidity with a corresponding increase in sugar content as the produce reaches maturity and ripens. The ratio of sugar to acid is used in fact, as an index of ripeness for several fruits.

Besides the acid/sugar composition, flavour depends to a great extent upon characteristic complex mixtures of volatile products and essential oils which a particular variety of plant produces in biochemical reactions as it grows and ripens. Many of these substances are present in extremely small amounts, only detectable by sophisticated scientific techniques, and yet they are able to contribute to the characteristic taste and smell of a fruit or vegetable.

The Harvesting and Storage of Fruit and Vegetables

While a plant is growing, a large number of complex chemical reactions are occurring continually. When vegetables and fruits such as potatoes, beans, peas, cabbages, brussels sprouts, pears, apples, etc. are harvested and stored, chemical

Table 6.6. Examples of fruits and vegetables – composition per 100 g of edible portion (Data adapted from McCance and Widdowson, 1978)

Food (fresh/raw)	Protein (g)	Fat (g)	Available Carbohydrates (g)	Energy Kilocalories	Water (g)	Edible matter as eaten. Expressed as a % of weight purchased
FRUIT						
Apples – eating	0.3	0	11.9	46	84.3	77
Apricots	0.6	0	6.7	28	86.6	92
Avocado	4.2	22.2	1.8	223	68.7	71
Banana	1.1	0.3	19.2	79	70.7	59
Blackberries	1.3	0	6.4	29	82	100
Cherries	0.6	0	11.9	47	81.5	87
Currants – black	0.9	0	6.6	28	77.4	98
Figs – green	1.3	0	9.5	41	84.6	98
Gooseberries	1.1	0	3.4	17	89.9	99
Grapes – black	0.6	0	15.5	61	80.7	81
Grapefruit	0.6	0	5.3	22	90.7	48
Lemons	0.8	0	3.2	15	85.2	99
Loganberries	1.1	0	3.4	17	85	100
Melon – yellow	0.6	0	5	21	94.2	59
Olives (in brine)	0.9	11	0	103	76.5	80
Oranges	0.8	0	8.5	35	86.1	75
Peaches	0.6	0	9.1	37	86.2	87
Pears	0.3	0	10.6	41	83.2	72
Pineapple	0.5	0	11.6	46	84.3	53
Plums – Victoria	0.6	0	9.6	38	84.1	94
Raspberries	0.9	0	5.6	25	83.2	100
Rhubarb	0.6	0	1.0	6	94.2	67
Strawberries	0.6	0	6.2	26	89.9	97
Tangerines	0.9	0	8.0	34	86.7	70

VEGETABLES						
Beans, runner	2.3	0.2	3.9	26	89	79
Beans, butter	19.1	1.1	49.8	273	11.6	100
Brussels sprouts	4	0	2.7	26	88.1	63
Cabbage, Savoy	3.3	0	3.3	26	89.9	53
Carrots	0.7	0	5.4	23	89.9	96
Cauliflower	1.9	0	1.5	13	92.7	62
Celery	0.9	0.1	1.3	8	93.5	73
Cucumber	0.6	0	1.8	10	96.4	77
Leeks	1.9	0	6	31	86	36
Lettuce	1.0	0.4	1.2	13	95.9	70
Mushrooms	1.8	0.6	0	13	91.5	75
Onions	0.9	0	5.2	23	92.8	97
Parsley	5.2	0	0	21	78.7	53
Peas	5.8	0.4	10.6	67	78.5	37
Potatoes	2.1	0.1	20.8	87	75.8	86
Swedes	1.1	0	4.3	21	91.4	86
Tomatoes	0.9	0	2.8	14	93.4	100
Turnips	0.8	0.3	3.8	20	93.3	84
Watercress	2.9	0	0.7	14	91.1	77

Table 6.7. *Examples of fruits and vegetables – vitamins and minerals per 100 g, edible portions*
(Data adapted from McCance and Widdowson, 1978)

Food (fresh/raw)	Vit A (μg)	Vit B$_1$ (mg)	Vit C (mg)	Sodium (mg)	Potassium (mg)	Calcium (mg)	Magnesium (mg)	Iron (mg)	Phosphorus (mg)
FRUIT									
Apples – eating	5.0	0.04	3.0	2.0	120	4.0	5.0	0.3	8.0
Apricots	250	0.04	7.0	0	320	17.0	12.0	0.4	21.0
Avocado	16.6	0.1	15	2.0	400	15.0	29.0	1.5	31.0
Banana	33.3	0.04	10	1.0	350	7.0	42.0	0.4	28.0
Blackberries	16.6	0.03	20	4.0	210	63.0	30.0	0.9	24.0
Cherries	20.0	0.05	5.0	3.0	280	16.0	10.0	0.4	17.0
Currants – black	33.3	0.03	200	3.0	370	60.0	17.0	1.3	43.0
Figs – green	83.3	0.06	2.0	2.0	270	34.0	20.0	0.4	32.0
Gooseberries	30.0	0.04	40.0	2.0	210	28.0	7.0	0.3	34.0
Grapes – black	0	0.04	4.0	2.0	320	4.0	4.0	0.3	16.0
Grapefruit	0	0.05	40.0	1.0	230	17.0	10.0	0.3	16.0
Lemons	0	0.05	80.0	6.0	160	110	12.0	0.4	21.0
Loganberries	13.3	0.02	35.0	3.0	260	35.0	25.0	1.4	24.0
Melon – yellow	16.6	0.05	25.0	20.0	220	14.0	13.0	0.2	9.0
Olives (in brine)	30.0	0	0	2250	91	61.0	22.0	1.0	17.0
Oranges	8.33	0.1	50.0	3.0	200	41.0	13.0	0.3	24.0
Peaches	88.3	0.02	8.0	3.0	260	5.0	8.0	0.4	19.0
Pears	1.66	0.03	3.0	2.0	130	8.0	7.0	0.2	10.0
Pineapple	10.0	0.08	25.0	2.0	250	12.0	17.0	0.4	8.0
Plums – Victoria	36.6	0.05	3.0	2.0	190	11.0	7.0	0.4	16.0
Raspberries	13.3	0.02	25.0	3.0	220	41.0	22.0	1.2	29.0
Rhubarb	10.0	0.01	10.0	2.0	430	100.0	14.0	0.4	21.0
Strawberries	5.0	0.02	60.0	2.0	160	22.0	12.0	0.7	23.0
Tangerines	16.6	0.07	30.0	2.0	160	42.0	11.0	0.3	17.0

VEGETABLES								
Beans, runner	66.6	0.05	20.0	2.0	280	27.0	27.0	0.8	47.0
Beans, butter	0	0.45	0	62.0	1700	85.0	164.0	5.9	320
Brussels sprouts	66.6	0.1	90.0	4.0	380	32.0	19.0	0.7	65.0
Cabbage, Savoy	50.0	0.06	60.0	23.0	260	75.0	20.0	0.9	68.0
Carrots	2000	0.06	6.0	95.0	220	48.0	12.0	0.6	21.0
Cauliflower	5.0	0.1	60.0	8.0	350	21.0	14.0	0.5	45.0
Celery	0	0.03	7.0	140	280	52.0	10.0	0.6	32.0
Cucumber	0	0.04	8.0	13.0	140	23.0	9.0	0.3	24.0
Leeks	6.66	0.1	18.0	9.0	310	63.0	10.0	1.1	43.0
Lettuce	166	0.07	15.0	9.0	240	23.0	8.0	0.9	27.0
Mushrooms	0	0.1	3.0	9.0	470	3.0	13.0	1.0	140
Onions	0	0.03	10.0	10.0	140	31.0	8.0	0.3	30.0
Parsley	1166	0.15	150	33.0	1080	330	52.0	8.0	130
Peas	50	0.32	25.0	1.0	340	15.0	30.0	1.9	100
Potatoes	0	0.11	Vble	7.0	570	8.0	24.0	0.5	40.0
Swedes	0	0.06	25.0	52.0	140	56.0	11.0	0.4	19.0
Tomatoes	100	0.06	20.0	3.0	290	13.0	11.0	0.4	21.0
Turnips	0	0.04	25.0	58.0	240	59	7.0	0.4	28.0
Watercress	500	0.1	60.0	60.0	310	220	17.0	1.6	52.0

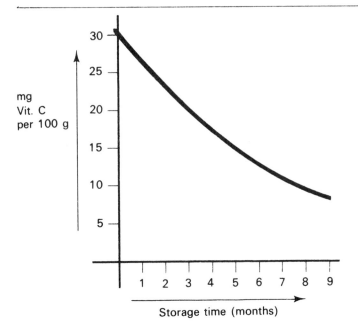

Figure 6.6 Graph showing decrease in vitamin C content with storage time for maincrop potatoes

Table 6.8. Main sources of vitamins in the U.K. diet.
Percentage of average total daily intake supplied by various foods
(From H. F. C. and E: 1984 HMSO 1986)

Food group	Thiamin (B₁)	Riboflavine (B₂)	Nicotinic Acid	Ascorbic Acid (c)	Retinol Equivalents (A)	Vitamin D
Milk, cream, cheese	10.7	37.4	2.6	5.2	17.7	9.3
Meat (all types)	13.6	18.0	40.3	1.8	36.5	0.9
Fish (all types)	1.0	1.2	4.1	0.1	0.1	14.1
Eggs	1.4	6.2	0.1	–	3.2	12.1
Fats and oils	–	–	–	0.1	18.2	52.2
Potatoes	8.4	2.7	10.7	21.9	–	–
Other vegetables	8.3	5.4	9.5	27.6	21.5	–
Fruit	3.6	1.6	2.8	40.2	1.0	–
Cereals	49.6	20.2	18.7	0.8	0.7	10.6
Total	96.6	92.7	88.8	97.7	98.9	99.2

reactions continue to take place. The speed at which these reactions continues is in part governed by temperature: generally, the higher the temperature, the more rapid the reactions. Hence a cool storage temperature is normally recommended, *see* Table 6.5 on the storage of fruit and vegetables.

Harvesting

There is a great deal of importance attached to the time chosen for the harvesting of fruit and vegetables. This time factor can be important in two ways; the age or stage of development of the particular plant; and the time of day at which a particular crop is harvested.

These general comments can be illustrated briefly by two examples:

(i) Carrots. If carrots are harvested when very young they will be relatively lower in vitamin A, than if they were cropped at a later stage. If the date for cropping is delayed for about two weeks, the same variety of carrots will yield a much higher vitamin A content; i.e. in terms of vitamins the carrots will have a higher nutritive content.

(ii) Peas. In one experiment, when 'Lincoln' peas were harvested at 4 a.m. in June the vitamin C content was 27 mg per 100 g of fresh peas, whereas the same variety, cropped at 11 a.m. yielded 30 mg per 100 g, while at 4 p.m. 29 g per 100 g were recorded.

These two examples show that carefully planned harvesting of fruits and vegetables can result in higher nutritive contents being achieved. Often when vitamin content is at a maximum other factors contributing to quality are also at an optimum, hence a good quality product is also obtained.

Storage

Delays between the harvesting and utilization of crops are inevitable, and fresh fruit and vegetables are especially prone to loss of quality and nutritive value during any intervening period.

As far as nutrient retention is concerned in fresh fruit and vegetables it is important that the commodities are handled very carefully to avoid mechanical damage. If the cells of fruit and vegetables are damaged by careless handling, enzymes are released from within the cells, and such nutrients as vitamin C will be destroyed by oxidation reactions. Other similar reactions will occur, contributing not only to a loss in nutritive value, but also to a loss of quality in the product.

Damage to quality and nutritive value will also occur if the commodity is badly stored. Vitamin C losses in fruit and vegetables stored for relatively short periods can be considerable if damage or wilting due to high temperatures and/or poor humidity has occurred.

It is also worth the caterer noting that cabbage left whole and stored in a dry cool place loses very little of its nutritive value in a week, and only about 30% in a month. However, if cut or minced, it may lose most of its vitamin C in a period of a few minutes. This shows the importance of preparing fruit and vegetables as near the time required as possible.

Table 6.9 gives an indication of how the vitamin C content of vegetables decreases with storage time.

Table 6.9. *Approximate loss of vitamin C content
of some vegetables when stored whole at 20°C.
(These losses would be much greater if the products
were fragmented in any way)*

Approximate Vitamin C Content mg per 100g		
Vegetable	Fresh	Stored 1 week
Brocolli tops	200	120
Brussels sprouts	150	120
Cauliflower	100	70
Cabbage	60	40
Spinach	60	10
Peas	25	12

Gas Storage

If fruits and vegetables are stored in modified or controlled atmospheres deterioration can be minimized and quality maintained for quite long periods. It has been found that disadvantagous reactions can be slowed down by storing fruit and vegetables in artificial atmospheres containing a low concentration of oxygen and a high concentration of carbon dioxide, thereby extending their storage life — a fact of great commercial importance.

Clearly such methods require expensive technology and would not be viable for most catering situations. However Table 6.5 shows how the caterer can best store his fruit and vegetables in his establishment.

7

Processed Fruits and Vegetables

The processing of fruits and vegetables serves five main purposes.

1. Produce which was previously subject to only seasonal availability is available throughout the year.
2. The processing methods are also methods of preservation which halt the deterioration of the produce ensuring their keeping properties for long periods.
3. Processing provides a means of presenting the food to the caterer in a very convenient form with little or no waste and often in a ready-to-use form.
4. The processing method in some cases makes available the produce in a different form from the original product, with a different appearance, texture and flavour, resulting frequently in a different catering use, e.g. fresh grapes are of a different form, and have different catering uses from dried currants, raisins, etc.
5. The range of produce in a country can be increased by importing processed fruits and vegetables which are far less difficult to handle and store than the fresh produce.

There are four main processing methods for fruits and vegetables.

1. Dehydration — fruits: e.g. currants, sultanas, prunes, figs, etc.
— vegetables: e.g. potatoes, carrots, peas, beans, etc.

2. Canning — fruits: e.g. grapefruit, rhubarb, peaches, pears, etc.
— vegetables: e.g. potatoes, carrots, peas, asparagus, etc.

3. Freezing — fruits: e.g. apples, strawberries, blackcurrants, etc.
— vegetables: e.g. potatoes, peas, carrots, beans, etc.

4. Crystallizing — glacé fruits and nuts
candied peels, crystallized fruits, and flavours

The processing methods are also a suitable means for classifying processed fruits and vegetables.

Each of these processes has its own particular advantages and disadvantages when compared with each other and with the fresh product. As prominent convenience type foods they all have these common factors.

Price Stability
The prices for canned, frozen, etc., fruits and vegetables tend to remain reasonably stable throughout every season of the year. This is an advantage to the caterer as he will know in advance what the costs for this range of produce will be.

Supply Stability
Unlike the markets for fresh fruit and vegetables there is far less likelihood of there being a sudden shortage or a fluctuating supply for processed fruits and vegetables.

Consistent Quality
The quality of processed fruits and vegetables is controlled critically by the food processor and at times by the grading standards laid down by a country. The caterer can select the particular standard to suit his type of business and keep to it, knowing that the standard selected will be constant.

Standard Yield
Processed fruits and vegetables, with little or no waste, give a standard yield each time when purchased from the same manufacturer and are of the same brand name; whereas fresh produce will frequently give a varying yield of unusable food.

Labour-saving
As the processed foods require little preparation before being used, the labour content of a menu item is minimized, making a significant saving to the caterer.

Variety
There is a great range of processed fruits and vegetables available throughout the year which further assists the caterer to provide attractive and exciting menus at all times.

Storage
The storage space required is far less than that required for fresh produce. The control of stock is also simplified in that all processed foods tend to be packaged in units and are easy and clean to handle.

The Selection of Raw Materials for Processing

It is important that the reader understands that processed fruits and vegetables are not inferior quality produce that would not sell on the fresh food market.

Today processed fruits and vegetables are of a very high quality in that:

(*a*) the fresh, raw produce is obtained from specially grown crops, often of a particular hybrid strain;

(*b*) the hybrid strain being the result of years of experimentation to produce a crop that is of a high yield, will mature evenly and be of a high standard of flavour, texture, colour, size, and shape;

(*c*) the hybrid strain also produces a crop that is relatively easy to harvest by machinery. This increases the speed of harvesting and reduces the time between harvesting and processing and therefore reduces the time for the produce to deteriorate;

(*d*) the crop produced also has to be suitable for the method of processing that it has to undergo. This means that different species and different hybrid strains will be grown when the method of processing will be different;

(*e*) by using hybrid strains it is possible to produce crops which have the minimum of uncontrollable defects;

(*f*) processing of the produce takes place within a few hours of it having been harvested.

The food processor aims to get his fresh fruit and vegetables to his factory in peak condition, with particular regard to the following:

(*a*) The produce should be uniform in size, shape, and physical condition. This means that the product should require less grading and be easier to process.

(*b*) The product should be at the 'firm ripe' stage when it is fully grown and harvested. When firm the produce will be easier for mechanical processing and when ripe will have the maximum characteristic flavour.

(*c*) The produce should be free of blemishes and bruising. This is for two reasons: first spoilage can occur quickly in bruised areas and render the produce unusable or of a lower grade; and second any damaged part will need to be removed.

(*d*) The produce should be of maximum flavour when harvested. This is because any heat treatment tends to reduce the general intensity of flavour of the produce and therefore a full rich flavour is desirable initially.

(*e*) The colour of the produce is also important, particularly for frozen and dehydrated produce. Canned and crystallized produce is aided at times by artificial colourings.

1. Dehydration

The general principle of dehydration as a method of food preservation is the reduction of the moisture content to a level below that at which bacteria moulds which cause decay can multiply. The reduction of the moisture content causes a reduction in the weight and volume, and affects the general appear-

ance of the food. It is without doubt one of the oldest methods of food preservation known.

There are three main methods of dehydration used for fruits and vegetables,
which are as follows.

Air-drying

This method may be subdivided into two methods for clarity.

Sun-drying

This method is mainly used today in the processing of dried fruits although it
was at one time used extensively for the drying of vegetables such as lentils,
butterbeans, and peas. The most common sun-dried fruits today are currants,
raisins, sultanas, prunes, dates, figs, apricots, and peaches.

It is usual for the picked, ripened fruit to be dipped into or sprayed with a
lye solution and olive oil before drying. This helps to increase the rate of
drying and to give a standard characteristic colour to the fruit. Drying is done
by placing the fruit on racks of wire mesh fully exposed to the sun. However,
certain refinements to this method can be made by drying the fruit in the
shade to produce a softer skin. The larger fruits such as apricots and peaches
must be halved, pitted, and arranged on trays with the cut side upwards and
then treated with the fumes of burning sulphur in a sulphur chamber. The
moist cut surface of the fruit absorbs some of the fumes. This acts as a preservative of colour and assists with the drying process. Drying by this method
increases the sugar content to about 75%.

Machine Air-drying

The fruit and vegetables are prepared initially as for canning (i.e. washed,
graded, peeled, sliced, etc. and blanched when necessary) except that in most
instances the fruit will be exposed to sulphur dioxide before drying. The
drying is usually done in tunnel dryers at a temperature of about $70°C$
($158°F$) until the moisture content is below 25% (usually in the range 12–24%
moisture). Fruit is then placed in 'sweat-bins' for the moisture to become
equal in all the fruit before being packed for sale.

Dehydrating

The term 'dehydration', although simply meaning 'removal of water', when
used in the description 'dehydrated fruit' has come to mean a product (particularly in the U.S.A.) which has had its moisture level reduced to about 2–10%.
The advantages of this product lie in its further reduced weight, and its longer
storage life (particularly in tropical climates).

These products are produced by taking the end-product of the air-drying
process (normally machine dried), cutting them into small pieces, laying them
on to shelves, and subjecting them to further drying under vacuum. More
moisture is removed, leaving a residual level in the range of 2–10%.

These products reconstitute in a similar way to air-dried products, but are
obviously fragmented.

Accelerated Freeze Drying (A.F.D.)
This is a recent process for the preservation of food, having previously been
an established process in the pharmaceutical and biological industries for
preserving blood plasma, etc.
    The process is in three stages:

The Preparation Stage
This is similar to that for freezing, canning, and drying. It involves the washing,
grading, peeling, and slicing etc., when necessary, and at times the blanching
of the produce. In addition thick-skinned produce such as peas and blackcurrants may be pricked or scratched to provide an easy path for the extraction
of moisture during the drying stage without damage to the final appearance of
the produce.

The Freezing Stage
This is identical to the normal process for freezing of fruit and vegetables and
is described in pp. 147—8.

The Drying Stage
The frozen food at a temperature of about $-20°C$ ($-4°F$) is sandwiched thinly
and evenly between sheets of expanded metal mesh which are inserted between
both a tray and lid and the food surfaces. The trays are placed in a vacuum
chamber and inserted between heating plates which are moveable so that
pressure may be applied to ensure that a close thermal contact is made to the
surfaces of the food. The amount of pressure applied depends on the type of
food being processed. The vacuum chamber is then rapidly evacuated of air,
to avoid any thawing taking place, to a pressure below 1 mm Hg.
    When the chamber is evacuated to a total pressure less than the vapour
pressure of the ice in the food, sublimation begins, and the food temperature
falls further to a minimum of $-30°C$ ($-22°F$). The heating plates are then
closed into light contact with the food and a source of heat applied to raise
the plate temperatures to around $140°C$ ($284°F$) for some 30 minutes and then reduced to around $60°C$ ($140°F$) for several hours. It is usual during this drying
period for the temperature of the food surface not to be allowed to rise above
$60°C$ ($140°F$). The ice in the food sublimates into water vapour and escapes
through the mesh of expanded metal. When drying is complete the cabinet
vacuum is broken by admitting dry nitrogen and the trays then unloaded. The
product is then packaged using a dry nitrogen or carbon dioxide gas packing
system so as to exclude any oxygen.
    It should be noted that this process is at present confined to particular
produce for specific purposes. Its main use is in the preparation of 'ready to
use' vegetable based soup mixes for which it is ideal as the reconstitution time
is almost instantaneous. Although it is possible to process most fruits and
vegetables by the A.F.D. method the end product is fragile and brittle causing
a major and expensive problem for packaging.

2. Canning

The general principle of canning as a method of food preservation is the application of heat to food at temperatures high enough either to partially or completely sterilize the food (the difference depends upon the product being processed) and the expulsion of air from the container after which it is then hermetically sealed to contain the vacuum created. The temperature applied to the food depends on the type of food being processed, but in general terms it is usual to apply higher temperatures to the non-acid foods such as vegetables and lower temperatures to the acid foods such as fruits.

As has been previously explained, most vegetables and fruit will have been grown specifically to be processed by a particular method. This applies also to canned fruit and vegetables. Some fruits and vegetables are processed as soon as they are fully grown and have reached their optimum quality, e.g. raspberries, strawberries, peas, beans, etc.; others may be stored because they will not perish quickly and are processed at a later convenient time, e.g. apples, pears, carrots, potatoes, etc.; whilst fruit salad and fruit cocktail are processed in large containers and later re-canned in smaller size units.

The canning process may be divided into stages.

First Stage
The initial grading and washing of the produce.

The Preparation Stage
This may be peeling, coring and slicing for produce such as apples and pears; dehulling for raspberries and strawberries; peeling and de-eyeing of potatoes, etc.

Blanching
This stage is carried out for nearly all vegetables and for fruit which are to be solid packed. The process stage is the immersion in boiling water or steam immediately after the preparation stage and immediately before being canned. The main reasons for blanching are:

(a) to destroy any surface bacteria;
(b) to deactivate enzymes which could cause unpleasant flavours and discoloration;
(c) to expel air and gases from the inter-cellular spaces in the foods;
(d) to reduce the bulk so that more of the produce may be packed into the cans, e.g. leaf spinach;
(e) to make the produce more pliable and therefore easier to pack;
(f) to fix the colour.

Filling
The correct filling of cans depends upon whether the blanching stage has been carried out satisfactorily. The main points to be noted at this stage are:

(a) That the correct weight or volume of food is put into the can, leaving the correct amount of head-space between the product and the top of the can. Should the can be filled completely there would be no room left for the produce to expand during retorting, resulting in additional strain on the seams of the can which may result in the can leaking or even bursting. If the can is not filled sufficiently too large a vacuum may be created during the exhausting stage resulting in the sides of the can being drawn in, giving the appearance of a badly dented can.

(*b*) That the correct quantity and proportion of all ingredients is put in the can. There should be the correct ratio of solids to liquids in the can, as it is frequently the volume of the drained weight of the produce that is important to the caterer. The density of the brix (or sugar syrup) for fruits or brine (salt solution) for vegetables depend on the type of produce in the cans, e.g. a heavier brix for raspberries and strawberries is required than for pears. The heavier brix gives some further protection to fragile produce.

Exhausting

It is necessary to remove the air from the produce in a can and from the head-space so that a vacuum is created in the sealed can when it is cold. The main reasons for this are:

(*a*) To reduce the pressure created in the can during the retorting stage so that no additional pressure is placed on the seams of the can. (N.B. Air will expand more than water, syrup, or steam when heated.)

(*b*) Air left inside the head-space of the can together with liquids can cause oxidation of the can to take place causing rusting and eventually leakage.

Exhausting may be done by many different ways depending on the produce being canned. With fruits and vegetables it is usually done by filling the can with cold, blanched, or unblanched products, passing the can through a hot water bath to heat the contents to the required temperature for exhausting. The heat from the contents drives out the air and fills the head-space with steam. On completion of the exhausting stage the lid is crimped on.

Processing

This is the stage at which the contents of the can are sterilized so as to ensure their safety as a food and a long shelf-life. The processing takes place in large retorts where steam and pressure can be regulated to meet the different processing temperatures to suit the fruit or vegetables being canned. The processed cans are then quickly cooled to prevent overcooking by spraying with cold water.

Inspection

All cans prior to being labelled, packed in cases and sent out to a customer are inspected. A can will pass inspection if it is seen to be clean and to have distinct concave ends. A can will *not* pass inspection at the cannery or later by a caterer should it have one of the following faults.

BLOWN CANS. This may be caused by a chemical change acting on the metal of the container, particularly with acid fruits. This causes the liberation of hydrogen gas which causes blowing, with the ends of the can obviously convex. A similar cause for gas-blown cans can be as a result of microbial (bacteria and yeast) action.

'SPRINGERS'. This refers to cans which have one convex end which when pressed becomes flat or concave and usually causes the other end to bulge. On opening and inspecting the contents they are usually found to be safe.

FLAT SOURS. This may only be detected on the opening of the can and noticing the sour smell. It is caused by certain bacteria which produce lactic acid but no gas.

LEAKING. This may be caused by inadequate sealing of the can or by perforation.

RUST. Severe rusting on the can surface is likely to erode through the can causing pinholing and leakage.

Code of Practice no. 4
This code describes the standards of fill, composition and size of canned fruit and vegetables which have been accepted as the recognized practice of the British canning industry. The minimum weight of prepared fruit and vegetables is stated for each can size, the syrup densities, and the proportions of any mixed contents.

Labelling
The purpose of labelling is to identify the contents of the can and to assist in marketing it. The label is required by law to state specific information such as the detailed contents of the can. The caterer should realise that the cannery will be frequently canning food of identical quality standards but fixing different labels for different suppliers, who no doubt will be selling them to caterers at different prices.

Can Sizes
The Code of Practice for canned fruit and vegetables, specifies minimum filled weights of prepared fruit or vegetables which must be used in a range of can sizes as specified (see Table 7.1).

3. Freezing
The general principles of freezing as a method of food preservation are two-fold:

(i) the lowered temperature slows down the rates of chemical reactions and multiplication of micro-organisms; therefore any activity leading to loss of quality will be greatly retarded;

(ii) the more importantly, the water within the product is immobilized as ice, so that it can no longer be utilized in chemical reactions or in microbial growth.

Hence at temperatures of $-18°C$ ($0°F$) and below virtually all deleterious activity in the food ceases.

Table 7.1. Can sizes and minimum filled weights

Can description	Nominal dimensions	Nominal capacity fl. oz.	ml
5 oz	211 × 202	5.53	157
8Z	300 × 208	8.20	233
Picnic	211 × 301	8.26	235
A1	211 × 400	11.10	315
14Z	300 × 401	14.00	398
16Z	300 × 410	16.1	457
A2	307 × 408	20.35	578
A2½	401 × 411	29.90	850
A6	603 × 600	93.00	2642
A10	603 × 700	109.10	3100

Note 1: Can sizes 8 oz, E1 and no. 1 tall may be used in place of the 8Z, 14Z and 16Z size cans respectively

Note 2: The dimensions refer to the diameter and height of a can, e.g. a can size 603 × 700 would be $6\frac{3}{16}$ in. in diameter and 7 in. high.

The initial stages of processing of frozen fruits and vegetables are almost identical to that of canning and will be only mentioned briefly here so that the reader is fully aware of the sequence.

Suitable Produce
Produce should be grown that will be suitable for processing by freezing. Whilst growing the produce will have been closely watched by field officers of the food processing company who advise the farmer in bringing the crop to maturity at a planned time in a perfect condition.

Grading and Washing
On being picked or taken to the factory to be machine picked, the produce will be graded and washed.

Preparation
When necessary the produce will be peeled, sliced, diced, etc.

Blanching
This applies to most vegetables but not to fruit. The reasons for blanching are to destroy surface bacteria, reduce the bulk, make the produce more pliable, fix the colour, etc. For fruit this stage is replaced by packing in sugar or syrup often with special additives to prevent enzymic oxidation and browning.

Cooling
Blanched vegetables are then quickly cooled either by immersion in iced water or by spraying with cold water.

Inspection

Inspection takes place before and after the blanching stage to remove any foreign items or low grade produce.

Filling

This stage applies to produce which is not to be individually quick-frozen. The produce is placed in waxed cartons; the wax prevents free water (either prior to freezing or after thawing) from soaking into the paper or cardboard, which clearly would be disadvantageous.

Quick-freezing

There are two basic methods used in commercial freezing.

PLATE OR CONTACT FREEZING. In this method the produce is packed in shallow cartons in a single layer between refrigerated shelves, compressed to ensure maximum contact, and frozen.
BLAST FREEZING. In this method the food is frozen as it floats on a cushion of supercooled air, while it travels along a freezing tunnel. This method provides extremely fast and uniform freezing of free flowing fruits and vegetables. This method is often referred to as 'individually quick freezing' (I.Q.F.).

Campden Specifications

There are some twenty different specifications, eighteen for vegetables and two for fruit, which are widely accepted in the frozen food industry throughout Europe. Each specification document includes a description of general quality, details of sampling methods, methods for measuring maturity of certain products, definitions of defects, tables of tolerances, grade descriptions and details of assessment of texture, colour and flavour.

4. Crystallizing

This is a well-established method of preservation which is mainly applied to certain fruits, nuts, and flower petals. The principle of crystallizing is the exchange of water in the fruit, nuts, and petals for a strong sugar syrup. The addition of sugar in concentration acts as the preservative and prevents bacterial action taking place.

The term crystallized is often used to describe three similar types of products: glacé fruits and nuts; candied peels; and crystallized fruits and flower petals. The produce which is to be processed in this manner should be of good quality, firm, just ripe and be in good condition.

Glacé Fruits and Nuts

The most commonly processed are cherries and chestnuts. Cherries are firstly graded by size and then placed in a solution of sulphur dioxide and water to cure the cherries and to bleach them of all colour. The stone is then removed and the cherries are gently cooked in a dilute sugar solution. They are then drained and placed in wire trays in a deep vessel and covered with a fresh and coloured sugar solution. The solution is brought to the boil for short periods over several days, during which the sugar solution becomes a dense syrup. The cherries when cool are packed after most of the excess syrup has been drained off. Chestnuts are processed similarly except that the skins are first removed and the sugar solution is not coloured.

Candied Peels

The most commonly processed are lemon, citron, and orange peels. The method of processing is similar in each case although the strength of the sugar solution and the processing time is different. All the peels are usually processed from special varieties of thick-rind fruits. The fruit is cut in half and the pulp extracted. They are then placed in a weak brine solution for several days to kill off undesirable flavours and to condition the peel so that it will readily absorb the sugar solution. The caps are then worked before being placed in a vessel of warm sugar solution. The fruit caps become fully saturated with sugar after passing them through a series of stronger solutions over a period of several days. They are then placed on wires to drain and are then dried in a hot cupboard which sets the sugar and hardens the caps. After cooling completely they are then packed.

Crystallized Fruits

The fruits used are usually, apricots, greengages, plums, pineapple, pears, and cherries. They are processed in a very similar way to glacé cherries except that the large fruits will have been cut into large pieces and that at the end they will be dried in a similar way to candied peels. Angelica, although not a fruit, is processed in a similar way.

Crystallized Flowers

The petals from violets and roses are those that are commonly processed. The petals are placed on wires in shallow containers and warm coloured sugar solutions are allowed to drip on to them repeatedly until they become saturated. They are then gently dried in hot cupboards.

Catering Uses

The catering uses of processed fruits and vegetables are shown in Table 7.2.

Scientific and Nutritional Aspects

Raw foods are not inert substances and unless man takes positive action they will deteriorate for three principal reasons:

(i) the activity of micro-organisms naturally present;
(ii) the reactions facilitated by the action of enzymes naturally present in the food;
(iii) the reactions termed hydrolysis and oxidation, which result from the action of water present in the food or environment, and oxygen from the air. These also may be speeded up by enzymes.

Table 7.2. Main catering uses of processed fruits and vegetables

Product	Main Catering Uses
1. *Dehydrated fruits and vegetables*	
Currants, sultanas, raisins	As an ingredient in cakes, puddings, etc.
Prunes, figs	As poached fruit, in puddings, etc.
Potatoes, carrots, peas, etc.	As a vegetable course, as part of a garnish to a main course, etc.
2. *Canned fruits and vegetables*	
Raspberries, peaches, pears, etc.	For the sweet course, to decorate flans, etc.
Plums, rhubarb, gooseberries, etc.	As poached fruit, hot pies, tarts, etc.
Potatoes, asparagus, peas, etc.	As a vegetable course, as part of a garnish to a main course, etc.
3. *Frozen fruits and vegetables*	
Strawberries, blackcurrants, etc.	For a sweet course, to decorate flans, etc.
Peas, broad beans, asparagus, etc.	As a vegetable course, as part of a garnish to a main course, etc.
4. *Crystallized fruits*	
Glacé fruits, e.g. cherries	As an ingredient in cakes, ice-cream etc.
e.g. chestnuts	As a petit fours, as an ingredient in some speciality ice-cream dishes, etc.
Candied peels, e.g. lemon, citron, orange	As an ingredient in cakes and puddings, etc.
Crystallized fruits, e.g. pineapple, damsons, pears, etc.	As a petit four, as an ingredient in some speciality ice-cream dishes, etc.
Crystallized flowers/petals	To decorate gateaux, ice-cream dishes, etc.

Food processing attempts to stop or slow down the deterioration caused by the factors described above. Table 7.3 summarizes the principles upon which the main food preservation methods depend.

Nutritional and Textural Changes in Food During Processing
As already said, the preservation and processing of food allow man a degree of independence from the climatic conditions and geographical locations which control his food supply. Without this measure of independence he would inevitably suffer a 'plenty followed by famine' food cycle. However, besides preserving food, so that it can be eaten at a time divorced from harvest, processing in some cases can also make food more palatable to man, and more easily digested. Nevertheless, it must be noticed that food materials do lose

Table 7.3. Summary of basic principles involved in some major food preservation processes

Process	Basic Principles Involved
Blanching	Deactivates enzymes and kills surface micro-organisms
Dehydration	Removes water, prevents microbial activity and hydrolysis
Cooking	Deactivates enzymes and destroys most micro-organisms
Canning and bottling	Deactivates enzymes, kills micro-organisms, removes and excludes oxygen
Chilling ($4°C$)	Slows down most deteriorating reactions
Freezing ($-20°C$)	Slows down most deteriorating reactions to a very slow rate. Removes water (as ice), therefore preventing reactivity of enzymes. Kills or stops multiplication of micro-organisms
Curing and pickling	Alters ionic concentration of solutions, inhibits activity of enzymes and micro-organisms
Candying and jamming	Increases concentration of sugar and the resultant osmotic effect inhibits activity of micro-organisms
Gas or vacuum packing	Removes oxygen, therefore prevents oxidation and inhibits aerobic micro-organisms

some of their nutritional value during processing and it is these losses which are briefly commented upon here, and it is hoped, put in their right perspective.

Food Preparation

It is important to be aware that the caterer (or housewife) often destroys more nutrients during food preparation, than does the large-scale food processor. Water soluble vitamins such as ascorbic acid, thiamine, riboflavin and niacin (nicotinic acid) are particularly susceptible to cooking losses — by being dissolved out of foods into the cooking water, which may be thrown away and not utilized. Ascorbic acid (vitamin C) is also very prone to destruction by oxidation, as are fat-soluble vitamins, to a lesser extent, when heated in air (or stored in air for long periods).

Because of the losses which can occur in food preparation, the actual vitamin contents of foods ready for service are often similar regardless of the type of process the food has undergone previously, *see* Table 7.4.

The Effects of the Stages in Processing on Vitamins and Minerals

Blanching

This is the initial process in most preservation methods for fruits and vegetables. These foods are blanched to inactivate enzymes and to destroy micro-

Table 7.4. Vitamin C content of prepared garden peas. Percentage retention at the stages indicated. (The data have been taken from various sources and are only intended to give an approximate guide to amounts.)

Fresh	Quick Frozen	Canned	Air Dried	Freeze Dried
	Blanching 75	Blanching 70	Blanching 75	Blanching 75
	Freezing 75	Canning 63	Drying 45	Drying 70
	Thawing 71			
Cooking 44	Cooking 39	Heating 36	Cooking 25	Cooking 35

organisms, which might otherwise affect adversely the flavour, colour, and vitamin content of the product.

Blanching in boiling water can cause losses of between 10 and 35% of water soluble vitamins and minerals, whilst steam blanching can reduce losses to below 10%.

Canning

Most vitamins, with the notable exceptions of riboflavin and niacin, are destroyed by heat to various extents. Therefore, some nutrient losses are inevitable. The longer the time taken in the process, the greater is the nutrient loss; hence high temperature, short time sterilization (HTST) is being increasingly used, because higher temperatures have a greater bacterial destroying capability, compared with their effects on nutrients, e.g. a $10°C$ ($18°F$) rise in temperature increases the bacterial destruction by *ten* times, whilst only *doubling* the rate of destruction of vitamins. Examples of beans and tomatoes canned in this way have been quoted as retaining up to 90% of their original vitamin content.

Drying

The governing factors of nutrient loss are again temperature and time. Also, if air is present as the product dries, oxidation of nutrients may occur. Vitamins most affected are A, C and E.

Freezing

This process does not in itself produce any significant losses in nutrients. Any losses in frozen foods occur either during the blanching process or during the thawing period, when water soluble substances may leach out in the 'thaw-drip'. (*See* later comments on textural changes.)

The Storage of Processed Fruits and Vegetables

Tables 7.5–7.8 give approximate storage times for a selection of processed fruits and vegetables, however some nutrient loss may occur during storage, even though eating quality may be little affected.

Vitamin losses during distribution and subsequent storage of canned products vary greatly, depending upon the temperature of the environment. Generally it is true to say that if canned products are stored in cool ($12°C$ or $54°F$) dry conditions, losses will be minimized.

Table 7.5. *Approximate storage times for DRIED products stored in cool (12°C/54°F), dry and well ventilated conditions*

Product	Satisfactory Storage Time (months)
Dried fruit	6
Dehydrated potato	4 unopened, 1 opened
Dehydrated vegetables	6 unopened, 1 opened
Dried peas	9
Dried herbs	4

Table 7.6. *Approximate storage times for CANNED products stored in a cool (12°C/54°F) dry place*

Product	Satisfactory Storage Time (months)
Grapefruit	4
Prunes	4
Rhubarb	3
Fruit juices	4
Carrots	12–24
Baked beans	12–24
Broad beans	12–24
Asparagus	6
French beans	6
Tomatoes	8
Peaches	12
Pears	10

Table 7.7. *Examples of storage times for FROZEN fruit and vegetables at −18°C/0°F (see Table 7.6 on storage of fruit and vegetables in general)*

Product	Satisfactory Storage Time (months)
Apples	9–12
Pears	9–12
Soft fruits	9
Potatoes	6–9
Root vegetables	6–9
Peas	3–6

Table 7.8. Examples of storage times for CRYSTALLIZED
fruits, nuts, and flowers

Product	Satisfactory Storage Time (months)
Glacé fruits and nuts	6–9
Candied peels	6
Crystallized fruits	6
Crystallized flowers	9–12

The keeping qualities and nutrient retention in dried products, depends
not only on temperature of storage, but also on whether or not the product is
in contact with air. Air, as mentioned before, permits oxidation, which affects
nutrient content adversely.

Temperature is also very important for the retention of quality and nutrient
content of frozen products. Storage at $-18°C$ ($0°F$) and below allows excellent
retention of both quality and nutrients for long periods of time. Packaging
also can play an important part, for as in dried products, if air comes in contact with the product, oxidation may result in losses. Higher storage temperatures definitely affect adversely the nutrient retention, e.g. peas, spinach,
beans, sprouts, etc. can lose up to 50% of their vitamin C content in 6 months,
when stored at $-10°C$ ($14°F$).

Textural Changes in Fruits and Vegetables During Processing

Canning

Because the canner wants to kill all bacteria that might be present in a food,
food must be heated for a minimum time to ensure that this occurs. Unfortunately some foods, particularly those low in acids, require longer heating
to achieve sterility. This heating time is often longer than the optimum for
palatability, and many canned foods consequently are overcooked and lack
the texture of the original food. Generally, fruits are more acid than vegetables,
and hence can be canned more successfully. In some cases the necessary heating time for some vegetables is so long that their texture is wholly unacceptable, and they cannot be canned successfully.

Dehydration

Whilst this method of preservation is probably the oldest known to man, and
in some countries sun drying is still used for certain products, more modern
methods predominate in developed countries. Modern methods fall into two
principal classes.

AIR DRYING. Air drying is carried out by heating the product at temperatures ranging between 40–100°C (104–212°F) in air or under reduced pressure. The loss of water causes an increase in concentration of dissolved substances in the tissues of the product, causing irreversible damage to the texture. In addition, textural changes associated with cooking will occur. These textural changes cause the tissues to shrink, and upon reconstitution they never regain their original volume or tenderness. The heating very often causes browning and other discolorations, which obviously affects the acceptability of the products.
FREEZE DRYING. Freeze drying is a fairly recent commercial process. The food is first frozen (and therefore suffers any damage associated with this process), and the moisture removed by sublimation under reduced pressure whilst still frozen – this avoids damage due to heating. The freeze-dried product has an open texture which re-hydrates fairly easily, giving a re-constituted product of quite good texture and flavour. The dry product however, having the porous open structure, is rather fragile and prone to oxidation, and therefore needs careful packaging.

Freezing

The location of ice formation is a critical factor in the quality of frozen products. Water exists in fruit and vegetables both within the plant cells and between the cells. These two areas remain separate only if the plant cells remain intact, and as was described in an earlier section on fruit and vegetables, the disposition of the water in the cells contributes markedly to textural pro-perties. If for some reason the cell walls rupture there will be a resulting change in texture of the product.

When a food is cooled, ice crystals begin to form between the cells. The rate of cooling obviously governs the rate of ice formation, and also the size of crystals formed. The slower the cooling, the larger the crystals that are formed, because water migrates from inside the cells to form ice crystals between the cells – this in turn sets up stresses within the tissues, which may rupture the cell walls, with resulting loss of texture on thawing. Fast freezing conversely causes smaller ice crystals to form more uniformly throughout the plant tissue, both inside and outside the cells, without much migration of water from the cell. Hence the cell structure is not damaged appreciably, and upon thawing there is little change from the original texture prior to freezing. Similarly there are few losses of water soluble nutrients (vitamins and minerals), because thawing of a successfully fast frozen product does not cause much 'thaw-drip', since few cells are ruptured.

Food Irradiation

Since 1963 various countries have approved of irradiation as a method of prolonging the shelf life of food for human consumption, but this process is at present prohibited in the U.K., except for the preparation of sterile foods for hospital patients requiring them as part of their treatment.

In 1986 a government committee, the Advisory Committee on the Safety of Irradiated and Novel Foods, investigated whether or not such processes should be permitted in the U.K. To quote from the resulting report 'we are satisfied, from our review of data and having regard to the likely uses of the process, that ionizing radiation up to an overall average dosage of 10 kilo Gray (kGy), correctly applied, provides an efficacious food preservation treatment which will not lead to a significant change in the natural radio-activity of the food or prejudice the safety and wholesomeness of the food'.

Food irradiation, if introduced, will provide an alternative to some of the existing methods of preservation or maintaining the quality of foods. It involves the exposure of food to ionizing radiation at varying intensities. Different doses would achieve different results (*see* Table 7.9). Low doses can be applied to inhibit the sprouting of vegetables, to delay the ripening of fruit and vegetables, to extend the shelf life of soft fruit, and to lower the level of insect infestation. Higher doses are needed to reduce the food's level of micro-organisms to achieve similar results to pasteurization. Levels required to achieve sterilization as in canning are much higher, and exceed the Report's maximum recommendations.

The food is exposed to gamma rays emitted by cobalt 60 or caesium 137 isotopes, and it is expected that, because of high cost, this will take place commercially, only in a small number of high capacity plants. This will facilitate the monitoring of the process, to ensure the necessary safety standards are adhered to.

Consumers, however, in the 1980s seem uneasy. Nuclear power and its associated problems, real or imaginary, have captured the public mind. It seems likely that food processors will advance very cautiously, and will only introduce food irradiation when the climate of public opinion is appropriate.

Table 7.9. Recommended doses of radiation for selected purposes
(adapted from 1986 Report from the Advisory Committee on
Irradiated and Novel Foods)

Desired outcome	Approximate dosage range (kGy)
Inhibition of sprouting	0.05–0.15
Delaying ripening of fruits and vegetables	0.2–0.5
Insect disinfestation	0.2–1.0
Elimination of various parasites	0.03–6.0
Shelf-life extension by reducing micro-organisms	0.5–5.0
Elimination of non-sporing pathogenic micro-organisms	3.0–10.00
Microbial sterilization	up to 50.0 (higher than recommended maximum figure of 10.0)

Conclusions

Losses, both in eating quality (texture) and in nutritional terms, must be balanced against the advantages. While it is true and sad, that there can be unnecessary losses due to poorly controlled processing, storage, or preparation, there may well be losses under the best conditions — these losses must be the price paid, if all the other advantages of preservation, processing, and preparation are required.

However, it is the duty of any processor of food, caterer and manufacturer alike to act responsibly in trying to optimize the balance between the process and retention of quality and nutrients.

8

Herbs, Spices, Condiments, Essential Oils and Essences, and Colourings

Herbs

From the early days of civilization, man has used a variety of herbs to vary and to enliven the flavour and aroma of monotonous basic foods and to disguise the unpleasant taste of food that is no longer fresh. Most herbs that we use originated from the hot and seasonally dry regions of the Mediterranean region, e.g. the bay laurel, sage, savory, and thyme, where they are still used today in national and regional dishes. The distinctive flavour and aroma of herbs is due to the presence of volatile oils which are contained in minute glands on the leaves and stems of most varieties, whilst in others the oils are within canals inside the leaves and fruits. Hence the need to chop the herbs in many cases to obtain a fuller flavour and aroma.

The classification of herbs may be done in several ways.

Botanical Names

The main varieties are grouped under botanical families as follows:

(a) Labiatae, e.g. basil, balm, marjoram, mint, rosemary, sage, savory, thyme.
(b) Umbelliferae, e.g. chervil, dill, fennel, lavage, parsley.
(c) Compositae, e.g. tarragon.
(d) Amaryllidaceae, e.g. chives.
(e) Lauraceae, e.g. bay laurel.
(f) Cruciferae, e.g. horseradish.

Catering Uses

(a) Soups, e.g. sweet marjoram, one of several herbs used in making turtle soup.
(b) Salads, e.g. chives in Fauchette salad.

158

(*c*) Sauces, e.g. tarragon in sauce Bearnaise.

(*d*) Fish dishes, e.g. dill with salmon trout.

Fresh or Dried

Herbs may be used fresh, but the majority of them today are purchased dried, either naturally or freeze dried. Ideally, herbs such as chives, mint, and parsley should be used when fresh. Most herbs have a strong flavour and so only small quantities should be used in any dish. Certain herbs have rather particular properties, e.g. when basil, marjoram, summer savory, and thyme are used the quantities of salt and pepper required in a particular dish can be reduced. Unfortunately the use of herbs in the regional foods of the U.K. is not very common which is rather a pity as a large variety of herbs are easily grown here.

The following are brief details of the most commonly used herbs.

Angelica

This is a tall plant which grows easily in damp areas. It is particularly cultivated for its aromatic hollow stem which is crystallized and used for cake decoration. The young leaf tips and stalks can be used when cooking acid-type fruits such as gooseberries and rhubarb to counteract their tartness and reduce the sugar content. The seeds are used in the production of gin and the liqueur Benedictine.

Basil

This can be grown in the U.K., but is particularly grown in warmer climates such as Italy and California, U.S.A. Its spicily fragrant leaves, similar to that of cloves, make it ideal for many uses in soups, salads, sausages, stuffings, fish, and pasta dishes. It is used in many Italian dishes and is also one of the ingredients found in a turtle soup herb bag.

Bayleaf

This is a member of the laurel family and is the original laurel used by the Greeks and Romans to make the ceremonial wreaths to crown their distinguished leaders. It is an evergreen tree, only the leaves of which are used. The leaves are elliptic, smooth, dark green on the upper surface and a paler green underneath when fresh. The leaves are very strong in flavour and are used in soups, sauces, and confectionery. The leaves are also used in a bouquet garni and in turtle herb mixtures.

Borage

A small, hairy, blue-flowered herb with a smell and flavour like that of cucumbers. The fresh leaves are used in salads, shell-fish cocktails and particularly as a decorative garnish in fruit cups and other mixed drinks.

Bouquet Garni

This is not a herb in the usual sense. It is a small bundle of standard herbs tied together and used to flavour sauces, soups and stews. It consists of a small bay leaf, a sprig of thyme; and a few parsley stalks tied together either between two small pieces of celery or leek stalk.

Celery Seed
This is the dried seed from celery which is used when fresh celery is either too expensive or is unobtainable. It is used in flavouring sauces, soups and stews.

Chervil
This is a small plant with a neat and much divided leaf with a very delicate aromatic flavour similar to aniseed. It is added to soups and salads, but is particularly used for decorating fish and poultry dishes. It is also one of the 'fines-herbs', a standard mixture of herbs used for many culinary preparations.

Chives
These belong to the same family as onions, leeks, and garlic but differ from them by their very mild flavour and their habit of growth. They grow as dense tufts of long, green, narrow, grassy, tubular leaves about 6–8 in. in length. They have a mild onion flavour and are used fresh when finely chopped on salads, sauces, and soups.

Dill
A hardy, aromatic annual herb which grows to about 2 ft tall and has an appearance like that of a young fennel. Its very divided, threadlike, bluish-green leaves are used in sauces, fish dishes and for pickling cucumbers.

Fennel
The leaves, which are similar to those of dill, grow out from the bulbous type vegetable. The fresh leaves have a pleasant sweet aniseed flavour and can be used for fish, poultry and salad dishes, as well as when finely chopped with many types of vegetables instead of using parsley.

Garlic
A small bulbous plant, related to the onion and shallot family. The root of the garlic plant is white when ripe and divides into segments called cloves. It is a very strong herb and must be used sparingly. Its uses are numerous and include many sauces, stews, and salads.

Horseradish
A strong growing pungent root, which when established in a garden or field is difficult to get rid of. The root is usually grated as an accompaniment to roast beef or in a hot or cold sauce with roast beef or various smoked fish.

Marjoram
There are three common varieties of marjoram, wild, pot, and sweet marjoram of which the sweet variety is used mainly. It has a rather strong aroma and

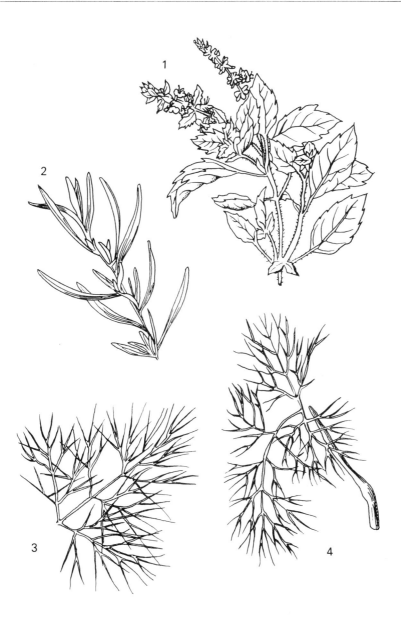

Figure 8.1 (1) Basil; (2) tarragon; (3) fennel; (4) dill

Figure 8.2 (1) Chevril; (2) chives; (3) rosemary; (4) borage

is used in many Italian regional dishes as well as being an ingredient of the turtle soup herb bag.

Mint
There are more than a dozen different types of culinary mint with a great variety amongst them, e.g. ginger mint, white peppermint, pineapple mint, etc. The mint commonly used for culinary purposes is the spearmint, although another variety, the 'Bowles mint', is claimed to be of superior quality. The common uses are mint sauce, mint jelly and to flavour and decorate new potatoes and garden peas.

Mixed Herbs
This consists of a mixture of dried herbs which are available in a ready-mixed form under several trade names.

Oregano
The name given to a variety of marjoram, imported from Mexico, which is more pungent than wild marjoram. It is used particularly in the preparation of Italian pizzas and Chili con Carne.

Parsley
The most commonly used herb in the U.K. not only for its flavouring properties in parsley sauce, stuffings, and bouquet garni, but also its sprigs are used fresh or deep fried as a garnish or decoration for many fish and meat dishes.

Rosemary
A hardy evergreen plant that is densely covered with pine-needle like leaves. The leaves are often used in Italian cookery particularly with veal.

Sage
A small, easily grown shrub with grey—green velvety leaves. It has a strong flavour and aroma, and is used in the stuffing for ducks and geese and for the flavouring of many types of sausages.

Sorrel
A large-leafed plant with leaves similar to small spinach leaves. It is served raw in salads or cooked like spinach. It is often used in a puree or leaf form in soups and omelettes.

Tarragon
A valuable culinary herb, with long (2—3 in.) thin leaves on tender stalks. It is used in salads and sauces, and is also used for decorative purposes on cold fish and meat dishes. It is one of the 'fines-herbes' as well as being used in the preparation of tarragon vinegar.

Thyme
A popular herb in the U.K., being used in bouquets garnis and as a flavouring in sauces, soups, stews, stuffings, and several types of sausage preparations.

Spices

Spices are aromatic vegetable products which are mainly available in a powder form, and are used to flavour raw, uncooked, and cooked foods. The powdered spices are processed by grinding and pulverizing certain parts of trees, shrubs, etc. which are dried after being picked. Unfortunately powdered spices are easy to adulterate with worthless material which only increases bulk to the spice but adds nothing else and this makes it more important for the buyer to deal with an established reputable spice manufacturer. The aroma and strong pungent flavour is due to the presence of essential oils which evaporate quite quickly during storage, particularly if the spice has been ground.

The classification of spices may be done in several ways.

Botanical Source

(a) roots — e.g., ginger, liquorice
(b) barks — e.g., cassia, cinnamon
(c) stems — e.g., angelica
(d) buds — e.g., cloves
(e) flowers — e.g., saffron
(f) fruits — e.g., caraway
(g) seeds — e.g., mace, nutmeg

Strength

(a) hot spices — e.g., cayenne pepper, ginger
(b) mild spices — e.g., paprika pepper, coriander
(c) aromatic spices — e.g., cinnamon, cassia, mace, nutmeg.

Particular Catering Uses

(a) e.g. in the manufacture of cakes — cinnamon, cloves, etc.
(b) e.g., in the manufacture of sausages — white pepper, nutmeg, ginger, mace, etc.

It is most likely that a mixture of these classifications will be used based mainly on the first classification given.

Like herbs, spices are very strong and so need to be used sparingly and carefully so that the finished food is not dominated by the spices but is blended with its own flavours to create an harmony of taste.

The following are brief details of the most commonly used spices.

Allspice

This spice is also known as pimiento or Jamaica pepper. It is the berries of a tree grown in the West Indies which are gathered whilst green and full of volatile oils, then dried, turning black in the process. Dried, whole allspice is about twice the size of black peppercorns and as the name implies has the flavour of several spices, namely pepper, cloves, nutmeg and cinnamon. It is used principally for pickling and sausage manufacture.

Aniseed

The seeds come from the anise plant, which is a member of the parsley family and grows in Egypt and several European countries. The seeds are of a grey–green colour, pear-shaped, and with a flavour similar to liquorice. Aniseed is used for flavouring cakes and the making of a liqueur called anisette.

Caraway

The most common of the dried aromatic fruit spices, it is obtained from a plant which is a member of the parsley family. It is grown commercially in Holland. The small, thin brown seeds have a strong, slightly hot flavour which resembles aniseed. It is commonly used in the making of cakes, bread, cheese and many Jewish dishes as well as for the making of the liqueur Kummel.

Cassia

An aromatic bark, of a light reddish-brown, similar to cinnamon but inferior in aroma and flavour. It is grown in China and India. It is used as a substitute for cinnamon when ground and as an ingredient of ground spice.

Cayenne Pepper

Prepared from the dried red, fully-ripened berries of one of the varieties of capsicums. The fruits are ground into a powder, mixed with some wheatflour and yeast and made into small flat cakes and baked. The cakes are then ground down into a powder and sieved. It has a very hot flavour and is used sparingly in sauces and as a table condiment.

Cinnamon

The dried bark is taken from the young branches of a tree of the laurel family, which grows in Ceylon. The cinnamon bark when dried is in the form of long cylindrical quills, having a yellow–brown colour and a furrowed outer surface. It is used in making cakes, syrups, puddings, punches, etc. as well as being an ingredient of mixed spice and curry powder.

Cloves

These are the dried, unopened flower-buds of an evergreen tree which grows in Sri Lanka, India and the West Indies. Cloves possess a hot, strong flavour and contain the essential oil of cloves. They are used with baked apple, baked ham and in stocks, soups, sauces, and braised stews.

Coriander

The small fruit of a plant, also of the parsley family, which is grown in southern Europe and India. The coriander is round shaped similar to white peppercorns but light brown in colour and also hollow. They have a fragrant smell and a mild flavour similar to sage. They are used particularly for flavouring syrups for savarins, etc., and for water ices.

Cumin

Cumin is the dried fruit of a plant grown in India and Egypt. The fruit resembles the caraway seed but is used mainly as an ingredient in curry powder and in munster cheese.

Curry Powder
A curry powder is a mixture of many various types of spices and herbs, the quality of which depends totally upon the manufacturer. Typical ingredients are often allspice, bay leaves, capsicum, cinnamon, chilli, coriander, cumin, ginger, mace, nutmeg, mustard seed, peppercorns, saffron, and turmeric.

Ginger
Ginger is a root which has some resemblance in appearance to a Jerusalem artichoke, and is grown in Jamaica and India. The root, on being dug up, is washed, trimmed, scraped, dried, and often bleached. It is obtainable in the U.K. fresh, as a dried root (peeled and unpeeled), preserved in a heavy sugar syrup, crystallized and in powder form. Its uses are mainly in cakes, biscuits, curry powder and mixed spice.

Juniper
These are the fruits of a shrub-like tree which grows wild in most parts of Europe. The dried black berries are used in the preparation of marinades, roasting game and the cooking of sauerkraut. The famous Limerick ham is smoked over juniper branches and berries. The berries are also used to flavour gin.

Mace
This is the husk of the nutmeg. The nutmeg tree which grows in the East and West Indies and Malaysia produces a fruit which is similar to a peach, which when fully ripe is split open, giving a skin with some flesh attached and a stone. The skin and flesh is carefully dried, turning to a buff colour and is known as Mace. It is available in pieces, known as 'blades', or finely ground. It has a much more delicate flavour than nutmeg and is used for flavouring fish dishes, sauces, and many types of sausages. It was used a great deal in English cookery during the sixteenth to nineteenth centuries.

Mixed Spice
This is a mixture of ground spices, the quality of which varies depending on the recipe used by the manufacturer. A typical mixture would contain rice flour (25%), cinnamon (30%), caraway (25%), coriander (3%), ground ginger (3%), mace (4%) and nutmeg (10%). The rice flour is added to increase the bulk and cinnamon is the predominating spice. Its uses are for puddings, cakes, and biscuits.

Monosodium Glutamate (M.S.G.)
This is not a spice at all and is only included here because it is sometimes added to dry spices. It is a white crystalline substance, rather like salt, obtained from the proteins of plants such as maize, soya bean and sugar beet by a form of hydrolysis. It enhances the natural flavours of foods by stimulating the palate. It is particularly used by food manufacturers in a very wide variety of foods.

Nutmeg

This is the kernel of the same fruit from which mace is obtained. It may be purchased whole or ground. Its uses are in milk puddings, custards and for flavouring mashed potatoes.

Paprika

This is obtained from a species of sweet capsicum peppers grown in Hungary. It is not so strong as many other types of peppers, but it has a delicate and sweet flavour as well as imparting a red colour to the foods. Its uses are in many Hungarian dishes such as goulash.

Poppy Seed

These are very tiny white and blue dried seeds obtained from the poppy plant. The seeds have a pleasant nutty flavour and are used in the manufacture of some types of bread and cakes. Poppy seeds are widely used in Balkan and Slav cookery.

Saffron

This is obtained from stigmas and styles of the saffron crocus. It is obtainable in the dried and the powdered form. It is of a deep-orange colour and has the property of not only imparting its particular and slightly bitter flavour but also its deep-orange colour to the food with which it is cooked. It is used in the preparation of fish and rice dishes as well as cakes.

Turmeric

Turmeric is a root of a plant belonging to the ginger family. The root is washed, trimmed, and dried before being ground to a powder. It has a characteristic sweet, spicy smell, with a slight bitter flavour and a bright yellow—gold colour. It is used for its colour which it imparts to food as well as its flavour and is found in curry powder, mustard sauces, and in piccalilli.

Condiments

The term condiments is a general one and refers to a number of seasonings which are added to prepared foods often at the table. There are four basic condiments: salt; pepper; mustard; and vinegar.

The classification is possible in several ways.

Plant or Other Origin

Some condiments are of plant origin (i.e. pepper, mustard, and vinegar) and some are not (i.e. salt which is a mineral).

Catering Uses

For example, salt is essential in the making of a good loaf of bread in that it confers flavour and palatability, it confers stability on the gluten, it has a controlling influence on the fermentation of the dough and therefore affects the colour of the crumb and crust and assists in the retention of moisture.

Like herbs and spices, the different condiments have to be used sparingly and carefully so as not to spoil the food and make it unpalatable.

The following are brief details of the four main condiments.

Salt

The chemical name for salt is sodium chloride. It is composed of two elements sodium and chlorine in the rates of four parts sodium to six parts chlorine. As separate elements they are deadly, but when combined in these proportions as common salt they are indispensable to the human body. Salt is found naturally in many parts of the world, in mines, in underground lakes and in the sea. The salt from mines is excavated and brought to the surface for crushing. When the mining becomes difficult it is necessary to sink wells and force water in and to pump out the resultant brine to be evaporated in shallow pans. Sea water is evaporated in shallow lagoons in many hot climates to extract the sea salt. The common types of salt available are as follows.

Rock Salt

This is a large coarse crystal-sized salt obtained from crushed mined salt in some cases or from a salt brine that has been evaporated very slowly. It is ideal for most culinary purposes.

Vacuum Salt

This is prepared by evaporating a purified salt solution in vacuum pans to produce a salt that is 99·9% pure. To these small cubical-form crystals is added a very small amount of magnesium carbonate to prevent caking and to allow it to remain free-pouring.

Dairy Salt

This is a 99·9% pure salt of a fine crystal size, which is used in the manufacture of butter, cheese, and margarine.

Dendritic Salt

This is a new grade of salt. It is very fine and has star-like crystals, and is used in the seasoning mixtures for sausage type goods where its particular shape assists in retaining an even mixture of all the spices and seasonings.

Celery Salt

This is a blend of crushed celery seed and vacuum salt which is purchased already prepared. It is frequently used when fresh celery is unavailable or just a small quantity is required.

Garlic Salt

This is a blend of crushed, dried garlic and table salt which is purchased already prepared. It is used for any dish where fresh garlic normally is used.

Iodized Salt

This salt contains 15–30 parts per million of sodium iodide (or potassium iodide).

Pepper
There are three main kinds of pepper which are commonly used.

Black and White Pepper
This is the fruit of a climbing plant, which is cultivated in India, Malaysia, and the West Indies. Black and white peppers are produced from the same plant, and are from just the same growth; the black peppercorns some from fruits picked before they are ripe and dried either in the sun or over a fire, whilst the white peppercorns are from ripe fruits which are soaked in water and then rubbed to remove the dark outer skin. The black peppercorn being the whole fruit is stronger in flavour than the white peppercorn. Both types of peppercorns are finely ground and sold either separately or as a mixture. Peppercorns are used in meat and fish stocks as well as being freshly milled to season meat before grilling or frying.

Paprika Pepper
This is a red pepper with a mild delicate flavour. Further details are contained in the section on spices.

Cayenne Pepper
This is a red pepper with a very hot flavour. Further details are contained in the section on spices.

Mustard
This is a mixture of the ground small seeds of the black mustard plant with the ground larger seeds of the white mustard plant, both coming from distinctly separate types of plants. The plants are grown in East Anglia, Holland, and Italy. The seeds or a mixture of them are ground and then sifted to produce a mustard flour. English mustard is a yellow paste made from mustard flour, wheatflour, turmeric, sugar, salt, 'other flavourings', and water. Continental mustard is much darker in colour, but more mild to taste and contains wine vinegar or wine in it and is often flavoured with herbs. Mustards are used in sauces such as mustard sauce, vinaigrette, and mayonnaise, as well as being served with roast or grilled beef.

Vinegar
This is one of the oldest of condiments, with several references to it made in the Bible. It is an acid liquid prepared from various substances by the acetous fermentation of alcoholic liquors, the alcohol being oxidized by fungi which convert the alcohol into acetic acid. The vinegar is fundamentally the national or regional alcoholic drink of a country that has become soured by acetous fermentation, e.g. malt vinegar in England, wine vinegar in France, cider vinegar in the U.S.A. and distilled vinegar in Scotland.
There are numerous types of vinegar, these are the main ones.

Malt Vinegar
This is prepared by an infusion of malt (partially fermented barley) which is fermented by yeast to produce alcohol. It is then allowed to aerate to en-

courage the growth of a vinegar fungi which converts the alcohol into acetic acid. It is then filtered off into vats where it matures for several months and develops its characteristic flavour and aroma. The colour may be adjusted by adding caramel prior to bottling.

Wine Vinegar

Wine vinegar is produced mainly in France, and is a by-product of the wine making industry, i.e. it is produced from wines that have turned sour.

Distilled Vinegar

All vinegars may be distilled so as to remove all traces of original colour. Distilled vinegar is particularly used for pickling vegetables, where a clear liquid and no discoloration of the food is required.

Fruit Vinegars

These are vinegars that are made from an initial fermentation with fruit such as apples, pears, and gooseberries.

Herb Vinegars

These are numerous and consist of a good quality vinegar into which some sprigs of a herb are added to give a particular flavour, e.g. tarragon, dill, thyme.

Vinegars are used as a preservative for vegetables and some fish dishes, in a marinade to tenderize meat and game prior to cooking, in court-bouillons, to flavour hot and cold sauces and as a table condiment.

Essential Oils and Essences

Essential oils (or volatile oils) are extracts prepared from a plant or a fruit and consist of the natural flavouring in the most concentrated form possible. The oil is extracted by pressure or by a steam distillation process. Although it is possible to extract oils from any part of a plant or fruit, they are obtained commercially from two main sources, from citrus fruits and from spices. Essential oils are very expensive.

Natural essences may be made by dissolving a small quantity of an essential oil in alcohol or other suitable substances, or, by mascerating natural flavouring materials, such as barks, fruits, roots, etc. in alcohol. Natural essences are expensive, but are cheaper than essential oils and easier to use when only small quantities are required.

Artificial essences are man-made essences, prepared by specialist chemists blending different organic compounds with a suitable solvent. Frequently artificial essences do not behave as consistently as natural essences when used at varying temperatures.

The main essential oils and essences produced are these.

Almond Oil

This is produced by a lengthy process after pressing the oil from bitter almonds. A cheaper type of almond oil is produced using the kernels from apricots and peaches.

Almond essence is obtained by making a 1% solution of almond oil in alcohol or suitable solvents.

Lemon Oil
This is produced as a by-product of the citrus fruit industry. It is obtained by hand or machine pressing the ripe lemon caps, spraying them at the same time with water to wash the oil from the fruit and then separating out the oil and water in a centrifuge and finally filtering the oil. In some instances it is separated by a distillation process, but the resultant oil is lacking in strength.

Lemon essence is made by diluting the essential oil with alcohol or other suitable substance.

Orange Oil
This is also a by-product of the citrus industry being produced by a similar process as that for the extraction of lemon oil. There are two types produced, a sweet and a bitter orange oil from the respective types of oranges.

Orange essence is made by diluting the essential oil with alcohol or other suitable substance.

Peppermint Oil
This is obtained from the peppermint plant by distillation with water. The oil has a pale green colour.

Peppermint essence is a weak solution of the oil in alcohol or suitable solvent.

Vanilla Essence
There is no such thing as a vanilla oil, it is always an extract and essence. Pure vanilla essence is obtained by mincing the prepared vanilla bean pods and mascerating the pulp in alcohol, which dissolves the vanilla crystals and some of the aromatic resins present. The liquid is then filtered.

Artificial Essences
These are the widest range of essences sold, mainly because they are relatively cheap. They cover all types of essences possible from an apple essence to a vanilla essence and seldom contain any natural oil or essence at all.

Colourings

These may be divided into a simple classification of natural colourings and synthetic colourings. Natural colourings mainly come from plants whilst synethic colourings are man-made with some originating from coal-tar products. Both types are obtainable in liquid and powder form. The use of colouring matter in food is closely controlled by legislation in every country as some are considered to be poisonous to varying degrees.

The most common natural colours used are as follows.

Brown
This is produced by simply caramelizing sugar to a dark colour and diluting it

with water. This dark brown liquid is used to colour gravies, sauces, soups, and confectionery.

The different types of brown sugars are added to various kinds of cakes to give flavour and a deep brown colour.

Chocolate

This may be obtained by using powdered, flaked, or melted cocoa or chocolate. If a prepared liquid chocolate colouring is used, this will have been prepared from a caramel and glycerine base with a chocolate extract for flavouring.

Coffee

This may be obtained from a strong infusion of ground roasted coffee beans. If a prepared liquid coffee colouring is used, this will have been prepared from a caramel and glycerine base with a coffee and chicory extract for flavouring.

Green

This can be obtained by extracting the natural green colouring from plants such as nettles and spinach. It is used in confectionery or green sauce.

Red

This is obtained from a small insect which is commercially produced in Mexico and the Canary Islands. The colouring (cochineal) is obtained from the female insect which is killed, dried, and then ground to a fine powder whilst in water. This red liquid is then boiled for a long period and stabilized with lime so that the colouring does not precipitate out. Cochineal may be processed further to produce a brighter red colouring called carmine.

Yellow

This is obtained from several sources already mentioned, such as saffron and turmeric. In addition it is obtained from annato which is obtained from the South American plant of the same name as well as from fresh or dried egg yolks.

Storage

Herbs

Fresh: should be kept in a cold room and used whilst very fresh.

Dried: keep in darkened screw-cap bottles, so as to exclude all light. N.B. They should never be stored in paper bags as the paper will absorb the aromatic oils, nor in plastic bags or containers as these tend to make the herbs 'sweat'.

Purchase dry herbs on a regular basis as they will lose their strength if stored too long.

Spices

Store in tight fitting containers.

All spices should be purchased on a regular basis as once they have been ground they lose their strength of flavour and colour.

Condiments

Pepper and mustard should be treated as spices. Salt should be stored in a dry room. Vinegar should be stored in a sealed container.

Essential Oils and Essences

Should be stored in dark bottles, well corked and in a dark cool room. Because they oxidize rapidly they should be purchased in small quantities on a regular basis.

Colourings

Prepared colourings should be stored in a cool dry room.

Scientific and Nutritional Aspects

Herbs and Spices

These are consumed in too small quantities for them to have any nutritional importance. Their original function was principally to mask off-flavours in food which was past its best — perhaps even beginning to putrefy. However, it has been found that some of these products do contain compounds which actually inhibit the growth of micro-organisms causing food spoilage, e.g. cloves and mustard.

Salt

Common salt, or sodium chloride as it is known by its chemical name, is an essential nutrient. The human body needs salts, of which this is an important example, to maintain its fluid balance. The diet therefore must supply this need. Salts are constantly being lost from the body via perspiration, breathing, the kidneys, etc., as the body excretes the water which either enters the body via food and drink, or is formed in the body by the oxidation of foodstuffs.

Sodium chloride also has an important function as a preservative, because in solution it exerts an osmotic pressure on the cells of micro-organisms (this pressure being stronger as the concentration of dissolved sodium chloride is increased), which dehydrates them. This effect certainly prevents multiplication of the micro-organisms in most cases; and in many cases high concentrations of salt can kill the micro-organisms.

Salting and curing (a process using sodium nitrates and nitrites) has been used for centuries for preserving a variety of foodstuffs — and nowadays these products are types of food in their own right, e.g. bacon and ham.

Vinegar

As has already been described, this product is formed by the oxidation of ethyl alcohol to acetic acid; it is the acetic acid which is the active ingredient in vinegar, whichever way it is manufactured.

Its preserving effect depends mainly on its acidic nature which inhibits the growth of most micro-organisms. It is a weak acid of a pH value of about 3, ionizing partially as indicated below

$$CH_3COOH \rightleftharpoons CH_3COO^- + H^+$$

| acetic | acetate | acidic |
| acid | ion | hydrogen ion |

Flavourings (including essential oils and essences)

The flavour of food is probably one of the most complex areas of food science, and very few natural flavours have been fully analysed, even though much research has been done, and is being done, in this field. Inevitably it is found that any natural flavour is contributed to by a number of chemical substances, for example at least 10 distinctly different chemicals have been isolated in the natural onion flavour, while 44 have been identified so far in the aroma of coffee!

Consequently any attempt the scientist makes at copying nature's flavours is never completely perfect but it is often cheaper than the real thing. Hence synthetic flavours are employed widely. There are over a thousand flavouring agents that can be used in food products and even though they are mostly used in a few parts per million concentration, concern is being expressed about their possible harm to health. Although in the U.K. there is no official list of permitted flavours to be used in foods as there is for permitted food colours, recommendations for prohibition have been made about those flavours which are thought to be harmful, and the Food Standards Committee has reported on this area of concern.

Colours

The colours used in foods fall fundamentally into three groups:

(i) Natural pigments extracted mainly from plant sources, a notable exception being cochineal, a vivid red dye obtained from the crushed female conchilla of Mexico.

(ii) Inorganic pigments of synthetic origin.

(iii) Dyes derived synthetically from coal-tar.

Most countries find those colours in groups (i) and (ii) acceptable for use in foods — but no two countries' experts can agree about the desirability of having any of those in group (iii) in foods. Such is the state of the confusion, that no single dye is permitted in foods in every country!

Tea, Coffee, and Chocolate

Tea, coffee, cocoa and chocolate are the processed parts of shrubs and trees of particular species which provide us with the basic ingredients of our major non-alcoholic beverages.

Tea

The Tea Plant and its Sources

Tea is a hardy evergreen tropical plant that belongs to the camellia family. Wherever tea is grown in the world it comes from two main types of the same plant, one a native of India (*Camellia assimica*) and the other a native of China (*Camellia sinensis*); however, with the modern advances of horticulture most tea plants are now of a hybrid variety offering many advantages such as resistance to disease, etc. and a higher yield. Tea plants require a tropical or sub-tropical climate and a well-drained, acid type soil with an even rainfall of not less than 70 in. per year. The plant in its wild state will grow to a height of 30 ft, but by constant pruning and shaping, the tea bush is kept to a height of 3–4 ft and made to produce large quantities of young shoots.

Tea is made from the young leaves of the plant, called the 'flush' and the leaves are picked by hand. Usually only two small leaves and a bud from each shoot are picked for the finest teas with picking taking place every 7–14 days depending on the altitude and location of the plantation.

The main producers and exporters of tea are:

(i) South Asia: mainly India and Sri Lanka (Ceylon) with smaller supplies from Bangladesh.

(ii) Far East: mainly China and Taiwan with small supplies from Japan. These are mostly green teas.

(iii) Africa: mainly Kenya, Malawi, Uganda, Mozambique with smaller supplies from Tanzania, Zaire (Congo), Rwanda, Mauritius and the Cameroons.

    (iv) South East Asia: mainly Indonesia with smaller supplies from
        Vietnam, Malaysia and Papua.

    (v) South America: Argentina and Brazil.

Classification

Teas may be classified under the following headings:

    (i) By their country of origin, e.g. India, China, etc.

    (ii) By their type (which includes also the general method of manu-
       facture), e.g. green tea, black tea, speciality teas, etc.

    (iii) By the method of manufacture, e.g. Orthodox, 'CTC', 'Legg-Cut',
       etc.

    (iv) By the grade of the leaf, e.g. Broken Orange Pekoe, Fannings, etc.

    (v) By the blend, e.g. teas may be sold under a brand name giving con-
       sistency of quality and taste at a standard price. They may also be
       blended to the particular requirements of a catering company to
       overcome problems from their water supply, etc.

    (vi) By their particular catering uses, e.g. for bulk production, for
       vending machines, etc.

The Manufacture of Tea

The manufacture of black tea by the orthodox method is in five main stages.

To Wither the Leaf

The plucked leaves, on reaching the factory which is usually situated centrally
to the plantation, are first weighed, then spread out thinly and evenly, on
special racks, where they lose by evaporation about 50% of their moisture.
This stage may take up to 24 hours depending on the temperature and humidity
of the air.

To Roll the Leaf

The leaves are put through rolling machines that break up the leaf-cells, thus
releasing the natural juices and bringing them into contact with the air. At
this stage the 'fine' leaf which includes the bud and first leaf are usually sifted
from the 'coarse' larger leaves and are then separately further processed.

To Ferment the Leaf

This is not a true fermentation but more correctly an oxidization stage, being
the oxidation of the tea tannin and the development of the colour, the aroma,
and flavour from the enzymes found in the leaf sap. The rolled leaves are
spread out on racks in a cool humid room for about 3 hours, during which time
they turn a bright, coppery red colour through the absorption of oxygen.

To 'Fire' the Leaf

To stop the fermentation stage, the leaves are 'fired' in a current of hot, dry
air for some 20–30 minutes. The leaves are then black, dry, and crisp.

To Sift and Grade the Leaf

The dry tea is next sifted, graded, and packed into foil lined tea chests and sealed to protect the tea from moisture and odours whilst *en route* to the blenders.

Further Notes on Methods of Manufacture

Green tea is processed similarly to black tea except that the fermentation stage is omitted. Because of this it does not have the characteristic flavour and aroma of black tea.

Oolong tea is also similarly processed but has only a partial fermentation stage.

'CTC' manufacture is a variation of the orthodox method of manufacture in which a special machine cuts, tears and curls the withered leaf all in a single process exposing more cells to the atmosphere. This method produces a browner leaf than does the orthodox method.

'Legg-Cut' is another method of manufacture in which the leaf is not withered, but is cut into small strips with a Legg-Cutter rather as the tobacco leaf is cut. After cutting, the leaf is lightly rolled, fermented for only a short period and then fired.

The Grading of Tea

To make the unsorted, processed tea leaf commercially marketable it is sorted into a large number of grades by passing it through a series of sieves of different mesh sizes.

There are four main grades of black tea:

(*a*) Leaf teas;
(*b*) Broken and small leaf teas;
(*c*) Fannings;
(*d*) Dust.

Leaf Teas

The gradings are:

(i) Flowery Orange Pekoe (F.O.P.)
(ii) Orange Pekoe (O.P.)
(iii) Pekoe (P.)
(iv) Pekoe Souchong (P.S.)

Leaf teas generally yield more flavour and fragrance than broken and small leaf teas.

Broken and Small Leaf Teas

The numerous gradings within this group consist of the smaller leaves sifted from the bulk, intentionally cut after firing to a smaller size or processed by the 'CTC' method.

The gradings are:

(i) Broken Orange Pekoe (B.O.P.)
(ii) Flowery Broken Orange Pekoe (F.B.O.P.)
(iii) Broken Pekoe (B.P.)
(iv) Broken Pekoe Souchong (B.P.S.)

Fannings

Fannings grades include B.O.P. Fannings, Pekoe Fannings, and Fannings. Fannings are small pieces of leaf.

Dust

This is the trade name for the smaller leaf particle size. These grades usually yield a darker and stronger tea with a shorter infusion time than leaf teas. The fanning and dust grades are suitable for teabags.

Each of the grade terms above refers to the appearance or the size of the leaf but not to the origin of the tea or its quality.

The Grading of Green Tea

There is no recognized grading of green tea simply because the sales are less than 2% of the total sales for all teas. Green teas are mainly produced in China and are classed according to the condition and size of the leaf and the district of production. The best known green teas are Gunpowders, Chan Mees, Sou Mees, and Hyson.

The Tasting and Blending of Tea

Teas imported into the U.K. are stored in special warehouses, where samples are taken from each consignment from a tea estate by the selling brokers for examination by the buyers. The selling brokers make up a catalogue of the teas they have to sell and they are distributed to the buyers prior to selling the tea by auction.

Teas purchased by a tea merchant would first be cleaned to remove any dust, wood splinters, pieces of metal, etc. Next, expert tea blenders would sample the teas by tasting the tea and examining the leaf, and assessing the tea for quality, flavour, strength, body, size, and style of leaf. The assessment is then compared with the cost of the tea. Tea from each sample is made in a separate pot and allowed to infuse for a standard time of six minutes. It is usual for some tea tasters to only allow an infusion time of three minutes for teas which are specifically for the catering trade. As the tasting is by comparison against a quality standard, each batch of tastings are standardized, that is, they are presented to the taster in exactly the same way, made with equal weights of leaf, equal quantities of fresh boiling water, equal infusion times, and finally with or without a measured amount of milk. After infusion, the tea is drained into a bowl, the infused leaf tipped into the pot lid and both placed against a sample of the dried leaf. The taster is then able to taste each tea, examine the infused leaf and the dried leaf and make his comparison against all the other samples and the standard for that type of tea.

Most of the black teas purchased today are blended teas and are prepacked. The blending is a highly skilled job to ensure that a standard product of high quality, flavour, and appearance is consistently available throughout the year at a standard price. To maintain the standard of a blended tea, the blenders would make up many samples of mixtures of teas from different estates, each with different characteristics, and taste and compare them against the original standard, before a quantity of a blend is made up in the factory.

Table 9.1. Typical blends of tea, their origin and characteristics

Blend	Origin	Characteristics
Broken Orange Pekoe A blend of Ceylon and other fine teas.	Broken Orange Pekoe teas are grown in the famous hillside tea gardens of Ceylon	Medium leaf – delicious bouquet smooth flavour
Earl Grey A blend of fine Oriental teas with flavouring	A secret blend of Indian and Chinese teas with the addition of oil of Bergmont	Delicately scented producing a pale clear liquor
Darjeeling A blend of Darjeeling and other fine teas	Darjeeling teas are grown in the Himalayan foot-hills of India	Muscatel flavour
Lapsang Souchong A blend of Lapsang Souchong and other fine teas	A blend from the Province of Fukien in China	Large leaf, pale liquor, slightly smoky flavour and aroma
Ceylon A blend of Uva Ceylon and other fine teas	Uva Ceylon teas are grown high on the hill-sides of Ceylon	Flowery bouquet – gold coloured 'light' liquor
Keemun A blend of Keemun and other fine teas	The tea of Old Imperial China	Produces a light liquor – delicately flavoured – free of 'tannin'
Assam A blend of Assam and other fine teas	Assam teas are grown in the Assam region of Northern India	Produces a full coloured liquor – the traditional British cup of tea at its best

Tea Bags

Tea bags contain up to 30 original teas which, like most teas, are blended together by expert tea blenders to produce a high standard of tea of the required flavour and strength. As tea bags are immersed in the tea cup or pot the material used to make the bag has been specially developed to avoid imparting any foreign flavours to the tea and also to give it sufficient strength so that it will not burst. Although usually costlier than loose tea, tea bags do have the advantages of the same measured quantity of tea being used each time thus simplifying costings plus offering a convenient and hygienic way of disposing of the used leaf.

Catering Packs

Catering packs are similar to tea bags except that they are packaged in bags to make specific large quantities of tea, e.g. $\frac{1}{2}$, 1, 3 and 5 gallon packs. They have the same advantages as mentioned previously for tea bags.

Instant Tea

This is made by spray or freeze-drying an infusion of tea and then packaging it in air-tight containers. It is produced for two distinctly different requirements, namely hot-water and cold-water solubility. The hot-water use for instant tea is mainly for automatic vending machines. The cold-water use for instant tea is for the popular iced tea product. The manufacture of this is more difficult as the final product has to be perfectly clear even after the addition of ice, the manufacture of it having to remove the normal precipitate in tea and to eliminate problems of hard water.

Speciality Teas

Yerba de Mate (Paraquay Tea)

This is not a true tea. It is made from the leaves and small stems of a species of the holly tree which grows in Paraguay and Brazil, and is processed in a similar fashion to black tea. It is usually drunk without milk and often for its claimed but unsubstantiated medical properties.

Scented Teas

These are made by adding such flavourings as dried Jasmine flowers, rose petals, cloves, orange zest or mint leaves to tea during the firing stage after which they may be sieved out. Scented teas are now commonly available in tea bags.

Coffee

The Coffee Plant and its Sources

The coffee plant is an evergreen tree or bush which is grown commercially in tropical climates throughout the world. It requires not only a hot climate but also a high rainfall, a rich soil and a relatively high altitude. The coffee plant is unable to survive any wide variations of temperature or any frost conditions.

The part of the plant that is processed and used for making into coffee is the ripened berries which grow along the stems in small clusters rather like holly berries. Commercially three varieties of coffee plant are grown.

    (i) *Coffea arabica* (Arabica coffee) which supplies the largest quantity and best quality coffee. It is renowned for its bold regular sized bean and its fine flavour. It grows best at high altitudes at 2,000 and 6,500 ft, but unfortunately is very prone to disease and requires very careful cultivation. It is grown in Brazil, Colombia, Costa Rica, Kenya, Jamaica, and India.

   (ii) *Coffea canephora* (Coffee Robusta) produces the second main type of coffee. The beans from this plant are usually smaller, of a lower quality and a more neutral flavour. It grows best from sea level to 2,000 ft and has the particular advantages that it produces a higher yield than arabica and is a more hardy and disease resistant plant. It is grown in East and West Africa.

  (iii) *Coffea liberica* (Coffee Liberica) produces the third main type of

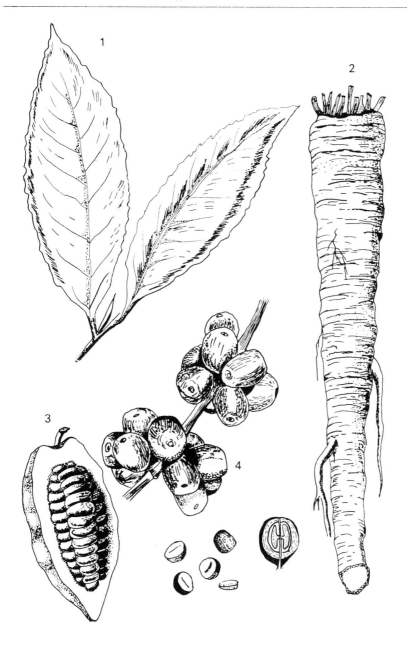

Figure 9.1 (1) Tea leaves; (2) chicory; (3) cocoa bean; (4) coffee berries and beans

coffee. It grows in similar conditions to the Robusta coffee plant, and is a robust plant often growing wild. The beans are large in size but lacking in quality, and are not of any commercial importance in the coffee trade in the U.K. It is grown in Malaysia and Guyana.

The main producers and exporters of coffee are Uganda, Kenya, Brazil, the Ivory Coast, Congo, Tanzania, and Colombia.

Classification
'Coffees' may be classified under the following headings:

(i) By their country of origin, e.g. Uganda, Kenya, Brazil, etc.
(ii) By their type, e.g. Arabica, Robusta, Libberica, e.g. green beans, roasted beans, etc.
(iii) By the grade of the bean, e.g. this depends on the country. The U.S.A. grade from 1—8 with 1 being the highest grade. In the U.K. grading is by name (*see* p. 181)
(iv) By the method of processing, e.g. the degree of roasting and grinding, e.g. coffee essence, A.F.D. coffee, etc.
(v) By the blend, e.g. coffees sold under trade names to give a quality standard of flavour, colour and aroma at a near standard price (e.g. coffee mixtures with chicory or figs).
(vi) By their catering uses, e.g. coffee processed specifically for use in espresso machines, vending machines, etc. or coffee concentrates, essences, etc., for use as a flavouring for bakery and confectionery uses.

The Processing of Coffee
When the berries are ripe, they are picked by hand and taken to a processing plant. The berries are about the size of a small cherry and consist of an external red skin, a layer of pulp, a tough parchment-like inner membrane, a thin silver skin and finally two beans, rounded on one side and flat on the other, with the flat sides together. Depending on the country in which the coffee is grown it will be processed by one of the following methods.

The Dry Method
This method is used in countries which do not have sufficient water supplies, or where the value of the cured beans does not warrant the extra costs of washing. The coffee berries are spread out thinly in the sun and left until the pulp shrivels tight on to the parchment. The berries are then put through an hulling machine which removes the parchment and pulp in one stage. Beans processed in this way will carry traces of the silverskin and lack the attractiveness of washed beans. Also in this method very little sorting out of inferior quality beans is done. Finally the beans are graded for export.

The Wet Method
This method is used in countries which have a sufficient water supply and where the quality of the bean being grown warrants the extra processing costs.

The berries are processed through a de-pulping machine, removing the fleshy part of the berry leaving the two seeds contained in their parchment jackets. They are then placed in large vats where they are allowed to ferment partially for 24 to 40 hours. The fermentation serves two main purposes, it is important for the development of the aroma of the finished cooked coffee bean and it assists the removal of any adhering pulp to the parchment. When the fermentation stage is completed the beans are thoroughly washed and then spread out in the sun to dry completely. The next stage is the removal of the parchment by machines to leave just the clean, olive green beans. The final stage is one of grading before exporting.

The Grading of Coffee
The designations of coffee grades varies with the country of origin, with letters and sometimes with the numbers used. The usual grades may be seen as being sub-divided into four groupings and are described as:

(i)	Bold or A	large, heavy, flat beans
	Second size or B	medium size, heavy, flat beans
	Smalls or C	small size, heavy, flat beans
(ii)	Peaberry 1	large, peaberry | almost round berries
	Peaberry 2	small peaberry | graded by weight
(iii)	Elephant	berries of above average size, often deformed in shape and being semi-hollow
(iv)	Triage or T	broken beans, usually of low quality
	TT	large broken beans
	CTT	mixed small flat and large broken beans

It should be noted that with different species of coffee bean being grown and different grading procedures in each country, the gradings are not identical. It is usually accepted that the largest normal shaped beans, i.e. Bold or A, are best in quality and possess a fuller flavour, aroma, and body than the other beans.

Coffee Roasting
The green coffee bean has little or no flavour. The flavour, aroma, and colour of the liquid coffee that we drink is developed by roasting the coffee bean, which causes the cell walls of the bean to be ruptured making the flavouring and aromatic qualities of the natural oil content in the bean readily available to extraction by hot water. Roasting can vary from light to dark and is graded by colour. A dark roast gives a slightly bitter characteristic and is widely used for espresso and after-dinner coffee. A light roast will give a mild taste suitable for general purposes. The correct degree of roasting is as important as any stage in the preparation of quality coffee.

It should be noted that roasted coffee is a cooked article and is liable to deterioration of quality. Any beans not used soon after roasting should therefore be stored in air-tight containers.

Coffee Grinding
The roasted coffee bean is next ground to enable the flavour, aroma, and colour

to be easily extracted by hot water. The degree to which the coffee bean is ground is very important indeed and is related to the type of coffee-making equipment that is being used. For example, a finely ground coffee made with equipment that includes the use of filter papers would take a long time to make and be usually cloudy and of 'muddy' characteristics. The prolonged infusion does not add anything of advantage to the liquor, except possibly bitterness.

It should be further noted that ground coffee deteriorates more rapidly than the roasted coffee bean because of the high volatility of the flavouring oils. Ground coffee in an unsealed container will lose about 20% of its freshness in one day and 50% in twenty days. Not only will ground coffee lose freshness but it will develop staleness as a result of the volatile oils being easily oxidized.

Ideally quality coffee is made from freshly ground roasted beans. Alternatively the ground coffee should be stored in an air-tight container or packaged in vacuum packs.

Coffee Blending
Many coffee blends are available from coffee merchants and are sold under trade names, the blends often being for breakfast, mid-morning or after-dinner use. The blending is skillfully done by experts, in a similar way to tea tasting and blending, to produce a standard product of high quality, flavour, aroma, and colour that is consistently available throughout the year at a standard price. Blends often have advantages in that they are lower in price than straight coffees and are more generally acceptable to a wide variety of consumer tastes.

Coffee Mixtures
Some well-known coffee brands available are mixtures of coffee with either chicory or figs. Coffee and chicory mixtures are usually sold as French Coffee, whilst coffee and figs are usually sold as Viennese Coffee or Cafe Vienna.

Chicory, a perennial herb, is extensively grown in India, Poland, and parts of Western Europe for use as a substitute or additive to coffee. The root of the plant, which is similar in appearance to the sugar beet, is washed, trimmed, cut, dried, roasted, and then ground before mixing it with ground coffee. Chicory mixtures are usually cheaper than pure coffee and produce a strong, heavy coffee to drink.

Figs are extensively grown in Spain and are prepared by washing, trimming, drying, and roasting before being ground and mixed with ground coffee. This mixture is not usually cheaper than blended pure coffee. It produces a distinct flavoured coffee with a sweetish taste and a smoother liquor to the mixture than that obtained with chicory.

The quantity of chicory or figs that may be added to coffee is strictly controlled by law in the U.K. with coffee and chicory mixtures containing at least 51% of coffee solids, and with coffee and fig mixtures containing at least 85% of coffee solids.

Instant Coffee
This is the convenience form of coffee which is so widely used today. It is

quick to make, needs no special coffee-making equipment, and is of an acceptably good standard.

Instant coffee is pure coffee in a soluble form and is made by brewing freshly blended, roasted and ground coffee in large extractors where a very strong coffee concentrate is produced. The liquid is then atomized to a fine mist into a drying chamber containing hot air where the water evaporates from each tiny droplet leaving a powder of pure coffee. A more recent development has produced an instant coffee that has the appearance of freshly ground coffee and is produced by the accelerated freeze dry method. Its particular advantages are its appearance and its ability to dissolve fully quickly.

Caffeine-free Coffee
Caffeine is the alkaloid substance found in coffee to which the stimulating property of coffee is due. It also is partly responsible for the bitterness of coffee. Most of the caffeine, up to 87%, can be extracted by processing the green beans under steam in a vacuum.

The reason for extracting the caffeine is to remove the stimulant content from coffee making it a suitable drink for people with heart complaints, etc., who advisedly should not drink ordinary coffee. De-caffeinated coffee by law must not contain more than 0·1% of caffeine.

Coffee Concentrates
These are concentrated extracts of coffee which are mainly used as a flavouring agent for confectionery and bakery goods.

Coffee Bags
These are similar to tea bags except that they contain ground coffee with, in some instances, a proportion of instant coffee.

Catering Packs
Again similar to the catering packs for tea. They are made up in units to produce specific quantities of coffee, e.g. $\frac{1}{2}$, 1, 3 and 5 gallon packs. The variety of blends, degree of roasting and grinding gives the caterer a very wide choice.

Cocoa and Chocolate

The Cocoa Plant and its Sources
The cocoa plant is a small tropical tree originally grown in Central and South America but now commercially grown in West Africa. Cocoa trees require a good soil in which to grow, a high rainfall, and a low altitude.

The part of the plant that is processed and used for making into cocoa and chocolate is the fruit that grows on the main trunk of the tree as well as on the branches. The fruit is a large pod 4—12 in. in length and about 4 in. in diameter, and has a hard leathery rind containing 25—75 seeds in 5 distinct rows embedded in a soft pulp.

The main producers and exporters of the cocoa seeds or beans are:

(i) West Africa, which produces almost 74% of the world's production.

(ii) North, Central, and South America, which produces almost 24% of the world's production.

(iii) Asia and Oceania, which produces almost 3%.

Classification

Cocoa may be classified under the following headings:

(i) By their country of origin, e.g. West Africa, Brazil, etc.

(ii) By their species, e.g. Criollo, Forastero, and many hybrid strains. With hybrid strains being widely used today the quality of the beans are not now judged solely on the species of the cocoa tree.

(iii) By their type (which includes also the general method of manufacture), e.g. drinking cocoa, drinking chocolate, chocolate couverture, etc.

(iv) By their particular catering uses, e.g. chocolate powder specifically processed for use in vending machines, chocolate couverture for chocolate moulding, ganache, icings, etc.

The Processing of Cocoa

The processing of the cocoa bean into cocoa powder is in seven main stages.

TO FERMENT THE BEANS. The ripe cocoa pods are collected, split open, and the beans and pulp surrounding them scooped out and fermented under controlled conditions. Fermentation usually takes place in 'sweat boxes' where the temperature is allowed to rise to 40–50°C (104–122°F). There are several reasons for the fermentation:

(*a*) to kill the germ and prevent germination of the seed, and decomposition of the bean;

(*b*) to encourage the enzyme reaction reducing bitterness and developing flavour. The beans absorb the liquid from the fermenting sugary pulp, which is then converted into alcohol and then to acetic acid. The fermentation is stopped as soon as the mass of beans passes into the acid stage. Should the fermentation be allowed to continue it would develop unpleasant flavours and odours in the beans.

TO DRY THE BEANS. This is done either by laying the beans out in the sun for two or three days and occasionally turning them over, or by passing them through a mechanical drying chamber. When completely dried the beans should have a moisture content of less than 4%.

N.B. At this stage the beans are exported unless they are to be processed into cocoa chocolate for consumption in the producing country.

TO ROAST THE BEANS. This stage is essential to develop the flavour and aroma of the bean and to give it an even colour. Moisture is lost at this stage which assists in the separation of the shell from the bean.

TO REMOVE THE SHELL (WINNOWING). This process is the removal of the shell from the cocoa bean, by passing it through a series of rollers and sieves. The de-shelled beans (now mostly broken pieces) are referred to as nibs.

TO ALKALIZE THE NIBS (DUTCH PROCESSING). This stage which further develops the flavour and colour is usually done by tumbling the nibs in a warm alkali solution. After drying, the nibs may be re-roasted to correct the moisture content.

TO GRIND THE NIBS. The nibs are ground into very small particles, a process which releases a large amount of fat and results in the mass becoming a thick syrup. The fat is cocoa butter, usually 50% of the nibs.

TO EXTRACT PART OF THE COCOA BUTTER. The cocoa-fluid (or mass or pâté) is then fed into felt-lined steel pans fitted with a movable perforated lid. When subjected to hydraulic pressure some of the fat is forced through the filter cloths leaving behind a solid residue known as press cake. This is removed from the pan, cooled to set the colour, pulverized and sieved. To this very fine powder, a small quantity of salt and flavouring (vanilla) is usually added before it is marketed as the familiar cocoa powder.

Chocolate

The Processing of Plain Chocolate

The processing of chocolate includes the first six stages as for the processing of cocoa and involves three further stages.

TO MIX THE COCOA (OR CHOCOLATE) MASS WITH SUGAR. The chocolate mass is thoroughly mixed with powdered sugar in large blending kettles. The fat content of the mass is strictly controlled to enable a standard product to be obtained. Additional cocoa butter is added where necessary to obtain the required consistency.

TO REFINE THE MIXTURE. This is done by passing the mixture through a series of five heavy steel rollers to reduce the size of the individual non-fat particles further so that the chocolate will be very smooth to the palate. This stage exposes the particles to the air reducing the moisture content, partially evaporating volatile substances, and lightening the colour of the mixture.

TO 'CONCHE', FLAVOUR, AND STANDARDIZE THE MIXTURE. This final stage is concerned with producing a standard quality of chocolate. Conching is the mechanical aigitation of the chocolate mass, with additional cocoa butter, if necessary, at a temperature of $60-70°C$ $(140-158°F)$ which further exposes the mass to the air, removing further undesirable volatile substances (resulting from the fermentation stage) and helps to develop the flavour. Additional desired flavours when required are added at the end of this stage prior to the chocolate being run off and set in moulds as bars, slabs, etc. The product is then also known as 'couverture'.

The Processing of Milk Chocolate

This is identical to the above process except that 'milk crumb' is added at the refining stage and the conching is at a lower temperature but for a longer time. 'Milk crumb' is a mixture of specially prepared condensed milk and chocolate mass which has been reduced to a powder form.

Drinking chocolate is a modern beverage drink prepared from chocolate powder or chocolate flakes and made in a similar manner to the cocoa drink by adding hot water or milk.

Catering Uses of Tea, Coffee, Cocoa and Chocolate

The catering uses of these products are shown in Table 9.2.

Table 9.2. The main catering uses of tea, coffee, cocoa, and chocolate

Product	Main Catering Uses
Tea	As a hot beverage drink usually with milk or lemon, and sugar As a cold beverage drink Sometimes used in the making of cakes and tea bread
Coffee – ground, bagged and instant	As a hot beverage drink on its own or with cream, milk and sugar. Also served with various liqueurs As a cold beverage drink with whipped cream or vanilla ice cream
– instant, concentrates	As flavourings, and colourings for ice-cream, buttercreams, fondant, and gateaux
Cocoa and chocolate – powder or flake	As a hot beverage drink As the flavouring and colouring for ice-cream Hot and cold chocolate sauces
Chocolate couverture	As a coating on its own or with fondant for cakes and pastries For piping as a decoration on cakes For moulding into Easter eggs, etc. Hot and cold chocolate sauces Chocolate ice-cream

Storage of Tea, Coffee, and Cocoa

Coffee, especially when roasted and ground, is particularly prone to loss of volatile aromatic substances which constitute much of its flavour and aroma, therefore care must be taken with storage. The problems are not so acute with tea and cocoa, nevertheless neither product has indefinite shelf-life without some loss of flavour. The staleness which might be detected in these products after long storage, is perhaps most due to loss of flavour components, which therefore allows the less volatile bitter tannin flavours to predominate – rather than any off-flavours actually developing.

The storage times for tea, coffee, cocoa and chocolate are given on p. 187.

Scientific and Nutritional Aspects

Man's body has a daily need for water of between 1 to 1·5 litres (2 to 3 pints approximately) to enable him to live comfortably. To meet this need therefore he must drink, and it would appear that he is not over fond of just plain water (sufficient though it is to satisfy his fluid needs). Man prefers to have his water flavoured with something else, if at all possible, from fruit cordials,

Table 9.3. Storage times for tea, coffee, cocoa, and chocolate

Product	Suggested Storage Period (weeks)
Tea − loose	4
− packeted, bags, etc.	8−16
Coffee − beans, roasted (vacuum packed)	52
− beans, roasted (loose)	2
− ground (vacuum packed)	40
− ground (loose)	1
− instant (unopened)	12
Cocoa, chocolate powder/flakes (unopened)	12
Chocolate couverture (unopened)	12

N.B. All the above products should be stored in a clean, dry and well-ventilated store-room, well away from items such as fruit, vegetables, spices, soap, cooking oils, etc. Where possible the products should remain sealed in their original containers (to reduce the absorption of moisture and taint). When tea and coffee are purchased loose, they should be placed in a clean dry air-tight storage bin. Never add new supplies of loose tea or coffee to old supplies.

to tea and coffee; and for many, the only way to quench thirst is by drinking water containing fermented products from varying sources!

At the moment we are considering a selection of non-alcoholic beverages, and whilst they are mainly drunk for their particular flavour, they do have various ingredients which are known to have pharmacological effects, and

Table 9.4. Composition of dry products from which beverages are made,
either by the addition of hot water or milk
(After McCance and Widdowson, 1978)

Dry product	Grams per 100 g				
	Water	Sugar	Protein	Fat	Kilocalories per 100 g
Bournvita	1.5	52	8.7	5.1	377
Cocoa powder	3.4	0	18.5	21.7	312
Coffee, ground, roasted	4.1	0	10.4	15.4	287
Coffee, instant	3.4	6.5	14.6	0	100
Horlicks	2.5	49.4	13.8	7.5	396
Ovaltine	2.3	73	9.8	3.8	378
Tea, Indian	9.3	3	19.6	2	108
Bovril	38.7	0	39.1	0.7	174

they may also provide man's diet with energy and nutrients. The major components of the dry products which are used to make common beverages are shown in Table 9.4.

Varieties of Tea

The Englishman's drink − the U.K. consumes about one-third of the world's total production of a little over one million tons.

Black Tea

After picking, the leaves are partially dried and then passed through rollers to break them up. The ruptured cells in the crushed leaves release enzymes (e.g. polyphenol oxidase) which bring about oxidation reactions — the so-called 'fermentation' process — which give rise to the characteristic colour and flavours associated with this type of tea. Obviously other factors such as shrub variety, nature of cultivation and type of leaf, also govern the final flavour of the product.

After fermentation is complete, the crushed leaves are dried more thoroughly at a higher temperature which deactivates the enzymes, and reduces the water content to about 3 to 5%. (This usually rises during further processing, packaging and transportation to about 9 to 10% moisture.)

Green Tea

After picking, the leaves are crushed and dried thoroughly at high temperature, which, because the enzymes are deactivated before 'fermentation' can proceed, results in a product which is lighter and contains more tannin than black tea. The missing fermentation stage also accounts for the major differences in flavour between green and black teas.

Uses of Tea

The beverage tea is made by pouring boiling water on a selected quantity of the dry leaves. The produce is best drunk after it has been infused for about 5 minutes, during which time all the products contributing to desirable flavour are leached out from the leaves. About 80% of the caffeine, 90—100% of the riboflavine and nicotinic acid, 60% of the tannin and other water-soluble substances are extracted in a 5 minute infusion. A long infusion brings out the rest of the water soluble substances, and while many of the more volatile substances contributing to good flavour are lost during standing, the components such as tannins which cause bitterness of taste, increase in concentration.

It is worth noting that when tea (and coffee) are infused with hard water, the dissolved calcium and magnesium salts may cause precipitation of some of the soluble extracts of the tea, resulting in a 'scum' formation and a change in flavour. It may, therefore, be said that one would obtain a 'better' cup of tea in a soft water area. Since increase in altitude lowers the boiling point of water, and the best extraction of tea flavour is obtained with boiling water, normally at 100°C, people living at high altitude cannot make a good cup of tea.

Caffeine is an alkaloid drug which stimulates the human nervous system, and seems to prevent temporarily mental fatigue, without becoming addictive. The leaves contain about 1·5—2·5% caffeine, resulting in about 12—15 mg per ounce of beverage. Since the dangerous dose level of caffeine is said to be in excess of 300 mg, one would have to drink a lot of tea for the caffeine intake to be dangerous.

Vitamins — two water soluble vitamins of the B group are present in the beverage, riboflavine and nicotinic acid, but since the infusion from about 4 oz of tea only gives about 1 mg of riboflavine and 6 mg of nicotinic acid, while the average man's daily recommended allowances are 1·7 mg and 18 mg — one would have to drink a great deal of tea for it to have any nutritional significance. However, since it is usual for sugar and/or milk to be added, the resulting beverage may contribute to total daily nutrient intake.

Coffee

As was implied in the case of tea, the chemical substances in coffee are also many and complex, and some of the major constituents are shown in Table 9.3. It has been suggested that there are as many as 200 different substances in coffee, most of which contribute in some way to its flavour.

Before the beverage can be made from the beans, they are roasted and ground. Roasting the beans at about 250°C drives most of the aromatic oils to the surface — does coffee smell better than it finally tastes? — and it is for this reason that coffee should be made from freshly roasted beans because they soon lose their flavour. Roasting also causes a number of chemical changes which contribute to the colour and flavour of the final product. The beans are ground prior to infusion so that the optimum extraction may be achieved in the shortest time with hot water at about 95°C (203°F). Two minutes is often suggested, because this time facilitates extraction of the desirable flavour, whilst being too short for the extraction of components contributing to bitterness. Hence the popularity of 'cafe filtre'.

Caffeine

This is probably the most notable substance extracted from the coffee bean. Even though coffee beans are lower in caffeine than tea, having about 1–2%, the resulting beverage is higher in concentration because more ground coffee is required to make the drink, than tea. A cup of coffee may contain about 18 mg of caffeine per ounce. (Truswell in 1975 showed that Londoners may get from 58 to 168 mg of caffeine in a cup of coffee and from 43 to 92 mg in a cup of tea.)

Decaffeinated Coffee

Decaffeinated coffee is coffee from which the drug has been removed by treating the aqueous extract of coffee with such chemicals as ethylene or methylene dichloride. The resultant drug-free extract is then dried — therefore giving rise to a decaffeinated instant coffee.

Instant Coffee

This is a modern form of coffee which is manufactured from aqueous coffee extract prepared by infusion of ground coffee beans in the factory. The aqueous extract is either spray-dried or freeze-dried, the latter process resulting in more of the volatile components being retained in the dry product. The dried product from both processes needs to be quickly packaged in air-tight containers to limit loss of aroma and flavour. The beverage is prepared simply upon the addition of hot water or milk.

Cocoa

The prepared, clean beans are first roasted, which causes a series of complex chemical reactions, resulting in the development of the characteristic flavour and aroma. The powdered cocoa, obtained by processing the inner part — the nib — of the roasted bean, when made into the beverage by the addition of hot water and/or milk, is wholly consumed. From Table 9.5 it can be seen therefore that cocoa can add significantly to the nutritional value of the diet, apart from added milk or sugar. Besides the major components of protein and fat, cocoa contains only traces of tannin and caffeine, consequently its stimulant effect is much less than that of coffee or tea — making it more suitable for a bedtime drink.

Chocolate

Whilst mentioning chocolate it might be appropriate to show its components compared with those of cocoa. The main additions to cocoa powder are cocoa-butter, obtained during cocoa manufacture, sugar in fairly large amounts, and in the case of milk chocolate, milk solids as well.

The comparative approximate compositions are given below in Table 9.5.

Table 9.5. Composition of cocoa and chocolate

	Grams per 100 g			
	Fat	Protein	Carbohydrate	Kilocalories per 100 g
Chocolate, milk	30.3	8.4	59.4	529
Chocolate, plain	29.2	4.7	64.8	525
Cocoa powder	21.7	18.5	11.5	312

From the figures in Table 9.5 it is clear that chocolate can contribute greatly to the energy component of the diet, and that there is very little difference between milk and plain chocolate in this respect. Being such a palatable concentrated energy food, it is easy to see why it is used in the emergency rations of climbers, explorers, servicemen, and the like.

10

Convenience Foods

Introduction and Classification

The majority of foods that we eat today would have seemed novel to our ancestors. From biblical times efforts have been made to make food more convenient from the point of preserving, preparing, cooking, and storing. For the past thirty years the emergence of a large variety of foods in a greater state of preparedness for the caterer and the housewife has led to the words 'convenience foods' having a special connotation. There are however several definitions used from different sources which unfortunately do not match well with each other and only add to the confusion of what is really meant by the term 'convenience foods'.

Reports of the National Food Survey Committee define convenience foods as 'those processed foods for which the degree of preparation has been carried to an advanced stage by the manufacturer and which may be used as labour-saving alternatives to less highly processed products'. The convenience foods identified by the Survey are cooked and canned meats, meat products, cooked and canned fish, fish products, canned vegetables, vegetable products, canned fruit, fruit juices, cakes and pastries, biscuits, breakfast cereals, puddings, cereal products, instant coffee and coffee essences, baby foods, canned soups, dehydrated soups, ice-cream bought to serve with a meal and all 'cabinet trade' quick frozen foods, but not including uncooked poultry or uncooked whitefish.

The report by Arthur D. Little Ltd to the Hotels and Catering and Food Manufacturing EDC entitled 'Convenience Foods in Catering' defines con-cenience foods as 'those foods that have been converted by a manufacturer into a form more readily stored and prepared for consumption by others. However, the definition is limited to those foods that are in common use by caterers or consumers in both raw or fresh and convenienced forms. Thus flour, for example, is not included even though the manufacturer has converted it from grain into a more readily used form.'

Articles in the trade and national press define convenience foods as 'pre-prepared and frozen foods ready to be served with only a minimum of preparation such as heating, plating and garnishing'.

These definitions which are widely used are not in agreement with each other and illustrate how claims for the growth of convenience foods can differ depending upon what definition the claims are based. If the reader is to accept the second definition given as being most suitable a definition for 'convenienc*ed* foods' could well be necessary to cover items such as cakes, pastries, puddings, breakfast cereals, etc. If the first and second definitions are used it does not mean that the foods have to be frozen to be classified as convenience foods, as is often the suggestion by some food manufacturers. A solution to the problem of an acceptable definition could be to classify all foods that have been partially or completely processed as 'convenient foods'.

The classification of convenience foods can be approached in a number of ways.

Process of Manufacture

This method of classification is an important consideration, as the processing of a food item dictates to a large extent the methods of handling, storing, and preparing as well as the equipment requirements and the level of skills necessary by the operators to produce an acceptable dish for customers. The manufacturing processes would include canning, freezing, dehydration, accelerated freeze drying, and irradiation. Each of these methods is described in detail for the processing of specific foods within this book.

Convenience Food Product Sectors

These are the four main sectors: frozen foods, dehydrated foods, canned foods, and prepared and partly prepared foods. Each of these sectors compete against each other continually for an increase of their sector of a very large and increasing market.

Degree of Preparation that has taken place

This is in three classes:

(*a*) Items with a low degree of preparation, meaning basically washed and prepared vegetables, filleted fish, dressed poultry, prepared butchers meats, etc.

(*b*) Items with a medium degree of preparation and requiring only to be cooked, heated or mixed in some way such as portioned cuts of meat or fish, frozen, canned or boil in the bag soups and entrees, ready to cook pies, etc.

(*c*) Items that are ready to serve such as cold meat or sweet pies, ice-cream, canned fruit segments, prepared, canned or fresh hors d'oeuvres, etc.

Categories within a Menu

For example, appetizers, soups, entrees, sweets, etc. would be convenient categories.

The Production of Convenience Foods

There are three main processing methods for the production of convenience foods:

(i) Dehydration, e.g. fruits — currants, sultanas, raisins, figs, etc., vegetables — potatoes, carrots, peas, etc., soups — chicken, celery, etc.

(ii) Canning, e.g. fruits — peaches, pears, raspberries, etc., vegetables — carrots, beans, peas, etc., soups — of all types, puddings — milk, sponge, etc.

(iii) Freezing, e.g. fruits — raspberries, apples, etc., vegetables — peas, beans, potato chips, etc., entrees — meat and poultry dishes of all types, including many classical special entrees.

Each of these processes has its own particular advantages and disadvantages when compared with each other and with the fresh product. Each of the main processing methods are detailed quite fully in Chapter 7 in this book but may be simply summarized as follows.

Dehydration

This age old method is based on the principle of reducing the moisture content to a low level, below that at which moulds and decay can multiply. The reduction of the moisture content causes a reduction in the weight and volume, and the general appearance of the food.

There are three main methods of dehydration commonly used:

(a) Air-drying, the food that can be sun-dried or machine dried

(b) Dehydration which is a further stage to air-drying and involves the further removal of water. The end product of which may be pulverized if used for soup mixes, etc.

(c) Accelerated freeze drying which is a more recent process.

Canning

The principle of canning is the application of heat to food at temperatures high enough either to partially or completely sterilize the food, and the expulsion of air from the container after which it is then hermetically sealed to contain the vacuum created. A development of this is for the can to be replaced by strong aluminium foil sachets.

Freezing

The general principles of freezing are two-fold; to lower the temperature such that the rate of chemical reactions and the multiplication of micro-organisms are slowed down; and also more importantly to immobilize the water within the food as ice so that it cannot be used in chemical reactions or in microbial growth.

There are three main methods of freezing commonly used.

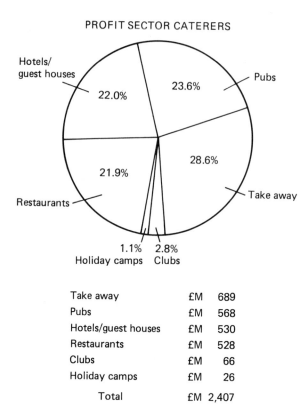

PROFIT SECTOR CATERERS

Take away	£M	689
Pubs	£M	568
Hotels/guest houses	£M	530
Restaurants	£M	528
Clubs	£M	66
Holiday camps	£M	26
Total	£M	2,407

Figure 10.1   Food and non-alcoholic drink purchases by profit sector
caterers (H.C.I.T.B., 1985)

Plate or Contact Freezing

This is used for flat products such as steaks, hamburgers, fish fingers, small
packages of vegetables and fruits, etc.

Blast Freezing

This is used for items that are individually frozen before being packaged such
as some fruits and vegetables and for entrée dishes that have an uneven top
surface and are unsuitable for plate or contact freezing.

Immersion Freezing

This is the immersion of the food in a type of refrigerant that will not con-
taminate the food. At present it has limited use mainly restricted to freezing
strawberries individually and for freezing shrink-wrapped poultry.

The Range of Convenience Foods

Convenience foods are manufactured in a very wide range covering all areas of the menu. The total number available being several hundreds with new products coming on to the market each week. The following are examples of some of the convenience products available under the main categories of a menu and in Table 10.1 the demand for each product is shown.

Table 10.1. The range of convenience foods

Food categories	Examples
APPETIZERS	Fresh fruit juices, orange and grapefruit segments, melon balls and pieces, stewed prunes and figs, chicken, duck, and pheasant patés, cheese and bacon flans, cannelloni and tomato sauce
SOUPS	A very full range from canned turtle soup and lobster soup to powdered tomato soup
FISH	Fish fingers, breaded fish portions, fish cakes, breaded or battered scampi, dressed crabs, lemon sole in prawns and mushrooms, lemon sole bonne femme
ENTREES	Sausage rolls, beefburgers, pizzas, cottage pies, cheese and onion croquettes, chicken and pork croquettes, meat and potato pies, cornish pasties, beef curry and rice, sliced beef/lamb/pork in gravy, steak pies, steak, kidney and mushroom pies
SPECIAL ENTREES	Beef bourguignonne, beef strogonoff, braised beef provençale, braised steak in cognac sauce, chicken chasseur, coq au vin, roast guinea fowl with peaches, duckling with orange sauce, duckling with honey and chestnuts, venison in red wine sauce
COMPLETE MEALS	(This refers just to the main course) roast beef, roast chicken, braised steak, boiled beef and dumplings, sausages with an onion sauce, savoury minced beef, liver and onions, haddock in parsley sauce. Each is complete with a portion of potatoes and of vegetables for customer's choice
VEGETABLES	Potato croquettes, potato chips (straight or crinkle cut), carrots (whole, sliced or diced), fluted carrot rings, cauliflower florets, corn on the cob, asparagus, stuffed cabbage, battered onion rings
SALADS	A full range of prepared salads, beetroot, potato, mixed, rice with peppers, cole slaw, etc.
SWEETS	Frozen gateaux of all types, cheese cakes, charlotte russe, profiteroles with a chocolate sauce, fruit flans, fruit pies, waffles, milk puddings, sponge puddings, fruit trifles, ice-cream of all types, speciality ices and gateaux

N.B. Many of the above items are available in single portion and multi-portion packs.

PRODUCT DEMAND – PROFIT SECTOR

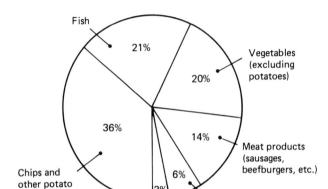

Figure 10.2 Catering demand breakdown for quick frozen convenience foods (data from Mintel, *Catering for Profit*)

N.B. 200,000 tonnes of quick frozen convenience products were sold into the catering industry in 1985, of which approximately 60% concerned the profit sector.

Table 10.2. *Profit sector sources of convenience food supply by value* (data from Market Power Survey 1984)

	% using		
	Direct purchasing	Wholesaler	Cash and carry
Hotels (large)	20	80	5
Hotels (small)	–	5	100
Restaurants	35	80	35
Pubs	–	80	40
Fast food	60	90	–
Travel	30	90	–
Cafes	–	40	60
Clubs	–	80	20

N.B. Dual use results in percentage adding up to more than 100%

The Role of Convenience Foods

The consideration of the role of convenience foods in the catering industry as a whole, would not give a true representation of the situation. The catering industry is itself made up of a great variety of outlets, from pubs, to hotels of every type, to restaurants, cafes, canteens, hospitals, school meals, and prisons. Each establishment is different and has peculiarities particular to its own operation and market, and thus its requirements for the use of any group or type of food will vary.

Without any doubt it can be stated that the use of convenience foods not only in the catering industry but also in the home is widespread and is likely to continue. The market penetration of convenience foods is in excess of 30% for many sectors of the industry and over 90% for some speciality fast-food chain operations.

The reasons for the growth of convenience foods are numerous, but amongst them are the pressures on the management of a catering operation to make a satisfactory profit (if operating in the commercial sector) or to operate within specified cost limits (if operating in the non-commercial sector); and the successful marketing by the manufacturers of all types of convenience foods.

Amongst the major problems facing a catering operation today are the following.

Food Costs
The maintenance of food costs at predetermined levels is of the greatest importance as it is in most cases the largest element of cost for an establishment. It is very difficult today to keep costs in line since due to matters such as increased production costs, inflation, etc., prices rise and also fluctuate more than in the past. When the price of purchasing a fresh food, together with the loss in preparation and cooking, becomes too high the caterer has the choice of taking the item off the menu, attempting to produce the same dish by using cheaper alternative fresh foods or by using a convenience food as an alternative. In most cases there will be a convenience food that is very similar to the original dish, and it is then up to the caterer to evaluate it with regard to cost, quality and acceptance by his type of customer.

Labour Costs
Next to food costs, labour costs are a significant element of the total cost of a prepared dish. The advantages of using convenience foods are that labour costs can be reduced because most of the preparation of the food has already taken place, fewer staff are needed and the number of highly skilled workers reduced.

Fuel Costs
The importance of fuel costs in the total costing of a dish has been of little significance in the past as fuels were very cheap. Today and in the near future fuels will not only be expensive, they will also be scarce and therefore they must be calculated and added to the total cost of a dish. High fuel costs will

be an important consideration to take into account in the future whenever a new catering establishment is being designed. The planned use of a high proportion of convenience foods will reduce the total fuel costs.

Capital Costs
The equipping of a new conventional kitchen (i.e. one that is designed to process all forms of fresh food) is very costly indeed. The equipping of a new kitchen that is required to process mainly convenience foods, for the same number of customers, is also costly but only half as much as that for a conventional kitchen.

Space Costs
Space is an expensive item and needs to be used correctly and efficiently. The conventional kitchen requires a very large amount of space, particularly for its storage and preparation areas, whilst the purpose planned convenience food kitchen requires on average only about 40% of the same space. The savings in space come from requiring less preparation and cooking areas.

It can be seen from the above that convenience foods do have some advantages to offer the caterer in five main problem areas and that they need to be seriously considered.

General Advantages and Disadvantages

Advantages

(i) The main cost elements of food, labour, fuel, capital, and space can be substantially reduced by a high usage of convenience foods.

(ii) There is a great variety of convenience foods available for the caterer to purchase, making it easy to select foods for the particular needs of his customers. This variety enables the menu to be interesting, exciting, and flexible.

(iii) By using the major manufacturers, the caterer is able to purchase products that are of a standard and consistent quality.

(iv) Purchases can be made in different forms, from single portion packs to 'catering packs' of 20–25 portions.

(v) The nutritional contents of most convenience foods are available.

(vi) The purchasing, receiving, and storage procedures are far less involved than when purchasing fresh foods. Stock control is much easier.

(vii) High level culinary skills are not required, as most of these foods are simply heated, plated, and garnished. Standard recipes as such are not required; in their place production and preparation instructions, with photographs, are substituted.

(viii) The over-production of food is reduced or eliminated as the preparation—cooking period is greatly reduced and food can easily be batch produced. The age-old problem of the use of 'left-overs' is eliminated.

(ix) Wastage due to poor preparation and over cooking is now no longer a problem.

(x) The standard of the food served to the customer is consistent even though there are long-term disadvantages as in (v) below.

(xi) The portion sizes for each dish can be easily standardized and are more easily controlled. The costing for each dish can be accurately determined.

(xii) Production space can be reduced considerably.

(xiii) Greater versatility is possible in handling production demands during off-peak service times and unexpected surges in business.

(xiv) The kitchen environment is more pleasant to work in, it is cleaner, the odours are reduced, the working temperature and humidity are lower, and it is more quiet and orderly.

(xv) Management time is freed from a lot of control work allowing more time to be spent on merchandizing the food to increase customer numbers and satisfaction.

Disadvantages

(i) A caterer with a specially designed convenience food kitchen is very much at the mercy of the food manufacturers with regard to supplies. It would be difficult for him to switch to producing fresh food dishes.

(ii) A high capital investment is necessary to purchase special equipment to process any quantity of convenience foods on a regular basis.

(iii) Power failures can result in major disruptions to the business.

(iv) Power failures can affect storage temperatures, cause partial thawing of frozen items and result in spoilage.

(v) There is little or no product standardization by manufacturers. There is also the problem of manufacturers changing their specification for a product without informing the caterer.

(vi) There is little or no packaging standardization by the manufacturers.

(vii) Packages do not have complete instructions for the recommended preparation procedures.

(viii) Distribution by manufacturers and wholesalers is limited reducing the range of foods available. Purchasing of less than one case is also a problem for the small unit that wishes to try a new product.

(ix) There is no guarantee by manufacturers that a particular product range will be produced for a definite minimum period.

(x) The claims by food manufacturers about their products are not substantiated by the experience of the caterer, e.g. a manufacturer claims that the contents of a package of dried peas will produce 100 x 2oz portions. The caterer after following precisely the instructions on the package is only able to obtain 90 x 2oz portions. Fake claims by manufacturers require the caterer to recost each item himself, a step that should be unnecessary.

(xi) The need for greater appreciation and imagination on the part of the food preparation and service personnel in order to plate and garnish convenience foods properly and attractively to make them more appealing to customers.

(xii) Unfortunately there is a built-in resistance by some food employees to handling convenience foods. Some are of the opinion that it is just another method by management to increase profits, whilst others fear it is de-skilling their job.

(xiii) There is a need for more government control in the general area of convenience foods. New legislation in such areas as the following would be a help to caterers:

(*a*) An extension of the grading of fruits and vegetables as required by the E.C. into frozen, dehydrated, and canned produce.

(*b*) A tightening of the labelling requirements on canned and frozen foods so that the contents of the major items are more accurately defined.

(*c*) The drained weights of canned foods to be clearly stated on all cans.

(*d*) A tightening of the laws to restrict fake claims, mainly of the number of portions obtainable, by food manufacturers in the advertising and labelling of their products.

(*e*) The date stamping of all produce at the time it is packaged.

(*f*) Some standardization of pack sizes, particularly with frozen entrée dishes.

The Problems of Quality and Cost Comparison

Most food manufacturers have as their first priority the supply of their products to the consumer market because it is a larger and more valuable market than the catering industry. However, in recent years food manufacturers have become aware of the size and the potential market for their products in the catering industry and are now very involved with supplying the industry in a major way, frequently producing items specifically for the industry.

The convenience food produced by a manufacturer can be measured simply in two ways; by the quality of the food; and by its cost.

Quality

'Quality' is a difficult subject to be precise about, because it has different meanings for different people. To the manufacturer or food technologist it is something which they can measure in precise terms such as the colour of a batch of tomato soup, the tenderness of green peas before and after freezing, the sugar content required in a can of strawberries, the gluten strength in a flour, etc. To the caterer it can mean many things most of which are subjective opinions of his own. It is common practice that catering companies will have an established practice of evaluating new products by a taste panel consisting of people such as the catering manager, head chef, restaurant manager and purchasing manager. They would 'blind test' (i.e. test products without knowing any details such as the manufacturer or the price) a range of similar produce and award marks for various points on a prepared score sheet. The marks awarded by each member of the taste panel for each food item under test would be added up and then compared against the cost information for each item. Ideally the food item scoring the highest number of points in total together with the lowest food cost would be chosen for purchase.

On testing cans of pears the typical headings on a score sheet could be as follows:

TEST ITEM . . . .

(*a*) Gross weight of can
(*b*) Net weight of contents
(*c*) Drained weight of contents
(*d*) Count (i.e. number of pear halves)
(*e*) Colour (max. 5 points)
(*f*) Taste (max. 10 points)
(*g*) Uniformity of size (max. 5 points)
(*h*) Absence of defects (max. 5 points)
(*i*) Quality of syrup (max. 5 points)
(*j*) TOTAL SCORE (max. 30 points)
(*k*) Cost per can
(*l*) Cost of each pear half

Any food item which would be heated or cooked prior to serving to the customer must be heated or cooked in the usual way before being tested. Similarly, if the item is likely to be held in a container on a service counter for half an hour before being served to a customer, it should only be tested after being held under identical conditions.

Some convenience food service systems depend on efficient packaging and this also has to be taken into account when selecting the suitability of an item. Good packaging will protect the food from micro-organisms, and prevent evaporation or dehydration. The packaging should be well labelled, rigidly constructed and be easily opened. The module type container package that remains intact throughout the entire operation from storage to service reduces many handling stages.

Cost

The costing of most convenience type foods is relatively simple, often the cost is of just the food item itself, at other times the cost of the garnish must be added. The prices paid by caterers for convenience foods are often considered to be too high when comparing the cost of a pound of a convenience food with its fresh equivalent. The food manufacturers of the product point out that the higher price includes the preparation, trimming and cooking at times, as well as the labour and expertise costs in its production, which the caterer does not now have to provide by using their convenience foods; the net effect being a cost saving to the caterer. The saving of preparation losses is easily acceptable, but to achieve the overall cost saving the caterer must save labour and this is not always easy. By saving a few hours work here and there in a total kitchen operation not necessarily one employee less will be required. The effect of using convenience foods but not reducing the labour force will result in an increase in costs.

What is more difficult to do is a true comparison between the cost of producing fresh food dishes in a conventional kitchen and producing dishes from convenient foods. This is because the cost of space, labour, fuel and equipment depreciation have also to be taken into account, as well as the problem of customer acceptance of convenience foods which may well affect the turnover and profit. Savings can be quite considerable if the catering operation changes over to a complete convenience food operation that is properly designed and marketed. However, it is not quite as simple as supposed, as to date no one food manufacturer's present list of products meet the needs of the large full meal service caterer. This causes the caterer the problem of having to deal with many food manufacturers to satisfy his total menu requirements as well as being faced with the complexity of different pack sizes, varying processing times for similar products, etc. In addition, there is the problem of having to produce salads and egg dishes by conventional means.

A solution to overcome the problems of using convenience foods produced by food manufacturers with the limitations as given above is for large catering establishments and companies to produce their own cook/freeze products. This has been done very successfully in the school meal and the hospital service where the food is prepared in a large production kitchen, cooked, portioned into 8–12 portion packs, frozen in a blast freezer within 90 minutes, stored at $-18°C$ $(0°F)$, transported in the frozen state and reheated in convection ovens 25 minutes before service. This method, operated by caterers is claimed to:

(i) give them full control of the quality of food they wish for their customers,
(ii) allow a better utilization of equipment and labour with a higher level of productivity as a result of separating the two elements of production and food service,
(iii) the range of dishes offered can be wider and take into account regional and local preferences,
(iv) the nutritional value is potentially better than food produced in a conventional kitchen.

The full control over quality and the wider range of dishes available are a distinct advantage over using just food manufacturer's products.

The Future of Convenience Foods

The future of convenience foods seems assured, subject of course to the food manufacturing industry not becoming too aloof from the catering industry and working in liaison with their customers, the caterers.

The main concern of the caterers regarding convenience foods are outlined in the disadvantages given earlier in this chapter, but are particularly those relating to the need for a consistent and acceptable product standardization as well as package size standardization.

The growth of the usage of convenience foods will continue, but not perhaps at the same rate as there has been in the past ten years. Several factors will contribute to this growth, the high cost of space for food preparation areas, an increase in the marketing of specialized type catering operations using convenience foods either totally or partially, the high cost of control when using conventional foods, the lack of highly skilled chefs, and an unwillingness for catering staff to work unsocial hours when workers in other industries are having increased leisure time awarded to them.

Developments are most likely to occur in the packaging of convenience foods with 'heat-in', 'serve-in' and 'drink-from' type packaging becoming commonplace in the near future replacing the conventional tin can or glass container, from which neither are totally suitable for storage, heating, and eating or drinking.

Scientific and Nutritional Aspects

It would seem that for the most part, present-day methods of food processing and food production, cause no major losses to food's nutritional value, and those that do occur are counter-balanced by the very mixed nature of most people's diet. Very few people confine their food intake to one type of processed food!

Much more food gets into the everyday diet of more people the world over, because of modern food technology. However, because technology is perfecting new methods of processing, and also fabricating new types of product, the nutritionist and food scientist must continue to monitor and evaluate processes in terms of safety and nutritional values.

On balance it can be safely said that modern processed foods — convenience foods — are playing an important and successful role in feeding modern man. They provide also a valuable source of materials from which the caterer can prepare his products for his customer — but he must make sure that he treats them with the care and respect with which he would treat a fresh commodity, otherwise the result can be far from satisfactory — the blame being placed on the caterer and not on the product.

11

Introduction to Meat

Meat is usually accepted as being the most important food purchased by the caterer. This is for two main reasons: first it is normally the central focus of a meal and its selection determines the other foods that will be served: and second it is common for 40–60% of the total expenditure on food to be spent on meat.

Meat is defined by the E.E.C. regulations as any part of a bovine (beef-type animal), pig, sheep, goat, horse, ass or mule that is fit for human consumption. The types of animals from which meat may be obtained indicates the variations of eating habits within the E.E.C. countries. In the U.K. the main sources of meat are from bovines, pigs, and sheep and include not only carcase meat but offal (liver, kidneys, etc.). The general term meat includes carcase meat often in the form of joints, offal such as liver, kidneys, etc., and processed meats such as pickled beef, hamburgers, sausages, etc.

Meat may be classified in seven main ways:

(a) by the type of animal, e.g. bovines (beef/veal), porcine (pork), ovines (lamb/mutton);

(b) by the country of origin, e.g. Scotland, Eire, New Zealand, etc;

(c) by the age and/or sex of the animal, e.g. steer beef, bull beef, cow beef, lamb, mutton, etc;

(d) the grade of the meat, e.g. a carcase of New Zealand lamb of high quality and with a weight range of 16·5–2·5 kg is sold by the grade of PH;

(e) by the particular cut of meat, e.g. sirloin of beef, saddle of lamb, etc;

(f) by the condition of the meat, e.g. fresh, chilled, frozen, pickled, etc;

(g) by their catering uses, e.g. suitable for roasting, frying, grilling, boiling, etc.

Breeds of Animals

The worldwide increase in the demand for meat brought about by the wealth of the developing countries, a general higher standard of living in developed countries and established advances in the preservation and transport of meat, has resulted in newer breeds of animals becoming established as meat-producing animals to meet the demand. The new breeds of animals are those which in the main are suitable for being reared by intensive farming methods, capable of consistently producing meat of a specific quality and weight range, having a high meat to bone ratio, and a high conversion rate (i.e. the efficiency by which the animals convert the intake of foodstuffs into an increase in their body weight). The new breeds of animals produced have to meet the demands of the caterer, general public and food processor as meat of a consistently high quality with a low fat content and at a reasonable price is required. A brief mention of specific breeds for different types of meat is given later in subsequent chapters on meat.

The Slaughter of Animals

The slaughter of animals which are for sale for human consumption is rigidly controlled by law to ensure that the animal suffers no pain at all, that the method of slaughtering and subsequent preparation of the carcases takes place under hygienic conditions in licenced slaughterhouses and that the meat is inspected by authorized officers and found to be fit before being permitted to be sold for human consumption.

The slaughtering of animals is in five main stages.

Ante-mortem inspection
Animals to be slaughtered are brought to the slaughterhouse and kept in lairages usually for a minimum of 24 hours. This resting has a beneficial effect on the quality of the dressed carcase. The inspection of each animal is done to identify any signs of disease, injury, distress, etc., prior to the animal entering the slaughterhouse. An animal identified as being unfit would be isolated from other animals and appropriate action taken often on the advice of a veterinary surgeon.

Stunning
Fit animals are taken into the slaughterhouse and individually stunned by one of the following methods.

Captive Bolt
This is the stunning of the animal by a captive bolt pistol and is used for large animals such as bovines and large male pigs. Bovines are also pithed to minimize any subsequent reflex muscular action which could take place during the sticking and dressing of the carcase. Pithing is done by inserting a long thin metal rod through the hole in the skull made by the bolt, which has the effect of destroying the part of the brain which controls the reflexes.

Electrical Stunning
This method is the passing of a small current of electricity through the brain of small animals such as baby calves, pigs, and sheep for at least 7 seconds. It is done by applying a pair of special tongs, connected to an electricity supply,

behind the ears of the animal. This method renders the animal unconscious for up to $1\frac{1}{2}$ minutes.

Carbon Dioxide Stunning

This method is used for stunning pigs. The pigs are placed on a moving platform which passes through a tunnel containing a mixture of CO_2 and air and renders the pigs unconscious. The particular benefit of this method is that the subsequent bleeding of the animal is more efficient.

Bleeding of the Animal

After the animal has been stunned it is bled by making a small incision along the side of the neck and cutting the main blood vessels. The animal is usually hung up by the hind legs during this stage. It is important that as much blood as possible should be removed from the body after death as blood is an ideal medium for the growth of the bacteria which causes decomposition. The flesh of an inefficiently bled animal putrefies very quickly.

Dressing the Animal

In this stage the hide of the animal is removed for bovines and sheep, and only the hair for pigs. The animal is cut open along the chest and stomach and the offal and viscera (intestines, etc.) removed. Large animals such as bovines and pigs are usually split down the vertebrae into two sides to facilitate handling.

Inspection

This is a continuous process in that as soon as anything unusual in the animal or carcase is noticed it is brought to the attention of a meat inspector. Any part of the animal that is removed from the carcase must, if required for sale for human consumption, be inspected and be identifiable with the carcase from which it came. That is, any blood, offal or viscera must be identifiable with the same tag number as the carcase just in case something of a serious nature is found which may result in all or part being condemned as unfit. The final inspection is of the carcase and usually takes place in the cooling room. All of the inspection is of a visual nature and is only helped by the cutting of certain parts of the carcase (e.g. lymph nodes) for detailed examination.

During the period in the cooling room the meat will go through a stage of setting (or rigor mortis) and the muscles and joints become stiff. After a period of time the setting passes off and the carcase becomes relatively limp again. After the carcase has passed inspection and has been cooled to below $7°C$ ($45°F$) it is ready for storage prior to sale or further processing (*see* Chapter 10).

The Animal Body

There are three main parts of the animal body that the caterer is mainly interested in: the skeletal structure; muscles; and fat.

Skeletal Structure

This consists of the framework composed of the bones of the animal which are joined together in their natural positions by ligaments and joints.

The importance of knowing the different bones and their position in the carcase of an animal is because meat cutting in the U.K. is based on the bone structure of the animal. It becomes of further importance when preparing purchasing specifications for joints and cuts of meat.

The skeletal structure may be divided up into the head, the trunk, and the limbs.

The Head

This consists of the skull, the upper jaw bone, containing the upper teeth, and attached to the skull and the lower jaw bone, containing the lower teeth, which is attached to the skull by ligaments. The head itself articulating with the first cervical (neck) vertebrae.

The Trunk

This consists of three main parts, the various vertebrae, the ribs and the sternum (or breast bone).

THE VERTEBRAE. There are five types of vertebrae which are named according to their position in the body.

(i) Cervical or neck vertebrae.
(ii) Dorsal or thoracic vertebrae – these are the vertebrae of the back on which the ribs articulate.
(iii) Lumbar vertebrae – situated in the loin region.
(iv) Sacral vertebrae – situated in the pelvic (hip) region. These bones are often fused together to form the sacrum and they articulate with the pelvic (or H bone) to form the pelvis.
(v) Coccygeal or tailbone.

THE RIBS. There are two main types of ribs.

(i) The true ribs which articulate directly with the sternum (or breast bone).
(ii) The false ribs which articulate with each other and are connected to the sternum by a piece of cartilage.

THE STERNUM (BREAST BONE). This is a long flat bone consisting of 6–8 pieces of bone held together by cartilage.

The Limbs

They consist of the fore-limbs and hind-limbs.

(i) Fore-limb – containing all of the bones from the shoulder blade to the elbow joint.
(ii) Hind-limb – containing all of the bones from the pelvic bone (H bone) to the hock bone (or tarsus).

See Figure 11.1 for the skeleton of a beef type animal.

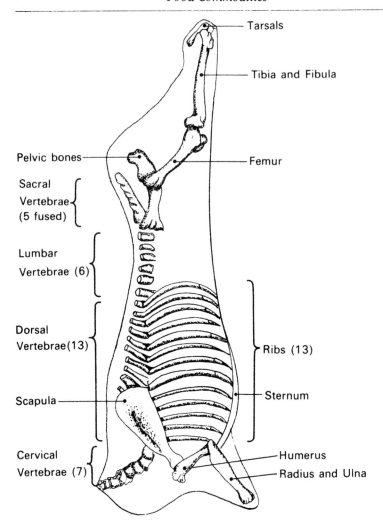

Figure 11.1 Skeletal structure of a beef carcase

The skeletal structure of bovines, sheep, pigs, and the horse are very similar, *see* Table 11.1.

Table 11.1. Comparison of vertebrae and rib bones in four food animals

Animal	Cervical	Dorsal	Lumbar	Sacral	Coccygeal	Ribs (pairs)
Bovines	7	13	6	5	18–20	13
Sheep	7	13	6–7	5	16–18	13
Pigs	7	14–15	6–7	4	20–23	14
Horses	7	18	5	5	18–20	18

Muscles

The movements of animals are caused by the muscles of the animal which have the power to contract. The size and shape of the muscles of the body giving the animal its particular shape. It is the muscle of the animal together with any associated fat that is commonly referred to as meat.

Muscles are divided into three types.

Skeletal Muscles

These are described as 'striped' ('striated') or 'voluntary', are attached to the bones and are under the control of the animal.

Plain Muscles

Plain muscles are described as 'non-striated' or 'involuntary' are those which are the tissue of the intestines, the liver and the kidneys. In general terms the offal of the animal.

Heart Muscle

This is 'striated' but different from voluntary muscles and not under the control of the animal.

Muscle Tissue

Muscle tissue is composed of very small elongated cells called muscle fibres, which are bound into bundles by connective tissue. 'Striped' muscle is composed of innumerable parallel fibres which show up under a microscope as fine transverse striations. The end of each skeletal muscle is extended to form a tendon which is inserted into an adjacent bone. (*See* Figure 11.2 for diagram of cross-section and Figure 11.3 longitudinal section of a skeletal muscle.)

The proportions of connective tissue in a muscle depend on the activity of the muscle in the live animal. The muscles in the lower part of the legs of a large animal, such as a steer, are subject to much greater stress during standing and walking and consequently contain a greater amount of connective tissue than the muscles in the small of the back, which has relatively little stress or strain applied to it. Connective tissue contains a large amount of a tough substance called collagen which can be converted by boiling to gelatin. Thus, any joints containing a high proportion of connective tissue (and therefore collagen) will require a moist and slow method of cooking (boiling and stewing) whilst those with little connective tissue may suitably be used for dry and quick methods (roasting and grilling).

The colour of the muscle depends on the type of animal, its age, whether it is fresh or preserved in some form and how long the cut surface has been exposed to the air.

Fat

Fat is deposited in and on an animal as a reserve store of energy or nourishment for its body. As a poor conductor of heat it also prevents loss of body heat. With the growth of the animal the fat is laid down in the following order, first around the intestines, then the kidneys, then in the rump region and finally

Blood vessels

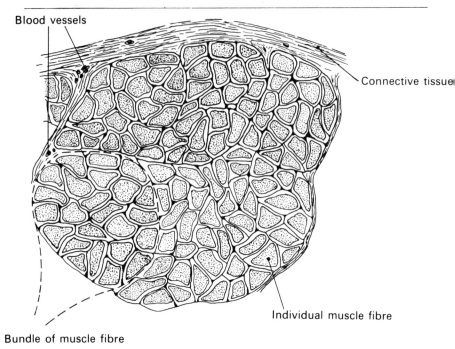

Connective tissue

Individual muscle fibre

Bundle of muscle fibre

Figure 11.2 Cross-section of muscle showing bundles of fibres

Tendon connected to bone

Connective tissue

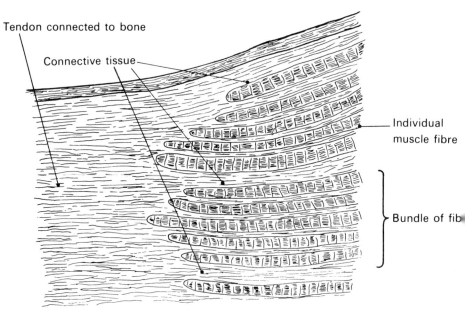

Individual
muscle fibre

Bundle of fib

Figure 11.3 Longitudinal section of voluntary muscle, showing bundles of
muscle fibres surrounded by connective tissue

along the back, the belly, neck, and lower parts of the legs. Therefore a very young animal such as a veal calf will have almost no visible fat to its carcase other than a small amount around the kidneys. Besides age, the type of feed will affect the quantity of fat laid down by an animal as also will its state of health. The colour of the fat will depend on the type of animal, the breed, the type of feed, its state of health and also its age.

An important point from the palatability aspect is the melting point of the different fats. External fats, the fats laid down on the surface of a carcase, have a relatively low melting point of about 32–35°C (90–95°F) whereas internal fats such as kidney fat (or suet) have a melting point of about 49°C (120°F). Fat is also deposited between muscle fibres and is known as 'marbling'. It is clearly seen on the cut surface of quality grade meats as tiny white flecks. It is an indication of quality and of the degree of finish to the carcase. The fat introduces flavour into cooked meats and whilst being cooked provides a constant basting effect to the muscle bundles, preventing the meat from being completely dry.

Composition of Meat

Meat as purchased contains blood vessels, fat, bones, connective tissue, muscle tissue and pieces of spinal cord. The tables below give some idea of the composition of various types of meat.

Table 11.2. Average composition per 100g in terms of protein, fat and water, of whole carcase meat is shown

Meat	Protein (g)	Fat (g)	Water (g)	Calories
Beef	15	28	56	312
Mutton	13	31	55	331
Pork	12	40	47	408

Clearly Table 11.2 only gives a very rough guide to composition and individual cuts vary greatly in their composition, and Table 11.3 gives a few examples for comparison.

The Constituents of Meat

Protein

(i) The contractile matter of the muscle consists mainly of two proteins, termed myosin and actin. During contraction the two join to form actomyosin — a similar condition exists shortly after the death of the animal in rigor mortis when the meat is rigid and tough.

(ii) Structural protein — the connective tissue — is also mainly composed of two proteins, collagen and elastin. It is these which contribute to toughness in the texture, and are formed in larger quantities in mature animals than in young ones. When meat is cooked in moist conditions collagen is converted into gelatine, a protein which is soluble in water — hence muscle is liable to fall apart when overcooked.

Table 11.3. Composition of various samples of meat per 100 g

Meat	Description	Protein (g)	Fat (g)	Water (g)	Kilocalories	Percentage* edible portion
Beef	Rump steak, raw	18.9	13.5	66.7	197	95
Beef	Rump steak, fried	28.6	14.6	56.2	246	70
Beef	Silverside, boiled	28.6	14.2	54.5	242	56
Beef	Stewing steak – stewed	30.9	11.0	57.1	223	60
Beef	Topside, roast	26.6	12.0	60.2	214	74
Lamb	Chops, loin, raw	14.6	35.4	49.5	377	82
Lamb	Chops, grilled	23.5	29.0	46.6	355	54
Lamb	Leg, roast	26.1	17.9	55.3	266	53
Pork	Chops, loin, raw	15.9	29.5	54.3	329	83
Pork	Chops, grilled	28.5	24.2	46.3	332	49
Pork	Leg, roast	26.9	19.8	51.9	286	60
Veal	Fillet, raw	21.1	2.7	74.9	109	100
Veal	Fillet, roast	31.6	11.5	55.1	230	75

*This column represents edible portion as an average percentage of weight purchased.

Fat

Adipose tissue (fat cells) often surrounds muscles, and also fat cells are formed within muscles themselves. It is the latter which give rise to the 'marbling' effect or sheen sometimes seen on cut meat. These fat cells contribute to the juiciness of the meat, helping to prevent moisture loss.

The colour and texture of the fat varies — beef fat is yellow, while that of mutton is white and harder, and that of pork white and softer (*see* Chapter 3 for explanation). The younger an animal is, then generally the less fat is associated with the meat.

Carbohydrate

The polysaccharide glycogen is present in living muscle, but when the animal is killed, it is converted into lactic acid by enzymes present in the cells. This process contributes to the ageing process which improves the tenderness of meat during hanging.

Colour

Principally the colour of meat is due to two iron-containing proteins.

HAEMOGLOBIN. The red oxygen-carrying protein of the blood contributes to the colour, because blood vessels run throughout the muscle, and even though much of the blood is drained at slaughter, some leaks out of the capillaries into the surrounding flesh.

MYOGLOBIN. Another pigmented protein, myoglobin, within the muscle contributes to colour in the following way: in freshly cut meat myoglobin imparts a purplish-red colour to the flesh; while if exposed to air it is converted to oxymyoglobin which is a brighter red. However, there is a further process which takes place as the meat ages converting the myoglobin into metmyoglobin, which is a brownish red. When meat is cooked this pigmented substance breaks down into brownish substances — the characteristic colour of cooked meat.

Flavour

So-called 'extractives' contribute to the flavour of meat. They are substances produced during living muscle metabolism including lactic acid, and end-products of protein metabolism, e.g. urea, uric acid, and some amino-acids. Other nitrogenous compounds also considered very important in this connection are creatine and creatinine. However, all the factors which go together to make meat flavour are by no means fully understood.

Nutritional Aspects

Meat is particularly valued because it is a good source of high biological value protein. It is also a good source of energy, because fat is always present in meat in varying quantities.

Meats are usually rich in iron and phosphorus (as phosphates) and provide significant quantities of B group vitamins, i.e. about 50% of the recommended intake of nicotinic acid comes from meat in the U.K., as does about 25% of the recommended intake of riboflavin. While thiamin is found in meat, there is very little vitamin A, and no vitamin D or C.

Post-mortem Changes in Meat

Muscle in the live state is not really the meat with which the caterer and the consumer is familiar. Although meat to a great extent does reflect the chemical and physical nature of the muscle from which it comes, it differs significantly because of the many and varied biochemical and biophysical changes which, initiated by slaughter, occur during storage.

A few hours after death rigor mortis occurs when the muscle tissue contracts because of the formation of the actomyosin complex in the absence of adenosine triphosphate (a compound which in life provides energy to the muscles allowing them to contract and relax normally). At this stage the meat is tough and rigid, it is therefore not consumed until after a period of storage (known as 'conditioning'). Probably maximum tenderness will be achieved after a fortnight's storage of $0°C$ (or 4–5 days at $10°C$).

During the conditioning period the acid content of the muscle goes up due to the formation of lactic acid from the glycogen stores in the muscle. For example, the pH might change from pH 7·4 to 5·5. Two notable things are affected by this pH change:

    (i) If the pH falls to about 5·5 then the myoglobin pigment's red colour is enhanced and the meat has a good appearance, while if a pH of only 6·6 is achieved a darker coloured meat is obtained (*see* earlier comments on colour also).

    (ii) A low pH of about 5·5 brings about denaturation of some of the protein which can improve tenderness, but at the same time may reduce water-holding properties.

Hanging produces an increase in flavour, because of enzyme action on proteins; proteins are partially hydrolysed, and the hydrolysis products, amino acids and other nitrogenous compounds, contribute to the flavour of the meat. The breakdown of proteins in this way also increases the tenderness of the product.

There are also some changes in the fat content during hanging or conditioning — especially at the surface. A small amount of lipolytic (fat-splitting) enzyme action proceeds to produce glycerol and fatty acids, and this rancidity contributes to the overall flavour of the meat. A darkening in colour of the fat is often associated with these changes during hanging.

Carcase Quality

The quality of the carcase of an animal is something which is extremely difficult to judge and requires years of experience to become proficient.

The quality of a carcase is affected at two main stages prior to it reaching the caterer.

The Ante-mortem Stage

Breed

The breed of an animal can affect the quality of a carcase in as much as specific breeds are suitable for specific purposes.

For example, the breeds of sheep may be placed into three general groups:

    (i) wool producing breeds;
    (ii) meat producing breeds;
    (iii) dual purpose breeds, i.e. those breeds with a good average quantity of wool and an average carcase quality.

Quite understandably the carcase quality from a meat producing breed would be much better than that from a wool producing breed.

Sex

The sex of an animal after several months growth will affect the quality of a carcase.

For example, a cow carcase in general has a low amount of muscular development with a poor meat to bone ratio. Bull beef will usually have very heavy forequarters, large muscular development and dark coloured meat with a coarse texture.

Age

The age of an animal will quite naturally affect the size and quality of a carcase.

For example, the carcase of English veal will be small in size, about 35–50lb, be of a pale pinkish colour and have little or no fat covering. The carcase of bull beef will be very large in size, about 700–800lb, be a dark red in colour and have often a dark yellow fat covering.

Type of Feed and Method of Rearing

For example, young beef calves fed on milk or milk substitutes will produce a very pale pink carcase, whilst those fed on grass will produce a much darker coloured carcase. Intensively reared young calves fed on barley will produce a larger carcase than if fed on grass and be of a pale red colour.

The Post-mortem Stage

The Slaughter Stage

This is without doubt the most important stage in obtaining quality meat. The efficiency of the slaughter stage from the resting of the live animal to the final dressing of the carcase can seriously affect the final quality of the carcase. A good grade of animal, if under stress prior to slaughter and inefficiently slaughtered, would result in producing a carcase of poor quality only.

The Storage Stage

The rate of rigor mortis, the efficiency of cooling of the carcase and the efficiency of the storage conditions will all affect the quality of a carcase. Too rapid a chilling stage produces a condition known as 'cold shortening', causing the cooked meat to be tough.

Judgement of Quality

The recognition of quality in a carcase as has been stated previously is something which requires years of experience to become proficient. It is usual to examine a carcase for quality under the three headings of conformation, finish, and quality.

Conformation
This refers to the shape and size of the carcase. It is usual that a good conformation in a carcase would be one that was compact in shape, be well and evenly fleshed with a high proportion of the more valuable joints of meat and a small percentage of bone.

Finish
This refers to the quantity, colour, and character of the fat on the carcase. A good carcase would have a smooth, even layer of external fat of the correct colour and texture. Also, small deposits of intra-muscular fat (marbling) would be expected to be evident in the cut surface of a major muscle. A high degree of finish, although indicating good feeding and quality for taste is not so readily acceptable today with consumer demands for lean meat.

Quality
This refers to the texture of the muscle in conjunction with conformation and finish. A fine, smooth texture with evidence of 'marbling' is the usual requirement. As stated previously quality can be affected by such things as breed, sex, age, etc. Age is determined by the texture of the meat and the amount of cartilage present at the extremities of the bones.

Grading of Meat

The grading of carcase meat is done by either the government departments of producing countries such as New Zealand and the United States of America or by local producers/packers as in Australia where there is no national grading scheme. Most methods use the species, the sex, the weight range, conformation, quality and finish as the framework for grading. Examples of grading by exporting countries are given in the next chapter. Unfortunately in the U.K. there is no national grading scheme at present for home produced meat. However, the Meat and Livestock Commission offers a carcase classification service to the British meat industry as an aid to better marketing. An example of the beef carcase classification scheme is given in Figure 11.5.

The advantages of an efficient grading scheme for the caterer are numerous and include such major points as:

(i) when it is a national grading scheme, the country concerned will enforce rigid inspection and quality control to ensure that a high and consistent standard is maintained;

(ii) it removes the need for the caterer to go to the market or wholesaler to select each carcase that he wishes to buy. All that he needs to do is to specify the grade he requires for his establishment;

(iii) with a standard carcase, it means that standard butchery procedures may be used, producing standard cuts of standard weights. all assist in making the food control aspects easier.

Effects of Preservation Methods on Meat

Freezing

Most authorities comment that this preservation method tends to increase tenderness, provided that the meat is prevented from drying (sometimes referred to as 'freezer-burn') i.e. protected by a moisture-proof film. Perhaps the major problem associated with frozen meat is that of 'thaw-drip' upon defrosting, when water soluble substances – vitamins and minerals – may be lost.

Canning

This process may be regarded as very similar to moist cooking. In general there is little nutritional change, with virtually no loss of protein and varying losses in B group vitamins, depending upon the cooking temperature, from 10 to 30%. The main changes are in terms of texture caused by denaturing, and consequently tenderizing, the meat proteins, and hydrolyzing the connective tissue with similar results. Overcooking results in the meat structure falling apart.

Drying

Textural changes occur here, the reconstituted product often being described as tough, fibrous, and stringy. However, there are few nutritional losses.

Salting and Curing

These processes do not significantly affect the nutritional quality of the product. The main points to note concern colour and flavour, the latter depending upon the concentration and nature of the added salts. Sodium chloride preserves by exerting an osmotic pressure upon bacterial cells thus killing them by dehydration, while sodium nitrate has a bactericidal effect by oxidation, itself being converted to sodium nitrite. This nitrite, whether formed in the way described, or added intentionally, combines with the pigment myoglobin to form pink nitrosomyoglobin. It is this latter pigment that accounts for the characteristic colour of bacon, ham, tongue, corned beef, and the like.

Storage of Meat and Meat Products

If meat has been frozen (imported perhaps), and is not to be stored in this state, then it should be thawed out in a cold room, not in a warm place, otherwise thaw-drip will be accentuated, and there will be a loss in quality.

Always store cooked meat well away from uncooked meat, to avoid cross-contamination.

The ideal storage temperature for fresh meat is $1°C$ ($30°F$) at a relative humidity of 90%. Safe storage times achieved under hygienic conditions are – beef: 3 weeks; veal: 1–3 weeks; lamb: 1–2 weeks; pork: 1–2 weeks; and edible offal: 4 days.

Frozen meat keeps well at $-18°C$ ($0°F$) for at least six months. While freezing inhibits microbial growth, long periods of storage below freezing point may produce considerable rancidity in the exposed fat, in particular the softer fat of pork meat.

Meat Analogues (Substitutes)

Meat is an expensive produce because of the time taken by animals to convert their food into muscle, which becomes our meat. Also as much as 90% of the protein in animal fodder is used simply to keep the animal alive, and often as little as 10% may be recovered as the final end-product, meat. If then, one could produce a vegetable substitute of a similarly high biological value, and palatably acceptable, one would get a much more efficient return on cultivated land — and hence, one hopes, a cheaper product.

If soya bean meal could be consumed directly by man then the 10% efficiency spoken of above could rise to about 70% but soya bean meal is not very palatable, therefore sophisticated processes are applied to it, in an effort to produce a product comparable to meat. It should be noted that soya flour has a comparatively high biological value, whereas many vegetable products have relatively low ones — for example, if meat on average is given a rating of 75 on a 'biological value scale', then soya flour has a rating of 67, whereas wheat has 49, and maize has 36, while egg achieves a rating of 83.

Production

The flow chart (Figure 11.4) indicates the various processes applied to soya in an effort to produce a meat analogue.

Uses

After initial production, the individual products can be ground (mince-like) or diced (stew-like). In this state they are analogous to cooked meat, and can be used in the same way, i.e. they can be frozen, canned or, as is most often the case, dehydrated (shelf-life one year approximately).

A simple comparison is shown below between the two basic varieties of product.

	Textured Vegetable Proteins	*Spun Proteins*
Advantages	Economical Fair texture Takes up flavour well Merges into made-up dishes well	Good texture
Disadvantages	Texture not as good as spun product	Price — almost as expensive as meat. To effect any saving has to replace wholly meat on a dish. Since it has to be used as a substitute, relies on artificial flavours, which are not always good.

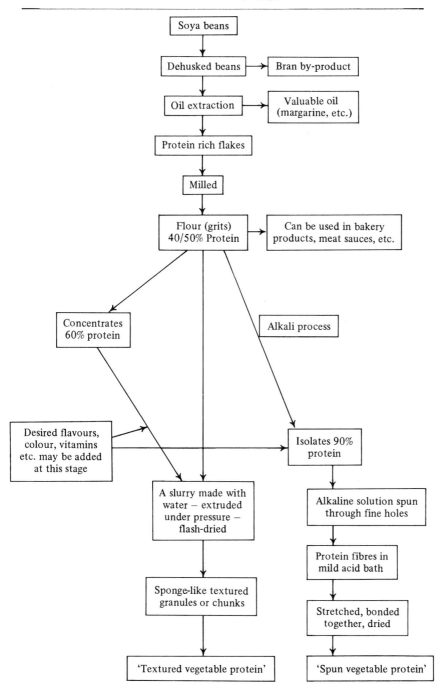

Figure 11.4 A flow chart showing important stages in the manufacture of meat analogues from soya

These products can be used to supplement the normal meat component of foods such as meat pies, minces, stews, sausages, etc. Under the Food and Drugs Act (1955) and compositional regulations, however, these soya products cannot count towards the minimum specified meat content. As far as institutional meals (those in hospitals, schools, old-people's homes, etc.), are concerned the Food Standards Committee report on Novel Protein Foods advised in early-1975 that 'the level of substitution in meals in institutions such as hospitals, schools etc., of hydrated vegetable protein food for meat should not on average exceed 10 parts by weight per 90 parts of meat, over a reasonable period'.

Since these products are of an acceptable nutritional standard there seems to be no reason why they should not be widely used domestically and commercially. However, it is important that people should know what they are eating — and the Trade Descriptions Act 1968 provides adequate protection for the consumer in this respect.

The M.L.C. Carcase Classification

The M.L.C. provides a classification service for beef, pigs and lamb.

Carcase classification describes characteristics of carcases which are important to meat traders. It is not a grading system, but it is a method of enabling purchasers to assess how much of the carcase they will be able to sell once bone, waste and fat have been removed — in other words, its yield of saleable meat.

Carcase classification is carried out to a common standard by experienced M.L.C. staff. It is independent, consistent and reliable.

Carcase classification describes carcases by:

(a) weight;
(b) sex (steer, heifer, cow, bull);
(c) conformation;
(d) fatness;
(e) age (optional).

Conformation

Conformation describes the overall shape of the carcase and is really an assessment of the thickness of lean and fat covering the skeleton. Conformation is divided into five main classes: E, U, R, O and P; classes U, O and P are subdivided into upper (+) and lower (−) bands. Conformation class E describes carcases of outstanding shape, particularly of the type produced by double-muscled cattle, but these represent only a small proportion of the national kill. Class P describes thinly muscled carcases of inferior shape, usually produced by cattle of extreme dairy breeds and by cows.

Fatness

Fatness is assessed in five classes from 1 (very lean) to 5 (very fat), with classes 4 and 5 being sub-divided into leaner (L) and fatter (H) bands.

The Classification Grid

When the quality of the carcase is expressed in classification terms, the conformation class is always given first. For example, the most common type of steer beef carcase would have a conformation class of R and a fat class of 4L. This would be written R4L, and its position is shown in the grid below.

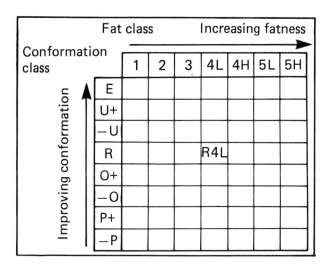

Figure 11.5   M.L.C. beef carcase classification

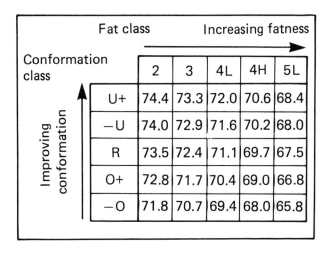

Figure 11.6   Saleable meat yield as a percentage of beef carcase weight

Saleable Meat Yield

The M.L.C. has conducted extensive tests and established average meat yields for the major classification classes. The yields obtained being confirmed by commercial tests. It is important to note that the final meat yield will depend on the actual cutting method and degree of trim. Reducing the fat content in a carcase has a far greater effect on increasing meat yield than improving conformation. An improved carcase conformation would yield a slightly higher percentage of more valuable cuts.

12

Beef, Veal–Lamb, Mutton–Pork

Beef and Veal

Introduction

Currently the beef and milk industries represent just over a third of the total
agricultural output for the U.K. Home production of both meat and milk have
increased considerably since 1960 enabling significant reductions to be made in
imports. The increasing production trend has not, and possibly in the future,
will not, be without periodic setbacks owing to such things as feeding costs,
labour costs and unexpected Government changes in policy (e.g. cuts in
subsidies) affecting the profitability for the farmer and hence affecting his
decision to increase or decrease his beef or dairy herds. This in turn affects
the number of beef animals being offered at the markets for sale and further
affects the price to be paid for meat by the caterer.

The relationship between beef and milk production is simply that the
majority of home produced beef is a by-product of the dairy herds. Pure beef
bred populations are small, their importance in beef production being through
cross-breeding. Cross-breeding has the objective of producing economically a
good quality animal of the correct size and weight in a short period of time
with the minimum amount of attention.

The breeds of bulls used in the U.K. are in order of importance, Friesian,
Hereford, Aberdeen-Angus, Charolais (imported originally from France),
Simmental (from Germany), and Limousin (from France). As with other food
animals many producers prefer to breed cross-bred animals on the assumption
that the best characteristic of both parents will be carried into their young.

Changes in production of beef in recent years has seen a change from
castrating young male bovines to feeding them intensively on concentrates to
produce a good quality carcase in under 14 months. An increase in quality veal
production in the U.K. has come about by feeding baby calves on a milk diet
and then on a high protein diet whilst keeping them under controlled ventila-

tion and lighting conditions in a factory environment. Slaughtering of the calves takes place between 4–6 months in age.

General Nomenclature

Entire Males
Bull	An adult entire male over one year old.
Bull calf	An entire male up to one year old.
Yearling calf	An entire male, at least one year old but not fully mature.

Castrated (de-sexed) Males
Steer calf	A castrated immature male, under one year.
Bullock or steer	Males over one year, then castrated.

Females
Heifer calf	An immature female under one year.
Heifer	An adult female that has not calved.
Cow	An adult female that has calved.

General Terms
Baby beef	Bovines specially prepared to sell as quality animals for slaughter between 11–14 months.
'Bobby' calf	Young bovines usually under three weeks of age, which are a by-product of the dairy industry. The carcase will be small, and the flesh greyish in colour, soft and very moist.
Veal calf	Young bovines about four months old especially reared for veal in indoor intensive feeding units. These animals are usually fed only on milk or milk substitutes to ensure a pale colour of the muscles.

Hindquarter of Beef — Wholesale Cuts
Hindquarter X (H$\frac{1}{4}$X)	A hindquarter minus the thin flank.
Hindquarter XX (H$\frac{1}{4}$XX)	A hindquarter minus the thin flank and kidney knob.
Top-piece (or top-bit)	Shank, topside, silverside, thick flank, aitchbone, cod or doug fat.
Rump and Loin	Rump, loin, wing end, kidney knob and fillet.
Rump and Loin X	Rump, loin, wing end and fillet.
Round of Beef	Top-piece minus the shin.
Buttock	Topside and silverside undivided.

N.B. The division of a side of beef into a hindquarter and forequarter is

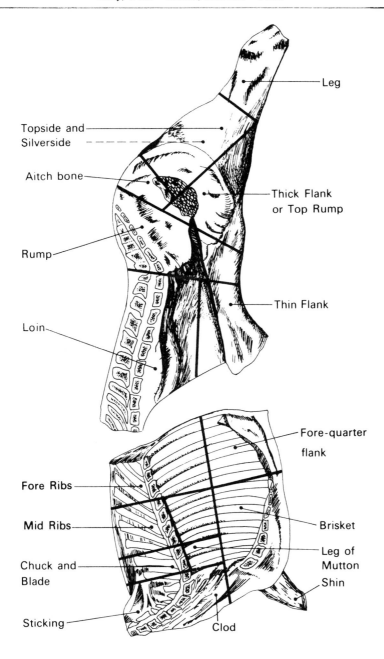

Figure 12.1 Traditional English style cutting of a hindquarter and fore-quarter of beef

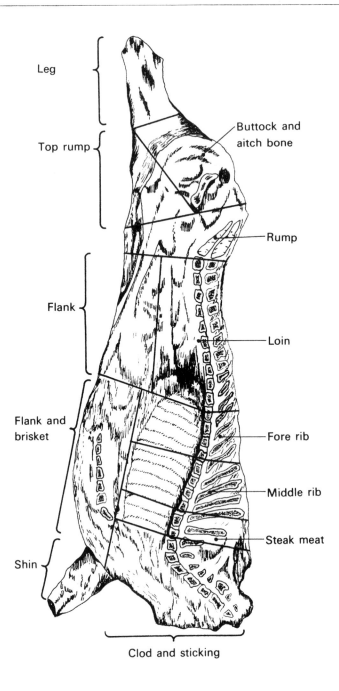

Figure 12.2 London and Home Counties cutting of a side of beef

made by cutting between the 10th and 11th ribs, leaving ribs 1–10 inclusive on the forequarter and ribs 11–13 inclusive on the hindquarter.

Forequarter of Beef – Wholesale Cuts

Forequarter X (F¼X)	A forequarter minus the plate or F¼ flank.
Forequarter XX (F¼XX)	A forequarter minus the plate and brisket.
Forequarter XXX (F¼XXX)	A forequarter minus the plate, brisket and shin. (Also known as an 'Australian crop'.)
Short forequarter	A forequarter minus the fore ribs and plate.
Crop (or rib and pony)	Two bone steak meat, middle ribs and fore ribs.
Short crop	Middle and fore ribs undivided.
Pony	Middle ribs and two bone steak meat undivided.
Steak piece	Leg of mutton cut, chuck and blade bone undivided.
Bottom piece	Shin, clod, sticking and steak piece.
Coast	Plate and brisket undivided.

General Terms

Baron of beef	A pair of loins undivided (frequently the rumps are also left attached).
Roasting	A half a baron of beef

Veal – Wholesale Cuts

Hindquarter Forequarter	the subdivision of a side of veal into a H¼ and F¼ by cutting between the 12–13 ribs, leaving 12 ribs on the F¼ and 1 rib on the H¼.
Oyster of veal	The shoulder minus the knuckle.
Fillet of veal	Any boneless cut from the leg (minus the knuckle).

Special Catering Cuts of Beef and Veal

Baron of beef	A pair of sirloins undivided. This large joint would have to be especially ordered well in advance as beef carcases are quartered in the slaughterhouse. (As stated previously the rumps are often left attached.)
Porterhouse steak	A large steak cut from the rump end of a sirloin. It would contain the main eye of meat from the sirloin, with the eye of meat from the fillet and held together by part of the lumbar vertebrae. (Also known as a T bone steak.)
Sirloin	The main eye of meat and fillet of beef contained attached to the lumbar vertebrae.
Contre-filet	The de-boned main eye of meat taken from the sirloin.

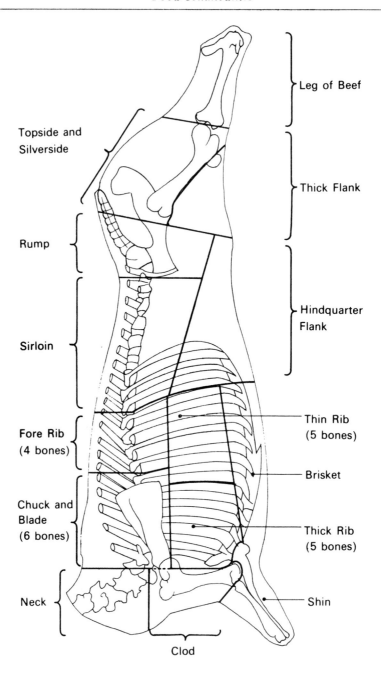

Leg of Beef

Topside and
Silverside

Thick Flank

Rump

Sirloin

Hindquarter
Flank

Fore Rib
(4 bones)

Thin Rib
(5 bones)

Brisket

Chuck and
Blade
(6 bones)

Thick Rib
(5 bones)

Neck

Shin

Clod

Figure 12.3 Primal cuts method 1. A specification prepared by the M.L.C. and
the D.H.S.S.

Entrecôte steaks

Steaks taken from the contre-filet. There are three common types of entrecôte steaks:

Entrecôte minute	a small steak flattened with a bat; usually 113.5 g (4 oz) each.
Entrecôte	a steak usually 170–227 g (6–8 oz) each.
Entrecôte Double	a large entrecôte usually 340–454 g ($\frac{3}{4}$–1 lb) each.

Fillet of beef

This is the most expensive joint from the beef carcase. It is usually 2.72–3.63 kg (6–8 lb) in weight and represents only about 1.5% of the carcase weight.

The fillet may be roasted whole or cut up into four types of steak meat:

(i) Chateaubriand steaks – these are cut from the head (widest and thickest part) of the fillet. It is a steak large enough for 2–3 persons, having a raw weight of at least 227 g (8 oz) per person.

(ii) Fillet steak – this is the next cut down from the head of the fillet. Each steak is an individual portion weighing 170–227 g (6–8 oz) each.

(iii) Tournedos steak – this is the next cut down from the fillet steak. It is a small individual steak weighing about 113.5 g (4 oz) each.

(iv) Filet mignon – this is a small flattened steak taken from the tail of the fillet. It is also cut into small fingers of meat for sauté dishes.

Growth in Beef Type Animals

A newly born calf will have long legs, a short body and a large head. Its actual size and weight depend on the breed of its parents. If the calf is fed on a good level of nutrition, growth will take place from the extremities and declines with maturity, e.g. the legs and neck, whilst the joints between the extremities all increase slowly for the first two years, e.g. sirloin, crop, and coast.

There are known factors which will assist in producing a quality beef animal in the shortest possible time and with a high proportion of the expensive joints. The castration of young male bovines assists by reducing the tendency of bulls to produce a carcase with heavy forequarters. However, this practice has been challenged in recent years as a result of extensive production studies in which it was found that the growth rate and the conversion rate is superior in bulls as compared to steers.

Further, the demand by consumers for beef with very little fat has encouraged producers to rear bull calves for beef production. Second, the increase of baby beef production by which young calves are weaned on milk substitutes and then fed on a high protein diet enables the farmer to produce beef animals of a desirable weight and a high quality carcase in about 12–14 months. In contrast to the previous methods of production, the meat from older animals may be tenderized by injecting commercial enzymes into the blood stream of the animal immediately prior to slaughter making the more active muscles more suitable for roasting and grilling.

Dressing Out Percentage
The dressing out percentage is a comparison between the live weight of the animal and the weight of the dressed, cold carcase.

The dressing out percentage is calculated by the following formulae:

$$\frac{\text{cold carcase weight}}{\text{live weight of animal}} \times \frac{100}{1}$$

e.g. an animal weighing 400 kg (950 lb) alive and yielding a cold carcase weight of 250 kg (560 lb) gives

$$\frac{250}{400} \times \frac{100}{1} = 62.5\%$$

The percentage figure obtained on any test would give a measure against the accepted standard percentage as to the efficiency of a particular breed combined with the type of feed, its age at slaughter, etc., and indicate its suitability for beef production.

A typical good dressing out percentage for beef animals is around 56%, giving a reasonably lean carcase. A higher dressing out percentage is usually only obtainable at the expense of a higher fat content. The dressing out percentage of 56 appears low at first, but this is because in the dressing of a carcase of beef, the head, hide, hooves, offal, and intestines are removed.

Carcase Quality in Beef and Veal

Beef
Hindquarter
CONFORMATION. The hindquarter should be compact in shape, well fleshed, have small bones and represent about 55% by weight of the side. The loin should be very well fleshed with a not excessively large kidney knob. The thin flank should be thick and full of meat. The rump and round should be full (i.e. well developed) and extending well down the leg. The bones should be pinkish in colour and when cut show evidence of blood in their structure. The extremities of the rib bones and spinal processes should be cartilaginous indicating a 'young' animal.
QUALITY. The cut surface of the hindquarter should show a well-developed

eye muscle, be a bright reddish-brown in colour, be resilient and smooth to the touch and have a fine texture. The eye muscle should show plenty of intra-muscular fat (i.e. marbling) and an absence of any gristle. N.B. the colour of a cut surface can be misleading and may be influenced by the age of the animal and the activity of the muscle. When a cut surface is first exposed to the air it tends to get brighter owing to the uptake of atmospheric oxygen and then later as the surface tends to dry out it becomes dull and a near black colour.
FINISH. There should be an even distribution of smooth creamy white fat not exceeding $\frac{3}{8}$ in. over the wing end and loin. The size of the kidney knob should not be excessive in relation to the size of the hindquarter. N.B. the colour can be influenced by the breed and the age of the animal.

Forequarter
CONFORMATION. The forequarter should be compact in shape, well fleshed, have a short neck and shanks, and represent about 45% by weight of the side. The ribs should be well fleshed, and have a good size of eye muscle. The brisket and plate should be well fleshed but short. The bones should show evidence of the forequarter coming from a young animal.
QUALITY. This is the same as for a hindquarter.
FINISH. There should be an even distribution of smooth creamy white fat not exceeding $\frac{1}{2}$ in. over the forerib. There should not be an excess of fat in the region of the brisket.

Veal Carcase
This is different from beef in that the carcase is not cut into four quarters. It is similar in size to a large carcase of mutton weighing often between 18–31 kg (40–70 lb).
CONFORMATION. The carcase should be compact, stocky, and very well fleshed. The loins should be very well fleshed, the legs well developed and rounded, extending well down the leg. The shoulders should be also well fleshed and the neck short and thick. The extremities of most bones should be cartilaginous.
QUALITY. The flesh should be a pale pinkish-white in colour, be resilient and smooth to the touch and have a smooth texture. Because it is immature bovine flesh there will be no signs of marbling.
FINISH. There is very little fat covering a carcase of veal. The fat that there is will be in a very thin layer covering the rump, loin, and shoulders. The fat is white in colour and contains trapped air as a result of the carcase being inflated to separate the hide from the flesh more easily. The kidneys should be reasonably covered with firm white fat.

Catering Uses and Weights of Beef and Veal Joints
The catering uses and weights of beef and veal joints are shown in tabular form (*see* Table 12.1).

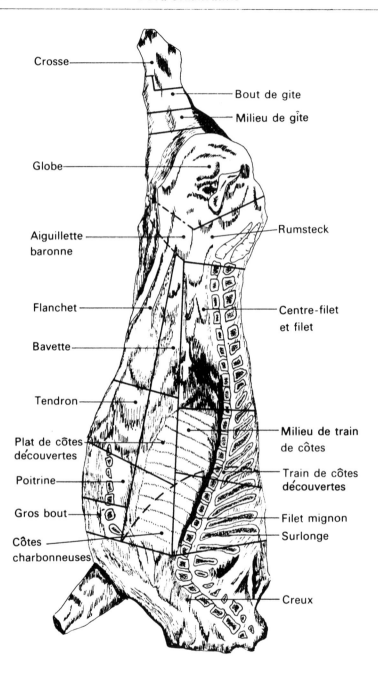

Figure 12.4 French method of cutting a side of beef

Table 12.1. *The French terms, catering uses and weights of beef and veal joints*

Joint	French Term	Approximate Weight kg	lb	Catering Uses
HINDQUARTER				
Shin	la Jambe	6.35–7.26	14–16	Consommé, stewing
Topside	la Tranche Tendre	8.17–9.07	18–20	Braising, stewing, second-class roast
Silverside	la Gite à la noix	10.89–11.79	24–26	Boiling, pickled, stewing
Thick flank	la Tranche grasse	9.98–10.89	22–24	Braising, stewing
Rump	la Culotte de Boeuf	8.17–9.07	18–20	Grilling, frying (as steaks)
Sirloin	l'Aloyou de Boeuf	9.07–9.98	20–22	First-class roast, grilling and frying as steaks
Wing ribs	la Côte de Boeuf	3.63–4.54	8–10	First-class roast, grilling and frying as steaks
Thin flank	la Bavette	8.17–9.07	18–20	Stewing, boiling, mincing, sausages
Fillet	le Filet de Boeuf	2.72–3.63	6–8	First-class roast, grilling and frying as steaks
Kidney knob		3.63–4.99	8–11	Kidney – stewing, braising Suet – suet paste, stuffings
FOREQUARTER				
Fore ribs	les Côtes Premières	6.35–7.26	14–16	First-class roast, grilling and frying as steaks
Middle ribs	les Côtes Découvertes	8.17–9.07	18–20	Roasting and braising
Chuck ribs	les Côtes de Collier	12.25–13.61	27–30	Stewing, braising, mincing
Leg of mutton cut	la Tallon du Collier	9.07–9.98	20–22	Stewing, braising
Plate	le Plate de Côtes	8.17–9.07	18–20	Stewing, boiling, mincing
Brisket	la Poitrine	15.42–16.33	34–36	Pickled, boiling
Sticking piece	la Collier	7.26–8.17	16–18	Stewing, mincing
Shank	la Jambe	5.44–6.35	12–14	Consommé, mincing
VEAL				
Knuckle	le Jarret	1.82	4	Stock, stew, mincing
*Leg	le Cuissot	4.54	10	Roasting, braising, frying
Chump or Rump	le Quassi	0.91	2	Roasting, braising, frying
Loin	la Longe	1.59	3.5	Roasting, grilling, frying
Best-end	le Carré	1.59	3.5	Roasting, grilling, frying
Breast	la Poitrine	1.36	3	Stewing, roasting
Neck end	les Basses Côtes	1.36	3	Braising, stewing
Scrag	le Cou	0.91	2	Stock, stewing
Shoulder	l'Epaule	2.72	6	Roasting, braising, stewing

*Leg of veal may be further divided into:

Joint	French Term	Approximate Weight kg	lb	Catering Uses
Knuckle	le Jarret	0.91	2	Braising, stock
Cushion	la Noix	1.36	3	Escalopes, braising, roasting

Table 12.1. cont.

Thick flank	le Quassi	0.68	1.5	Escalopes, roasting, sauté
Under cushion	le Sous Noix	1.59	3.5	Escalopes, braising, roasting

Purchase Specification

Striploin – Special Trim (i.e. Contre-filet)
The purchase specification for striploin is shown in Table 12.2.

Table 12.2. An example of a purchase specification for a catering cut of beef

Striploin – Special Trim (i.e. Contre-filet)

DEFINITION	(i) Taken from a $H\frac{1}{4}$ of Scotch beef
	(ii) Taken from a Sirloin XX
WEIGHT RANGE	(i) Between 10.89–12.70 kg (24–28 lb)
	(ii) Average weight per delivery of 10 striploins 11.79 kg (26 lb)
SURFACE FAT	(i) An even covering of fat not exceeding a thickness of $\frac{3}{4}$ in. (19 mm)
SUET DEPOSITS	(i) To be completely removed
LENGTH OF 'TOPS' (FLANK)	
	(i) Not to exceed 1 in. (25 mm)
DEPTH OF 'EYE' MUSCLE	(i) The main 'eye' muscle to be not less than 3 in. (75 mm)
GRISTLE CONTENT	(i) All small 'caps' of gristle on the underside of the 'eye' muscle to be removed
	(ii) 'Backstrap' gristle, which is situated on top of the striploin together with its covering of surface fat to be completely removed.
SIDE CHAIN	(i) To be completely removed
BONING	All boning to be done cleanly so that:
	(i) No bone fragments remain
	(ii) No rib fingers remain
	(iii) No knife cuts deeper than $\frac{1}{2}$ in. (12 mm)

Lamb and Mutton

Introduction
The breeds of sheep in the U.K. can be broadly divided into three main groups:

    (*a*) mountain and hill breeds (e.g. Blackface, Cheviots, Swalesdale, etc.);

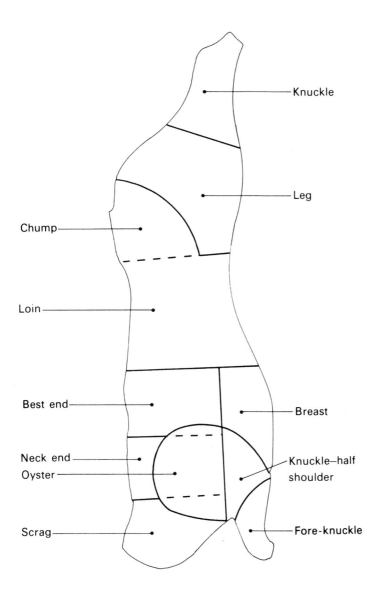

Figure 12.5 Veal cutting. N.B. Similarity of lamb and mutton cutting

(*b*) arable or down breeds (e.g. Southdown, Suffolk, Dorset Down, Hampshire Down, etc.);

(*c*) grassland breeds (e.g. longwool breeds such as Leicester, Romney Marsh, Lincoln, etc.).

The above breeds, as their names suggest, are best suited to hill, arable and grasslands respectively. This is mainly because the hill breeds can exist on poorer quality grazing than the others, whilst the arable breeds do not make full use of the best grasslands. In spite of the above mentioned breeds the crossing and second crossing of breeds is widely practised, to secure stock which will do particularly well in certain environments, to increase the fertility and milk production in the ewe and growth in the lamb, and to produce small, lean and fully fleshed carcases.

The hill breeds tend to produce a good small size carcase which has slightly long legs and deep ribs. The flesh is of a very good flavour due to the type of feed. The arable or down breeds produce the ideal carcase for the caterer, with a food conformation, quality and finish. The grassland breeds, originally bred for the quality and quantity of their wool, do not produce such a good carcase as the arable or down breeds, but by slaughtering the animals at an early age it is possible to produce a moderately acceptable carcase before the animal puts on too much, rather tallowy, fat.

Sheep farming systems are numerous and varied with their end-products being divided into five main categories:

(i) Lowland production from grass is of great importance in England. Lambing takes place from the end of January to March, with the young lambs being fed on a high quality milk produced by the ewes from the early spring grass. These lambs are mainly marketed in the autumn.

(ii) Mountain or hill production of fat lambs has become more important in recent years. Lambing takes place in April and May, by which time a reasonable amount of herbage is available. The quality lambs are marketed in the autumn and the remainder kept on for finishing in sheltered areas and marketing later.

(iii) Hoggets, young male sheep not yet sheared, are from lowland or hill farms which have been bought as stores in the autumn and fattened on roots and forage crops and marketed from late December to April.

(iv) Out-of-season lambs produced on lowland farms provide for a small quality market of new season lambs for December to Easter. It is a growing practice for these lambs to be produced by intensive farming methods similar to that for beef.

(v) Ewes and rams, being the adults of the species, are marketed in the last six months of the year. Ewes are sold mainly as mutton carcases with the ram carcases sold for manufacturing purposes.

It is obvious from the above that we are not fully able to supply lamb and mutton of sufficient quantities throughout the year. The supplies of home produced lamb and mutton are supported by the importation of chilled and frozen New Zealand, Australian, and South American carcases.

General Nomenclature

Entire Males
Ram lambs or hoggets	A young male up to its first shearing
Shearing ram or tup	A male after its first shearing

Castrated Males
Wether	A castrated male up to its first shearing
Shearing wether	A castrated male between first and second shearing

Females
Ewe lamb or gimmer	A young female up to the stage of being weaned (i.e. 2–3 months old)
Ewe teg or ewe hog	A female between being weaned and first shearing
Ewe	A female that has produced young (at least $1\frac{1}{2}$ years old)

General Terms
It is usual under the Fatstock Guarantee Scheme in the U.K. to classify sheep type animals (ovines) simply according to their age into lambs, hoggets, and sheep.

Carcase of Lamb and Mutton – Wholesale Cuts
Trunk	A whole carcase without the haunches (hind legs)
Jacket	A trunk minus the two shoulders
Targets (pair)	A jacket minus the saddle
Target	A pair of targets split down the vertebrae (i.e. scrag, middle neck and breast undivided)
Saddle	A pair of loins undivided
Chines and ends	A saddle with a pair of best-ends undivided
Haunches (pair)	Two hind legs undivided with the 'chumps' attached
Haunch	A hind leg with a 'chump' attached
Chumps	Small joint between the hind legs and saddle. Equivalent to rump in beef

Special Catering Cuts of Lamb and Mutton
Baron of lamb	Two hind legs and saddle undivided
Long leg of lamb	A leg with the 'chump' still attached
Short leg of lamb	A leg minus the 'chump'
Long saddle	A pair of loins and 'chump' undivided

Short saddle	A pair of loins undivided
Crown chop	A chop obtained by cutting across a short saddle, i.e. it would contain the two 'eyes' of meat from the loin and underneath have two halves of kidney. About 10oz each
Rosette of lamb	Similar to crown chop except that it would be boned and not contain the kidneys
Chop	Obtained from cutting across a loin (split short saddle)
Barnsley chop	The name given to a double lamb chop
Noisette of lamb	Obtained by cutting small steaks at an angle from a boned loin
Best-end	The small joint containing ribs 6–12 inclusive
French trimmed best-end	A well prepared best-end of which the bark (outer skin) and chine bone have been removed and the extremities of the ribs exposed and cleaned.
Cutlet	A cut taken from a best-end and containing a complete rib bone

Growth in Sheep

A newly born lamb is nearly all head and legs with a very short and shallow loin region. Its actual size and weight depend on the breed of its parents. With early maturing breeds the developmental growth takes place more quickly than in slow maturing breeds. Under normal feeding conditions the lamb develops with the body lengthening and deepening so that the proportion of the more valuable cuts of meat increases. When this happens the ratio of bones, head, and legs in the carcase decreases.

One of the questions most often discussed regarding this type of animal is 'when does lamb become mutton?' There is not a definitive answer to this question. The answer involves the age, the size, and the breed of the animal. In general terms sheep under 12 months of age are referred to as lamb in the U.K., whilst New Zealand lamb exported to the U.K. is from animals usually under 6 months of age. Age in meat animals can only efficiently be determined by the dentition of the animal. However, the carcases of lamb or mutton do not contain the head, and so age may only be partially determined by the state of the bones. The size of the animal is related to its breed, its level of feeding and its age. The smaller the size the more likely it is for it to be sold as lamb almost irrespective of age as against a young but heavy carcase.

Dressing Out Percentage

The dressing out percentage, as explained previously, is a comparison between the live weight of the animal and the weight of the dressed, cold carcase.

The dressing out percentages for lambs and sheep are low because in the dressing of the carcase the head, the skin and wool, hooves, offal, and intestines are removed. The wool in particular often weighing in excess of 2.27 kg (5 lb). Another relevant point is the intestinal content of the animal which will depend upon the quantity of the last feed and the period of fasting prior to being slaughtered.

A typical dressing out percentage for lambs would be in the region of 55–60% and for sheep in the region of 50%. Naturally the percentage figures would be lower for a poor quality carcase and higher for a carcase with a good finish (i.e. high fat content).

Carcase Quality in Lamb and Mutton

CONFORMATION. The carcase should be compact and rectangular in shape with well-sprung ribs, it should be heavy in relation to its size and uniformly fleshed throughout. The saddle region (loins) should be broad and well developed. The hind legs should be plump and full with the meat carried down to the shanks. The shoulders should be thick, full, and smooth. The neck should be short and compact. There should be clear indications in a good quality carcase of visible lean meat on the shoulders and legs.

The bones of a young animal when cut are porous showing some blood in their structure, whilst the breast bones and the end of the scapular are quite flexible and cartilaginous. The bones of an older animal are hard, dense, and white, with a tendency to splinter. The rib bones of a young animal should be narrow and red in colour. On a good carcase the legs, shoulders, and loins should represent 73–75% of the total dressed weight.

QUALITY. The cut surface should show the flesh to be firm and a light red colour. There should be some moderate fat streakings in the inside flank muscles and between the ribs. 'Marbling' should be evident in the region of the loin.

FINISH. The exterior fat covering the carcase should be smooth, evenly distributed and moderately thick over the back region. The fat covering the kidneys should be adequate but not excessive. The fat should be quite hard, brittle and flaky in texture and white to pale cream in colour.

Catering Uses and Weights of Lamb and Mutton Joints

The catering uses and weights of lamb and mutton joints are shown in tabular form (*see* Table 12.3).

Purchase Specification

Best-end Neck of Lamb – (Frenched)

The purchase specification for best-end neck of lamb is shown in Table 12.4.

The Grading of New Zealand Lamb and Mutton

This grading system is given to illustrate a recognized grading system with the choice of variety of some 25 different grades with weight ranges of from 8.0–36.0kg, which are freely available on the market at different prices.

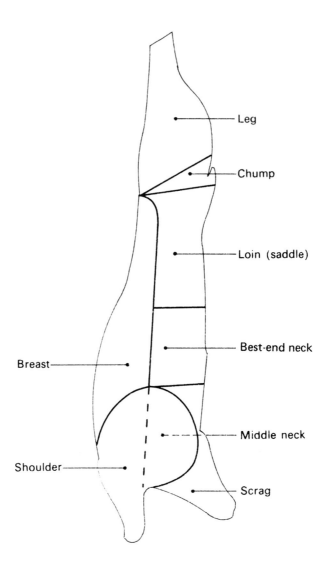

Figure 12.6 London and Home Counties cutting of lamb and mutton

Table 12.3. The French terms, catering uses and weights of lamb and mutton joints

Joint	French Term	Lamb kg	lb	Mutton kg	lb	Catering Uses
Legs (2) – short	le Gigot	3.17	7	4.99	11	Roasting, boiled for mutton
Saddle – long (including chump ends)	la Selle	3.17	7	4.99	11	Roasting, grilling or frying
Breast	la Poitrine	1.36	3	2.27	5	Roasting, stewing
Best-end	le Carré	1.81	4	2.72	6	Roasting, grilling, frying
Middle neck	les Basses Côtes	1.81	4	2.72	6	Stewing, braising
Scrag end	le Cou	0.45	1	0.91	2	Stewing, broth
Shoulders	l'Epaule	2.72	6	4.08	9	Roasting

Lamb Grading

A lamb is a sheep less than 12 months of age. Animals born in the N.Z. spring will be termed lambs until 30th September in the following year.

Lamb carcases are allocated to one of five grades on the basis of fat content.

Fat content	Almost devoid	Light	Medium	Heavy	Excessive
Grade symbol	A	Y	P	T	F

A grade lamb carcases are lightweight and almost devoid of external fat.

Grade symbol	Weight range (kg)
A	Less than 9.0

Y grade lamb carcases have a light fat content.

Grade symbol	Weight range (kg)
YL	9.0–12.5
YM	13.0–16.0
YX	16.5 and over

P grade lamb carcases have a medium fat content.

Grade symbol	Weight range (kg)
PL	9.0–12.5
PM	13.0–16.0
PX	16.5–20.0
PH	20.5 and over

Table 12.4. An example of a purchase specification for a catering cut of lamb

Best-end Neck of Lamb — (Frenched)

DEFINITION	(i)	Taken from a crown best-end (i.e. ribs 6–12 inclusive), split cleanly down the vertebrae
GRADE OF MEAT	(i)	Taken from Y M grade New Zealand lamb carcases
WEIGHT RANGE	(i)	All prepared best-ends to weigh between 1.25 kg (20 oz) and 1.48 kg (23 oz)
SURFACE FAT	(i)	An even covering of fat not exceeding $\frac{1}{4}$ in. (6 mm) in thickness
DEGREE OF PREPARATION	(i)	The chine bone to be removed
	(ii)	The bark to be removed
	(iii)	Tip of blade bone to be removed
	(iv)	Length of 'tops' not to exceed $1\frac{1}{2}$ times depth of main 'eye' of meat. Maximum length of rib bone to be $5\frac{1}{2}$ in. (140 mm)
	(v)	Extremities of all ribs to be exposed to a depth of $\frac{1}{2}$ in. (13 mm)
DELIVERY NOTES	(i)	All best-ends to be delivered still in the frozen state. Individually vacuum packed
	(ii)	To be packed in containers of 20 best-ends

T grade lamb carcases have a heavy fat content and will be cut and trimmed of excessive fat prior to export as cuts.

Grade symbol	Weight range (kg)
TL	9.0–12.5
TM	13.0–16.0
TH	16.5 and over

F grade lamb carcases have an excessive fat content and will be cut and trimmed of excessive fat prior to export as cuts.

Grade symbol	Weight range (kg)
FL	9.0–12.5
FM	13.0–16.0
FH	16.5 and over

Carcases that are not eligible for export in carcase form due to trimming or mutilation are graded Cutter. Intact cuts from these carcases may be exported. This grade comprises carcases which have at least 3 of the 4 hind primal cuts (legs and long loins) acceptable as exportable cuts.

Grade symbol	Weight range (kg)
CL	9.0–12.5
CM	13.0–16.0
CH	16.5 and over

The manufacturing grade includes carcases which:

    (*a*) are too thin for export in carcase form or as primal cuts;
    (*b*) are damaged but fail to meet the Cutter criteria;
    (*c*) weigh less than 9 kg but are too fat for the A Grade.

Grade symbol	Weight range (kg)
M	All weights

Conformation

While there is no specific grading for conformation 'leggy' carcases are excluded from the 'PL' and 'PM' grades.

    The various grades are summarized below.

	Export carcase grades				Fabrication grades		
Symbol	A	Y	P	T	F	C	M
Fat content	Almost devoid	Light	Medium	Heavy	Excessive	Mixed	Mixed
Less than 9.0 kg	A						
9.0–12.5 kg		YL	PL	TL	FL	CL	
13.0–16.0 kg		YM	PM	TM	FM	CM	M
16.5–20.0 kg		YX	PX	TH	FH	CH	
20.5 kg and over			PH				

Ram Grading

An adult uncastrated male sheep having more than 2 permanent incisors in wear.

    There is one grade covering all weights and fat contents.

Grade symbol	Weight range (kg)
R	All weights

Hogget Grading

A hogget is a young male sheep or maiden ewe not qualifying for the lamb grade and having no more than 2 permanent incisors in wear.

    Hogget carcases are allocated to one of two grades on the basis of fat content.

Fat content	Light	Medium
Grade symbol	HX	HL

HX grade carcases have a light fat content.

Grade symbol	Weight range (kg)
HX	All weights

HL grade carcases have a medium fat content.

Grade symbol	Weight range (kg)
HL	All weights

Manufacturing type carcases (i.e. those devoid of external fat) are not eligible for inclusion in the hogget grades and are graded as mutton i.e. MM.

Carcases with heavy or excessive fat content are graded as mutton, i.e. MH or MF.

Carcases that are not eligible for export in carcase form due to trimming or mutilation are graded as mutton, i.e. MP.

Mutton Grading

Mutton carcases include both ewes and wethers with more than 2 permanent incisors in wear. A wether must not show any of the accessory male characteristics.

Mutton carcases are allocated to one of 5 grades on the basis of fat content.

Fat content	Almost devoid	Light	Medium	Heavy	Excessive
Grade symbol	MM	MX	ML	MH	MF

MM grade carcases are almost devoid of external fat.

Grade symbol	Weight range (kg)
MM	All weights

MX grade carcases have a light fat content.

Grade symbol	Weight range (kg)
MX	Up to and including 22.0 22.5 and over

ML grade carcases have a medium fat content.

Grad symbol	Weight range (kg)
ML	Up to and including 22.0 22.5 and over

MH grade carcases have a heavy fat content.

Grade symbol	Weight range (kg)
MH	All weights

MF grade carcases have an excessive fat content.

Grade symbol   Weight range (kg)
MF   All weights

Carcases that are generally not eligible for export in carcase form due to trimming or multilation are graded Processor and should be cut and/or boned.

Grade symbol   Weight range (kg)
MP   All weights

The various grades are summarized below.

Symbol	MM	MX	ML	MH	MF	MP
Fat content	Almost	Light	Medium	Heavy	Excessive	Mixed
Up to 22.0 kg						
22.5 kg and over						

Further to the grading given above, the ticket attached to the leg of a carcase will identify the grade and weight range by the appropriate symbols and like the external wrapping will be colour coded. Full details of ticket colours and outer wrap colours are obtainable from the New Zealand Meat Producers Board.

Pork

Introduction
There are some eleven breeds of pig in the U.K., with the Large White and the Landrace being the most popular. As with beef and sheep production, there is a considerable amount of cross-breeding to obtain a high quality carcase for a particular market from breeds that produce large litters and have a high conversion rate (i.e. the efficiency by which they convert food into body weight).

There are some distinct differences between the production of pigs and that of sheep and cattle. Gilts (young female pigs) are ready to breed at eight months of age and the gestation period (pregnancy period) is only 16 weeks. Young piglets are usually weaned at about 8 weeks and the sow is then shortly ready for further breeding. This gives a reproductive cycle of about 6 months. Pigs are also extremely prolific, producing litters of over 8 pigs, giving a typical production of about 16 piglets per sow every 12—14 months. Further, the period from the birth of a piglet to slaughter is short, varying from 16—30 weeks, depending on the particular market for which the animal was produced. Pig production is mainly in factory-type buildings with controlled temperature and ventilation conditions and with controlled feeding. As the pig has only a simple stomach (one compartment) it requires a diet of concentrated foods in preference to grass and other bulky foods.

Pigs are produced for two main markets, for pork and for bacon. Pork is produced at two weight ranges, 110–150 lb (49.90–68.04 kg) and 150–185 lb (68.04–83.92 kg). Bacon is produced also at two weight ranges, 185–240 lb (83.92–108.86 kg) for the traditional bacon pig and 240–280 lb (108.86–127.01 kg) for the special Wall's hybrid bacon pig.

There is little seasonality for the marketing of pigs throughout the year. The trends that there are show an increased demand for pork in December and a move from pork to bacon in the summer months.

General Nomenclature

Entire Males

Boar	An adult entire male used for breeding
Boar pig	A young entire male not yet used for breeding

Castrated Males

Brawner	A young male that has been castrated after having been used for breeding
Stag	An adult male, castrated after having been used for breeding
Hog (or clean hog)	A young male castrated at or before weaning

Females

Sow pig	A young female not yet weaned
Gilt (or yilt, yelt or hilt)	A young female not yet serviced by the boar
Sow	A female that has produced young

General Terms

Sucking (or suckling) pig	Young pigs of either sex not yet weaned
Store pigs	Young pigs of either sex just weaned

Carcase of Pork — Wholesale Cuts

Side	A carcase divided into two sides by cutting down the spinal column and through the head
Jacket	A side minus half the head and the hind leg
Long loin	The complete loin with the neck-end still attached
Short loin	A long loin minus the neck-end
Hogmeat	The loin with the rind and excessive back fat removed
Hand and spring	The lower part of the shoulder, including usually the lower part of the 1st rib
Hand and belly	The hand and spring and belly undivided
Middle	Short loin and belly undivided
Fore end	The neck end and hand and spring undivided
Trotters	The feet
Rind	The outer skin of the pig (N.B. only the hair has been removed)

Growth in Pigs

Growth in pigs is related to the breed of the parents, i.e. whether they are of an early maturing breed or not, and also to the type of feed. As pigs for all purposes are usually slaughtered within 30 weeks from birth, the breeder has to produce a suitable animal for a particular market in a very short period of time. In the early maturing breeds the body proportions become balanced quite quickly whereas in a slow maturing breed this takes place at a much later stage of development. The growth in pigs starts with the bone followed by muscle and then fat.

However the type of feeding can also affect considerably the amount of muscle development and in particular the amount of fat put on. Danish bacon type pigs are fed on a high level of protein from birth to 16 weeks to develop the bones and muscles and then until being slaughtered are fed on a lower but controlled protein diet to increase weight further and to develop the correct proportions of fat. The 'Wall's Hybrid Bacon Pig' though, being a larger animal, is first fed on a low protein diet and later on a high protein diet to produce the required amount of lean meat. 'Porkers' and 'Cutters' are also fed first on a low protein diet and then on a high protein diet.

Dressing Out Percentage

The dressing out percentage is a comparison between the live weight and the weight of the dressed cold carcase.

The dressing out percentages for all types of pigs is high simply because in the dressing the head, feet, skin, and tail are left on, whereas in other food animals they are removed. The heavier the pig the higher the dressing out percentage. The percentage will vary between 68–80%.

The Main Groups of Pigs

These are shown in Table 12.5.

Carcase Quality in Pork

CONFORMATION. The carcase should be of a good weight for the particular purpose it is to be used. The carcase should be heavily fleshed and have a rectangular outline whether viewed from the back or the side. A long carcase with a good depth to the loin is desirable as this is the most valuable part. The hand and hindleg should be well developed. A large kidney is accepted as a good sign of a well muscled and finished carcase. The shanks should be short and the shoulders and head should be small. The bones should be pinkish in colour and when cut show some blood in their structure. The extremities of some young bones should be cartilaginous, e.g. scapula and spinal processes.
QUALITY. The cut surface should show the flesh to be firm, of a pale pink colour, with a fine smooth texture together with evidence of 'marbling'.
FINISH. The rind should be thin, smooth and free from any deep rooted bristles. Skin pigmentation should be avoided unless the rind is to be removed. The external fat should be evenly distributed but not excessive. The thin end of the bellies should be well lined with smooth 'leaf fat' which extends up to the kidneys. The fat should be firm, have a smooth texture, and be white in colour. The fat is slightly oily when compared with beef and lamb fat.

Table 12.5. The live and carcase weights, approximate age and dressing out percentages of the main groups of pigs

Type	Live Weight		Approximate Age (weeks)	Carcase Weight		Dressing Out %
	kg	lbs		kg	lbs	
Porker	49.90–68.04	110–150	16–18	34.02–47.63	75–105	68–70
Cutter	68.04–83.92	150–185	20–22	45.36–61.24	100–135	67–73
Bacon pigs	83.92–108.86	185–240	24–26	61.24–83.92	135–185	73–77
Heavy hogs (including Wall's Hybrid)	108.86–127.01	240–280	26–30	86.18–102.06	190–225	79–80

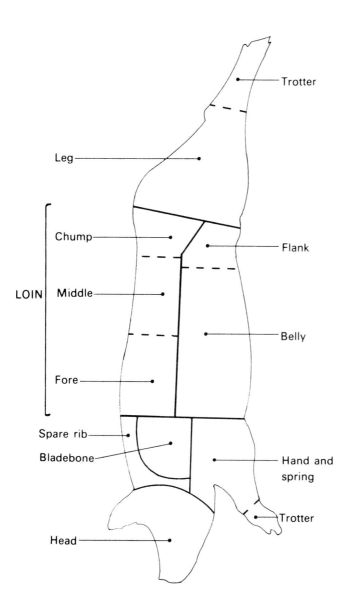

Figure 12.7 London and Home Counties cutting of a side of pork

Catering Uses and Weights of Pork Joints

The catering uses and weights of lamb and mutton joints are shown in tabular form (*see* Table 12.6).

Table 12.6. The catering uses and the weights of pork joints obtainable from a side of pork

Joint	French Term	Approximate Weights kg	Approximate Weights lb	Catering Uses
Head	la Tête	1.81	4	Brawn, boarshead
Shoulder (hand and spring)	l'Epaule (Plat de Côtes)	2.72	6	Roasing, sausages
Spare rib	la Basse Côte	1.36	3	Roasting, pies
Loin	la Longe	5.44	12	Roasting, grilling, frying
Belly	la Poitrine	1.81	4	Boiling, braising
Leg	le Cuissot	4.54	10	Roasting, boiling
Trotter	le Pied	1.81	4	Boiling, brawn

Purchase Specification

Short Loin of Pork (De-rined)
The purchase specification for short loin of pork is shown in Table 12.7.

Table 12.7. An example of a purchase specification for a catering cut of pork

Short Loin of Pork (De-rined)

DEFINITION	(i) Taken from a middle
	(ii) To include ribs 5–13 inclusive
	(iii) Leg removed by a square cut approximately 1 in. (25 mm) from the round of the aitch bone
WEIGHT RANGE	(i) All prepared short loins to weigh between 5.44–6.35 kg (12–14 lb)
DEGREE OF PREPARATION	(i) Rind to be removed
	(ii) Backfat to be removed where necessary, leaving a maximum external fat covering of $\frac{1}{2}$ in. (13 mm)
	(iii) Kidney and flare fat to be left intact
	(iv) Belly meat to be removed parallel to the chine bone. 'Tops' not to exceed the height of the main 'eye' muscle
DELIVERY NOTES	(i) All prepared short loins to be delivered individually wrapped
	(ii) To be delivered in a 'chilled' state

13

Offals–Bacon–Processed Meats

Offals

Offal may be defined as the edible or useable parts of meat other than the carcase, that are obtained from an animal at the time of slaughtering.

Offals may be classified under the three headings of:

(i)' Edible offals. This group is the one which is of particular importance to the caterer. It includes the tongue, brains, cheek sweetbreads, heart, liver, skirt (thick and thin), spleen, tail, kidneys, stomach, feet, bones, fats, lungs, and blood.

(ii) Inedible offals. The only interest to the caterer in this group of offals is that the established sale of inedible offals does help in a small way to keep the cost of edible meat down. It includes the hide, horns, feet, bones, blood, and intestines.

(iii) Pharmaceutical offals. The extraction of specific small offals for pharmaceutical use would only take place in very large modern slaughterhouses. This group includes the thymus, spleen, thyroid, ovaries, testes, red bone marrow, pituitary, pancreas, etc.

The Edible Offals

Tongue
All tongues are available to be purchased fresh as either long- or short-cut tongues. The long-cut tongues still have the hyoid bone, the root of the tongue and some fat attached, whilst the short-cut tongue has the root, hyoid bone, and any excess fat removed.

    (a) Ox/calves   (i) the largest of the tongues weighing 1.81–2.72 kg (4–6 lb)

                        (ii) a pointed tip and a prominent dorsal ridge (lump) on the upper surface

(b) Sheep	(i) weighs about 113.4–170.1 g (4–6 oz)
	(ii) a rounded tip with a small notch in it, and a dorsal ridge
(c) Pigs	(i) weighs about 170.1 g (6 oz)
	(ii) long and narrow with a pointed tip, but no dorsal ridge

Brains

The brain is a part of the central nervous system and is connected to the spinal cord. It has a limited use in catering. It is a very soft meat to handle, is covered by a fine membrane, is full of small blood vessels and has the general appearance of a mass of intertwined small white tubes. The most frequently used brain in cookery is the calf's brain.

Head Meats

This term is used to describe any meats taken from the head other than the brains and tongues. Whilst head meat has some value, it frequently will be discarded for animal feeding unless the quantity handled is large enough to warrant a factory type butchery section.

(a) Ox/calves	The cheek meat may be removed and used for manufacturing meats. At times a whole calves head may be boned out and all surface flesh and cheeks used to make a classical entrée known as a calf's head.
(b) Sheep	No head meats are usually removed from a sheep's head.
(c) Pigs	The lower cheek of the pig can be removed, cured and smoked like bacon to produce 'Bath chaps'. The cheeks could otherwise be used for sausage meat.

Hearts

(a) Ox/calves	(i) the largest of the hearts weighing 1.81–2.72 kg (4–6 lb)
	(ii) has two small bones against the opening to the aorta artery
	(iii) has some fat evident on the upper portion of the heart
	(iv) three distinct ventricular furrows or grooves filled with fat
	(v) a very dark red colour
(b) Sheep	(i) a small heart weighing 113.4–170.1 g (4–6 oz)
	(ii) similar shape to a calf's heart but with a pointed apex
	(iii) three ventricular furrows

	(iv)	firm white fat on the upper part of the heart
(*c*) Pigs	(i)	a small heart weighing about 6 oz
	(ii)	a blunt apex
	(iii)	two distinct ventricular furrows
	(iv)	any fat attached to the heart will be soft and greasy.

Kidneys
(Part of the excretory system)

(*a*) Ox/calves	(i)	the largest of the kidneys weighing about 340 g ($\frac{3}{4}$ lb)
	(ii)	lobulated with 15—25 lobules
	(iii)	reddish brown in colour
	(iv)	encased in suet
(*b*) Sheep	(i)	a small kidney, weighing about 85 g (3 oz)
	(ii)	smooth, bean-shaped and unlobulated
	(iii)	dark brown in colour
	(iv)	encased in a small amount of hard, white fat
(*c*) Pigs	(i)	a small kidney, weighing 113.4—141.7 g (4—5 oz)
	(ii)	smooth, bean-shaped, but more elongated than sheep's kidneys, unlobulated
	(iii)	dark brown in colour
	(iv)	encased in a small amount of creamy white fat which is soft and greasy.

Liver
When purchased the liver should not have the gall bladder left attached to it nor show any green—yellow staining from the gall. A liver may show that clear cuts have been made into the meat. This is not evidence of poor dressing at the slaughterhouse but necessary cuts made by the meat inspector during inspection.

(*a*) Ox/calves	(i)	largest of the livers weighing 5.44—6.35 kg (12—14 lb)
	(ii)	three lobes (pieces of meat). A thin left lobe and a thick right lobe to which is attached a small prominent lobe known as a cordate lobe or thumb piece
	(iii)	a dark red colour
(*b*) Sheep	(i)	similar to a calves liver, but with a prominent division between the right and left lobes. Weight about 0.45—0.68 kg (1—1$\frac{1}{2}$ lb)
	(ii)	a small pointed cordate lobe which is not visible at all when the liver is placed face side up

(c) Pigs	(i) very distinct, it has five lobes and weighs 0.91–2.72 kg (2–6 lb)
	(ii) the surface has the appearance of Moroccan leather.

Spleen (or melt)

This is part of the blood vascular and lymphatic systems. (It acts as a filter of foreign bodies from the main blood stream, manufactures white blood corpuscles, produces antibodies, stores iron and blood.)

(a) Ox/calves	(i) largest of the spleens, weighing up to 0.91 kg (2 lb)
	(ii) elongated oval shape
	(iii) reddish-brown in calves to greyish-blue in cows
(b) Sheep	(i) flat oyster shaped, weighing about 85 g (3 oz)
	(ii) both surfaces convex
	(iii) reddish-brown in colour
	(iv) soft and elastic to touch
(c) Pigs	(i) long, narrow and tongue shaped, weighing about 142 g (5 oz)
	(ii) triangular in cross-section
	(iii) a long ridge on inner surface
	(iv) deep red in colour.

Skirt

This is meat obtained from the diaphragm (the muscular wall between the lung and abdominal cavities) of bovines. The 'thick skirt' is the central muscular portion of the diaphragm and the 'thin skirt' is the outer muscular part which is attached to the ribs. Part of the thin skirt is left on a forequarter of beef.

Stomach

The stomach of cattle and sheep, both ruminants, is complex and consists of three fore-stomachs and a true stomach, whilst the stomach of a pig is simple and sac-like. The stomachs have limited catering uses. Three of the stomachs of cattle and sometimes also sheep are processed into tripe. Sheep's stomachs may also be used as the container for haggis.

Intestines

These are simply divided into large and small intestines, the actual size depending on the type of animal. Like stomachs these are processed by specialist firms. The main uses being as containers for the many different kinds and sizes of sausages. The middle of the large intestines of a pig are processed to make 'chitterlings'.

Sweetbreads (or thymus)

These are classified as ductless glands and are thought to have a role in the growth of young animals and in the formation of antibodies. The thymus is of a pinkish white colour and is clearly lobulated. It consists of two portions, a thoracic portion found in the chest cavity and a neck portion found on either side of the windpipe. The thoracic portion or 'heartbread' is in the shape of the palm of the hand and is the largest, whilst the neck portion or 'neckbread' is smaller and elongated. The sweetbreads are largest when the animal is about 6 weeks old, after which it gradually shrinks. Calf's and lamb's sweetbreads only are used since the calf's 'heartbread' is as heavy as 0.68 kg ($1\frac{1}{2}$ lb) and a lamb's 'heartbread' about 113 g (4 oz).

Tails
The only tail that is commonly used is the ox tail which is by far the largest weighing 1.36–2.27 kg (3–5 lb). There is however a demand in some areas by the immigrant populations for pig's tails to make dishes of their homeland.

Feet
Pig's and calf's feet only are used, but the demand is somewhat limited.

Beef Offals and Catering Uses
The catering uses of beef offal are shown in tabular form (*see* Table 13.1).

Table 13.1. Catering uses of beef offal

Offal	Catering Uses
Ox cheek and head trimmings	Brawn, sausages
Calf's cheek and head trimmings	Calf's head
Tongue	Fresh or pickled, boiling, braising
Brain	Poaching
Sweetbreads	Braising, grilling, frying
Heart	Braising
Liver	Ox – braising
Liver	Calf's – frying, grilling
Kidneys	Stewing
Tail	Braising, soup
Spleen	Ingredient in manufactured goods
Skirt – thick ⎫ Part of the	Stewing
Skirt – thin ⎭ diaphragm	Stewing
Stomach – rumen, reticulum, abomasum	Cleaned and prepared for tripe
Udder	Boiled, smoked, and fried
Fats – suet	Suet pastry, mincemeat
– fat	Dripping

Lamb and Mutton Offals and Catering Uses
The catering uses of lamb and mutton offals are shown in Table 13.2.

Special Terminology
PLUCK. This consists of the windpipe, lungs, heart, liver, and spleen. In some areas of the country it is the practice for the head to be left attached.

Table 13.2. Catering uses of lamb and mutton offals

Offal	Catering Uses
Tongue	Boiling, braising
Brain	Poaching
Sweetbreads	Braising, grilling, frying
Heart	Braising
Liver	Frying, grilling
Lungs	Frying, stewing
Kidneys	Grilling, sauteing
Spleen	Ingredient in manufactured goods
Stomach — rumen	Tripe
Stomach — reticulum	Container for haggis
Intestines	Casings for sausages, etc.

Pig Offals and Catering Uses

The catering uses of pig offals are shown in tabular form (*see* Table 13.3).

Table 13.3. Catering uses of pig offal

Offal	Catering Uses
Head	Brawn
Head cheek	Smoking, boiling
Tongue	Fresh or pickled, boiling, braising
Brain	Poaching
Heart	Braising
Liver	Braising
Lungs	Frying, stewing, faggots
Kidneys	Grilling, stewing
Spleen	Ingredient in manufactured goods
Intestines	Chitterlings, sausage casings
Fats	Lard, dripping
Blood	Blood sausages
Trotters	Poached

Special Terminology

PIG'S PLUCK. This consists of the windpipe, lungs, heart and liver.
PIG'S FRY. This consists of the liver, heart, spleen together with the caul and mesenteric fat.

Bacon and Cured Meats

Bacon is obtained by processing (curing and sometimes smoking) the trimmed sides of pork or specific choice joints from a side of pork.

Cured meats are made by processing joints of pork that are not required for bacon production and from other meats such as the brisket, silverside and tongue from beef carcases and also turkeys and ducks.

The processing stage that this type of meat goes through is known as curing. Briefly this is the introduction of salt into the meat, with or without other ingredients, to preserve it and to give it a characteristic colour and flavour. The meat may also go through another stage, that of smoking.

The type of pig used is the Landrace or the Landrace/Large White cross which gives a large carcase. As mentioned previously the normal bacon pig will have a carcase weight of 61.24–83.92 kg (135–185 lb), whilst the Wall's hybrid pig has a carcase weight of 86.18–102.06 kg (190–225 lb). The Wall's hybrid pig (a heavy hog) is not specifically bred just for bacon, the 'middles' of a side are used for bacon whilst the remainder is used to produce bacon joints, ham, a variety of manufactured products such as sausages and pork pies, and fresh pork.

The Production of Bacon

For simplicity this may be broken down into some four main stages.

Preparation of the Meat

Not all of a side of pork is processed into bacon. From the side the following are removed: the head, the feet, the spinal column, the breast bone, scapula (shoulder blade), aitchbone, tail, kidneys, fillet, flare fat and most of the diaphragm (skirt). The side is then trimmed if necessary and chilled. When 'middles' are taken from a side they are removed by cutting around a template so that a standard size is always obtained.

Curing

Two clearly defined processes can be identified when examining the methods of meat curing, there are 'traditional curing' and 'rapid curing'.
TRADITIONAL CURING. The significance of traditional curing is first the customer interest in products which have an unusual but special flavour and second the advantages to the processor of being able to process a near complete side of pork. The disadvantages are the length of time for the curing to take place, with the consequent large stocks of meat being in process, and the dependence on the quality of the cured meat solely by the distribution of the curing salts by diffusion.

Traditional curing has been done over many years by two basic methods. *The Dry Method.* The principles for dry curing are the withdrawal of some of the moisture from the tissues and the replacement of it by salt in a sufficient concentration to prevent the growth of micro-organisms. The cut surfaces are well rubbed with a mixture of salt, salt petre (added as a preservative and to produce the characteristic red colour of cured meat) and sometimes a small quantity of sugar (to mask the saltiness) and other flavourings. The sides are laid with the rind-side down, covered with a layer of the curing mixture and further sides placed on top, each being covered with a layer of the curing mixture. The stack of sides would be broken and re-stacked weekly for about 5–6 weeks. The sides would then be brushed free of salt and kept in a cool dry place for at least 2 weeks to mature before being used. When fully matured this kind of bacon would be known as 'green bacon'.
The Tank Method. This is a much quicker method of curing than the dry method and is the method used to produce the mild cured Wiltshire bacon.

The sides are prepared as for the dry method, chilled for 24 hours and then injected with a brine solution in 23–32 places per side at a minimum pressure of 80lb. The sides are then packed into vats, with the cut surfaces upwards and covered with a light layer of a salt and salt petre mixture. When the vat is two-thirds full it is battened down and a cover brine solution is pumped in to cover the sides well. (N.B. the cover brine solution is weaker than the solution that was injected into each side.) The sides remain in the vats for between 96–120 hours before being removed and being stacked, rind-side upwards, for at least 7 days at a temperature of between 6–9°C (43–48°F). When matured this bacon would also be known as 'green bacon'. Any surplus brine from the tank must be strained and its strength checked before being used again.

RAPID CURING. The importance of the development of rapid curing techniques in recent years offers a complete spectrum of processing methods to the processor, enabling him to manufacture products more quickly, more precisely and more economically. The product will have a determined quantity of fat, be fast cured with a high level of cured meat pigment production, have moist lean meat of a uniform texture and colour, and possess excellent flavour and eating properties. An additional important factor to the processor is the flexibility of carcase utilization and the products which therefore can be obtained.

The basic difference from the traditional (time consuming) curing methods is the elimination of the slow diffusion process as the prime means of distributing the curing salts in the meat, and the dependence on a microbiological process to blanket the product whilst the curing takes place.

Rapid curing is done by four basic methods.

Arterial Pumping. In order to assist in this method the main arteries are left exposed where possible in the dressing of the carcase at the slaughterhouse. The arterial system of the animal is used to carry the brine to all the extremities of the carcase or joint. A double action pump, large brining needles and a prepared brine solution are all that is required. The needles are inserted into the appropriate artery and the brine pumped through them with a continuous flow until the brine solution seeps out of the extremities of the meat. The meat is then fully and efficiently cured. The only problem with this method is that the cut surfaces tend to resemble the appearance of fresh meat. This is overcome by placing the side or joint into a vat of brine for about 2 hours.

Multiple Injection Method. This is an automated method in which sides of pork or joints are injected with brine by a large number of needles to ensure that a predetermined quantity and strength of brine is evenly distributed throughout the meat.

Slice Curing Method. This method is used by some of the large bacon processing firms. It is an automated method in which chilled sliced pork is passed through a mild brine solution for several minutes only, followed by a maturing stage of 3–4 hours. The brine may contain sugar in some form so as to give a 'sweet cure'. This method enables the processor to produce a uniformly cured sliced bacon within a few hours.

Tumble Method. This method is not often used for the production of sides of bacon but is a modern curing method for joints of pork, hams, and of beef.

This method produces cured meat more quickly than the traditional method and also a more tender meat with a higher yield on cooking.

'Tumblers' are large rotating cylinders which have fixed vanes positioned on the inside. As the cylinder rotates, the joint rubs against other pieces of meat and the brine is mechanically massaged into the fibres of the meat, giving a faster and more uniform distribution of the brine throughout the meat. In addition there is some breakdown in the fibrous structure of the meat giving an improved texture to the finished product.

There are many variations of this method but the following are two typical methods:

(a) A predetermined quantity of meat and brine are tumbled together until all of the brine is taken up by the meat.

(b) Tumbling of the meat, followed by the injection of a predetermined quantity and strength of brine. The meat is then tumbled again for a sufficient period of time such that any brine that is forced out of the meat by the action of tumbling is re-absorbed.

Maturation

In order to obtain the full flavour of the cured meat it is necessary to allow the meat to mature for a period prior to being sold. The maturing time depends mainly on the size of the piece of meat. During the period of maturation the salt, salt petre, sugar, etc. gradually become more evenly distributed throughout the meat, in which time the characteristic flavour of the bacon is developed and the colour of the flesh changes from the dull pink of pork to the rose-pink colour of bacon.

Pork that has been cured and is matured is known as 'green bacon'. Its particular characteristic is its mild flavour.

Smoking

Like curing, the practice of smoking meat and fish has been carried out for hundreds of years originally very much as an art. In recent years smoking has become more scientific, reducing not only the time taken but by varying the density of smoke and the temperature required very accurately, it is possible to obtain a range of standard products. The smoking process contributes in three distinct ways to the product.

PRESERVATION. The drying of the surface of the meat inhibits the multiplication of bacteria, with their growth being further retarded by the smoking process in which the smoke deposits minute substances on the meat which act rather as germicides. The usual 'cold smoking' process operates at a final temperature of $32-49°C$ ($90-120°F$). When a 'hot smoking' process is used (i.e. when the 'cooking' and smoking process is carried out at the same time) as in the preparation of certain types of smoked sausages, the surface of the meat is well dried restricting the growth of bacteria even further.

FLAVOUR. Smoking reduces the possibility of rancidity occurring in the fat and imparts the characteristic flavour and aroma of smoked meat by the vapours distilled from the burning sawdust. The different kinds of sawdust used, such as hickory, oak or other available hardwoods, give subtle flavour distinctions, which are most pleasant and attractive.

COLOUR. Smoking gives the meat an attractive colour which is brought about by the minute deposits from the smoke on the surface of the meat.

The Process of Smoking

The old type of smoke house consisted of a large brick built room in which meats were hung over smouldering piles of sawdust until they were judged as smoked. The process was one of chance with the end product depending very much on the skill of the smoke house operative.

A modern smoke house consists of a large room in which the meats may be mechanically handled and where the density of the smoke, the temperature, humidity and the rate of air circulation can be controlled, thereby reducing the total processing time. The smoke is fed into the smoke house from a separate chamber by controllable ducts, with the temperature of the smoke, or air, being controlled by heaters positioned in the ducts. The humidity is controlled by the heaters and by steam injection into the room, and the air circulation is assisted by fans. The advantages of modern smoke houses is that a clean, standardized product may be obtained much more economically than previously.

The actual smoking of a side of bacon is in four steps:

(i) The cured sides are well washed with clean cold water and left to drain well to remove any excess moisture.

(ii) The flesh sides are evenly covered by a thin layer of freshly sieved pea-meal. The pea-meal helps to ensure a good golden brown colour to the flesh side and to contribute to the flavour of smoked bacon.

(iii) The sides are then carefully hung in the smoke house so that no sides touch nor restrict a good circulation of air or smoke. The important features are the removal of some of the moisture in the meat, the penetration of the acidic vapours and the control of the temperature of the meat. 'Cold smoking' has a final temperature range of 32–49°C (90–120°F) beyond which 'cooking' will start and some of the fatty substances in the meat begin to soften.

(iv) On completion of the smoking, the sides must be allowed to cool and 'set off' before being handled otherwise their appearance and keeping properties may well be affected.

More recent advances in the smoking of meats have seen the introduction of a smoked salt so that the smoke flavour can be imparted to the meat during the curing stage. This however does not give the meat the additional preservative effect that true smoking does, nor does it give the traditional colour. Also, 'liquid smoke' has been used, made by distilling smoke and diluting it with water, but it is suitable only for small products such as sliced bacon and certain types of sausages.

Bacon that has been smoked is known as 'smoked bacon'.

Wholesale Cuts of Bacon

Wiltshire-cut side	A side of baconer pig that has been cured whole by the traditional Wiltshire method (i.e. tank cured)
Spencer	A Wiltshire-cut side of bacon minus a square-cut gammon
$\frac{3}{4}$ Side	A side of bacon minus the fore-end
Middle	A side of bacon minus the gammon and fore-end
Fore-end	The collar and fore hock undivided
Back	The loin and ribs (5–13 inclusive)
Streaky	The belly meat
Gammon	A hind leg cut off 'square' from a Wiltshire-cut side
Ham	A hind leg cut off 'round' below the aitchbone from a side of pork and cured separately
Picnic or shoulder ham	The fore hock from a baconer pig, cut off 'round' and cured separately

Catering Uses for Cuts of Bacon

The catering uses of cuts of bacon are shown in tabular form (*see* Table 13.4).

Table 13.4. The joints, average weights from a 65 lb side of bacon and the general catering uses

Joint	Average Weight kg		lb		Catering Uses
Gammon					
(i) Hock of gammon	1.59 ⎫		$3\frac{1}{2}$ ⎫		Boiling
(ii) Middle of gammon	3.40 ⎬ 7.03		$7\frac{1}{2}$ ⎬ $15\frac{1}{2}$		Grilling, frying
(iii) Corner of gammon	2.04 ⎭		$4\frac{1}{2}$ ⎭		Grilling, frying
Back-bacon	4.54 ⎫ 7.94		10 ⎫ $17\frac{1}{2}$		Grilling, frying
Thick back-bacon	3.40 ⎭		$7\frac{1}{2}$ ⎭		Frying, boiling
Best streaky	3.17 ⎫		7 ⎫		Grilling, frying
Thin streaky	1.81 ⎬ 6.35		4 ⎬ 14		Grilling, frying, lardons
Flank	1.36 ⎭		3 ⎭		Boiling, frying
Collar	3.63 ⎫ 8.17		8 ⎫ 18		Boiling
Fore-hock	4.54 ⎭		10 ⎭		Boiling
	29.48		65		

Other Cured Meats

Hams

Hams are the hind leg from a baconer pig which is taken from a side of pork and processed separately. It is usual in order to obtain a large ham, and one that has a good appearance, for it to be removed by a 'round' cut just below the aitchbone and taking in part of the flank fat.

Hams may be classified under the following headings:

(a) by the country of origin, e.g. England, Italy, U.S.A., Germany, etc.
(b) by the catering use of each ham, e.g. Parma ham is eaten raw as an hors d'oeuvre.
(c) by the method of processing, e.g. dry cured, wet cured, unsmoked, smoked, etc. and combinations of these.

Examples of some of the most well-known hams generally available are given below. It must be stressed to the reader, that the exact methods of processing, and the ingredients used for curing and smoking are closely-guarded secrets of the manufacturers. The subtle differences in the flavour between the various types of ham being not just in the particular refinements of curing and smoking but also in the type of feed given to the live animal and the temperature and humidity of the ham during the drying and maturing stage.

English Hams

YORK HAM. This is the traditional ham of England, which has a worldwide reputation. It is a particularly long cut ham, having a distinct banjo shape. It is prepared by dry curing for about a month, the joint is then washed, dried and placed in a calico bag and allowed to mature for about six months. During this period the hams are frequently inspected and the bags changed whilst at the same time the storage temperature is gradually lowered. When fully mature the ham will have a greenish-blue mould on its surface. It is boiled or baked and served either hot or cold.

BRADENHAM HAM. A well-known ham from Chippenham in Wiltshire. It is dry cured initially followed by a 'basting cure', in which the ham is placed in a pickle of molasses, brown sugar and spices. The ham is turned and basted daily. It is then hung to dry and mature for several months. When fully mature the outside is of a coal-black colour, and the flavour mild and sweet. It is usually boiled and served cold on a buffet table at a special function.

SUFFOLK HAM. This is one of the many 'county' types of hams produced in England. The ham is cured by the 'basting cure' method. The ham first has a mixture of salt and salt petre well rubbed into the surface and is then placed into a container and partially covered by a pickle of old ale, black treacle, brown sugar, and spices. The ham is turned and basted daily for about one month and then hung to dry and mature for about three to four months. It may be boiled, baked or braised and served either hot or cold.

Italian Hams

PARMA HAM. This is the classical Italian ham. The legs are taken from pigs which are claimed to be fattened on parsnips. It is dry cured often under the pressure of other hams or weighted boards so as to give it its flattened shape. After a long maturing period of about a year, the ham is soaked in tepid water for a short time to soften the rind. It is then dried and stored for a short period before being sold. It is served raw as an hors d'oeuvre or lightly fried in butter as a garnish for egg and pasta dishes.

CULATELLO DI ZIBELLO. Another speciality ham from the province of Parma. It is a rump or pork which has been cured in a similar way to Parma ham. Before cutting a fresh ham is often steeped in white wine for 2–3 days to soften the rind and make the ham more moist.

French Hams

JAMBON DE BAYONNE. A dry cured and smoked ham. Eaten raw as an hors d'oeuvre or as a garnish in stews or egg dishes.

JAMBON DE CAMPAGNE. A sweet cured and well smoked ham. Eaten raw as an hors d'oeuvre or as a garnish in stews and egg dishes.

OTHER FRENCH HAMS. Jambon Blanc, jambon demi-sel, jambon de Paris are very similar to the English York ham except that they are very lightly smoked. They may be cooked and served hot or cold. Other French hams are available from Brittany, Lorraine, Touraine, Alsace, and Auvergne.

German Hams

There are many German hams, of which six are well known. The Mainzer, Westphalian, and Schwargwalder are eaten raw as an hors d'oeuvre whilst the Hamburger, Stuttgarter, and Gochaer are either baked, braised, or boiled and may be eaten either hot or cold.

American Hams

VIRGINIA HAM. This is the classical American ham. It is dry cured for about seven weeks and after brushing off all of the salt it is 'basting-cured' with a mixture of molasses, brown sugar, black pepper, and salt petre for a further two weeks. It is then well drained and hung up to dry and mature for up to twelve months. It is served boiled, baked, or braised and can be served either hot or cold.

SMITHFIELD HAM. This is a ham from the Smithfield area of Virginia. The hams are processed from pigs which are claimed to be fed on a diet consisting mainly of peanuts. The ham is dry cured, well rubbed with black pepper and then cold smoked for up to one month, followed by a long maturing stage of ten to twelve months. It may be served either raw or boiled, baked, or braised and eaten hot or cold.

Picnic or Shoulder Hams

These are not true hams in that they are the fore-hock (front leg) of a baconer pig which has been cut 'round' in the ham fashion and cured separately. They are usually sold already cooked and boneless and either wrapped in cryovac or canned. They may be used for the same purposes as hams, but as they will be much cheaper they will be widely used in general catering.

Gammons

A gammon is obtained by removing the hind leg from a side of bacon in a
square cut fashion. It may be either cured (i.e. taken from a side of 'green
bacon') or cured and smoked (i.e. taken from a side of 'smoked bacon'). They
may be purchased raw in which case they may be cut into three joints (*see*
Figure 13.1) and used for boiling, grilling, or frying; or they may be boiled or
baked whole. They may also be purchased as boneless cooked hams either in
a vacuum pack or canned.

Silverside

A silverside is a cut from the 'top piece' (or 'top bit') of a hindquarter of beef.
It is cured initially by the arterial method and it is then steeped in a brine
solution for up to twelve hours to bring out the true colour of cured beef. It
is usually boiled and served either hot or cold.

Brisket

A brisket is a cut from the breast region of a forequarter of beef. It is usual
to bone out the brisket first before curing by the multiple injection method
followed by steeping for several hours in a brine solution. Like cured silver-
sides they are usually boiled and served either hot or cold.

Tongues

The tongues of ox, sheep, or pigs are all used. The tongues may be either
'long cut' or 'short cut'. They are first well cleaned by washing and scraping
to remove any slime. Curing is initially by the arterial method followed by
steeping in a brine solution for several days to ensure that the taste and colour
of the meat is uniform. They are usually boiled or braised and served hot or
cold. Tongues may also be purchased as canned tongues in which case they
will have been well trimmed and tightly packed after being cured and any space
filled with a seasoned aspic glaze.

Ducks and Turkeys

The breasts of ducks and turkeys and sometimes whole turkeys are cured and
then gently smoked to produce a speciality item. The meat is sliced very thin
and eaten cold as an hors d'oeuvre in exactly the same way as raw smoked
ham.

Processed Meats

'Processed meats' covers a wide variety or products from the vast variety of
sausage type products to products such as brawn and haggis. For simplicity
the classification may be as follows:

    (i) The various 'sausage types':

        (*a*) fresh sausages, e.g. beef, pork, etc.
        (*b*) cooked sausages, e.g. frankfurters, black puddings, etc.
        (*c*) dry sausages, e.g. salami, mortadella.

    (ii) Other meat products, e.g. brawn, faggots, etc.

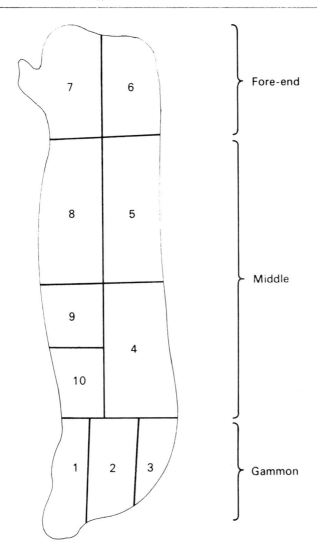

Fore-end

Middle

Gammon

Figure 13.1 Bacon cutting

1. Hock of Gammon
3. Corner of Gammon
5. Thick Back-Bacon
7. Fore-Hock
9. Thin Streaky

2. Middle of Gammon
4. Back-Bacon
6. Collar
8. Best Streaky
10. Flank

'Sausage Types'

Fresh Sausages

These are made from raw meat, fat, a filler (rusk, bread, flour, etc.), water, and seasoning, and are filled into casings (animal intestines suitably prepared or edible cellulose containers). They are purchased in the raw state and need to be cooked by grilling or frying before being served. Unlike other types of sausages these are very much a perishable product and should be used within a few days of making or purchasing.

The quality of a sausage cannot be better than its ingredients and special care should be taken to ensure that good quality ingredients are used so as to obtain an acceptable and consistent standard of product.

The recipes for making each type of 'fresh sausage' vary only slightly, the differences between each type being caused by the following:

(i) the main type of meat used and its quality, e.g. fresh clod and flank meat are used for beef sausages;

(ii) the type of quality of fat used, e.g. pork back fat is used for pork sausages;

(iii) the ratio of lean meat to fat and the percentage of both in the total product, e.g. a ratio of 4 : 1 of lean pork to back fat in a commercial pork sausage, with both representing 65% of the total product;

(iv) the type of filler or binder, and the quantity used, e.g. dry rusks for making pork or beef sausages, boiled rice for making the traditional 'Cambridge' type pork sausage;

(v) the types, quality, and quantity of the spices and seasonings used. N.B. the quantity used would depend on the region where the sausages are sold;

(vi) the method of manufacture, e.g. this depends very much on the machinery available.

A typical recipe is given below:

PORK SAUSAGE

Ingredients		Seasoning	
kg	lb	gm	oz
5.44	12	113	4
1.36	3	28	1
1.36	3	28	1
1.81	4	14	$\frac{1}{2}$
		14	$\frac{1}{2}$

Method

1. Pass lean meat through a $\frac{3}{16}$in. plate on a mincer.
2. Cube fat by hand to approximately $\frac{1}{4}$ in. cubes.
3. Place lean meat in bowl chopper, add seasoning, then the soaked rusks and finally the cubed fat. Continue until meat is of a fine consistency.
4. Fill into narrow pigs' casings and link eight to the pound. Refrigerate the sausages.

The common 'fresh sausages' include beef, pork, 'Cambridge' type pork, veal, chipolata, cocktail, and 'Cumberland' sausages. The main differences between them are outlined above.

Cooked Sausages

These are made from the same kinds of ingredients used for making 'fresh sausages' except that the filler or binders used may be cornflour, rice flour, or oatmeal and that a small quantity of onion or leek may also be used depending on the particular type being made. This type of sausage is precooked and requires no further cooking before being served. The exception to this is that some require a degree of heating prior to serving, e.g. frankfurters, black puddings, etc.

The cooking of the prepared raw sausage may be done in several ways detailed below, but what is important is that during the cooking the temperature of the meat inside the sausage reaches a high enough temperature partially to sterilize it (e.g. minimum temperature for pork meat should be 140°F). The cooking and smoking in some instances, is done in the following ways:

- (i) Smoking, followed by cooking in water;
- (ii) Cooking in water, followed by smoking;
- (iii) Adding a 'smoke powder' to the mixture then followed by cooking in water.

N.B. Depending on the particular sausage it may be cooked in water containing a dye to give it a particular colour.

The following is a very brief description of a few kinds of 'cooked sausages'.

PORK LUNCHEON SAUSAGE. Finely minced pork, potato flour, and seasoning, are smoked then cooked in water.

BOLOGNA SAUSAGE. Coarsely minced lean beef cured for 36—48 hours, is then added to a binder of cornflour and all finely chopped in a bowl chopper together with diced pork fat and seasoning. The mixture is placed into large containers then smoked for 3 hours and cooked in water containing a brown dye for up to 3 hours.

POLONY. Finely chopped lean pork, back fat, rice flour, rusks, and seasoning are placed into medium size containers and tied off into 0.45 kg (1 lb) rings. They are cooked for about 45 minutes, dipped into polony (red) dye and then dipped in cold water to set the colour.

BLACK PUDDINGS. These are made from fresh pig's blood (defibrinated to prevent clotting), cubed fat, cooked pearl barley, oatmeal, cooked onion, and seasoning. They are tied off into 0.45 kg (1 lb) rings and cooked in water (with a black dye) for about 45 minutes.

LIVER SAUSAGE. This is made from finely chopped pig's liver, pig's head meat, cornflour, onions, and seasoning. It is placed in large casings and cooked in water.

FRANKFURTERS. These are made of pork, pork fat, veal, a small quantity of filler, and seasoning. The meat may be precured or cured in the casings. They are smoked and then cooked in water.

Dried Sausages

These are made from similar ingredients to other sausage types, the main differences being that they are the largest of the sausages, that the meat is precured before processing or is cured early in the preparation and then dried under controlled conditions. They usually do not require any cooking at the preparation or serving stages, but many are smoked at relatively high temperatures. Dry sausages are mainly imported from countries such as Italy, Poland, Hungary, Germany, France, and Denmark. Those originating in the hot Mediterranean regions tend to be more heavily salted and spiced than those from Poland, Hungary, Germany, and Denmark.

The following is a brief description of a few kinds of 'dry sausages'.

GERMAN SALAMI. This is made from lean beef and pork with pork fat, which is finely minced, cured, then mixed with garlic and seasoning, and moistened with Rhine wine. It is placed in hog bungs, dried in the air for 2 weeks and then cold smoked.

ITALIAN SALAMI. This is similar to German salami but no wine is added, nor is it smoked. It is usually dried under controlled conditions for 10 weeks.

CERVALET. There are many recipes for cervalet depending on the country in which it is made, e.g. Cervalet polse is a Danish beef and pork sausage. The meat is minced, cured, seasoning added, and then packed into ox runners. It is air dried for one day and then cold smoked.

LANDJAEGER. This is made in Germany from dry cured beef and pork, together with garlic and seasoning. The meat is finely minced, seasoning added and filled into hog casings before being pressed flat, cold-smoked and dried.

MORTADELLA. This is made in Italy from cured beef, pork, and pork fat with fresh pork fat and seasoning. The seasoning includes sugar, rum, ground aniseed, and garlic. The cured meat is finely minced and then added to diced fresh pork fat and seasoning and placed into beef bladders or synthetic casings. It is then wrapped with string, air dried and then hot smoked for about 24 hours.

BLOOD AND TONGUE SAUSAGE. This is made from pork back fat, cooked and cured pork tongues, cooked pork rinds, pig's blood, and seasoning. The blood is heated and has added to it finely minced rinds, diced back fat, diced tongues and seasoning. It is thoroughly mixed and placed into large ox bungs or synthetic casings whilst still hot and then cooked for approximately 4 hours in water.

Other Meat Products

This group contains all the small goods that are not easily classified into one of the 'sausage types' explained previously. The number of products is endless, with many simply as specialities for local regions. The meat used tends to be the trimmings and offal left over from producing the more major joints and products.

The following is a brief description of some of the more common 'other meat products'.

BRAWN. This is made from the cured meat of pig's heads, ox cheeks, and beef trimmings. The meat is cooked, cut up into dice of different sizes, seasoned, placed into a mould and covered with a good clear gelatinous stock made from the cooking liquor.

FAGGOTS (OR SAVOURY DUCKS). These are made from meat remnants that are cooked, finely minced, and added to rusks, stock, and seasoning. The mix is then made into balls of about 3 oz each, wrapped in pig's caul fat and roasted. They are re-heated prior to serving.

SAVELOYS. These are made from minced beef and/or pork trimmings. The meat is minced, a filler and seasoning added, and placed into hog casings. It is hot smoked for a short period, then cooked in water with a brown dye.

HAGGIS. This is made from partially cooked sheep's lungs, liver, heart, and spleen all coarsley chopped and mixed with oatmeal, stock, and seasoning. The mixture is placed into sheep's stomachs and boiled. They are steamed for several hours prior to serving.

HASLETS. These are made from coarsley chopped lean fore-end of pork, rusks, and seasoning. The mixture is moulded into small loaf shapes, wrapped in pig's caul fat and roasted.

Table 13.5. The suggested storage temperatures and life of the edible offals, bacon, other cured meats, and processed meats

Type of Meat	Suggested Storage Temperatures $^\circ$C ($^\circ$F)	Approximate Storage Life
Edible Offals		
Fresh	0–2°C (32–35°F)	2–4 days. N.B. The offal should be wiped clean and placed on to clean trays each day
Frozen	–18°C (0°F)	3 months. N.B. When thawed out the offal should be used within 2 days
Bacon		
Green Bacon	4–7 (40–45)	7–8 days
Smoked Bacon	4–7 (40–45)	8–10 days
Other Cured Meats		
Hams – raw	4–7 (40–45)	Up to 4 months depending on type
Hams – cooked	1–4 (35–40)	8–14 days
Gammons – raw	4–7 (40–45)	1 month
Gammons – cooked	1–4 (35–40)	8–14 days
Silverside etc. – raw	4–7 (40–45)	14 days
Silverside etc. – cooked	1–4 (35–40)	8–14 days
Processed Meats		
Fresh sausages	1–4 (35–40)	2 days
Fresh sausages – frozen	–18°C (0°F)	2 months
Dry sausages	1 (35)	3–4 months, most varieties
Other meat products	1–4 (35–40)	1 week

HAMBURGERS. These are made from minced beef trimmings and pork fat, cooked chopped onions, breadcrumbs (or rusks), and seasoning. The mixture is moulded into patties of about 71–85 g ($2\frac{1}{2}$–3 oz) each, and fried or grilled prior to serving.

CREPINETTES. These are made from beef, veal, or pork. They consist of a dice of good quality lean and fat meat enclosed in a small quantity of sausage meat (of the same type) moulded into different shapes of about 57–85 g (2–3 oz) each and wrapped in pig's caul. They are fried or grilled prior to serving.

Storage of Offal, Bacon and Processed Meats

The storage and life of offal, bacon and processed meats are shown in Table 13.5.

14

Poultry, Game, and Eggs

Introduction

The term poultry is applied to birds reared for their meat and/or for their eggs, and includes chickens, ducks, geese, guinea-fowls, pigeons, and turkeys.

The start of the broiler chicken industry, since the derationing of feeding stuffs in 1954, has been one of the most remarkable stages in the agriculture industry this century. From being very much a luxury food item eaten only at Christmas and on special occasions poultry is now available throughout the year at a very competitive price with other meats. The intensive rearing of table chickens by the battery method has been also used for the production of most other types of poultry. Coupled with this has been the development of particular cross-breeds of birds to give particular strains and so achieve a faster growth rate, a good conversion rate (i.e. that is the rate at which the bird converts foodstuffs into flesh) and a good conformation with plenty of meat.

The classification of poultry is in four main ways:

- (a) by the type of poultry, e.g. chickens, ducks, geese, etc;
- (b) by the particular method of rearing, e.g. intensively reared by the broiler method or by the open range method;
- (c) by the condition of the meat when purchased, e.g. fresh, frozen, portioned, etc;
- (d) by their particular catering uses, e.g. guinea-fowl, may be served as a less expensive alternative to pheasant (a game bird).

Breeds of Poultry

Since the wide acceptance of poultry by the public throughout the year there has been the development of a large breeding industry concerned with the selection and development of strains to meet the demand. The requirements by producers are for birds with a fast growth rate, good conversion rates, and a good conformation with plenty of meat. The requirements by caterers are, in particular, a good conformation with plenty of breast meat and a consistency of quality and weight.

The typical breeds today are:

Chickens:	Brown leghorn x light Sussex
	White Rock. White Rock x light Sussex
	Rhode Island Red x light Sussex
Turkeys:	Norfolk, Cambridgeshire, American Bronze
Ducks:	Aylesbury, Pekin, White Pennine
Geese:	Embden, Toulouse, Chinese White
Guinea-fowl:	No specific breeds are known to the author. Birds are imported from Italy and France to supplement home supplies
Pigeon:	No specific breeds are known to the author. The wild pigeon is smaller and has a stronger flavoured flesh than those that are domestically reared. Supplies are supplemented by imports from Britanny and Bordeaux.

General Nomenclature

Chickens

Cock	An adult entire male
Hen	An adult female, mainly used for the production of eggs
Pullet	A young female up to the stage when she is capable of laying eggs (i.e. up to 20−22 weeks old)
Battery hen	Adult females, kept in cages where they are automatically fed and watered. Their main purpose to a producer is the maximum production of eggs. When the egg laying performance of the bird falls off, the birds are slaughtered and frequently used either in manufactured poultry products or those having a good conformation as boiling fowls for the retail and catering industries
Broiler	Young chickens of either sex. They are mass produced either by the deep litter method (i.e. housing the birds in large, well heated and ventilated buildings and allowing them to live on a deep litter floor of wood shavings or sawdust) or by confining them in cages like battery hens. This latter method is particularly used for the production of the smaller type of birds such as poussins. This mass production method is known as the batch system in which 5−10 thousand birds of only one age group and species are kept in a production house at any one time. The birds are fed on a high protein diet so that they can put on as much flesh weight in the shortest possible time. On reaching the desired weight range which is achieved

between 6–12 weeks of age they are all killed. The production house is then thoroughly sterilized, fresh stock brought in and the process repeated four to five times a year. This system reduces the risk of disease which would happen if fresh stocks of young birds were brought in periodically amongst growing birds. Since they are so young broiler birds have less flavour in comparison with an older bird. The present annual production of broiler birds is in excess of three million

Single poussin
: A young bird of either sex of some 5–6 weeks of age and produced by the batch system

Double poussin
: A young bird of either sex of some 6–7 weeks of age and produced by the batch system

Spring chickens
: The original name given to young open-range birds sold during spring. Now generally accepted as an alternative term to broilers

Capons
: Originally, a true capon was a male chicken from which the testes (sex organs) had been removed by a simple surgical operation, or suppressed by the implantation of oestrogen near to the base of the skull, or by mixing oestrogenic compounds in with the foodstuffs. This gave a treated bird the advantages of a much longer growing period, an increase in weight and a more tender and juicy flesh. These methods of treatment are now illegal.

The term capon today refers to a table bird, usually in excess of 2.72 kg (6 lb) in weight.

Table 14.1. Average percentage figures obtained from good quality chicken of average weight 1.8 kg (4 lb) liveweight, based upon the empty liveweight

	%
Feathers and blood	11.5
Head and shanks	6.5
Digestive tract	9.5
Lungs	0.5
Heart	0.5
Liver and gall bag	1.7
Kidneys	0.5
Neck	3.0
Carcase	63.3
Loss	3.0
Total	100.0
Total bone in dressed carcase	15.0%

Poularde
: A de-sexed female chicken which is allowed to grow to a large size. These are not frequently seen on the market

today mainly because of the availability of capons and the fact that female birds are likely either to be killed when under 12 weeks of age or used for egg production

Boiling fowls   These are, in the main, adult female birds which were originally used for the production of eggs. When their egg laying performance declines, they are killed, dressed, and sold to enable the egg producer to off-set the cost of his next egg laying flock. This means that the birds will be about one and a half years old when killed and will therefore be not only larger than the typical sized broiler bird but will have much more flavour

Ducks

Drake   An adult male

Duck   An adult female, although generally the term applies to an adult bird of either sex

Duckling   A young duck, usually produced by the batch system like broiler chickens, about 10–16 weeks of age when slaughtered

Geese

Gander   An adult male

Goose   An adult female

Gosling   Young birds of either sex

Turkeys

Poults   Very young turkeys. Usually only available on the market in September and October

Stag   A mature male, used for breeding

Cock   An entire male, produced by the batch production system. Heavier than the female of a similar age

Hen   A female bird, produced by the batch production system

Mini-turkey   A much smaller hybrid strain of turkey produced to popularize Turkeys throughout the year as against the more traditional times of Christmas and sometimes Easter

Guinea-fowl   Birds of either sex produced today by the batch production system. Killed at 14–20 weeks of age

Pigeon   Birds of either sex, killed at 8–12 weeks of age

See Table 14.2 for a summary of the poultry which are readily available from wholesalers.

The Slaughtering of Poultry

The slaughtering of poultry for sale to the public is rigidly controlled by law to ensure that the method of slaughtering and subsequent preparation of the carcases take place under hygienic conditions in licenced slaughterhouses and that the meat is inspected by authorized officers and found to be fit before being permitted to be sold for human consumption. The E. C. regulations require particularly stringent conditions regarding the slaughtering and subsequent dressing of poultry.

The complete slaughtering process of poultry is in eight main stages.

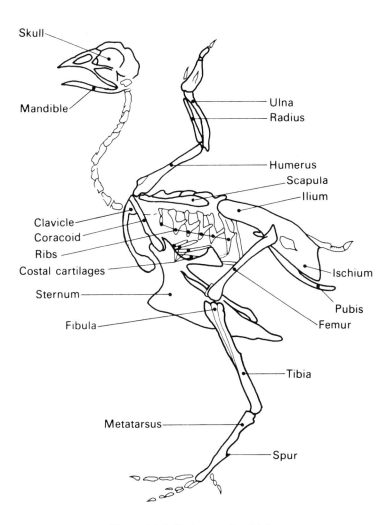

Figure 14.1 Skeleton of a chicken

Table 14.2. A summary of the poultry readily available from wholesalers, their approximate age at slaughter and their average weight range, oven ready

English	French Term	Average Weight (oven ready) kg	lb	Average Age
Poussin—single	le Poussin	227—283 gm	8—10 oz	5—6 weeks
Poussin—double	le Poussin	283—397 gm	10—14 oz	6—7 weeks
Spring chicken	le Poulet de Grain	0.91—1.13 kg	2—2$\frac{1}{2}$ lb	8—10 weeks
Broiler chicken	le Poulet Reine	1.13—1.81 kg	2$\frac{1}{2}$—4 lb	8—12 weeks
Boiling fowl	la Poule	1.81—2.72 kg	4—6 lb	12—18 months
Capon	le Chapon	2.72—4.08 kg	6—9 lb	5—8 months
Large roasting chicken	la Poularde	1.81—3.63 kg	4—8 lb	5—6 months
Turkey—cock	le Dindon	5.44—11.34 kg	12—25 lb	6—10 months
Turkey—hen	le Dindonneau	4.54—7.26 kg	10—16 lb	6—10 months
Turkey—mini	le Dindonneau	2.72—4.54 kg	6—10 lb	10—16 weeks
Duck	le Canard	1.81—2.72 kg	4—6 lb	12—16 weeks
Duckling	le Caneton	1.36—1.81 kg	3—4 lb	8—12 weeks
Goose	l'Oie	3.63—6.35 kg	8—14 lb	6—9 months
Gosling	l'Oison	1.81—2.72 kg	4—6 lb	4—6 months
Guinea-fowl	la Pintade	0.68—1.13 kg	1$\frac{1}{2}$—2$\frac{1}{2}$ lb	4—6 months
Pigeon	le Pigeon	283—397 gm	10—14 oz	6—10 weeks

Ante-mortem Inspection

Birds to be killed are brought to the slaughterhouse, which is usually situated on the same site that the birds are produced on, in a regular flow of batches of birds. Birds will be starved of food for some 4—6 hours so that the minimum amount of food is in the intestines when they are killed. Should birds be starved for longer periods they would start to lose body weight, which is the last thing that a producer would wish for. An adequate supply of drinking water is always available as it is essential not only for birds to maintain a normal body temperature in warm weather but also to prevent them from becoming distressed. Birds which show evident signs of malformation, illness, or distress are put to one side for further detailed inspection and do not enter into the slaughterhouse proper.

Killing and Bleeding

The large-scale processing of birds will be by a semi-automatic conveyor line system so that a large number of birds can be handled each hour. Birds will be placed upside-down in funnel type containers, to restrict the flapping of their wings and subsequent bruising, with the head hanging downwards. The birds travel along the conveyor and pass through a small area where they are electrically stunned — but not killed. They are killed by an operator who makes an incision with a sharp knife across the neck causing a rapid loss of blood. This results in a carcase which is clean to eviscerate, reasonably white in general appearance and that will keep well.

Plucking

The birds are taken out from the funnels and hung on hooks by their feet. They then pass through a water bath 52–54°C (126–130°F) for a few minutes and then through automatic plucking machines before being hung by their heads with the final plucking being finished by hand. The plucking of ducks and geese is slightly different in that they are usually dipped into hot wax and not water. This results in a carcase with a better appearance and with dry feathers which is more readily sold offsetting the processing costs. The carcases are then cooled to 4°C (40°F) to prevent bacterial spoilage if they are not going to be eviscerated immediately.

N.B. At this stage there is usually a physical division in the slaughtering process to separate completely the bleeding and defeathering stages from the eviscerating stage when the carcase is cut open so as to restrict any contamination.

Evisceration

A final cut is made by an operator between the end of the keel (sternum) and the vent to allow easy access to the abdomen, and a second cut made along the length of the neck to allow the crop and neck to be removed. The intestines are removed together with the liver, heart, and gizzard, and are separately inspected and washed before being sent with the neck to the giblet packing section. The opened carcase, after the head and feet have been cut off, is then thoroughly washed and inspected.

Cooling

This stage is the cooling of the cleaned carcase in troughs of water and ice chippings so as to reduce the temperature of the carcases to 4°C (40°F). The carcases to be propelled in a direction opposite to the flow of water.

Trussing

The giblets, which are usually wrapped in small polythene bags, are then inserted in the abdomen space of the drained carcases and are trussed either with string or rubber bands to reshape the carcases.

Weighing

The carcases are then weighed and separated into their particular weight ranges.

Packing

The carcases are then usually wrapped in polythene bags to keep them clean, to prevent any dehydration and if they are to be frozen, from such damage as freezer-burn.

Purchasing of Poultry

Poultry may be purchased as either open range or batch system birds.

Open Range Birds

These are birds which have had a more natural mode of life, living in large houses with free access to open ground and fed on a diet of natural foods.

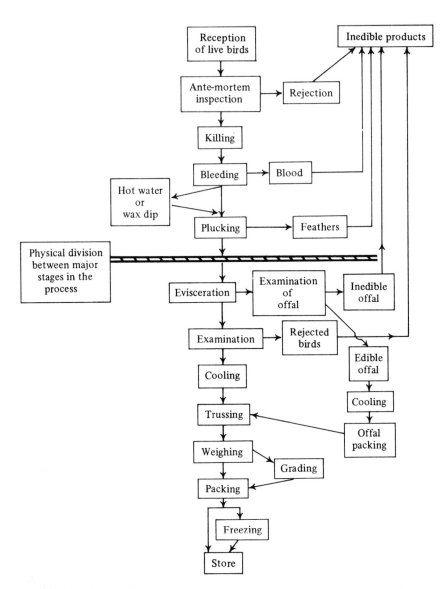

Figure 14.2 A flow diagram of the slaughter process for poultry. Although it bears similarities to the processing for larger animals, a large modern poultry production unit will be dealing with the slaughter of some 10–20 thousand birds a day.

These birds will generally be older (and have more flavour) than mass produced birds of the same weight.

Batch System Birds

These are birds that have been mass produced by intensive farming methods. They are the broiler type of birds previously described in this chapter. They are produced from specific cross-breeds in the shortest possible time, and are therefore very young birds.

Irrespective of whether they are open range or batch system birds they are available in the following forms.

Rough Plucked

This form of bird has had most of the external feathers cleanly removed. They are mainly purchased in the fresh state.

Eviscerated

This sort of bird has been fully dressed, i.e. all external feathers and hairs removed, has been fully drawn and has been trussed with the giblets placed inside the carcase.

N.B. Drawn poultry looses approximately 25% of its original weight. The giblets (neck, heart, liver, and gizzard) should not represent more than 10% of the total weight of the prepared eviscerated bird. They are purchased either in the fresh or frozen state.

Portioned

These birds have been cut up into portions (*see* Figure 14.3 for the cutting of a chicken). It is usual that portioned poultry will be sold as leg meat or breast meat, although for high class catering it is possible to buy fully prepared suprêmes. Again, it is possible to purchase these in the fresh or frozen state.

Quality Recognition

The quality of poultry will differ according to the type of poultry, the particular breed, the age and how well the bird has been fed.

The following main points are taken into consideration:

(i) The skin should be of a pale colour: white for chickens and turkeys, a rich cream/white for ducks and geese and grey/white for guinea-fowls and pigeons.

(ii) The skin should be unbroken with no cuts, blood patches, or evidence of bruising.

(iii) The breast should be straight, broad, and very well fleshed.

(iv) The breast bone should be pliable at the extremity. N.B. The breast bone or keel in poultry is rather pointed except for ducks and geese which have a square-ended breast bone.

(v) The flesh should be firm but pliable with a very fine texture. It should also have a pleasant and characteristic smell.

(vi) The wings should be compact.

(vii) The legs should be compact and well fleshed.

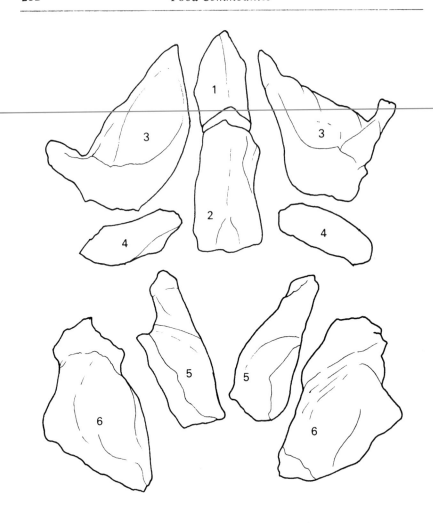

1 and 2—Breast (Poitrine)
    3—Wing Fillet (Filet, Aile, Suprême)
    4—Small Wing End (Ailerons)
    5—Leg (Pilon)
    6—Thigh (Gras de Cuisse)

Figure 14.3 The cutting of a chicken for sautéing

(viii) The bones should be fine.

(ix) The quantity of fat on the bird should be small, particularly in the abdominal cavity.

Game

Introduction

The term game refers to animals which are hunted and the flesh of which may be eaten by humans. Although this general definition is still correct many types of game are today produced by domestically rearing them like poultry.

Unlike poultry, game is specifically protected by legislation which was originally designed to give protection during the breeding periods and to restrict the hunting to certain months of each year. Each particular type of game has a closed season during which they must not be hunted nor sold. Furthermore, game must only be sold by shops and wholesalers who are licensed to sell game.

There are two basic kinds of game, namely:

(*a*) feathered game, e.g. pheasant, partridge, grouse, wild duck, etc;

(*b*) furred game, e.g. venison, hare, wild rabbit, wild boar, etc.

Game may be classified in the following ways:

(i) by the basic kind of game, whether feathered or furred;

(ii) by the individual species of game within its basic classification, e.g. pheasant (a feathered game);

(iii) by the season that it is specifically available for use by the caterer, e.g. grouse is available in the fresh state only between 12 August and 12 December;

(iv) by the particular catering uses, e.g. the mature hare is specifically used in dishes such as jugged hare.

Differences with the Meat from Game

Feathered Game

Game birds are different from poultry birds in several respects.

AGE. The age at which game birds are shot and available on the market is not so controllable as that of poultry which are domestically reared, and therefore it is not unusual to purchase game birds of different age groups, thus having different catering uses.

ACTIVITY. Game birds will have been much more active than poultry and therefore the muscles of the legs in particular will have been developed and are likely to be tough. Birds required for roasting should be young and ideally purchased early in the season.

FAT. There is very little fat to be found on game birds apart from those of the duck family. In order to prevent the breast meat from being too dry when cooked, it is the usual practice to cover the breast meat with either streaky bacon or larding bacon (salted pork fat).

HANGING OF GAME. It is usual to consume some types of game after hanging it for a period after it has been killed and prior to it being cooked. It is normal for the birds not to be cleaned prior to being hung. The stage of hanging allows the characteristic 'game flavour' to develop and also assists in tenderizing the meat. It really is a stage of meat decomposition which ends in a condition of putrefaction when the game would be maggoty, the flesh greenish in colour, quite soft and totally unfit for human consumption.

Furred Game

The above four points are also relevant to furred game.

AGE. The age of furred game is not so controllable as that of cattle, sheep, and pigs.

ACTIVITY. The animals will have led a very active life in order to obtain food for themselves and to survive, and therefore the meat apart from that of young animals will be tough.

FAT. There is very little fat to be found on game animals and the meat is usually larded with salted fat pork to prevent it drying out completely during cooking.

HANGING. All furred game is hung prior to cooking to tenderize the meat and to develop the characteristic 'game flavour'. Unlike feathered game, it is usually treated by a further stage of being marinaded for 12–24 hours in a mixture of red wine, carrots, onions, and various herbs.

Recommended Hanging Times

Feathered Game

Grouse Ptarmigan Capercaille Blackcock Pheasant Partridge Quail	Up to 7 days
Wild duck Teal	1–2 days
Corncrake	1–2 days
Plover Snipe Woodcock	Hung until clearly 'high'
Woodpigeon	2–3 days

Furred Game

Hares Rabbits (wild)	2–3 days
Venison	Up to 3 weeks
Wild boar	Up to 3 weeks

Game Seasons

These are shown in Table 14.3.

Table 14.3. The English and French names and seasonal availability of game

English Name	French Name	Season Available
Feathered game		
(1) Grouse (red)	la Grouse	12 August–10 December
Ptarmigan	la Poule de Neige	12 August–12 December
Capercaille	le Grand Tétras	20 August–12 December
Blackcock	le Tétras	20 August–12 December
(2) Pheasant	le Faisan	1 October–1 February
Partridge (young)	la Perdreaux	1 September–1 February
Quail	la Caille	1 July–30 September
(3) Wild duck	le Canard Sauvage	12 August–1 March
Teal	la Sarcelle	12 August–1 March
(4) Corncrake	le Râle de Genet	12 July–12 September
(5) Plover	le Pluvier	1 October–15 March
Snipe	la Bécassine	12 August–31 January
Woodcock	la Bécasse	12 August–31 January
(6) Woodpigeon (wild)	le Ramier	1 August–15 March
Furred game		
Hares	le Lièvre	September–March
Rabbits (wild)	le Lapin	September–April
Venison (buck)	la Venaison	August–October
(doe)		October–February

N.B. The Seasons listed above refers only to that for fresh game. It does not include deep frozen game, some of which may be obtained throughout the year.

The numbers beside the feathered game, relate to the group to which each species of bird belongs to: (1) The grouse family (2) The pheasant family (3) The duck family (4) The rail family (5) The sandpiper family (6) The pigeon family.

A Brief Description of the Different Game

Feathered Game

THE GROUSE FAMILY

Grouse. The famous grouse that is used most commonly is the red grouse which is shot on the Yorkshire or Scottish moors on 'the glorious Twelfth', the 12 August. It is a small reddish-brown bird, speckled with black feathers, possessing white down feathers on its lower legs. The birds are prepared and trussed like chicken except that the breast will be covered with thin slices of salted pork fat or streaky bacon. Grouse are usually only large enough for one or two persons.

Ptarmigan. A native bird (known also as white grouse and rock partridge) of the north of Scotland, it is the only British bird with the Arctic trait of assuming a pure white plumage in winter. During the rest of the year its plumage is a brown colour mottled with black with only its wings and under-parts being white. The prepared bird is about the size of a pheasant.

Capercaille (or capercailzie). Another native of the north of Scotland, it is the largest game bird (excluding the swan). Its plumage is grey—black with a dark green breast and a large fan tail. The male bird is much larger than the female and can weigh up to 4.54 kg (10 lb) with the female weighing up to 2.72 kg (6 lb).

Blackcock (or black grouse). This member of the grouse family is found in Scotland, Wales, and the north of England. The male is recognized by its blue—black plumage and a distinctive white lyre-shaped tail, whilst the female, a much smaller bird, has a chestnut and buff plumage with a forked tail and feathered legs. The cock will weigh 1.36—1.81 kg (3—4 lb) and the hen 0.91 kg (2 lb).

THE PHEASANT FAMILY

Pheasant. This is one of the most common of game birds, found throughout the U.K., where its wild population has increased in recent years. The male is recognized by its copper plumage and the multi-coloured plumage of its head, its ringed neck, and its long 18 in. tail, whilst the female is recognized by its mottled brown plumage and a shorter 9 in. tail. The typical weights for the cock are 1.13—1.59 kg ($2\frac{1}{2}$—$3\frac{1}{2}$ lb), and the hen 0.91 kg (2 lb).

Partridge. There are several varieties of this species with the common ones being the red-legged and the grey-legged. They are found throughout the U.K. Both varieties have a brown plumage with the red-legged having rich chestnut barring (stripes) on grey flanks, whilst the grey-legged has a dark horseshoe pattern on its breast. The typical weights are 0.34—0.45 kg ($\frac{3}{4}$—1 lb).

Quail. This tiny bird was originally imported from Egypt and India, but today they are produced on quail farms in the U.K. The birds resemble young partridges having a sandy brown plumage. The birds are so small (weighing only 57.85 gm (2—3 oz) each) that they are dressed and packed usually in small boxes and sold by the dozen.

THE DUCK FAMILY

Wild Duck. Two common varieties of this species are available to the caterer, the mallard and the wigeon.

(i) The mallard is the best known of the wild ducks and is found throughout the U.K. The duck is recognized by its brown plumage, whilst the drake has a glossy green head and white ringed neck and a purple brown breast. The dressed weights of the birds are 0.68—1.13 kg ($1\frac{1}{2}$—$2\frac{1}{2}$ lb).

(ii) The wigeon is found mainly in Scotland. It is a slightly smaller bird than the mallard and is distinguished from a mallard by its pointed tail. The drake has a cream coloured fore-head and a white forewing and grey upper parts, whilst the duck is darker in colour with a grey—green wing patch. The dressed weights of the birds are 0.68—0.91 kg ($1\frac{1}{2}$—2 lb).

Teal. The smallest duck commonly used by caterers is found mainly in Scotland and Ireland and to a lesser extent in Wales and the north eastern parts of England. Both sexes are recognized by having a distinct green patch bordered by black and white on the rear of the wings. The drake is separately identified by having a metallic green stripe around the eye. The dressed weight of the birds is only about 0.27 kg ($\frac{1}{2}$ lb).

THE RAIL FAMILY

The Corncrake. A less well-known game bird (also known as the landrail) belonging to the same family as the moorhen and the coot. Although some fifty years ago it was a very common bird throughout the U.K., today it is only found in the western parts of Ireland and Scotland. Both sexes have a near identical plumage of brown feathers with dark brown streaks on the back. The dressed weight of the birds is 0.27–0.34 kg ($\frac{1}{2}$–$\frac{3}{4}$ lb).

THE SANDPIPER FAMILY

These are small long and thin beaked birds which characteristically are dressed differently to other game birds and poultry. The differences are that only the gizzard, the gall bladder, and the intestines are removed. This is done by making a small incision under one of the legs. Second, the neck and head are not removed, but are skinned and the eyes removed, with the beak used to truss the bird.

The Golden Plover. One of the many varieties of the plover species. It is found in Scotland, North Wales, and the north of England. It is a small bird recognized by both sexes having spangled gold and black feathers on its upper parts and a black face. The dressed weights of the bird are about 113 g (4 oz).

The Snipe. There are several varieties of this bird, a few of which only are used for food, in particular the common, great, and jack snipes. They are recognized as small birds, with brown streaked plumage and a long thin straight beak. The dressed weight of a bird is 113–170 g (4–6 oz).

Woodcock. A bird that is similar when fully dressed to a snipe. It is recognized by its russet colour feathers and the dark bars on its head and underparts. When fully prepared for cooking it is often slightly larger than a snipe having a weight of 170–227 g (6–8 oz) and is further identified from a snipe by having a slight curve to its long thin beak.

THE PIGEON FAMILY

Woodpigeon. The wild woodpigeon can be classified as a game bird simply because in order to obtain them they have to be shot. They are recognized by having grey feathers on their head, neck, and tail and grey–brown feathers on their back and wings. The adult is identified by having a white patch on the side of the neck. The dressed weight of a bird is 227–340 g (8–12 oz).

Furred Game

HARES

There are two kinds of hare in the U.K., the mountain hare (also known as Scotch Blue in Scotland) and the common hare. The mountain hare is smaller and is claimed to have a finer flavour. Hares are best when under one year old, although the meat from females remains tender even up to two years of age. Easily distinguished from a rabbit as the hare is heavier 2.27–4.08 kg (5–9 lb), has a cleft lip and two large incisor teeth on the upper jaw and larger and much longer hind legs and ears. When purchased they will often still have the fur left on and only be partially dressed or paunched (i.e. only the lower intestines will have been removed, with the chest cavity remaining intact to collect the blood which may be used to thicken the sauce for jugged hare). In a young animal the ears should tear very easily.

RABBITS

Rabbits are similar to hares but much smaller 1.36–1.81 kg (3–4 lb). Ideally, they are best when 3–4 months old. The flesh is often flavoured by the wild rabbit's diet which may include such things as wild thyme or tree bark. Its flesh is paler than that of a hare, and is more easily digestible.

VENISON

This is the most common of hoofed game and refers to the flesh of the deer species, e.g. fallow-deer, red dear, roebuck, and stag. The stag should be killed at about three years of age when it is at its best; after this age it develops a strong flavour and the flesh becomes coarse and dry. Other deer should be killed when four to five years old when the fat should be bright and clear and the lean flesh not yet coarse and tough. The bucks (male) are considered to be at their best in the early autumn, whilst the doe (female) is at her best in the early winter. The dressed carcase of venison is similar in size to that of a large carcase of mutton, although it will have longer legs. The main difference is the colour of the meat which is a very dark blood-red colour, and the fat (although minimal) is whitish, hard, and crisp. It is the usual practice to dust the surface of the carcase with a mixture of salt, freshly ground black pepper and flour, and to hang the carcase in a cold room for two to three weeks to allow it to develop the characteristic game flavour. Venison is butchered in a similar way as that for lamb or mutton and is often marinaded like hares prior to cooking.

WILD BOAR

This animal although quite common in parts of Europe and the U.S.A. is seldom available in the U.K. It is a wild pig and may be treated in the same manner as pig meat. It may be purchased at times in the U.K., smoked like ham, or as small boars which have been boned, stuffed, and cooked for serving cold on a buffet table.

Purchasing of Game

Game may be purchased as either open range or domestically reared livestock.

(a) Open Range Birds and Animals

These will have lived naturally in the environment and will have been hunted.

(b) Domestically Reared Birds and Animals

This method is becoming much more common today in order to meet the demand for the supply of game.

The main difference between (*a*) and (*b*) above is that in (*a*) there is the possibility that the carcase may be bruised with large haemorrhages present in the flesh and also lead shot may be found. A second difference is that the age of the birds and animals can differ quite a lot and therefore some selection is necessary to ensure the correct type and age is chosen for a particular method of cooking.

Game birds may be purchased as follows.

Complete
These are complete with all feathers and uncleaned.

Rough Plucked
A bird that has had most of the external feathers removed is called rough plucked.

Fully Dressed
These birds are eviscerated, trussed, and in most cases the breast meat is covered with slices of larding bacon.

Frozen
In this case the bird will normally be eviscerated.

Furred game may be purchased in three ways.

Dressed Carcase Meat
These are fully prepared and ready for butchering into joints.

Prepared Joints
An example is a saddle of venison.

Prepared Meats
Hare paté, terrine of venison, or boar's head are examples of prepared meats.

Quality Recognition
The quality of game will differ according to the particular type of game, the age and how well it has been fed.
The following main points are taken into consideration.

Game Birds
Similar points as for poultry are to be considered.

   (i) The beak should break easily indicating a young bird.
  (ii) The extremity of the breast bone should be pliable.
 (iii) The breast should be broad and well fleshed.
  (iv) The skin should be unbroken with no cuts or excessive blood patches or evidence of severe bruising.
   (v) The flesh should be firm, but pliable, with a fine texture. It should also have a pleasant and characteristic smell and not be too 'high'.
  (vi) The legs should be compact.

Furred Game
HARES AND RABBITS
   (i) The ears should tear easily and the lower jaw should easily break with the fingers.
  (ii) Young hares should only have a faintly defined harelip.
 (iii) The claws on the feet should be easily broken.
  (iv) The meat should be firm and pliable to the touch. (The smell should be pleasant and characteristic but not too 'high'.)

(v) The animal should be well developed particularly in the hind legs
and the saddle.
(vi) There should be no evidence of bruising.

VENISON

(i) Ideally the carcase should be from an animal under five years of
age.
(ii) The meat should be firm and pliable with a fine texture. It should
also have a pleasant and characteristic smell, but not too 'high'.
(iii) The fat should be clear, bright, and thick.
(iv) There should be no evidence of excessive bruising.
(v) The carcase should be well developed, particularly in the regions
of the hind legs and the saddle.

Catering Uses of Poultry and Game

The catering uses of poultry and game are shown in tabular form (*see* Table
14.4).

Table 14.4. The main catering uses of poultry and game

	Main Catering Uses
Poultry	
Poussin	Roasting, grilling, pot-roasting
Spring chicken	Roasting, grilling, sauté, pot-roasting, pies, suprêmes
Broiler chicken	As above
Boiling fowl	Boiling, pot-roasting, soups, stocks
Capon	Roasting or pot-roasting
Turkey	Roasting
Duck	Roasting, braising, sauté
Goose	Roasting, braising
Guinea-fowl	Roasting, pot-roasting
Pigeon	Roasting, braising, pies
Game	
Game birds – young	Roasting
– old	Braising, pies, terrines, pâtés, special consommés
Furred game	Roasting, braising, pies, terrines, pâtés

Storage of Poultry and Game

The storage and life of birds are shown in Table 14.5.

Scientific and Nutritional Aspects

Nutrition

The compositions of the meat from poultry and game are shown in Tables
14.6 and 14.7, and from these figures it is clear that such meat forms an
excellent source of protein in the diet, comparing favourably both in content

Table 14.5. The suggested storage temperatures and time of poultry and game

Type	Suggested Storage Temperatures °C (°F)	Approximate Storage Time
Fresh poultry (all kinds)	0–2 (32–36°)	1 week N.B. The poultry should have the giblets removed and be wiped clean and placed on to clean trays each day.
Frozen poultry (all kinds)	–18 (0°)	1 year N.B. The poultry should be fully thawed out before cooking. When thawed out it should be used within two days.
Fresh feathered game	0–2 (32–36°)	1 week N.B. Care should be taken not to allow the birds to become too 'high', particularly waterbirds.
Frozen feathered game	–18 (0°)	6 months N.B. Treat exactly as frozen poultry.
Fresh furred game	0–2 (32–36°)	2–3 weeks. N.B. Storage can be lengthened by a further 1–2 weeks if the game is cut up into joints, after the initial hanging, and marinaded in wine, root vegetables, and herbs.

Table 14.6. Percentage edible matter and approximate composition
of poultry meats
(data adapted from McCance and Widdowson, 1978)

Food type	Percentage of normally edible portion	Percentage of composition of flesh		
		Protein	Fat	Water
Chicken, roast	40	24.8	5.4	68.4
Duck, roast	21	25.3	9.7	64.2
Goose, roast	39	29.3	22.4	46.7
Pigeon, roast	28	27.8	13.2	57.2
Turkey, roast	46	28.8	2.7	68.0

Table 14.7. Percentage edible matter and approximate composition
of game meats
(data adapted from McCance and Widdowson, 1978)

Food type	Percentage of normally edible portion	Percentage of composition of flesh		
		Protein	Fat	Water
Grouse, roast	51	31.3	5.3	61.6
Partridge, roast	39	36.7	7.2	54.5
Pheasant, roast	45	32.2	9.3	56.9
Rabbit, stewed	35	27.3	7.7	63.9
Venison, roast	58	35	6.4	56.8

and quality with other types of meat such as beef, mutton, and pork (*see* Table 11.2).

While perhaps game for the most part is still regarded as luxury fare, poultry, chickens in particular, have become almost an everyday dish. A little over twenty years ago chicken was still regarded as a symbol of prosperity; now, new techniques of breeding and new methods of marketing have made this one-time luxury into an inexpensive (relatively) and important part of the normal diet in the U.K.

Poultry and Game Meat: Constituents
The comments made under the various headings in the chapter on meat are largely applicable to poultry and game — but perhaps the following points need to be noted.

COLOUR
Dark and light meats are characteristic, the darker usually being associated with muscles used a great deal during life. The darker meat also has more of the pigmented protein myoglobin.

FAT
More fat is generally associated with dark meat, and contributes to its greater juiciness. A comparison of Tables 14.6 and 14.7 with the similar ones in the chapter on meat, will show that in general poultry and game are less fatty than other meats (duck being a notable exception).

FLAVOUR
Similar explanations apply here as in the case of other meats, however, particularly in the case of game, extended periods of hanging are sometimes recommended. Besides ensuring that all effects of rigor have passed, these long hanging times allow characteristic flavours to develop as enzymes naturally present cause the proteins to degrade to amino-acids and other related nitrogenous compounds. Game which is said to be 'high' is at a stage of putrefaction — a stage at which some gourmets are said to prefer some of these meats.

Poultry Processing
Although this has already been discussed, perhaps the following points need further clarification.

Use of Oestrogens

It was found that a castrated cockerel, put on more flesh in a given time, for a given intake of feed, than a similar uncastrated cockerel. Therefore, if large mature birds are required for the table, this caponization process would be advantageous, since not only is a larger, more fleshy bird of high quality produced, but its flesh is also more tender. There are, however, several problems about surgical caponization, and because of these, chemical caponization was preferred. This later process involved implantation of pellets of female hormones (oestrogens — usually synthetic) just under the skin of the bird, which suppress completely the maleness of the bird, rendering it docile, with the attendant advantages of flesh production mentioned earlier.

However, the bulk demand today is for the broiler, a chicken of 10–12 weeks of a particular strain with a high growth rate. Caponization using chemicals is now an illegal method of production in the U.K.

Polyphosphates

These complex phosphates may be added to chickens for example (and many other meat products) because they cause the protein to retain more water and are said thereby to improve the texture of the final product — it may be argued (perhaps unreasonably) that this enables the producer to sell the consumer a product containing more water!

Hygiene

Poultry are exposed to organisms during their life which may give rise to food poisoning in man if appropriate conditions prevail. Even the feed meal may contain salmonellae organisms, which may cause the poultry subsequently to carry the organisms.

In recent years the rapid growth of the broiler industry for chickens (and to some extent similarly for turkeys and ducks), has had associated with it, an increased rate of infection of birds and carcases. This is because there is likely to be a greater cross-contamination of poultry carcases during bulk production, than in previous small-scale processes.

The implications for the caterer and domestic consumer are obvious.

(i) Great care must be taken to avoid raw poultry coming into contact (even indirectly via dirty preparation surfaces, etc.) with other food.

(ii) Frozen poultry must be thawed thoroughly before cooking, otherwise bacteria might survive and multiply during the cooking process, and hence cause food-poisoning in the consumer. This has happened a number of times with lethal consequences.

(iii) All poultry should be thoroughly cooked prior to service. Longer times should be allowed for birds which have been stuffed to ensure that any bacterial contamination has been destroyed because it should be noted that even though a bird appears to be cooked on the outside, the inside, particularly if stuffed, could still be at a temperature which would encourage bacterial multiplication.

Storage
Mention has been made about hanging poultry and game for effects of rigor to pass and for flavour to develop, but for long-term storage, where minimal changes in flavour and texture are desired, freezing is the principal method employed. It is stated by many authorities that chicken meat particularly increases in tenderness with frozen storage.

Eggs

The bulk of all egg purchases are of hens' eggs, although the eggs of ducks, geese, turkeys, and seagulls are used at times in the catering industry.

Eggs may be classified under one or a combination of the following:

(a) the type of egg, e.g. chicken or duck, etc;
(b) whether a fresh or processed egg;
(c) the method of processing, if applicable — e.g. frozen, dried, etc;
(d) the catering uses — specific types of processed eggs should be purchased for particular purposes, so as to ensure a satisfactory end product.

The Function of Eggs
Eggs are one of the most versatile ingredients used in food preparation and are to be found throughout the menu.

Their main functions are:

(a) for general use in the diet as they are of a high nutritive value;
(b) to act as moistening agents in cooked goods;
(c) as enriching agents in the products made, as a result of their chemical composition;
(d) as aerating agents, because of the property they possess of film formation when they can take up large quantities of air when whisked, forming a stiff and stable foam;
(e) as emulsifying agents — the yolk of an egg contains the powerful emulsifying agent, lecithin;
(f) as a colouring agent.

The Structure and Composition
Shell eggs may be considered as consisting of three main parts.

Shell
This constitutes about 12% of the whole egg and consists mainly of phosphate and calcium carbonate deposited on a thin membrane which encloses the liquid portion of the egg. The shell of an egg is porous and unfortunately will allow odours, flavours, bacteria, and air to enter and affect the quality of the egg. The size of the air sac in a shell egg is an indication of quality and freshness.

Egg White
The egg white, or albumen, constitutes about 58% of the whole egg and consists mainly of a complex mixture of proteins such as albumen and globulin,

etc. and mineral salts. This liquid part of the egg is enclosed in a firm fibrous material, which forms membraneous cells throughout the mass. It is this membraneous matter which is important for the production of a stiff foam when egg whites are whisked. Stale eggs tend to have weak and watery whites which make whisking, poaching, and frying of eggs not only difficult but also the end product unattractive.

Egg Yolk

This constitutes about 30% of the whole egg and consists of a very complicated complex of proteins including nuclein and vitellin, as well as a fatty substance lecithin, which is the important emulsifying agent in the yolk. The chemical composition is even more complex than that of the white of an egg. It is the yolk which is the substance provided by nature to feed the embryo chick during its period of development and which, therefore, contains more food value than that of the white.

Table 14.8 shows the percentages of the constituent parts of egg whites, yolks, and whole eggs.

Table 14.8. The percentages of the constituent parts of an egg

	White %	Yolk %	Whole Egg %
Water	87·7	48·5	65·6
Protein	10·6	16·6	12·1
Fat	0·03	32·6	10·5
Minerals and carbohydrates	1·5	2·1	11·8
Vitamin groups	B	ABDEK	ABDEK

Grading of Shell Eggs

Shell eggs are graded as a result of an inspection and weighing of each egg. In order to be inspected the eggs are 'candled', that is they are held against a strong light, as the method for determining the quality of the eggs. Candling shows clearly the size of the air cell (or sac), the position of the yolk, the presence of any blood clots, meat spots, moulds, developing embryo and cracked shells. As eggs deteriorate the air sac increases in size and the yolk becomes displaced and tends to settle against the shell, instead of being firmly suspended in the white of the egg. Blood spots (or haemorrhages) are usually found in the white of the egg and will tend, like meat spots, to decompose in a short time.

The weighing of shell eggs is into bands of weights for the seven weight grades.

The quality standard for shell eggs sold in the E.C. countries in three classes.

Class A — first quality eggs.

Class B — second quality or preserved eggs.

Class C — non-graded eggs, intended for the manufacture of foodstuffs for human consumption.

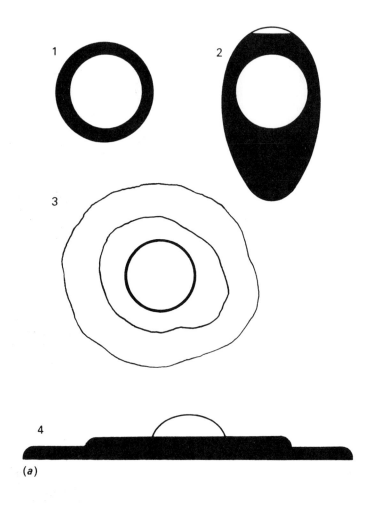

Figure 14.4 (*a*) First quality egg
  (1) Yolk central;
  (2) Small air cell at broad end of the egg;
  (3) and (4) Yolk central and standing bold, surrounded by a
      clear translucent white of a gelatinous consistency and an
      outer layer of thin white.

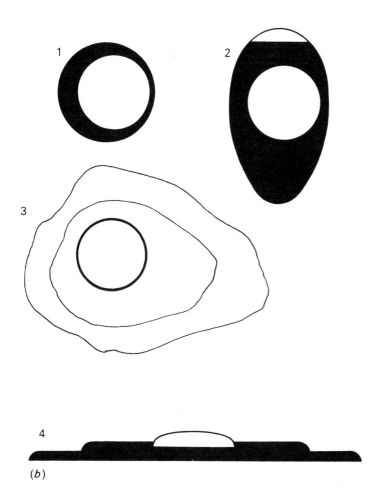

Figure 14.4 (*b*) Second quality egg
      (1) Yolk off-centre;
      (2) Air cell increasing in size;
      (3) and (4) Yolk off-centre and flattening. Two layers of
          white mingling and spreading out.

Table 14.9 shows further information on the quality standard for eggs.

Table 14.9. The quality standard for Class A, B and C eggs

	Class A	Class B	Class C
Shell and membrane	Normal, clean, intact	Normal, intact	May be visibly cracked
Air cell	Not exceeding 6 mm in depth	Not exceeding 9 mm in depth	Not exceeding 9 mm for incubator cleans
Egg whites	Clear, translucent, gelatinous consistency, free of foreign substances of any kind	Clear, translucent, free of foreign substances of any kind	All eggs not of class A or B, but suitable for the manufacture of foodstuffs for human consumption
Yolk	Visible under candling as a shadow only, without apparent contour not moving perceptibly from its central position when the egg is rotated. Free of foreign substances of any kind.	Visible under candling as a shadow only (not required for lime preserved eggs) Free of foreign substances of any kind.	
Embryo	No perceptible development		
Smell	Free of all foreign odours		

N.B. All eggs that do not fall into Classes A, B or C are classed as 'Industrial Eggs' and may not be used for human consumption, either in the manufacture of foodstuffs or otherwise.

The weight grading for Class A and B eggs is as follows:

Grade 1 : 70 g or over   per egg
Grade 2 : 65 g and under 70 g per egg
Grade 3 : 60 g and under 65 g per egg
Grade 4 : 55 g and under 60 g per egg
Grade 5 : 50 g and under 55 g per egg
Grade 6 : 45 g and under 50 g per egg
Grade 7 : under 45 g   per egg

N.B. (i) Class C eggs need not be weight graded.
    (ii) A 10% tolerance is allowed on weight grading, e.g. out of 100 eggs claimed to be of Grade 3, there may be 10 eggs from Grade 2 and 4, but of the 10 eggs, not more than 6 may be of Grade 4.

Processed Eggs
Frozen liquid eggs are readily obtainable in three forms, whole eggs, egg yolks, and egg whites. Before being frozen, they are usually filtered and up to 5% of

sugar or glycerine is added prior to the pasteurization of the eggs. Care must be taken to defrost the eggs slowly, but on defrosting the egg should be quickly used as they will rapidly decompose.

Dried eggs are available in two basic forms, as whole eggs or as egg whites. They are processed into the dried form by spray-drying, roller drying or accelerated freeze drying. Dried whole eggs are reconstituted by adding 90 g of water to 30 g of whole egg powder. This produces a thick liquid that has similar properties to fresh eggs except that it lacks the usual whipping properties. Dried egg whites are reconstituted by adding 60 g of water to 9 g of dried egg white powder and leaving for about three hours to dissolve completely.

Catering Uses
The catering uses for eggs are too numerous to mention in detail, but may be summarized by their uses throughout a menu.

Hors d'oeuvre	Egg mayonnaise.
Soups	As part of the liaison to thicken soups such as Germiny and various Veloutés. Also in the preparation of garnishes for consommé.
Egg dishes	As a menu course. Simple and garnished egg dishes cooked in various ways such as boiled, en cocotte, sur le plat, poached, scrambled and omelettes.
Farinaceous	For the making of pastes for ravioli, etc.
Fish	In the preparation of coating fish prior to breadcrumbing and for frying batters.
Sauces	As the basic ingredient for hot and cold egg based sauces, e.g. mayonnaise, hollandaise, bearnaise, etc. To enrich many other hot sauces, e.g. mornay, etc.
Meat	As a binding agent for made-up items such as hamburgers, etc. Also in the preparation of coating meat prior to breadcrumbing.
Salads	Hard boiled eggs included in many salads, e.g. Monte-Cristo.
Sweets	As a thickening agent, e.g. bavarois mixtures, various custards, soufflés, etc.
Savouries	As a major ingredient, e.g. cheese soufflés, savoury flans, etc.
Bread and cakes	As an enriching and moisture retaining agent, e.g. various breads and rolls. As an aerating and enriching agent, e.g. sponges, gateaux, etc.

The Storage of Eggs
Fresh shell eggs should be stored still in their packing trays, blunt end upwards in a refrigerator at a temperature of 7–13°C (45–55°F), and at a relative humidity of 70–80%. Under these conditions first quality eggs can be kept

for a month with little evident deterioration taking place. The higher the temperature in which eggs are stored the shorter is the time in which they will keep fresh. Also, as the eggs are porous they should be kept away from strong smelling foods such as onions, cheese, and fish.

Frozen eggs will keep safely for up to a year. When defrosted they should be used up the same day.

Dried eggs will keep safely for up to a year if kept unopened, in the original container, in a cool dry storeroom. Once a bag of dried egg is opened, the contents must be used as quickly as possible.

15

Fish

Introduction

No sector of the food industry in recent years has had a more worrying time and faced as many difficulties as the fishing industry. Some five years ago, fish was still a relatively cheap food and was looked upon often as a cheap substitute for meat. Today unfortunately prices have soared making fish in most cases as expensive as meat. Traditionally U.K. deep-sea fishermen have fished the seas over the continental shelf of Iceland for cod, haddock, hake, halibut, and plaice for many decades, but since two Icelandic Cod Wars and an international fishing agreement between Iceland and the E.C., the fishing permitted from these traditional fishing grounds has been considerably restricted. In addition to this has been the slowness of the U.K. to declare its own fishing limits around its shores, with the result that some foreign countries have overfished certain U.K. fishing grounds without any interest or concern for the conservation of the fish species.

All these problems have had two main effects on the fish market: first prices are much higher than in recent years; and second some varieties of fish, cod in particular, are in short supply. The U.K. has traditionally used cod as part of its diet and the replacement of it by acceptable alternatives is not without difficulties. Although there are alternatives available the public are reluctant to try them either because they associate the name with what was a cheap variety of fish or the fish has never been heard of before and has an unattractive name. Present day alternatives to cod are hake, whiting, coley and mackerel, whilst new varieties which are subject to research by the White Fish Authority and the Ministry of Agriculture and Fisheries for Scotland include the scabbard, grenadier and the blue whiting, with the latter being the most promising.

A solution to the problem of countries restricting fishing around their own coastline by foreign countries, together with the advantages of providing fish of a specific size and weight for retailers, caterers and food processors and

within acceptable price ranges is that of fish farming. The farming of fish is
not an entirely new subject; oysters and mussels have been 'farmed' for decades
and in more recent years carp and trout also. The level of accuracy that can
be obtained by farming can be illustrated by the fact that trout are readily
available on the market at two specific weight ranges when cleaned of 4–5 oz
and 5–6 oz.

Marine fish farming in the U.K. began mainly in the early 1960s and has
progressed at a very fast rate, in that several species have become domesticated
and adaptable to intensive rearing systems. Today the position is that fish
farming is moving from the research stage to the commercial stage. In order
to achieve commercial viability the fish chosen to farm were those that were
by tradition highly priced. Those that are viable at present are the salmon and
rainbow trout, with the turbot and Dover sole expected to become viable in
the near future. The success of fish farming of a species is that living in a
protected environment, the survival rate is very much higher, the feeding can
be controlled and fattening to a specific weight also. All this is not without
the problems that farmed fish come under the same restrictions as wild fish
regarding minimum permitted sizes and the close season for salmon. However
fish farming is held back from making rapid progress because it is not as
legally protected or financially assisted by the government as is the agricultural
industry.

The classifications of fish is possible in several ways.

(i) By the strict biological classification. Although accurate it is
difficult to learn and understand fully unless one is trained as a
biologist or zoologist.

(ii) By their different shapes, which for simplicity may be divided
into five main groups:

  (a) tapering, thicker at the head and slightly flattened out at the
  sides (e.g. cod);
  (b) arrow-shaped, a fairly even cross-section throughout and with
  the fins set well back (e.g. pike);
  (c) flattened, either horizontally (e.g. skate) or vertically (e.g.
  plaice);
  (d) serpentiform, long, round (e.g. eel);
  (e) contained within a shell. Those with legs, claws, etc. (lobster,
  crabs, etc.) those without (oysters, mussels, etc.).

(iii) By the general grouping of their species. This classifies fish into
marine, fresh-water, estuarine and migratory species.

(iv) By the condition of the fish, e.g. chilled, frozen, smoked, salted,
etc.

(v) By their catering uses, e.g. suitable for deep frying, for serving
whole, for stuffing, etc.

The most common method of classification, however, is a mixture of the
above in a not too scientific way into sea fish, river and lake fish and processed
fish, with further classification within each of these three main groups.

Sea Fish

These may simply be divided into two major groups, the round and flat species; and shell fish.

Round and Flat Species

These include the commonly known types of fish such as the cod, turbot, halibut, herring, etc. For purposes of identification they are grouped under the two headings of pelagic fish and demersal fish.

Pelagic Fish

This group comprise of fish that spend most of their life at or near the surface of the sea. They are the small, round, migratory, shoaling, seasonal fish such as herrings, pilchards, sprats, mackerel, and the larger tunny fish.

Demersal Fish

This group is the largest of the industrially caught fish. They spend most of their life at or near the sea bottom and are generally referred to as 'white fish'. There are basically two types of demersal fish, the round and the flat fish. The round fish include the cod, haddock, whiting, dog fish, etc. and the flat fish include the Dover sole, lemon sole, plaice, turbot, halibut, etc. Flat fish may also be further divided into two groups, one with the body depressed from above downwards such as those of the skate family and those with the body compressed from side to side and includes all types of flat fish other than members of the ray and skate families.

Shell Fish

These include the well-known types of shell fish such as crabs, lobsters, prawns, oysters, mussels, etc. For purposes of identification they are grouped under the two headings crustaceans and molluscs.

Crustaceans

These are articulated organisms, without any bones and possessing outer skins which contain calcareous deposits rendering them hard and shell-like. Unlike other forms of fish they possess limbs for locomotion and for grasping. Unfortunately crabs and lobsters are notoriously 'foul' feeders and so it is essential to purchase them from a reputed dealer to ensure that they have been thoroughly cleansed or obtained from a safe, clean water area. Failure to do so could result in customers suffering from gastro-enteritis after consuming the lobsters or crabs. The main crustaceans include, lobsters, crabs, crawfish, shrimps, prawns, and scampi.

Molluscs

These are distinguishable from crustaceans in that they do not possess any easily seen limbs for locomotion. Molluscs are of two distinct types. BIVALVES. These have two distinctly separate shells joined by a flexible hinge, which when the fish is relaxed holds the two halves open, but on being alarmed will tightly close both shells together. The common bivalves include the oyster, scallops, queens, mussels, clams, and cockles.

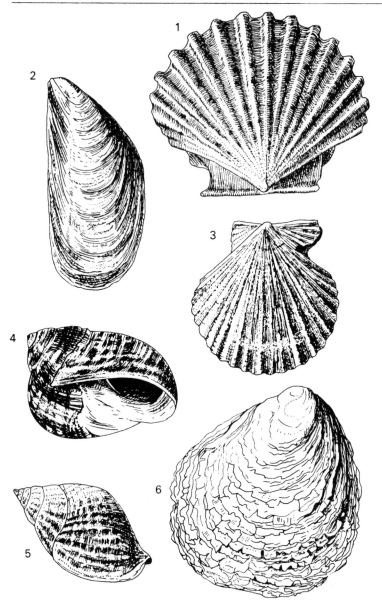

Figure 15.1 MOLLUSCS: (1) Scallop; (2) mussel; (3) Queen; (4) whelk; (5) periwinkle; (6) native oyster

UNIVALVES. These have just the one shell which tends to grow unevenly and usually is of a twisted spiral shape. The common univalves include the whelks and winkles.

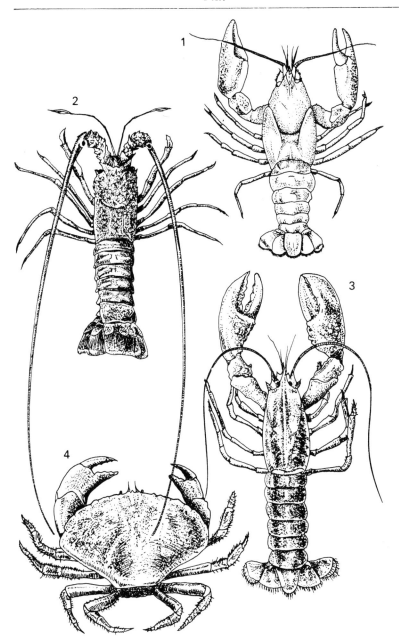

Figure 15.2 CRUSTACEANS: (1) Crayfish; (2) crawfish; (3) lobster; (4) crab

River and Lake Fish

These are fresh-water fish and are far fewer in species and quantity than sea fish. Basically there are of two types, round fish and shell fish.

Round Fish

It is worth noting at this stage that there are no common flat fish found in rivers or lakes, only round fish. They include carp, perch, and pike from lakes and trout, salmon, sturgeon, rudd, chub, roach, and fresh-water bream from rivers.

Shell Fish

The only common river shell fish is the crayfish, which resembles a very small lobster.

Processed Fish

This includes the processing of a whole fish: e.g. kippers, bloaters, buckling, etc; the processing of part of a fish, e.g. a side of smoked salmon, kipper fillets, anchovy fillets, etc; and manufactured fish products such as fish cakes, fish fingers, fish sausages, fish potatoes, etc.

The methods of processing include drying, salting, smoking, marinading, and manufacturing.

Fish Names

By tradition the names given to fish differ in various parts of the country, e.g. the common dogfish was also known in various areas as the rock salmon, flake, rock eel, huss, and Dutch eel. The confusion was mainly amongst the least expensive fish. Fortunately due to the efforts of the White Fish Authority and their publication (the *List of Recommended Names for the Sale of Fresh or Frozen Fish by Retail*) this problem is not now so prevalent. Clarification of the correct name to be used may also be found in the appropriate regulations for food labelling.

Recognition of Fish

To be able to identify the common types of fish it is necessary to be able to recognize the main features which are common to all fish and particular to the species being examined. This can be done under a variety of headings such as those in Table 15.1.

See Figure 15.3 for the main identifying features of a cod.

Fresh and Frozen Fish

The following is a brief description of the main species of fresh and frozen fish available on the U.K. market.

It should be noted however, that the same species of fish can differ in appearance and texture depending on the location of the fishing grounds at which they were caught. It is accepted that the reason for this is the different nature of the feeding stuff available on the seabed at the different fishing grounds. To a lesser extent it can also affect the keeping qualities of the fish.

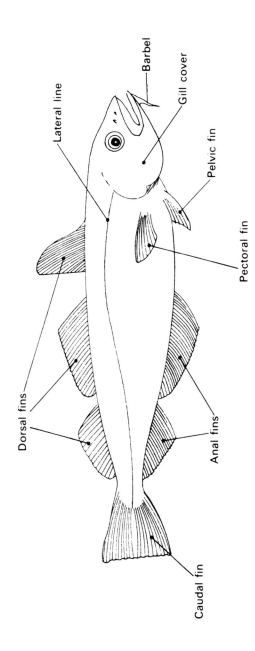

Figure 15.3 The major identifying features of a cod

Table 15.1. The ways in which fish can be identified

Headings	Identifying features
Type of fish	Flat or round?
Size	Small, medium, or large?
Shape	Is it torpedo shaped, arrow-shaped, flat and diamond shaped, flat and oval shaped, etc?
Distinguishing features	Position and shape of fins, has it a distinct barbel, prominent coloured spots or markings, right- or left-handed, etc?
Colour	This can vary a great deal within a species but nevertheless can be a valid point of identification.
Lateral line	Is it prominent, straight, curved, or hook shaped?
Mouth	Small or large, prominent, strong, teeth on one or both jaws, does the snout protrude over the lower jaw, etc?

Quality Recognition

It is essential for the reader to know the main points to look for when examining fish for quality. The quality of a particular species of fish is mainly concerned with freshness, although such factors as the time in the season, the weight, and yield obtainable is also of importance. Absolute freshness is essential if the best is to be obtained from any fish dish to ensure full flavour, texture, and nourishment. Unfortunately fish deteriorate in quality quite quickly unless carefully handled and stored correctly.

Fish goes bad (from two causes) after being caught, from self digestion by natural enzymes in the flesh which remain active, and by bacteria which are present in the gills, guts and on the skin of the fish and which multiply after the fish is dead, living on the flesh which they use for food. Fresh fish can be kept for several days if packed in ice and thoroughly chilled. Frozen, fresh fish is now a very good second in quality and accounts for the majority of fish readily available in the markets today.

Although many attempts have been made to develop standard laboratory tests for freshness in fish, the most common method is still visual inspection. The main points of inspection are as follows.

Fresh Fish

General Appearance
FRESH FISH. A clean and bright appearance to the fish. Skin smooth to touch and glistening. Moist with a transparent outer slime. Pleasant characteristic smell. If gutted, the belly flaps should be clean and show no discoloration nor unpleasant smell.

STALE FISH. Would show, if any, few of the above characteristics. Be lifeless in appearance, dry and rough to touch. Scales would rub off easily. The belly flaps would be discoloured and the smell unpleasant.

Flesh

FRESH FISH. Firm and elastic to the finger touch, so that when pressed the impression quickly disappears. The true characteristic colour – for white fish this would be white or a bluish white and translucent. The flesh should adhere firmly to the bones. Blood around the back bone should be a good red in colour.

STALE FISH. Soft and limp to the finger touch. When pressed with the finger the impression remains. The flesh is no longer firmly attached to the bones. Brown discoloration along the backbone.

Gills and Eyes

FRESH FISH. Gills should be brightly coloured and free from any slime or unpleasant smell. Eyes should be fresh looking and full. The pupil should be black and convex, the cornea transparent.

STALE FISH. Gills usually a dull brown colour, slimy and with an unpleasant smell. Eyes sunken and dull looking.

Frozen Fish

Frozen fish requires to be thawed out and examined in the same way as fresh fish. Ideally if purchased in any quantity frozen fish should be bought by using a purchasing specification. *See* Table 15.2 for an example.

Fillets of Fish

FRESH FISH. Firm and elastic to the finger touch, so that when pressed the impression quickly disappears. The true characteristic colour – for white fish this would be white or a bluish white and translucent. The flesh should be free of any bones. The belly flap area should be clean. The fillets should have a pleasant smell. All the fillets should be well prepared and of an equal size and weight.

STALE FISH. Soft and limp to the finger touch. When pressed with the finger the impression remains. Dull appearance – lack of characteristic colour. The fillets tear easily and are sticky when handled. The fillets develop an unpleasant smell.

Shell Fish

FRESH FISH: CRUSTACEANS. Always buy from a reputed dealer and purchase the fish alive whenever possible. The fish should feel heavy in relation to its size. All claws should be intact. The fish should show evidence of being alive in that the limbs should be active and the tail (as in lobsters, etc.) very springy. Should have a pleasant smell. (Shrimps and prawns always feel crisp when handled.)

N.B. If purchased already cooked from a reputed dealer, ensure that fresh supplies are purchased regularly and used within two days.

STALE FISH. Unpleasant smell. Little if any evidence of being alive. Possibly light in relation to its size.

FRESH FISH: MOLLUSCS. Always buy fresh from a reputed dealer whenever possible. The shells of bivalves (mussels, etc.) should be closed or close on being handled. (The body of univalves (whelks, etc.) should recede into the shell on being touched.) The smell should be pleasant. There should be an absence of barnacles.

STALE FISH. The shells of bivalves would be open or gaping. (The body of univalves would be inactive and often be discoloured.) The smell would be unpleasant.

Smoked Fish

FRESH FISH. The fish should be bright, glossy, and dry. The texture should be firm and springy to the touch. Smell pleasant with a slight smoky aroma.

STALE FISH. The fish would be dull in appearance and sticky. The flesh would be soft, flabby, and wet. Possibly gaping or separation of the flakes. Very stale fish would have an objectionable smell.

Table 15.2. The identifying features of fish

Fish	Classification	Approximate Size (ft)	Main Identifying Features
Catfish (rockfish or rock salmon)	Sea, demersal, round	3–4	Head resembles that of an ugly cat, with distinct teeth. Dark grey to blue–grey colouring with black bands.
Coalfish (saithe or coley)	Sea, demersal, round	2–3	Medium-sized mouth with prominent lower jaw and small barbel. Black colouring on back and distinct white lateral line. Very small scales.
Cod	Sea, demersal, round	2–4	Large mouth with barbel on chin. Grey to olive green colouring with dark blotches. Three dorsal fins.
Haddock	Sea, demersal, round	Up to 3	Similar in shape to a small cod. Small mouth and small barbel. Dark grey on back merging to a dull silver below

Table 15.2. cont.

Fish	Classification	Approximate Size (ft)	Main Identifying Features
			the distinct black lateral line. Black marking above each pectoral fin (known as the 'Apostle's' or 'Peter's thumb-mark'). Coarse scales and three dorsal fins.
Hake	Sea, demersal, round	Up to 4	Dark grey colouring on the back and silver grey on the belly. Large mouth, sharp teeth but no barbels. Distinct dark lateral line. Large coarse scales and only two dorsal fins.
Mullet (red)	Sea, demersal, round	Up to $1\frac{1}{2}$	Red colour, large scales. Small mouth but two long barbels. Distinct lateral line, slightly raised. Two dorsal fins.
Mullet (grey)	Sea, demersal, round	Up to $1\frac{1}{2}$	Silver−grey colour, large scales. No lateral line. Two dorsal fins with the anterior fin having four fin-rays.
Sea bream	Sea, demersal, round (but compressed and perch-like)	Up to $1\frac{1}{2}$	Short plump body with large scales. Reddish colour to the back with silver sides and belly. Large black thumb mark above the pectoral fin and on the lateral line. Distinct, dark lateral line. Small mouth and large eyes.

Table 15.2. cont.

Fish	Classification	Approximate Size (ft)	Main Identifying Features
Sturgeon	Round, anadromous habits (i.e. it migrates from the river to sea and back to the river)	Up to 20	Yellow−brown on back, grey colour underneath. Recognized mainly by its size, plus distinct single rows of bony scales along the back, belly and sides. Pointed head with a small mouth. One dorsal fin only.
Whiting	Sea, demersal, round	Up to $1\frac{1}{2}$	Brownish-olive green colouring above the lateral line, white below. Small black blotch at the base of the pectoral fin. Greenish coloured lateral line, curved over the pectoral fin. Large mouth, sharp teeth on both jaws.
Herring	Sea, pelagic, round	Up to $1\frac{1}{6}$	Blue−black colouring on the back, silver−white below. Small mouth with no teeth. No lateral line and only one dorsal fin.
Mackerel	Sea, pelagic, round	Up to $1\frac{1}{6}$	Blue−black, zebra striped markings on the back, silver−white colourings underneath. Very streamline shape to the body. Faint lateral line. Two main dorsal fins.
Pilchard	Sea, pelagic, round	Up to $1\frac{1}{6}$	Blue−black colouring on the back, silver−white below. Similar to the herring but rounder in shape and with larger scales. No lateral line and only

Table 15.2. cont.

Fish	Classification	Approximate Size (ft)	Main Identifying Features
			one dorsal fin (set more forward than that of the herring).
Sardine	Sea, pelagic, round	Up to $\frac{1}{2}$	The young of the pilchard family.
Sprat	Sea, pelagic, round	Up to $\frac{2}{3}$	Very similar to a small young herring. Main identification is the presence of very sharp bony hooks along the edge of the belly.
Whitebait	Sea, pelagic, round	Up to $\frac{1}{6}$	The young or 'fry' of herrings and sprats.
Brill	Sea, demersal, flat, left-handed	Up to $2\frac{1}{2}$	A large oval shape. Light brown, speckled colouring to upper side. Faint lateral line, curved over pectoral fin. Small, smooth scales.
Dab	Sea, demersal, flat	Up to $1\frac{1}{2}$	Similar in shape to plaice. Light brown colour with dark spots. Distinct curve to the dark lateral line over the pectoral fin. Scales rough to the touch.
Halibut	Sea, demersal, flat	Up to $\frac{1}{2}$	A large, long, flat, narrow body. Brown with some darker mottling on the upper side. Raised lateral line, curving over the pectoral fin. A large mouth with strong teeth on both jaws.
Plaice	Sea, demersal, flat	Up to $2\frac{1}{2}$	Oval in shape, with a dark brown colouring with orange spots on the upper side. The underside is

Table 15.2. cont.

Fish	Classification	Approximate Size (ft)	Main Identifying Features
			white and has a ribbed appearance.
Skate (common)	Sea, demersal, flat	Up to 8	A member of the ray family, identified by its large, flat, diamond shape with a long slender tail projecting from the rear. The upper surface is of a grey brown mottled colour. The large fleshy pectoral fins are commonly sold as 'skate' or 'rokar wings'. The internal parts of the fish and the organs are unusable.
Sole (Dover)	Sea, demersal, flat	Up to $1\frac{1}{2}$	Oval in shape, light–dark brown with darker mottling down the centre. A faint, straight lateral line. Very rough to touch if rubbed towards the head. The mouth is set back in the head.
Sole (lemon)	Sea, demersal, flat	Up to $1\frac{1}{2}$	Oval in shape, yellowish-brown colour with dark spots on the upper surface. A distinct golden rim along the edge of the gill cover. A raised, darkened lateral line, curving over the pectoral fin. A very smooth slippery skin and a small mouth.
Turbot	Sea, demersal, flat, left-handed	Up to 3	Diamond shaped body. A mottled light brown colour on the upper side

Table 15.2. cont.

Fish	Classification	Approximate Size (ft)	Main Identifying Features
			with numerous bony tubercles. A smooth slippery skin. Lateral line curved over the pectoral fin.
Carp	Lake, round	Up to 2	Resembles a large goldfish, although it may also be silver or black in colour.
Perch	Lake, round	Up to 1	Resembles a gold-fish in shape. Olive green along the back and yellowish below. Has two dorsal fins the front one being particularly large.
Pike	Lake, round	2	A long slender fish with a protruding snout with many teeth. A greenish colour on its back and white underneath.
Trout (rainbow)	Mainly fish farmed, round	Up to $\frac{5}{6}$	Brownish-green with rainbow coloured shades. Darker above the lateral line.
Trout (brown)	Round, river	1	Similar to rainbow trout but larger, brownish in colour with distinct spots.
Salmon	Round, anadromous habits (i.e. it migrates from the river to the sea and back to the river) N.B. The average age of a mature salmon is nine years. It is known under specific names up to maturity as:	3	Silver to steel-blue colour with dark shadings along the back. A long slender body, tapering at the base to a forked tail. The flesh is of a deep pink colour.
	Salmon parr	$1\frac{1}{2}-2$	A young salmon up to 2 years of age,

Table 15.2. cont.

Fish	Classification	Approximate Size (ft)	Main Identifying Features
			still living in the river in which it was born.
	Salmon smelt	$2-2\frac{1}{2}$	Between 2--3 years of age. This period is spent in the sea.
	Salmon grilse	$2\frac{1}{2}-3$	Between 3–4 years of age. This period is partially spent in the river where it spawns for the first time.
	Salmon grilse kelt	3	A spent salmon. i.e. of poor quality as a result of spawning. The spent salmon returns to the sea and returns annually to spawn again.
Salmon trout	Sea, round	2	Similar to salmon, but smaller and bulkier in appearance. The body is rounded at the base of the tail which is almost straight.
Crab	Crustacean, sea	Up to 1 (in breadth)	A large oval, hard rigid shell to the body. It has two large claws and eight distinct legs. It is of a light red–brown colour.
Crayfish	Crustacean, river	Up to $\frac{1}{2}$	Resemble miniature lobsters, but not very common in the U.K. Usually only the tails are eaten as the claws are small and contain little meat.
Crawfish (rock lobster)	Crustacean, sea	$1\frac{1}{2}-2$	Similar to a lobster but very much larger and without claws. The main body is covered with

Table 15.2. cont.

Fish	Classification	Approximate Size (ft)	Main Identifying Features
			spines and has two very long antennae. Will weigh 5–12 lb.
Dublin Bay prawns (scampi or Norwegian lobster)	Crustacean, sea	Up to $\frac{1}{2}$	Resemble miniature lobsters. Usually only the tail meat is eaten. The true scampi is obtained from the Adriatic.
Lobster	Crustacean, sea	$\frac{5}{6}$ to $1\frac{1}{4}$	Possibly the most common of crustaceans. Blue–black in colour when alive (bright red when boiled). Two large claws containing valuable meat and a tail with five articulations in the male and seven in the female. Will usually weigh 1–3 lb.
Prawns	Crustacean, sea	Up to $\frac{1}{3}$	Distinguished by a long beak projecting from the front of the shell. Almost transparent when alive, red and opaque when boiled.
Shrimps	Crustacean, sea	Up to $\frac{1}{6}$	Similar to prawns but smaller and with no beak. The front pair of legs are thickened and terminate in a pair of claws. Two main types of shrimps: the brown shrimp which is caught on sand-flats; and the pink shrimp which is caught further out to sea are found.

Table 15.2. cont.

Fish	Classification	Approximate Size (ft)	Main Identifying Features
Cockles	Molluscs, bivalve, sea	Up to $\frac{1}{12}$ diameter	White−cream in colour, a near circular shaped shell with ribs radiating out from the hinge
Mussels	Molluscs, bivalves, sea	Up to $2\frac{1}{2}$ in.	Oval in shape, being rather pointed towards the hinge. A smooth shell, blue−black in colour.
Oysters	Molluscs, bivalves, river estuary-sea	Up to $\frac{1}{3}$	Nearly round in shape. The lower valve of the shell is almost flat, the upper valve is convex. The colour of the shell is of a greenish-grey. The outside of the shell is uneven and ridged.
	N.B. There are two main species of oyster available in the U.K.: (i) The native oyster (ii) The Portuguese oyster		(i) As described above, coming from such sources as Whitstable, Colchester, and the Helford river. (ii) Similar to the above, but more elongated, a much more ridged shell and of greater depth. Used mainly for cooking.
Periwinkles	Molluscs, univalve, sea	$\frac{3}{4}$ in.	Small, snail-like shell, black−dark-brown in colour
Whelks	Molluscs, univalve, sea	Up to $\frac{1}{3}$	A spiral-like shell, muddy yellow or brown in colour
Queens	Mollusc, bivalve, sea	Up to $\frac{1}{4}$	Similar to the scallop, being fan shaped and fluted.

Table 15.2. cont.

Fish	Classification	Approximate Size (ft)	Main Identifying Features
			It is much smaller than the scallop. Has both shells convex and is pink in colour.
Scallops	Molluscs, bivalve, sea	Up to $\frac{5}{12}$	Fan shaped and fluted shell. The upper valve is flat and reddish in colour whilst the lower valve is convex and white.

Table 15.2 gives an example of a widely used purchasing specification for frozen fillets of white fish.

Table 15.3. An example of a purchase specification for frozen fish

Model Purchase Specification (White Fish Authority/Torry)

Frozen Fillets of White Fish
(A) *Scope of this Specification*
This specification applies to whole fillets purchased frozen, of the following species:

Cod (*Gadus morhua*)
Haddock (*Melanogrammus aeglefinus*)
Whiting (*Merlangius merlangus*)
Plaice (*Pleuronectes platessa*)
Lemon sole (*Microstomus kitt*)

Coley (*Pollachius virens*)
Redfish (*Sebastes* sp.)
South Atlantic hake (*Merluccius* sp.)
Greenland halibut (*Reinhardtius hippoglossoides*)
Dover sole (*Solea solea*)

(B) *Definition of Fillet*
Fillets are slices of fish muscle which have been removed from the carcase by cuts made parallel to the backbone and from which all internal organs, head, fins, bones (other than pin bones), and all substantially discoloured flesh have been removed.

(C) *Specification of Product as Delivered*
The fish on delivery shall meet all of the following requirements.

(1) Colour (blemishes)   Bruises and blood clots and other localized discoloration that materially affect the appearance of the fish and/or eating quality shall be absent.

Table 15.3. cont.

(2) Bones, skin, and belly lining/flap	The fish shall be free of bones except pin bones. The fish shall be supplied *skin on/skinless. (Fish which has more than 10 cm^2 of skin per half-stone (3·2 kg) unit shall not be deemed skinless.)* No more than 15 cm^2 of belly lining shall be permitted per half-stone unit. An excessive amount of belly flap must not be present or constitute more than 10% of the total weight.
(3) Worms and other parasites	The maximum tolerance for nematode worms is three worms per half-stone (3·2 kg) unit. No other parasites are permitted.
(4) Size of fillets	Individual fillets must be not less than . . . lb (. . . g) or more than . . . lb (. . . kg) each in weight (insert required weights).
(5) Eating quality	The fillets must not gape nor exhibit abnormal textural faults (e.g. due to the use of spent or starved fish) nor must they contain abnormal intrinsic odours or flavours such as 'weedy' or 'diesel' flavours common in fish from certain grounds at certain seasons.

At the time of delivery the fish must meet the following freshness standards:

1. Free of spoilage or rancid flavours;
2. A minimum score of 6 in the Torry taste panel system for assessing freshness.

Fish with stale or sour odours and flavours is not acceptable. In the case of cod, haddock, coley, and redfish the concentration of trimethylamine (TMA) must be no greater than 10 mg TMA nitrogen per 100 g of flesh.

The fillets on cooking must be free of the following:

1. Objectionable cold-storage odours and flavours;
2. Toughness and dryness resulting from cold-storage deterioration;
3. Gelatinous texture.

In the case of cod and haddock the values indicated below on the Torry taste panel system for assessing cold-storage deterioration must not be exceeded.

Cold-storage flavour	3·0
Firmness	4·5
Dryness	3·0

Table 15.3. cont.

(6) Packaging	The frozen fish fillets must be wrapped so that they are protected from bacterial and other contamination and from dehydration during storage and transportation. Any container used for the delivery of frozen fish fillets must be constructed of such material that taint is not imparted to the fillets. *Fillets should be packaged for delivery in units of . . .lb (. . .kg).*
(7) Temperature at delivery	The temperature of the frozen fish fillets at the time of delivery must be no higher than 5°F (−15°C).
(8) Freezing and cold storage	Freezing must be carried out according to the WFA code of practice for quick freezing. Storage prior to delivery should be at 0°F (−18°C) for no longer than three months. Longer periods of storage must be at −20°F (−29°C). Cold storage temperatures must not be allowed to fluctuate. The italicization in Section C of this specification indicates that options are to be exercised by purchasers.

N.B. TMA is formed in marine fish as they become stale. The TMA value taken from a sample of fish would be the measure of freshness of the fish.

The Basic Cuts of Fish

The basic cuts of a fish are in the main related to the actual size of the fish being prepared and the particular dish for which it is to be used. Naturally a very large fish would not be served to one person, nor would it be always necessary to fillet a small fish if it was of a single portion size.

The basic cuts are as follows.

Whole Fish

With a large fish such as a salmon, turbot, pike, etc. it is common to descale the fish, clean it by removing the gills and intestines, and to poach it whole and to portion it afterwards for the customer.

A small fish such as a trout, Dover sole, whiting, etc. could be cooked in many different ways and served whole as a portion to the customer. Very small fish such as whitebait, sprats, sardines, etc. would also be served whole to the customer, but many are required to make up a portion size.

Fillets

From a flat fish such as plaice, turbot, halibut, etc. four fillets are obtainable, two long fillets and two short fillets (with the belly flaps). Cross-cut fillets are taken from small flat fish. This consists of the long and short fillets taken off a fish together from each side of the fish.

From a round fish two fillets only are obtainable.

Suprêmes

This is a term applied to portions of a fillet that have been cut on the slant and taken from large fillets, e.g. halibut.

Delice

This is a term applied to neatly folded fillets of a small fish, e.g. Dover sole.

Paupiette

This is a term applied to fillets of a small fish that have been stuffed with a farce (of fish, shellfish, or vegetables) and neatly rolled into a barrel shape.

Goujon

This is applied to fillets of fish (usually flat fish) that have been cut into long strips of approximately $3 \times \frac{1}{4}$ in.

Darne

This is a steak of fish taken from a large round fish by cutting across the length of the fish, e.g. salmon.

Tronçon

This is a steak of fish taken from a large flat fish. The fish is usually split into two down the backbone and steaks taken off of each half.

Processed Fish

Smoked Fish

Fish is smoked today mainly to give it a pleasant flavour and aroma rather than to preserve it. The method of processing used nowadays will not keep the produce edible for much more than a week at ordinary temperatures as the fish is only slightly salted and smoked. Smoked fish that need to be stored for more than a week before being sold is usually quick frozen immediately after being smoked.

The following is a brief description of the method of processing used for the production of smoked salmon. The method used is similar for other types of fish. For simplicity the method of production may be broken down into three stages.

Preparation of the Fish

A very important factor in the smoking of fish is that only good quality fresh or frozen fish is used. Fresh fish must be chilled quickly immediately after being caught, and kept chilled until processed. This particularly applies to fatty type fish such as salmon and herrings as they deteriorate quickly. It should be noted that poor quality fresh or frozen fish cannot be turned into quality smoked fish, and also that the quality of the fish being processed will affect the storage life of the smoked fish.

The two fillets or sides are taken from the salmon, leaving in the shoulder bones and lugs, which are necessary to give support to the sides when hung for smoking. The belly bones and fins are removed to improve the appearance. If the fish fillets are particularly thick it is usual to make three cuts across the width on the skin side to allow uniform curing to take place.

Curing

There are two basic methods used for curing, either brining or dry salting.
BRINING. The prepared side (fillet) is washed to remove any traces of blood and then soaked in a 80° brine for several hours depending on the size. A 4lb side of good quality and high fat content may take about 6 hours, whilst a similar side but of low fat content, may take only 3 hours. This time can be further reduced if the brine is pumped into the thicker parts of the side initially. The fillets are then removed from the brine and left to drain overnight to allow a good salt gloss to form.
DRY SALTING. The prepared sides (fillets) are washed to remove any traces of blood and then gently rubbed all over with dry salt. The sides are then laid skin-side down on a bed of salt in a box of similar size and covered with more salt. A thinner covering of salt is applied to the thinner parts of the sides. Several more sides may be stacked on top and similarly salt treated. When the stack of sides is completed it is pressed by placing a piece of wood and a 10lb weight on top. After pressing and dry salting the sides are then washed, placed in a 30° brine for up to 1 hour to even out the salt concentration and then left to drain overnight.

It is not uncommon for the sides prior to being dry salted to be rubbed with brown sugar or molasses and for a small quantity of herbs to be added to the dry salt to give an especially attractive flavour.

Smoking

Two types of smoking kiln are used, the traditional chimney kiln and the more modern Torry mechanical kiln. Fish are in general terms either cold smoked, when the temperature in the kiln does not rise above 30°C and the fish remains uncooked, or hot smoked when the temperature may be as high as 80°C and the fish becomes cooked in the process.

The smoking of sides of salmon is in a cold smoke at a temperature of around 26°C (80°F). After several hours of smoking, when the sides become fairly dry a short period with the smoke at 38°C (100°F) is applied to bring some of the natural oil to the surface and to give an attractive glossy appearance. After smoking the sides are removed from the kiln and allowed to cool and 'set off' before packaging.

The finished product, sides of smoked salmon should have an attractive appearance, be not too dry, smell pleasantly and slice easily rather like ham.

The main types of smoked fish and their methods of production are given in Table 15.4.

Table 15.4. *The main types of smoked fish*

Type of Fish	Product	Preparation	Salting	Smoking	Approximate Total Weight Loss %
Cod	(a) Single fillets	Filleted	Brined often with a dye	Cold smoked	50–55
	(b) Cod's roe	Removed from female, washed	Dry salted or brined and dyed	Cold smoked	20–30
Eel	Whole fish	Gutted only	Dry salted and brined	Hot smoked	35
Haddock	(a) Single fillets	Filleted	Brined often with a dye	Cold smoked	35
	(b) 'Finnans'	Headed, split up belly, flattened and gutted	Brined often with a dye	Cold smoked	35
	(c) Smokies	Whole gutted fish, headed and cleaned	Brined	Hot smoked	45

Herrings	(a) Bloaters	Whole, ungutted	Dry salted	Cold smoked to give partial drying	15
	(b) Buckling	Whole, ungutted	Dry salted	Hot smoked	20
	(c) Kippers	Split along back, cleaned, opened flat	Brined and dyed	Cold smoked	35
	(d) Kipper fillets	Filleted	Brined and dyed	Cold smoked	45–50
Salmon	Side (or fillet)	Filleted trimmed	Dry salted or brined	Cold smoked using oak or juniper wood	30
Trout	Whole fish	Whole gutted	Dry salted or brined	Cold	20

Salted Fish

This is not such a common method of processing fish today, although it is necessary for preparing certain dishes.

Fish for salting are usually of the cod family. The fish is beheaded, split, and cleaned leaving a small piece of the backbone near the tail for strength. They are then packed in large tanks with a layer of salt between each fish and left for up to seven days during which the fish becomes impregnated with a saturated salt solution. The fish is then removed from the tank, washed and stacked again with salt. The fish is periodically restacked and salted so that the fish at the top of a stack ends up at the bottom and is subject to pressure to reduce its moisture content. The fish is washed and is then dried naturally or in heated chambers until the moisture content is between 10–30%. The whole process takes several months to complete.

Fish Fingers

These are processed from frozen blocks of filleted white fish which are cut to the required size, dipped into a batter and breadcrumbs, and then refrozen. Similarly, portion size fillets of white fish may be similarly treated.

Fish Cakes

These are most commonly processed from frozen, filleted white fish, which is first steamed and then minced and added to a puree of freshly boiled potatoes together with herbs and seasoning. The mixture is then portioned into fish cakes, dipped into a batter and then breadcrumbs and frozen.

Marinaded Fish

This is the preservation of pelagic fish, in particular herrings, with wine vinegar, salt, herbs, and spices. The fish is cleaned, then usually filleted and packed into glass or earthenware containers with alternating layers of herbs and spices and then completely covered with equal quantities of wine vinegar and water. The container is then sealed and the contents not eaten for at least seven days, e.g. bismark herrings and rollmops.

Delicatessen Fish Products

These are not commonly known but could well develop in future years as a by-product of fish farming. Amongst the many varieties of products are:

Frying Sausage

These are made from skinless white fish fillets together with pork fat, rusks, water, and seasoning, and put into natural or synthetic casings. The product is similar in appearance to a beef or pork sausage and needs to be fried or grilled.

Slicing Sausage

This has similar ingredients to the frying sausage, but is placed into larger casings of a similar size to a polony. They are then poached, cooled, and chilled. It is also possible to hot smoke this sausage to vary the flavour, aroma, and appearance.

Fish Chips
These are made from a puree of skinless white fish or herrings together with dried potato powder, water and seasoning. The mixture is extruded from a machine, cut off in lengths of 2–3 in. and then partially deep fried for 3–5 seconds. After draining off excess fat they are quick frozen.

The Catering Uses of Fish

The catering uses of fish are shown in tabular form (*see* Table 15.5).

Table 15.5. The catering uses of fish

Type of Fish	Main Catering Uses
Flat fish	
All flat fish may be filleted, portioned, e.g. halibut, plaice, turbot, etc.	Poached, grilled, shallow or deep fried
Medium sized 'quality' fish, e.g. turbot, brill	Boned (but keeping fish whole) stuffed, poached, and portioned in front of the customer
Small fish, e.g. Dover sole, plaice, etc.	Served whole, poached, grilled, shallow or deep fried
Round fish	
Large fish, e.g. salmon, pike, etc.	Poached or stuffed and baked whole
Large fish may be filleted, portioned, e.g. cod, hake, salmon	Poached, grilled, shallow or deep fried
Small fish, e.g. herring, trout, whiting	Served whole, poached, grilled, shallow or deep fried
Very small fish, e.g. sprats, whitebait	Deep fried
Shell fish	
(*a*) Crustaceans	
Crabs	Soup, boiled and dressed, served cold
Crayfish	Soup, boiled, grilled, shallow fried
Crawfish	Soup, grilled, boiled and decorated and served cold
Dublin Bay prawns	Soup, grilled, shallow or deep fried
Lobster	Soup, grilled, boiled and served cold
Prawns	Soup, boiled and served cold
Shrimps	Soup, boiled and served cold and potted
(*b*) Molluscs	
Cockles	Boiled, served cold
Mussels	Poached
Oysters	Eaten raw, soup, poached, grilled
Periwinkles	Boiled, served cold
Whelks	Boiled, served cold
Queens	Poached, deep fried
Scallops	Poached, shallow or deep fried

Table 15.5. cont.

Type of Fish	Main Catering Uses
(c) Smoked fish	
Cod	Poached
Eel	Served cold
Haddock	Poached
Herrings: bloaters	Paste, grilled
buckling	Served cold
kippers	Paté, grilled, poached
Salmon	Served cold
Trout	Served cold

Scientific and Nutritional Aspects

Nutrition and Composition

Fish, like meat and poultry, is of value in the diet, mainly for its protein content, but some fish do contain significant amounts of fat in the form of oil, as Table 15.6 indicates.

Table 15.6. The composition in terms of protein, fat and water of selected fish in g per 100 g
(adapted from McCance and Widdowson, 1978)

Food	Protein	Fat	Water	Kilocalories	Percentage Edible portion
Cod, raw	17.4	0.7	82.1	76	89
Haddock, raw	16.8	0.6	81.3	73	87
Lemon sole, raw	17.1	1.4	81.2	81	45
Plaice, raw	17.9	2.2	79.5	91	42
Herring, raw	16.8	18.5	63.9	234	55
Pilchards, canned	18.8	5.4	70	126	100
Sardines, canned (drained)	3.7	13.6	58.4	217	83

The flesh of fish has far less connective tissue than meat and the flesh of poultry — there is an absence of elastin, and the collagen present is converted easily during cooking to gelatin, yielding a very tender textured, and easily digested product.

Fish is a useful source of phosphorus in the diet, and in the cases where the bones are eaten, also of calcium. Only sardines are notable for their iron content. Oily fish, like herring and trout provide the fat soluble vitamins A and D and some B group vitamins — while white fish only provide small amounts of the latter.

Preservation

The comments made under similar headings in other chapters are generally applicable in the case of fish. However, it is necessary to emphasize that fish is a very easily spoiled product, and even at 0°C (32°F) fish can only be stored for a few days without beginning to take on the characteristic 'stinking fish' odour caused by bacterial formation of a substance called trimethylamine. Therefore, since fishing fleets are having to go increasing distances to provide sufficient fish for the market, freezing fish at sea at temperatures approaching −20°C (−4°F), has become increasingly important.

Storage

Since 'fresh' fish is always some days old by the time the caterer or housewife obtains it, an obvious general rule would be 'the sooner you eat it, the better'. However, fish can be kept safely for varying periods, under suitable conditions, as Table 15.7 shows. Oily fish generally does not store as well as white fish, since the oil it contains is prone to oxidation, producing rancid off-flavours.

Table 15.7. The suggested storage temperatures and approximate storage life of fish

Type	Suggested Storage Temperatures °C (°F)	Approximate Storage Life
Fresh fish (including fresh shell fish)	0 (32)	7 days maximum
Frozen fish (including shell fish)	(−20)	6 months maximum (except cooked lobster meat, 3 months maximum)
Smoked fish,		
Fresh	0 (32)	4−10 days
Frozen	−30 (−22)	4 months
Salt fish	Below 5 (40)	1 year
Marinaded fish	Below 5 (40)	6 months
Delicatessen	−30 (−22)	9 months

N.B. The above recommended storage times are the maximum under ideal storage conditions.

Irradiation of Fish

Considerable research has been conducted in the U.S.A. on the irradiation of fish as a means to extending its shelf-life. The U.S. food industry is optimistic that governmental approval will be granted for the commercial use of irradiation at pasteurization doses, doubling the shelf-life for many types of fish and shellfish. The success of this method, however, may depend on consumer reaction to it and also to the specific and detailed labelling requirements.

Appendix 1 Legislation Relating to Specific Foods

1. Cereal Products

The Bread and Flour Regulations, 1984 (S.I. 1984: 1304)
Biscuits. Ministry of Food Code of Practice, C.P. 20 (1949)
The Food Labelling Regulations, 1984

2. Sugars, Preserves and Confectionary Gums

The Specified Sugar Products Regulations, 1976 (amended S.I. 1982: 255)
Sweeteners in Food Regulations, 1983
The Jam and Similar Products Regulations, 1981

3. Fats and Oils

The Margarine Regulations, 1967 (S.I. 1967: 1867)
Food Standards (Suet) Order, 1952 (S.I. 1952: 2203)
Shredded Suet. Ministry of Food Code of Practice C.P. 12 (1949)

4. Dairy Type Foods (Milk, Cream, and Ice-cream)

The Food Act, 1984
The Drinking Milk Regulations, 1976 (S.I. 1976: 1883)
The Milk (Special Designation) Regulations, 1977
The Condensed Milk and Dried Milk Regulations, 1977
The Cream Regulations, 1970 (S.I. 1970: 752)
The Milk and Dairies (Heat Treatment of Cream) Regulations, 1983
    (S.I. 1983: 1509)

Code of Practice for Composition and Labelling of Yogurt
The Ice-cream Regulations, 1967 (S.I. 1967: 1866)
The Ice-cream (Heat Treatment, etc.) Regulations, 1959 and 1963

5. Dairy Type Foods (Butter, Cheese)

The Butter Regulations, 1966
The Cheese Regulations, 1970 (amended S.I. 1974 and 1984)
The Cheese (Amendment) Regulations, 1974 and 1984

6. Fresh Fruits and Vegetables

The Agriculture and Horticulture Act, 1964
Grading of Horticulture Produce (Amendment) Regulations, 1973
European Community Regulations for the Common Quality Standards for
    Fresh Horticultural Produce

7. Processed Fruits and Vegetables

Canned Fruit and Vegetables. Local Authority Joint Advisory Committee
    Codes of Practice: 4 (1965)

8. Herbs, Spices, Condiments, Essential Oils and Essences, and Colourings

Herbs and Mixtures of Herbs. Ministry of Food Code of Practice: 17 (1949)
Vinegars. Food Standards Committee Report, 1971
Essences and Flavourings. Ministry of Food Code of Practice: 18 (1949)
The Colouring Matter in Food Regulations, 1973 (S.I. 1973: 1340)

9. Tea, Coffee and Chocolate

Tea and Coffee. Ministry of Food Code of Practice: 10 (1949)
The Coffee and Coffee Products Regulations, 1978 (S.I. 1978, S.I. 1982)
The Cocoa and Chocolate Products Regulations, 1976 (S.I. 1976, S.I. 1982)

10. Convenience Foods

As for Chapters 7, 13 and 15

11. Introduction to Meat

The Slaughter of Animals Act, 1958 (S.I. 1958: 2166 amended by S.I. 1959:
    1493)
The Meat Inspection Regulations, 1963 (S.I. 1963: 1229 amended by
    S.I. 1971: 1179)
The Meat (Treatment) Regulations, 1964 (S.I. 1964: 19)
Novel Protein Foods. Food Standards Committee Report, 1974

12. Beef, Veal — Lamb, Mutton — Pork

As for Chapter 11

13. Offals — Bacon — Processed Meats

The Offals in Meat Products Order, 1953
The Meat Products and Spreadable Fish Products Regulations, 1984

14. Poultry and Game

The Slaughter of Poultry Act, 1967 Extension Order, 1978 (S.I. 1978: 201)
The Poultry Meat (Water Content) Regulations, 1984 (S.I. 1984: 1145)
Poultry Dressing and Packing. Food Hygiene Codes of Practice No. 5 (1961)
The Meat Products and Spreadable Fish Products Regulations, 1984

15. Fish

The Public Health (Shellfish) Regulations, 1934 (S.R. & O. 1934: 1342
     amended by S.I. 1948: 1120)
The Food Standards (Fish Cakes) Order, 1950 (S.I. 1950: 589)
Fish Pastes and Fish Spreads, Ministry of Food Code of Practice (1950)

Appendix 2 References and Further Reading

1. Cereal Products

Fance, W. J. *Breadmaking and Flour Confectionary* (Routledge and Kegan Paul)

Kent, N. L. *Technology of Cereals* (Pergamon Press)

Martin, C. R. A. *Practical Food Inspection* (9th edition) (H. K. Lewis)

T.A.A.C. Report *BREAD: an assessment of the British bread industry* (Intermediate Publishing)

Ranken, M. *Food Industries Manual* (21st edition) (Leonard Hill)

The Bread and Flour Regulations 1984 (H.M.S.O.)

2. Sugars, Preserves, and Confectionary Gums

Kollist, E. J. *The Complete Patissier* (MacLaren)

Ranken, M. *Food Industries Manual* (21st edition) (Leonard Hill)

McCance, R. A. and Widdowson, E. M. *The Composition of Foods, 1978* (H.M.S.O.)

3. Fats and Oils

Martin, C. R. A. *Practical Food Inspection* (H. K. Lewis)

Ranken, M. *Food Industries Manual* (21st edition) (Leonard Hill)

Masefield, G. B., Wallis, M., Harrison, S. G. and Nicholson, B. E. *The Oxford Book of Food Plants* (Oxford University Press)

Vegetable Oils and Fats (Unilever Educational Booklet)

Margarine and Cooking Fats (Unilever Educational Booklet)

Vegetable Oils and Oilseeds 1967 (H.M.S.O.)

4. Dairy Foods (Milk, Cream, and Ice-cream)

A Handbook of Dairy Foods (National Dairy Council)
Ranken, M. *Food Industries Manual* (21st edition) (Leonard Hill)
Martin, C. R. A. *Practical Food Inspection* (9th edition) (H. K. Lewis)
Kollist *The Complete Patissier* (MacLaren)

5. Dairy Foods (Butter and Cheese)

Davis, J. G. *A Dictionary of Dairying* (Leonard Hill)
A Handbook of Dairy Foods (National Dairy Council)
Davis, J. G. *Cheese, Volume 1* (J. and A. Churchill)
Ranken, M. *Food Industries Manual* (21st edition) (Leonard Hill)
Martin, C. R. A. *Practical Food Inspection* (H. K. Lewis)

6. Fresh Fruit and Vegetables

Duckworth, R. B. *Fruit and Vegetables* (Pergamon Press)
Kotschevar, L. H. *Quantity Food Purchasing* (Wiley)
Arthey, V. D. *Quality of Horticultural Products* (Butterworths)
Masefield, G. B., Wallis, M., Harrison, S. G. and Nicholson, B. E. *The Oxford Book of Food Plants* (Oxford University Press)

7. Processed Fruits and Vegetables

Martin, C. R. A. *Practical Food Inspection* (H. K. Lewis)
Fance, W. J. *The Students' Technology of Breadmaking and Flour Confectionary* (Routledge and Kegan Paul)
Ranken, M. *Food Industries Manual* (21st edition) (Leonard Hill)
Food Preservation (Unilever Education Booklet)

8. Herbs, Spices, Condiments, Essential Oils and Essences, and Colourings

Bennion, Stewart, Bamford *Cake Making* (Leonard Hill)
Parry, J. *Spices* (Food Trades Press)
Masefield, G. B., Wallis, M., Harrison, S. G. and Nicholson, B. E. *The Oxford Book of Food Plants* (Oxford University Press)

9. Tea, Coffee, and Chocolate

Bramah, E. *Tea and Coffee* (Hutchinson)
Cakebread, S. *Sugar and Chocolate Confectionery* (Oxford University Press)
Martin, C. R. A. *Practical Food Inspection* (H. K. Lewis)
Minifie, B. W. *Chocolate, Cocoa and Confectionery: science and technology* (J. and A. Churchill)

10. Convenience Foods

Little, Arthur D. *Convenicne Foods in Catering* (N.E.D.O.)
Thorner, M. E. *Convenience and Fast Food Handbook* (A.V.I.)

11. Introduction to Meat

Gerrard, F. *Meat Technology* (Leonard Hill)
Martin, C. R. A. *Practical Food Inspection* (H. K. Lewis)
Wilson, A. *Practical Meat Inspection* (Blackwell)

12. Beef, Veal — Lamb, Mutton — Pork

Gerrard, F. *Meat Technology* (L. Hill)
Martin, C. R. A. *Practical Food Inspection* (H. K. Lewis)
Cetre, F. *Practical Larderwork* (Pitman)
Kotas, R. and Davis, B. *Food and Beverage Control* (Intertext)
Meat and Livestock Commission *Cutting and Preparing Beef* (Meat and
    Livestock Commission)
New Zealand Meat — A Trade Guide (New Zealand Meat Producers Board)
Moore, Stone, Tattersall, *The Meat Buyer's Guide for Caterers*
    (International Thomson Publishing)

13. Offals — Bacon — Processed Meats

Ranken, M. *Food Industries Manual* (21st edition) (Leonard Hill)
Gerrard, F. *Meat Technology* (Leonard Hill)
Gerrard, F. *Sausage and Small Goods Production* (Leonard Hill)
Martin, C. R. A. *Practical Food Inspection* (H. K. Lewis)
The Bacon Curing Industry (N.E.D.O.)

14. Poultry and Game

Martin, C. R. A. *Practical Food Inspection* (H. K. Lewis)
Wilson, A. *Practical Meat Inspection* (Blackwell)
Table Chickens, Bulletin No. 168 (H.M.S.O.)

15. Fish

Simon, A. *A Concise Encyclopaedia of Gastronomy Section II Fish* (Wine
    and Food Society)
Specifications for the Purchase of Fish Sea Fish Industry Authority
Torry Advisory Notes 1–59 (H.M.S.O.)
Borgstrom, G. (ed.) *Fish as Food* (Academic Press)

General

Diet and Cardiovascular Disease   Committee on Medical Aspects of Food
Policy, DHSS H.M.S.O., 1984
Diet, Nutrition and Health   British Medical Association, 1986
Eating for a Healthy Heart   Joint Advisory Committee on Nutrition
Education, British Nutrition Foundation and Health Education Council,
1985
Guide to Healthy Eating   Health Education Council, 1986
Proposals for Nutritional Guidelines for Health Education in Britain
National Advisory Committee on Nutrition Education, Health
Education Council, 1983
Report on the Safety and Wholesomeness of Irradiated Foods   Advisory
Committee on Irradiated and Novel Foods, DHSS, H.M.S.O., 1986
D. A. T. Southgate   MAFF/MRC   H.M.S.O., 1978

Appendix 3 Glossary of Scientific Terms

Alcohol

The alcohol most often referred to in food areas is more correctly called
ethanol or ethyl alcohol. A colourless liquid with a boiling point $78°C$, and a
calorific value of 7 kcal (q.v.) per g, compared to that of carbohydrate 4 and
fat 9. It is formed during the yeast fermentation of sugars, and has the
characteristic property of causing intoxication in most animals.

Amino-acids

These are molecules which form the basic units of proteins. They have within
their structure the carboxylic acid group ($-COOH$) and the amino group
($-NH_2$), and it is by means of these that they can be linked together to form
the much larger protein molecules (q.v.).

Biological Value (B.V.)

This is a description of quality often applied to proteins. If a protein had a
biological value of 100 this would mean that it would be wholly utilized by
the human body. Measurement of B.V. is carried out on man by feeding a
certain protein under controlled conditions, and determining the amount of
protein that is retained by the body. Examples of values obtained: egg 95,
cow's milk 75, bread 50, etc. The B.V. of a given protein is limited by the
proportion of limiting essential amino-acid (q.v.) present in the protein.

Bleaching

A process by which coloured materials are rendered colourless, usually
brought about either by removal of oxygen (reduction) or by the addition of
oxygen (oxidation). Sulphites and sulphur dioxide are examples of reducing
bleaches, whilst hypochlorites and chlorine are examples of oxidizing bleaches.

Carbohydrates

Substances containing the elements, carbon (C), hydrogen (H) and oxygen (O) in such a way so that a general formula for them can be written as $C_x(H_2O)y$. Digestible carbohydrates in the diet can provide energy for the body (measured in calories or Joules). Starches and sugars are among such substances.

Carbon Dioxide

A gas at room temperature which is formed during yeast fermentations, and by chemical-raising agents such as sodium bicarbonate. The gas aerates the products in which it is formed, giving a resultant open texture.

Catalyst

A substance which has the property of being able to alter (usually accelerate) the speed of a chemical reaction, without being changed by the reaction.

Colloids

These are systems involving the dispersion of small particles (but very much larger than small simple molecules) in a second medium. The table below gives some examples.

Disperse Phase (small particles)	Continuous Phase (dispersion medium)	Name of Resulting Colloidal System	Examples
Liquid	Solid	Gel	Table jelly
Liquid	Liquid	Emulsion	Milk, salad cream
Gas	Liquid	Foam	Beaten egg white, whipped cream

Dehydration

The removal of water from a product, a term usually used in connection with dried processed foods.

Dextrinization

The name of the process by which heat causes the partial breakdown of starch to simpler products called dextrins (q.v.).

Dextrins

A mixture of compounds formed by the partial breakdown of starch, of complexity intermediate between that of starch and simple sugars. This is formed, for example, when bread is toasted.

Elasticity

The property of a material which enables it to stretch and return to its original dimensions. Something which was 100% elastic would be able to be stretched and return to its original dimension, with no permanent deformation.

Enzymes

Protein molecules produced by living cells which act as catalysts (q.v.) in chemical reactions — each reaction needing a specific catalyst.

Essential Amino-acids
About twenty or so amino-acids occur commonly in nature and of these, eight cannot be synthesized by the adult human body, i.e. iso-leucine, leucine, lysine, methionine, phenylalanine, threonine, tryptophan, valine. It is suggested by some that arginine and histidine are essential for children.

Fermentation
A term usually used to describe a process by which a micro-organism liberates energy from nutrients without oxygen; and often whilst doing so, produces by-pr ʾducts of interest to man, e.g. alcohol from the yeast fermentation of sugars.

Gelatinization
The process by which a gel (q.v.) is formed.

Essential Amino-acids
About twenty or so amino-acids occur commonly in nature and of these, eight cannot be synthesized by the adult human body, i.e. iso-leucine, leucine, lysine, methionine, phenylalanine, threonine, tryptophan, valine. It is suggested by some that arginine and histidine are essential for children.

Fermentation
A term usually used to describe a process by which a micro-organism liberates energy from nutrients without oxygen; and often whilst doing so, produces by-products of interest to man, e.g. alcohol from the yeast fermentation of sugars.

Gamma-rays
Radiation of very short wavelength produced by the nuclear disintegration of the atoms of certain radioactive isotopes of certain elements e.g. cobalt 60 or caesium 137.

Gelatinization
The process by which a gel (q.v.) is formed.

Gel
A colloidal (q.v.) system in which a framework of large molecules holds liquid particles in suspension — the result is a semi-solid material, e.g. a table jelly.

Gray (Gy)
The international unit for measuring radiation, which equals the absorption of 1 joule of energy per kilogram of material. An older unit, the rad, is still in use to some extent and 1000 Gy = 100 rad, i.e. 1 kiloGy or 1 kGy = 100 rad.

Hydration
The addition of water to a product, the opposite of dehydration (q.v.).

Hydrogenation
The process by which liquid or soft fats are hardened by the addition of hydrogen to the double-bonds in the unsaturated fat or oil molecules. A catalyst of finely divided nickel is usually employed to facilitate the reaction.

Hydrolysis

The chemical action whereby water molecules react with a substance, breaking it down to simpler substances. A process usually catalysed (q.v.) by the action of heat, acid, or enzymes.

Examples of hydrolysis reactions:

proteins + water	amino-acids
starch + water	sugars
fats + water	glycerol + fatty acids

Irradiation

The treatment of food with ionizing radiation (from a radio-active source material) to kill micro-organisms. However, doses required to render food sterile are so large, that they cause unpleasant flavours and textures to develop. This method is useful in prolonging storage life by preventing sprouting in some root crops.

Joule

The International Unit of Energy. However the Kilocalorie (or Calorie) is still commonly used when expressing the energy value of foods and diets. The relationship of the two units can be shown as:

	4.18 joules = 1 calorie
or	4.18 kilojoules = 1 kilocalorie = 1 calorie

Limiting Essential Amino-acids

These are the amino-acids which limit the body's use of a given protein, i.e. they lower the Biological Value of a given protein, because they are present in proportionally lower amounts than the other essential amino-acids. For example lysine is the limiting amino-acid in bread, accounting for the B.V. of 50.

Micro-organism

A general term, used to describe bacteria, moulds, and yeasts — organisms which can only be seen with the aid of a microscope.

Osmosis

The process by which water (or another solvent) passes through a semi-permeable membrane (i.e. a membrane which will permit the molecules of solvent to pass through it, whilst preventing the passage of dissolved substances), from a solution low in concentration of dissolved substances to one of higher concentration.

Pasteurization

A mild heat treatment of a food which will kill the normal cells of many bacteria — used as a means of prolonging the shelf-life of a food, but only for a limited period. Legally, pasteurization of milk involves either (i) holding the milk at 63–66°C (145–150°F), followed by immediate cooling; or (ii) a 'high-temperature, short-time' process (HTST) in which the milk is held at 72°C (161°F) for about 15 seconds.

Pathogenic micro-organisms

Those micro-organisms known to be harmful to man.

Polyunsaturated fatty acids (PUFA)

The constituent fatty acids of an oil or fat which have more than one carbon–carbon double bond per molecule e.g. linolenic and arachidonic acids.

Polyunsaturated fatty acids are to be found in greatest abundance in some vegetable oils such as Soyabean and Safflower, and in fish oils.

Proteins

Substances containing the elements carbon (C), hydrogen (H), and oxygen (O) and more importantly nitrogen (N). They are large molecules consisting of long chains of amino-acids (q.v.) linked together. They are essential nutrients in the diet, being necessary for growth, repair and working of the cells of the body.

Solubility

The extent to which a substance will dissolve in a solvent, usually water.

Vitamins

A group of chemically unrelated substances, but having in common the fact that they are essential in relatively small amounts for the body's metabolism. They are therefore essential elements in a balanced diet.

Index